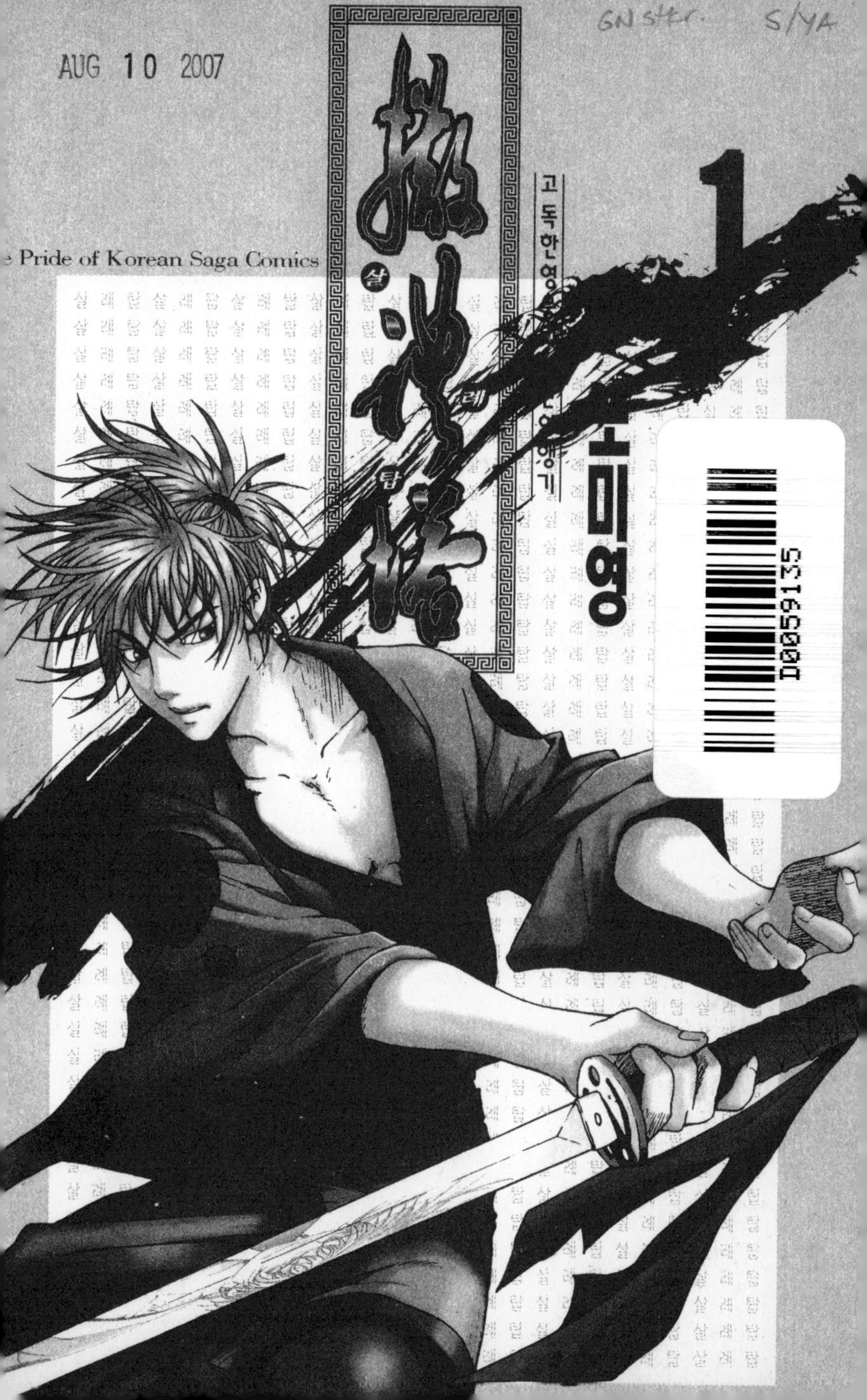
살 례 탑
고 독 한 영 웅 의 방 랑 행 기
1
미영
Pride of Korean Saga Comics

Threads of Time Vol. 1
Created by Mi Young Noh

Translation - Jihae Hong
English Adaptation - Luis Reyes
Retouch and Lettering - James Dashiell
Production Artist - Sophia Hong
Cover Artist - Patrick Hook

Editor - Luis Reyes
Digital Imaging Manager - Chris Buford
Pre-Press Manager - Antonio DePietro
Production Managers - Jennifer Miller and Mutsumi Miyazaki
Art Director - Matt Alford
Managing Editor - Jill Freshney
VP of Production - Ron Klamert
President and C.O.O. - John Parker
Publisher and C.E.O. - Stuart Levy

A  Manga

TOKYOPOP Inc.
5900 Wilshire Blvd. Suite 2000
Los Angeles, CA 90036

E-mail: info@TOKYOPOP.com
Come visit us online at www.TOKYOPOP.com

ISBN: 1-59182-780-9

First TOKYOPOP printing: September 2004
10 9 8 7 6 5 4 3 2 1
Printed in the USA

Threads of Time™

撤神塔

Volume 1

By
Mi Young Noh

S

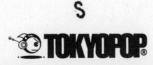

HAMBURG // LONDON // LOS ANGELES // TOKYO

contents

Threads of Time

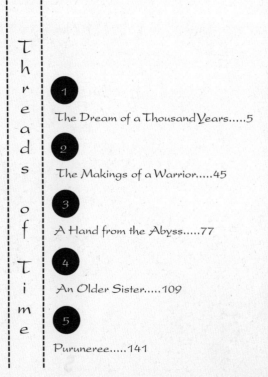

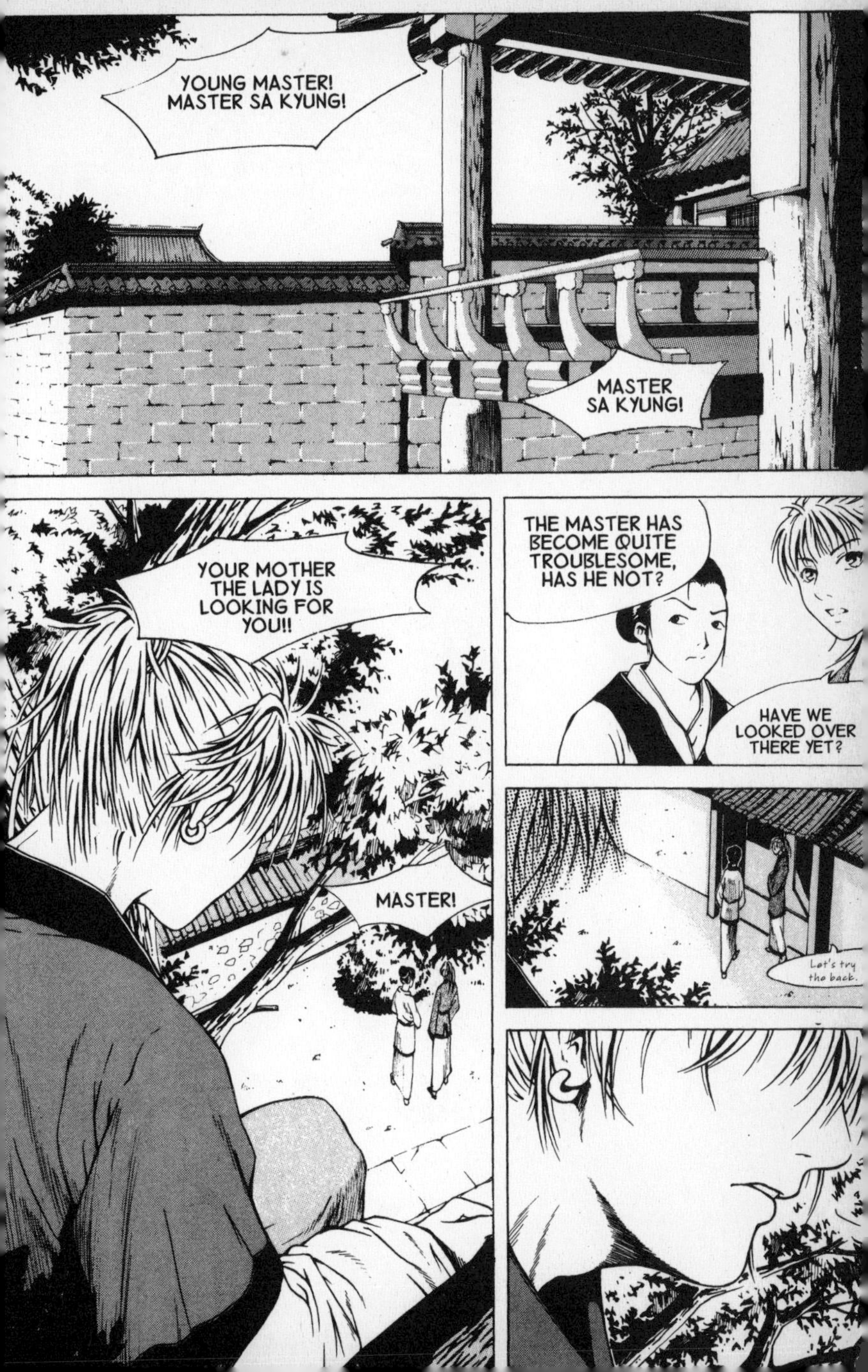
YOUNG MASTER! MASTER SA KYUNG!
MASTER SA KYUNG!
YOUR MOTHER THE LADY IS LOOKING FOR YOU!!
MASTER!
THE MASTER HAS BECOME QUITE TROUBLESOME, HAS HE NOT?
HAVE WE LOOKED OVER THERE YET?
Let's try the back.

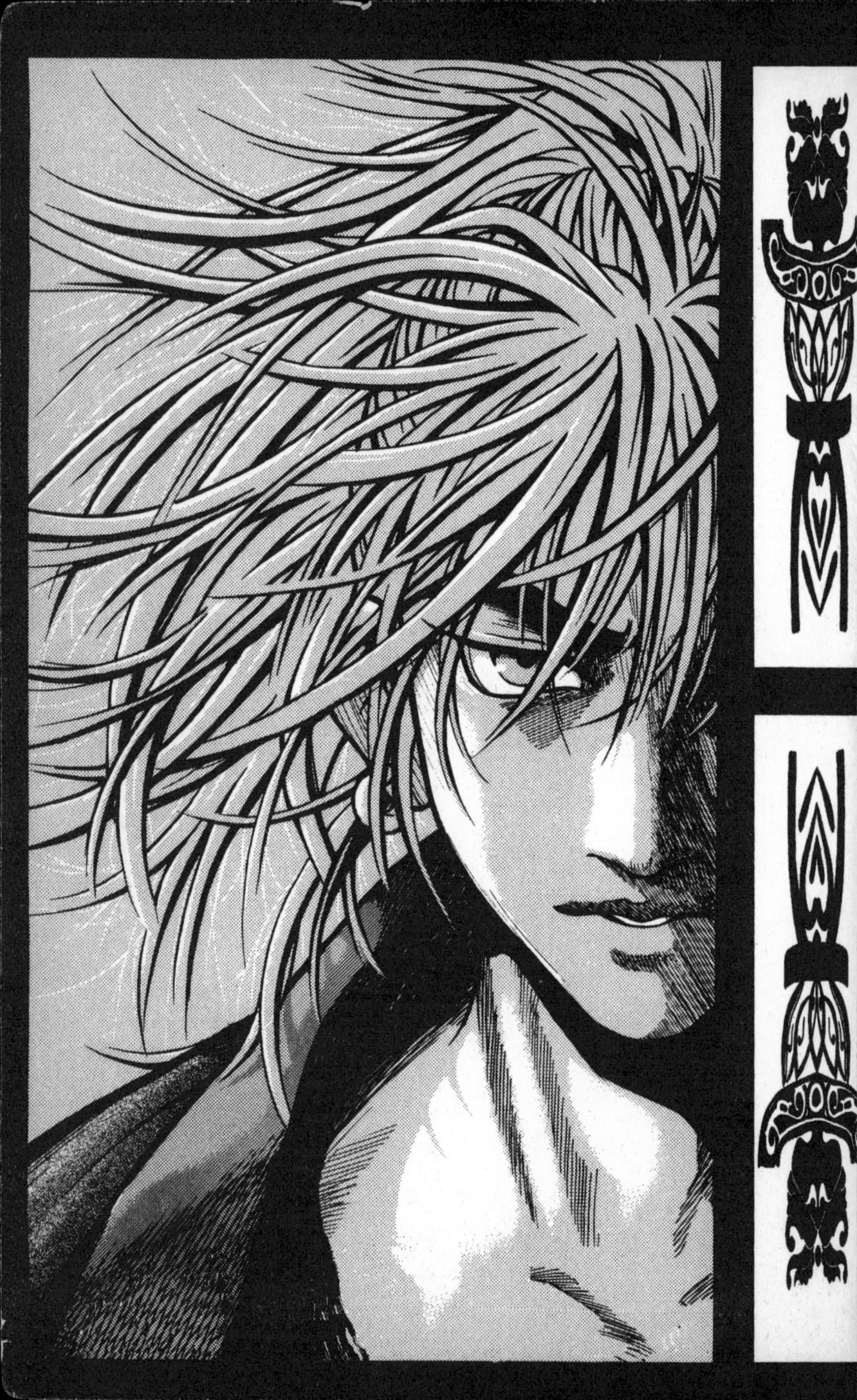

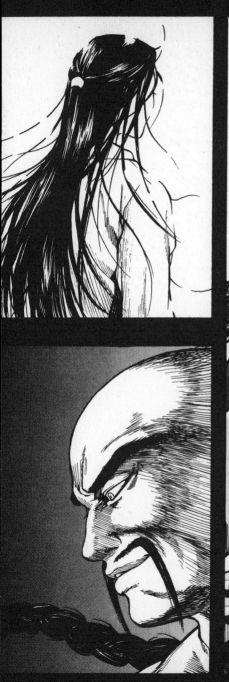

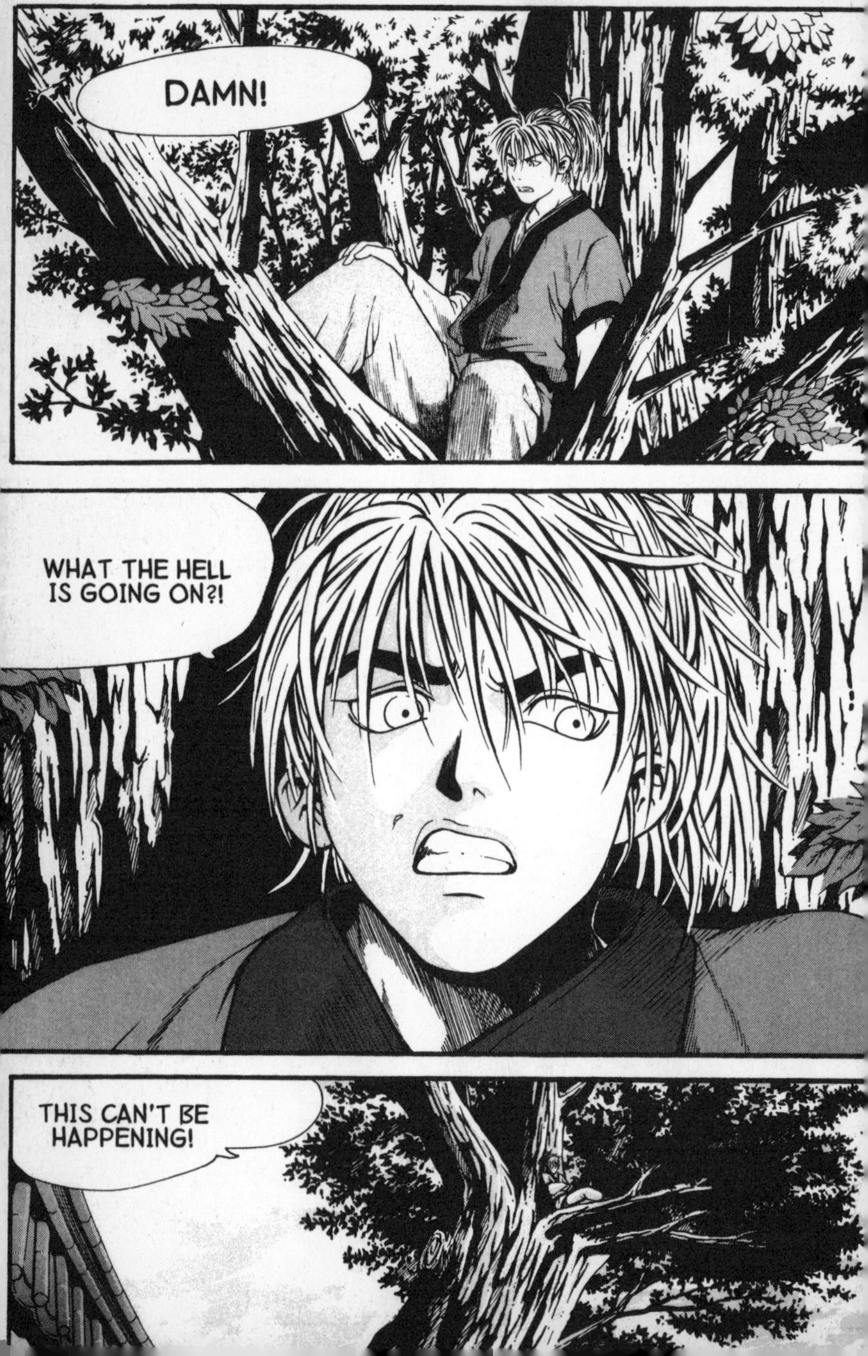
DAMN!
WHAT THE HELL IS GOING ON?!
THIS CAN'T BE HAPPENING!

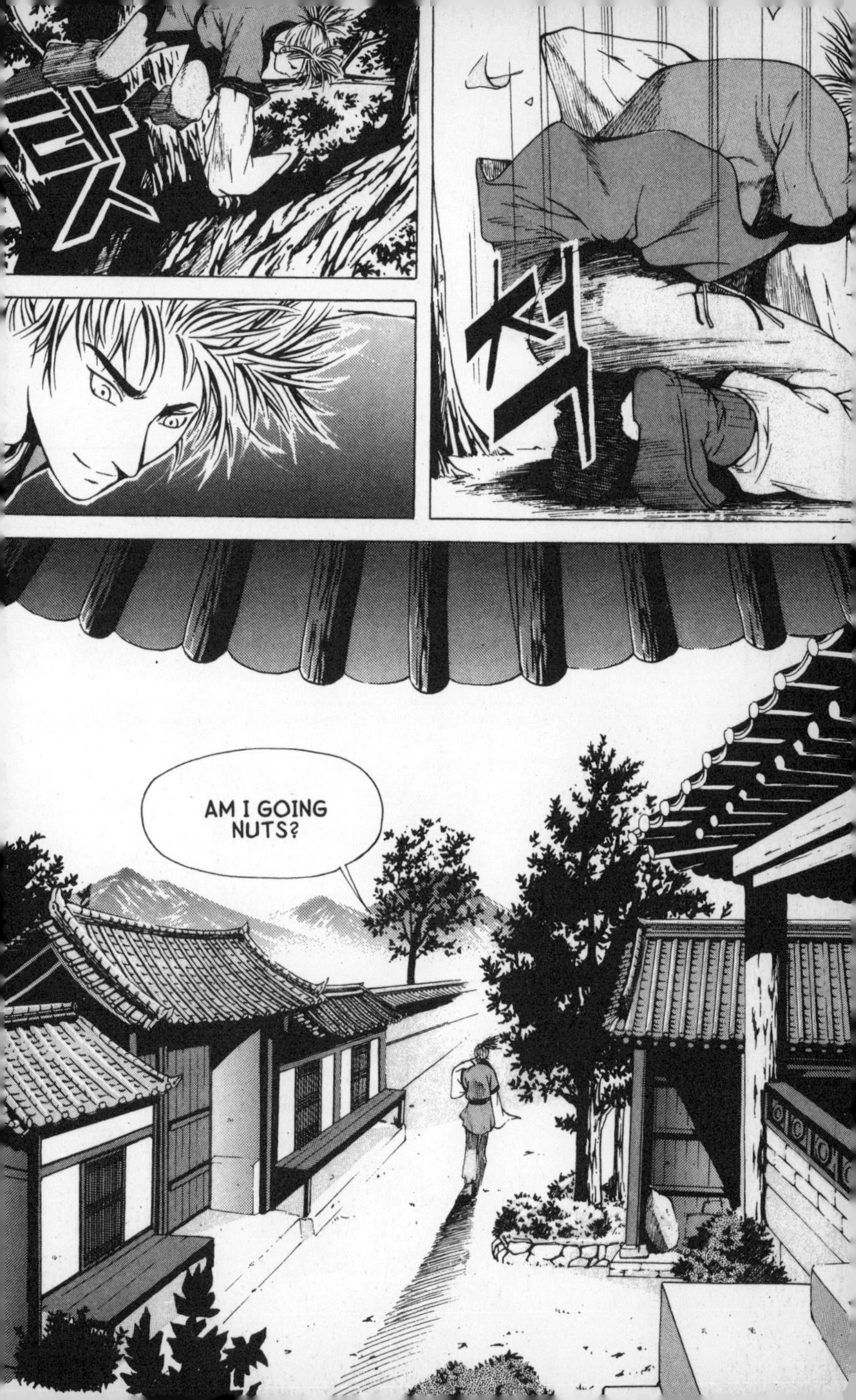
AM I GOING NUTS?

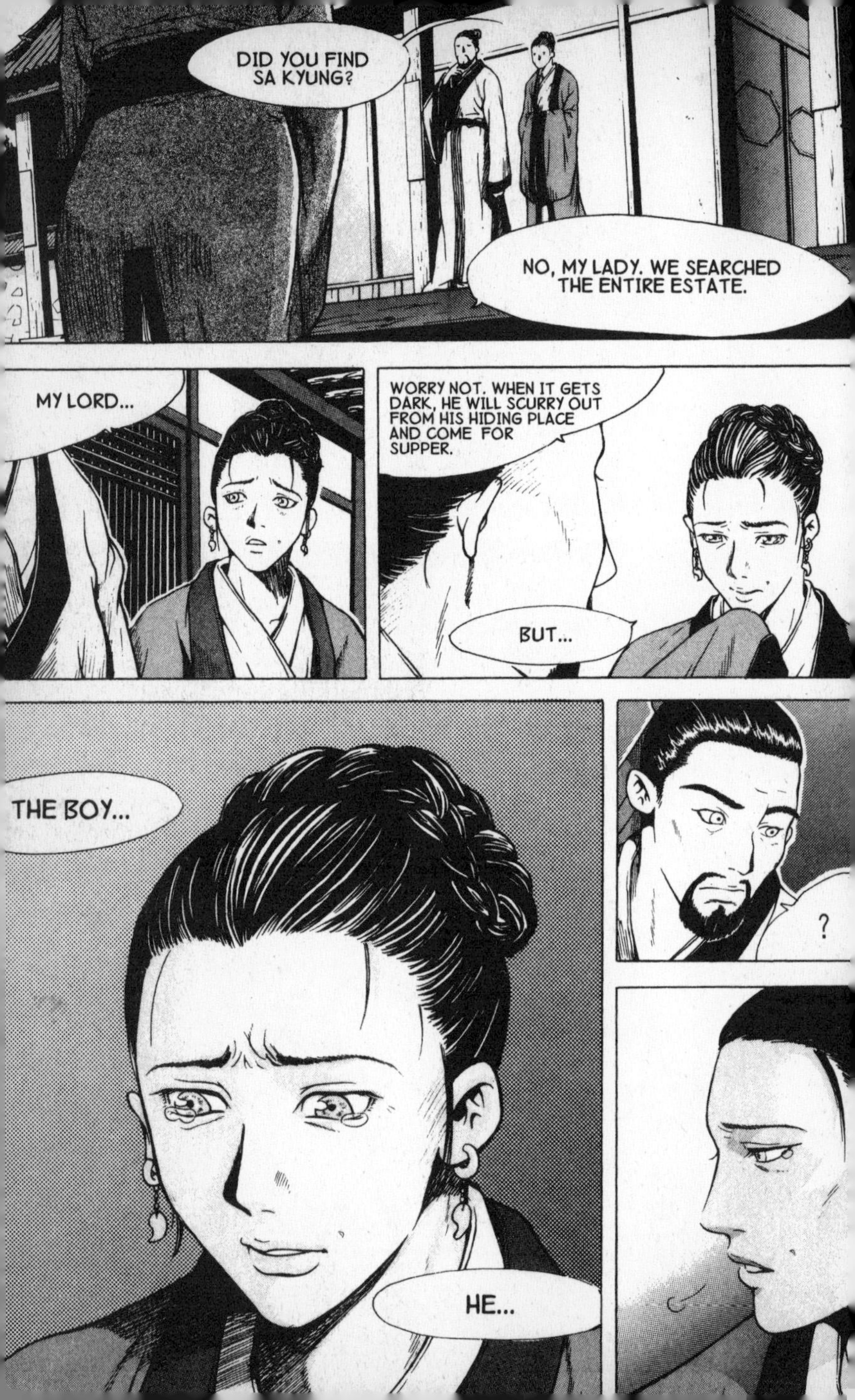
DID YOU FIND SA KYUNG?
NO, MY LADY. WE SEARCHED THE ENTIRE ESTATE.
MY LORD...
WORRY NOT. WHEN IT GETS DARK, HE WILL SCURRY OUT FROM HIS HIDING PLACE AND COME FOR SUPPER.
BUT...
THE BOY...
HE...
?

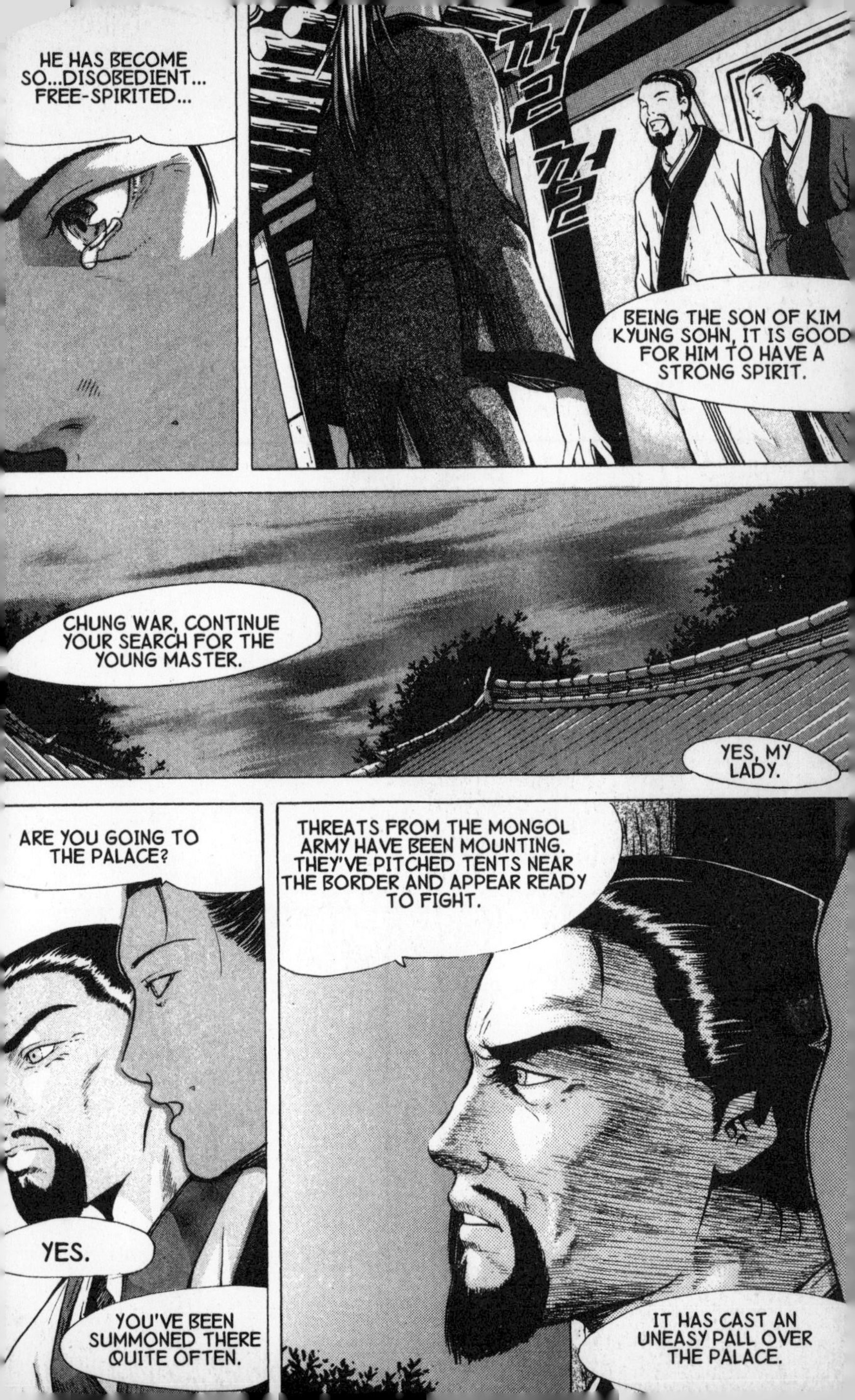
HE HAS BECOME SO...DISOBEDIENT... FREE-SPIRITED...
BEING THE SON OF KIM KYUNG SOHN, IT IS GOOD FOR HIM TO HAVE A STRONG SPIRIT.
CHUNG WAR, CONTINUE YOUR SEARCH FOR THE YOUNG MASTER.
YES, MY LADY.
ARE YOU GOING TO THE PALACE?
YES.
YOU'VE BEEN SUMMONED THERE QUITE OFTEN.
THREATS FROM THE MONGOL ARMY HAVE BEEN MOUNTING. THEY'VE PITCHED TENTS NEAR THE BORDER AND APPEAR READY TO FIGHT.
IT HAS CAST AN UNEASY PALL OVER THE PALACE.

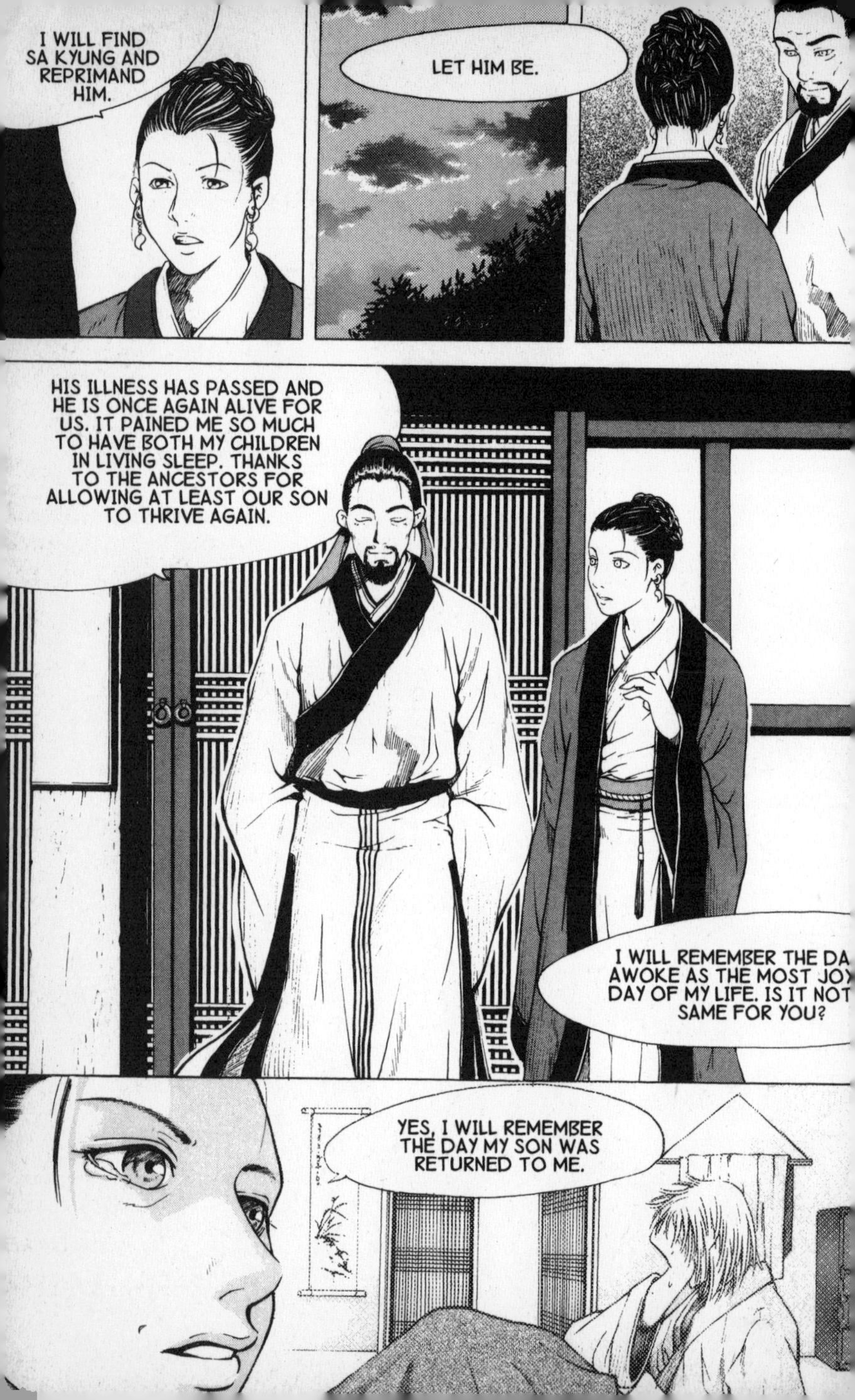
I WILL FIND SA KYUNG AND REPRIMAND HIM.
LET HIM BE.
HIS ILLNESS HAS PASSED AND HE IS ONCE AGAIN ALIVE FOR US. IT PAINED ME SO MUCH TO HAVE BOTH MY CHILDREN IN LIVING SLEEP. THANKS TO THE ANCESTORS FOR ALLOWING AT LEAST OUR SON TO THRIVE AGAIN.
I WILL REMEMBER THE DA AWOKE AS THE MOST JOY DAY OF MY LIFE. IS IT NOT SAME FOR YOU?
YES, I WILL REMEMBER THE DAY MY SON WAS RETURNED TO ME.

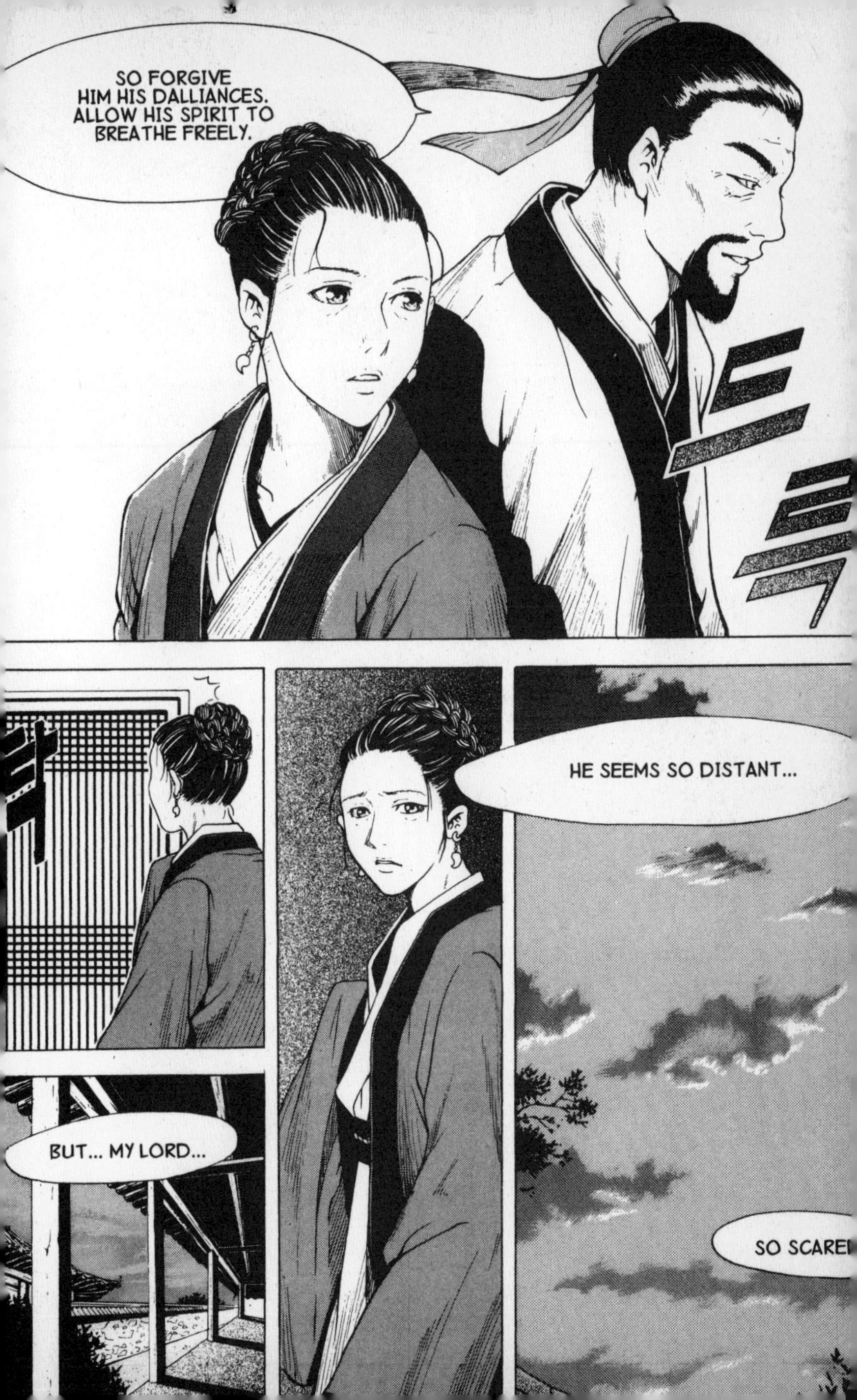
SO FORGIVE HIM HIS DALLIANCES. ALLOW HIS SPIRIT TO BREATHE FREELY.
BUT... MY LORD...
HE SEEMS SO DISTANT...
SO SCARE

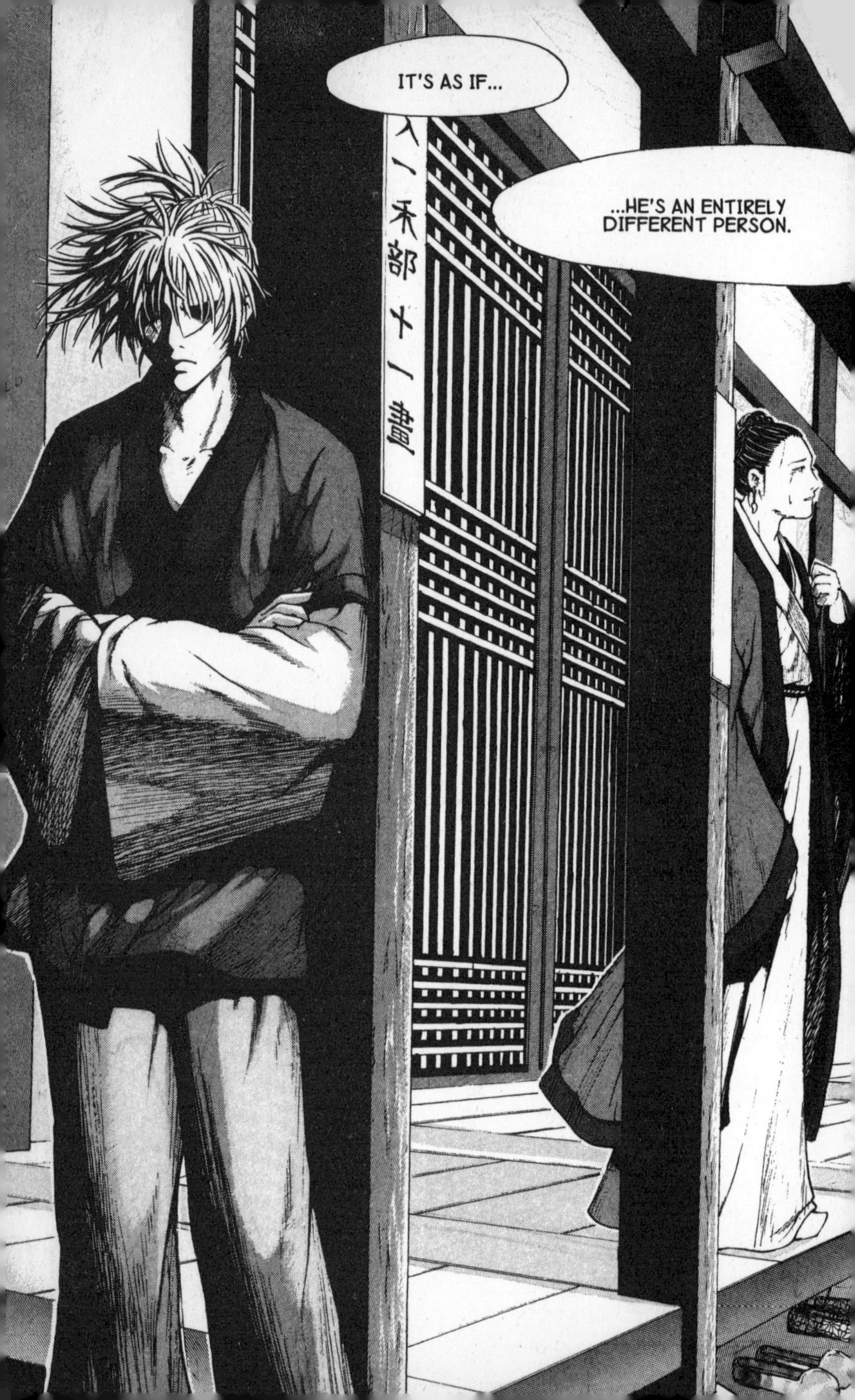
IT'S AS IF...
...HE'S AN ENTIRELY DIFFERENT PERSON.

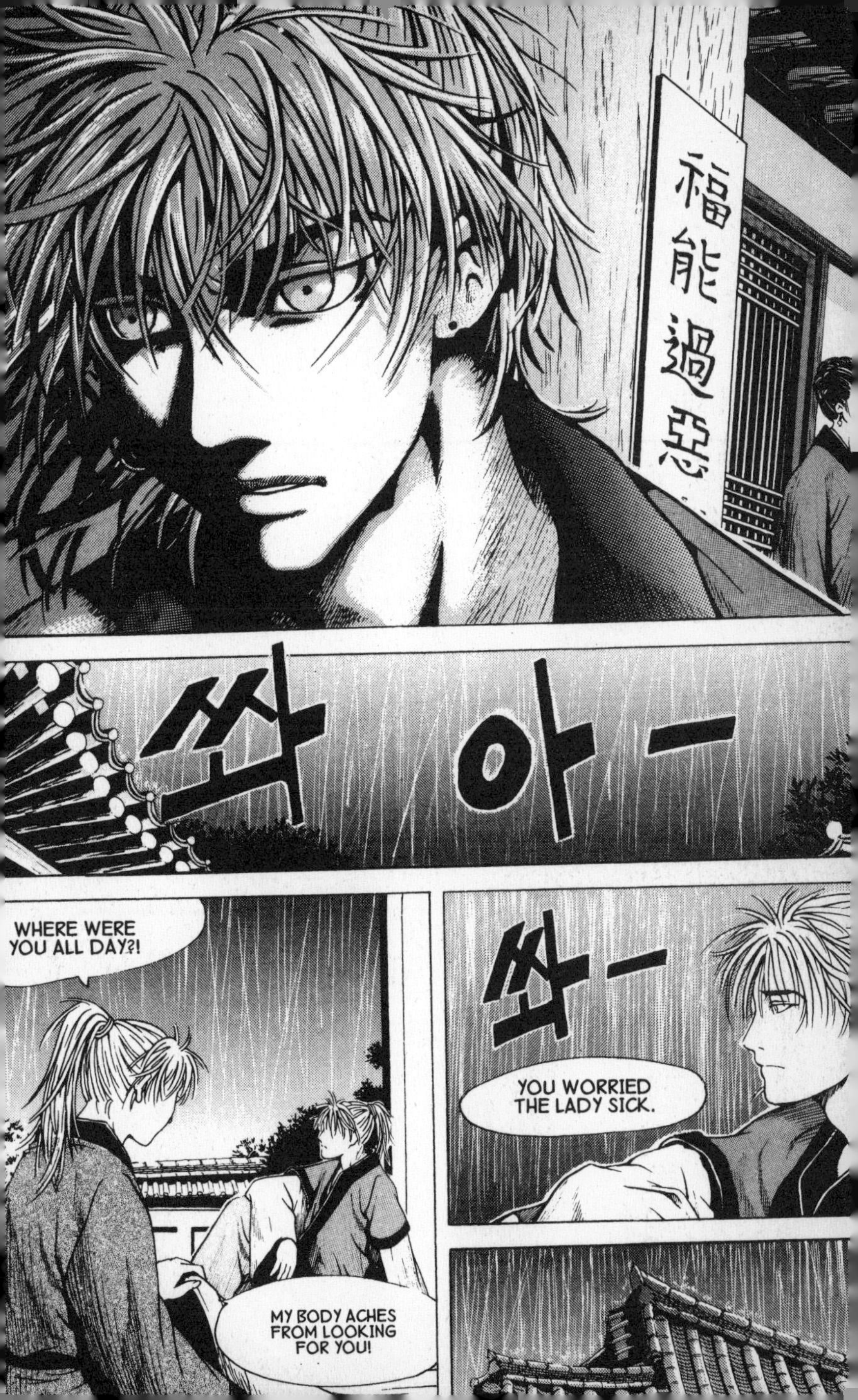
福能過惡
쏴 아 ㅡ
WHERE WERE YOU ALL DAY?!
MY BODY ACHES FROM LOOKING FOR YOU!
쏴ㅡ
YOU WORRIED THE LADY SICK.

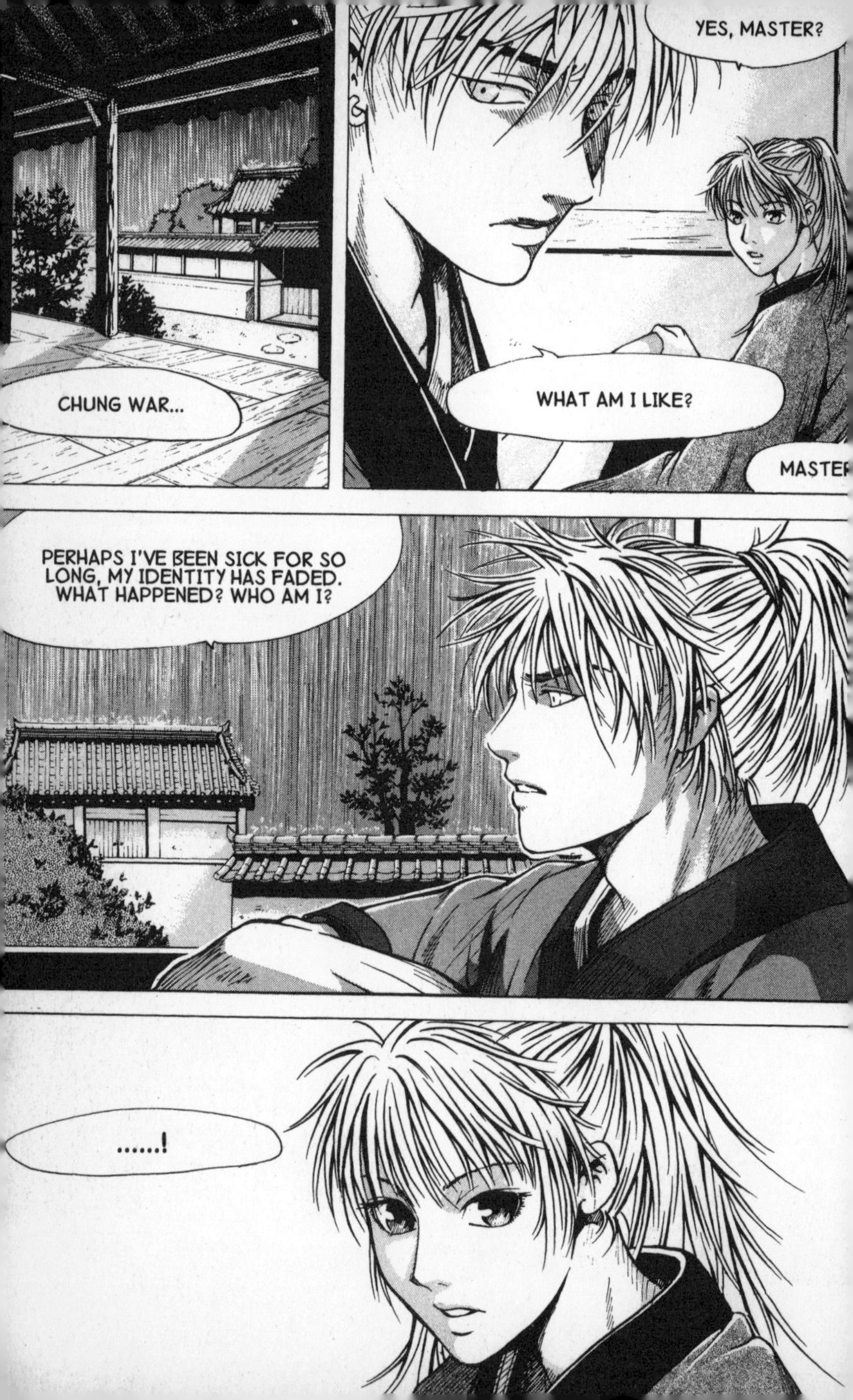
CHUNG WAR...
YES, MASTER?
WHAT AM I LIKE?
MASTER
PERHAPS I'VE BEEN SICK FOR SO LONG, MY IDENTITY HAS FADED. WHAT HAPPENED? WHO AM I?
......!

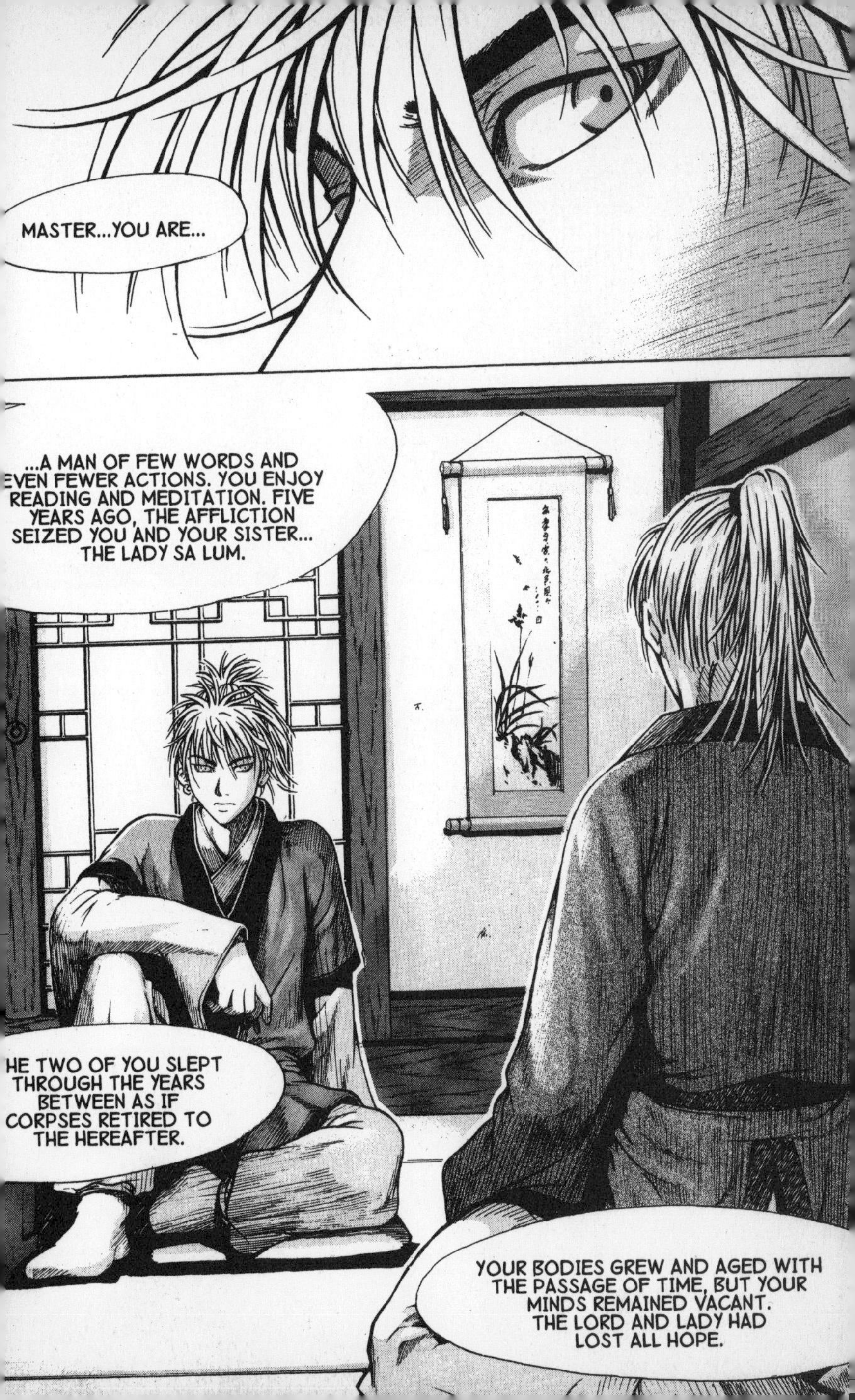
MASTER...YOU ARE...
...A MAN OF FEW WORDS AND EVEN FEWER ACTIONS. YOU ENJOY READING AND MEDITATION. FIVE YEARS AGO, THE AFFLICTION SEIZED YOU AND YOUR SISTER... THE LADY SA LUM.
HE TWO OF YOU SLEPT THROUGH THE YEARS BETWEEN AS IF CORPSES RETIRED TO THE HEREAFTER.
YOUR BODIES GREW AND AGED WITH THE PASSAGE OF TIME, BUT YOUR MINDS REMAINED VACANT. THE LORD AND LADY HAD LOST ALL HOPE.

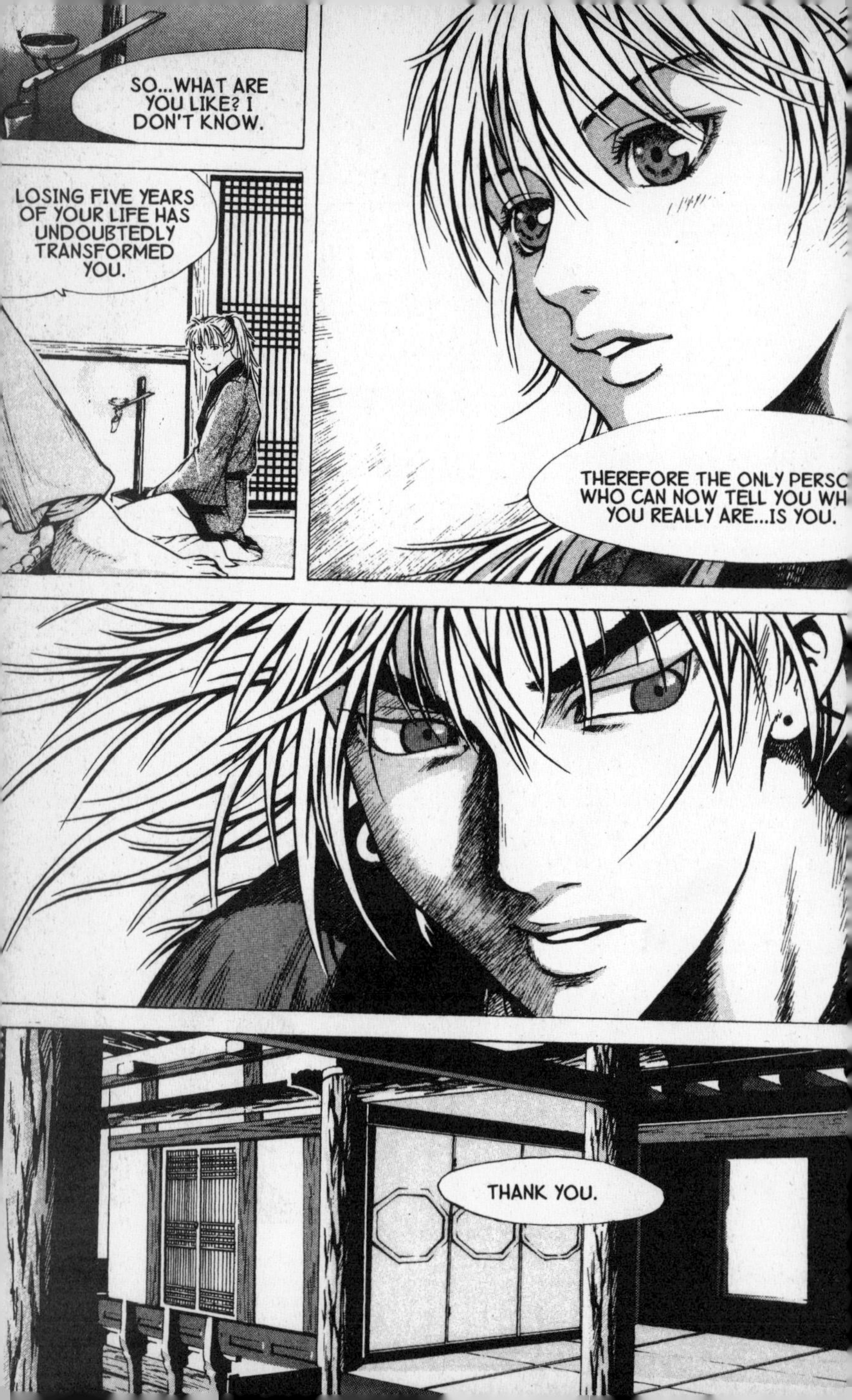
SO...WHAT ARE YOU LIKE? I DON'T KNOW.
LOSING FIVE YEARS OF YOUR LIFE HAS UNDOUBTEDLY TRANSFORMED YOU.
THEREFORE THE ONLY PERSO WHO CAN NOW TELL YOU WH YOU REALLY ARE...IS YOU.
THANK YOU.

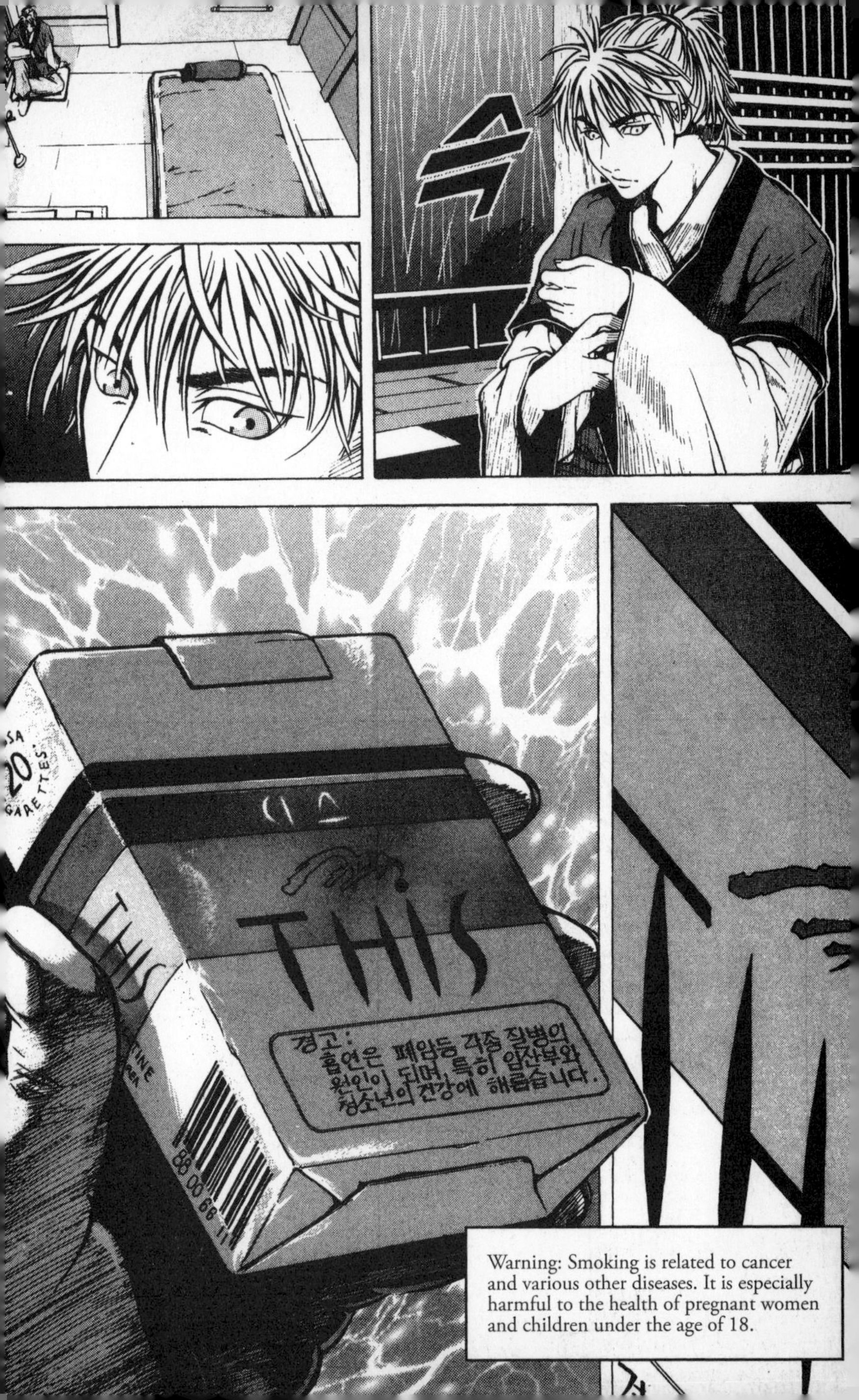
THIS
경고:
흡연은 폐암등 각종 질병의
원인이 되며, 특히 임산부와
청소년의 건강에 해롭습니다.
Warning: Smoking is related to cancer and various other diseases. It is especially harmful to the health of pregnant women and children under the age of 18.

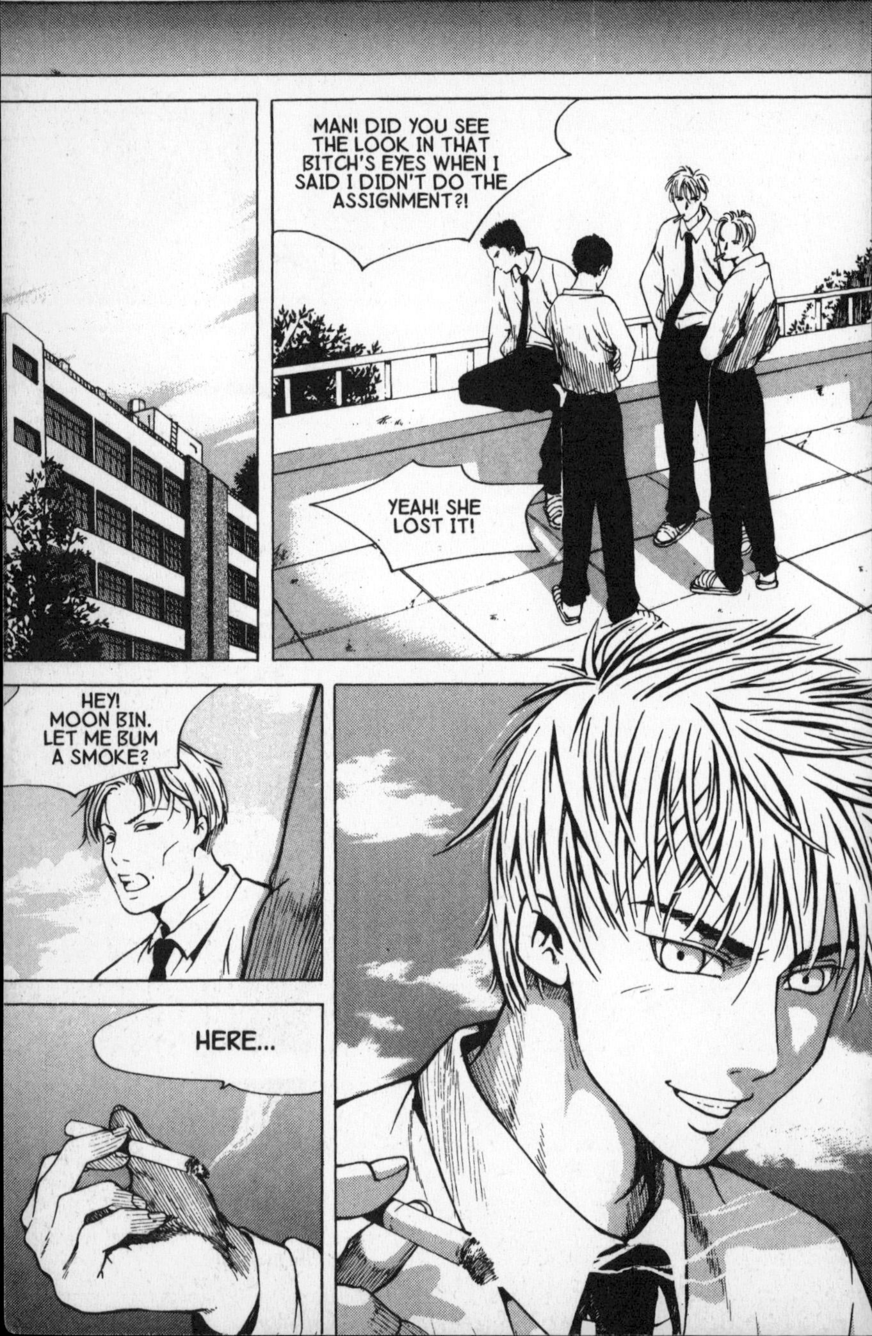
MAN! DID YOU SEE THE LOOK IN THAT BITCH'S EYES WHEN I SAID I DIDN'T DO THE ASSIGNMENT?!
YEAH! SHE LOST IT!
HEY! MOON BIN. LET ME BUM A SMOKE?
HERE...

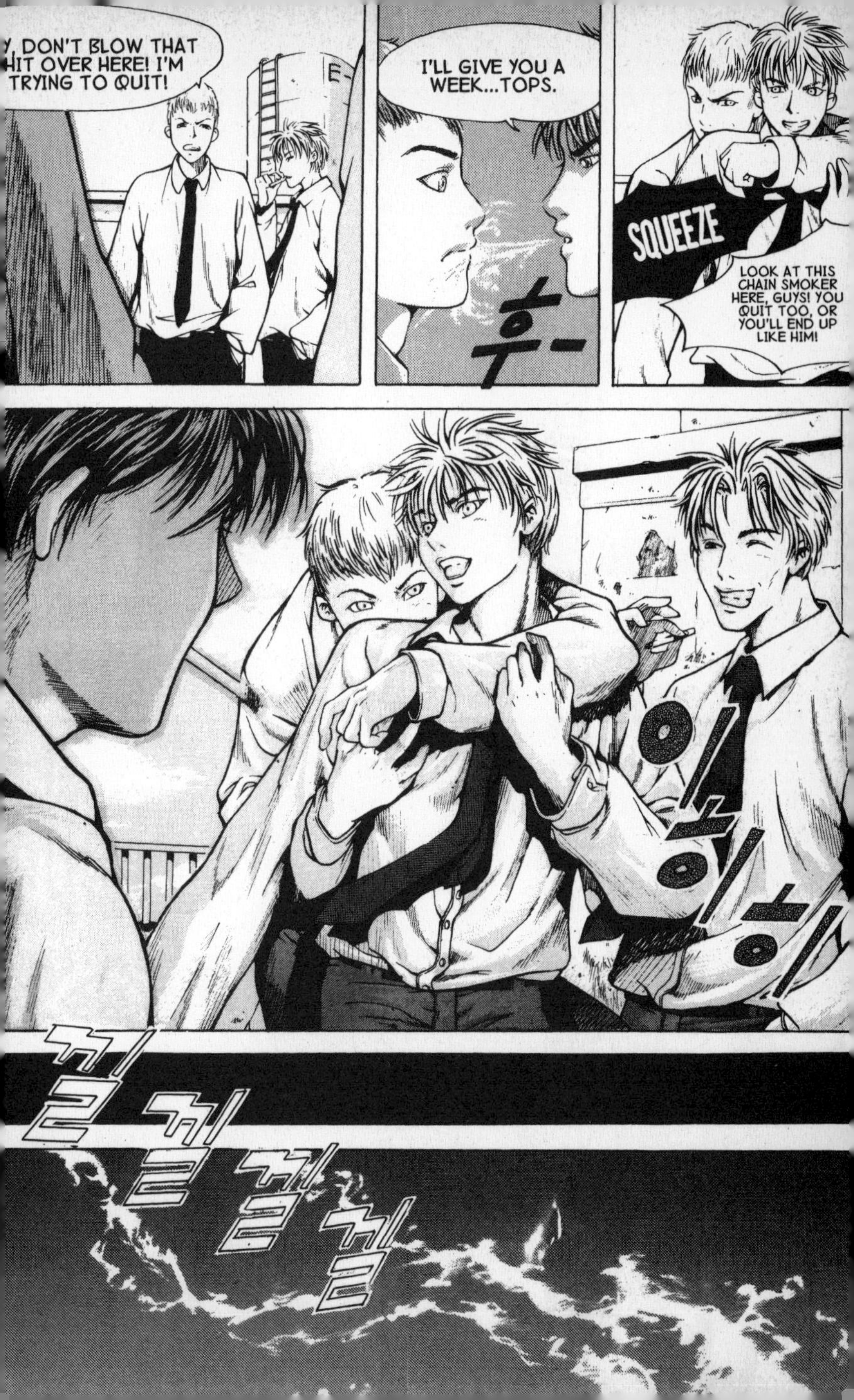
Y, DON'T BLOW THAT HIT OVER HERE! I'M TRYING TO QUIT!
I'LL GIVE YOU A WEEK...TOPS.
후-
SQUEEZE
LOOK AT THIS CHAIN SMOKER HERE, GUYS! YOU QUIT TOO, OR YOU'LL END UP LIKE HIM!

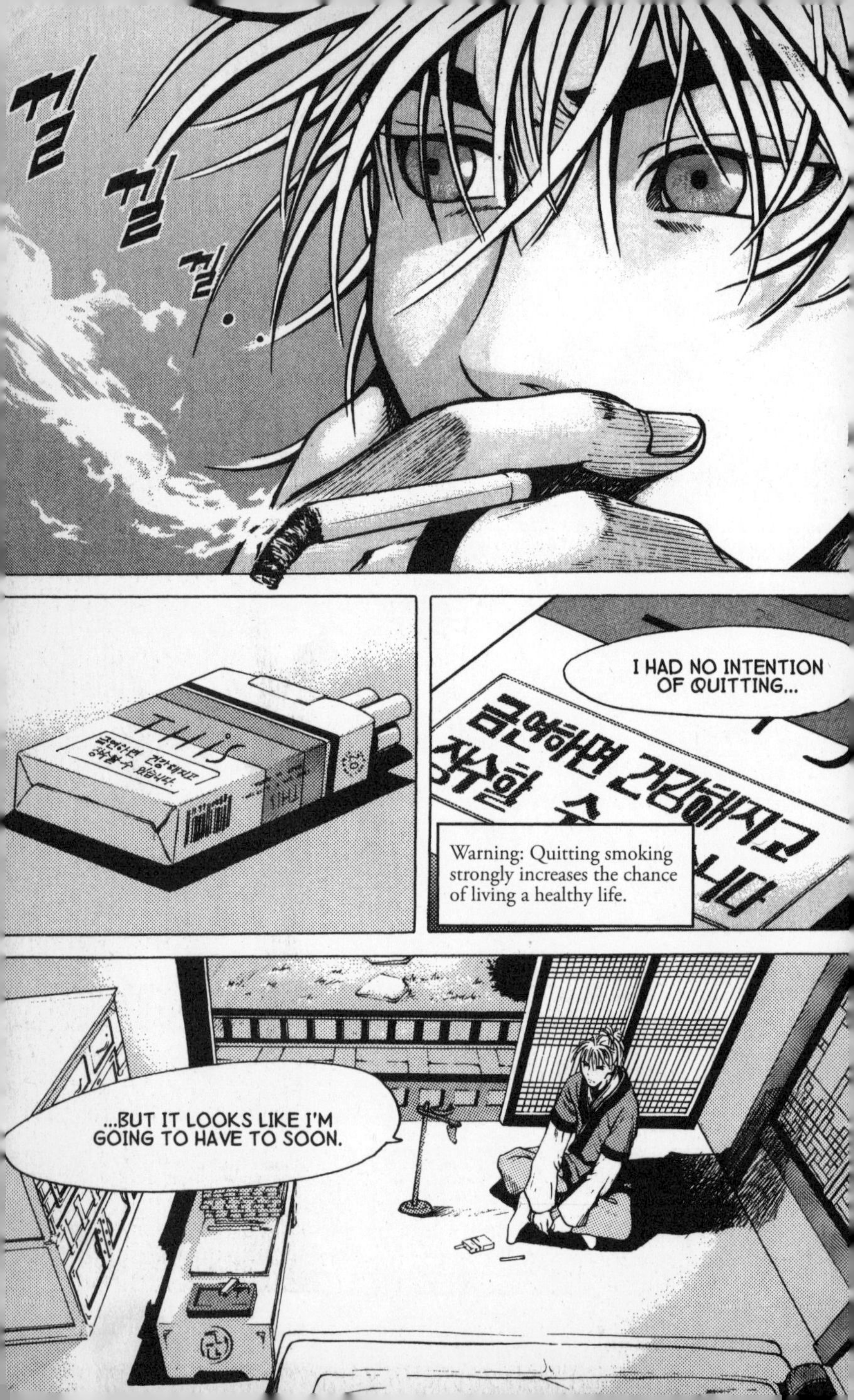
금연하면 건강해지고
I HAD NO INTENTION OF QUITTING...
Warning: Quitting smoking strongly increases the chance of living a healthy life.
...BUT IT LOOKS LIKE I'M GOING TO HAVE TO SOON.

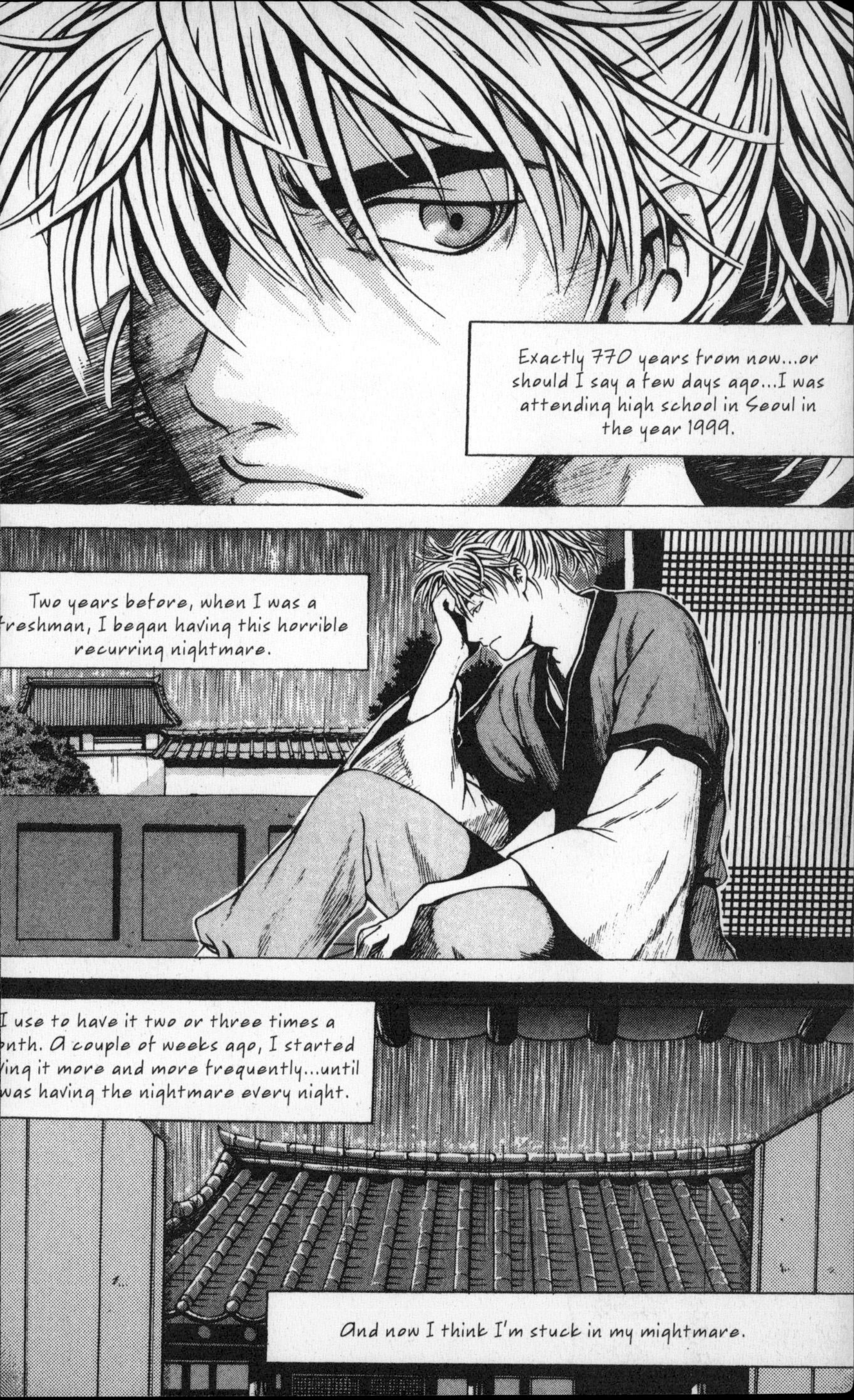
Exactly 770 years from now...or should I say a few days ago...I was attending high school in Seoul in the year 1999.
Two years before, when I was a freshman, I began having this horrible recurring nightmare.
I use to have it two or three times a onth. A couple of weeks ago, I started ving it more and more frequently...until was having the nightmare every night.
And now I think I'm stuck in my mightmare.

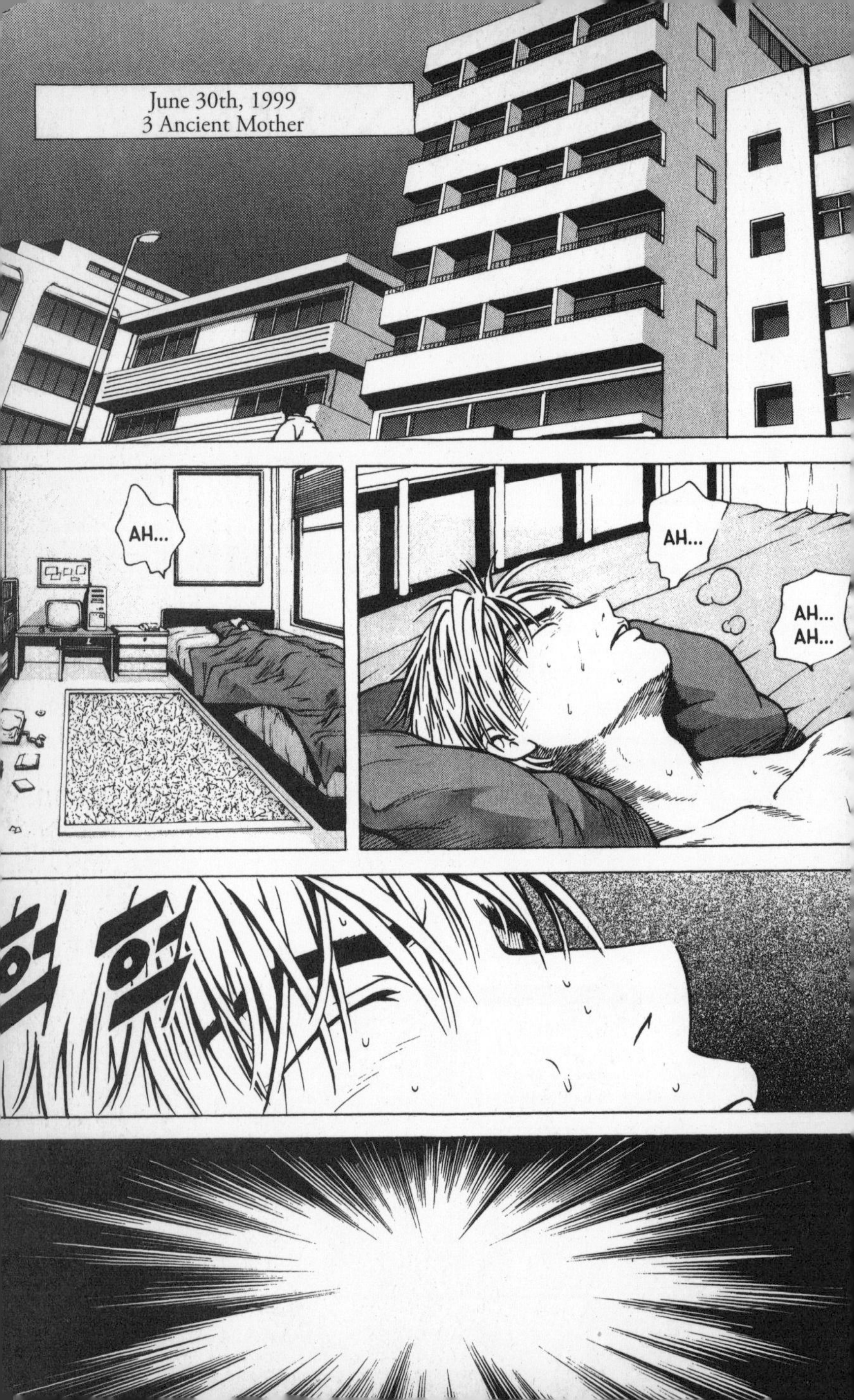
June 30th, 1999
3 Ancient Mother
AH...
AH...
AH...
AH...

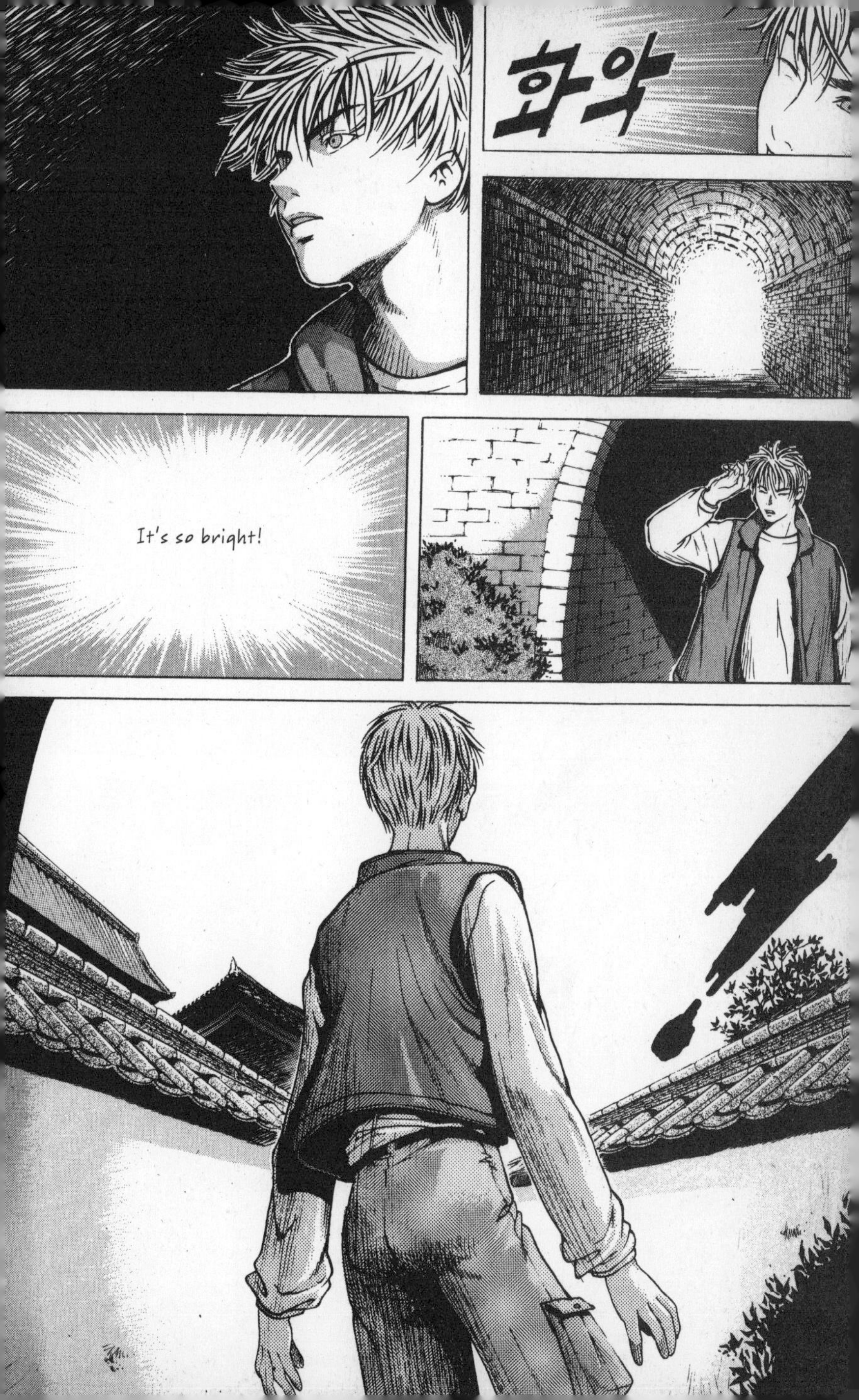

화악
It's so bright!

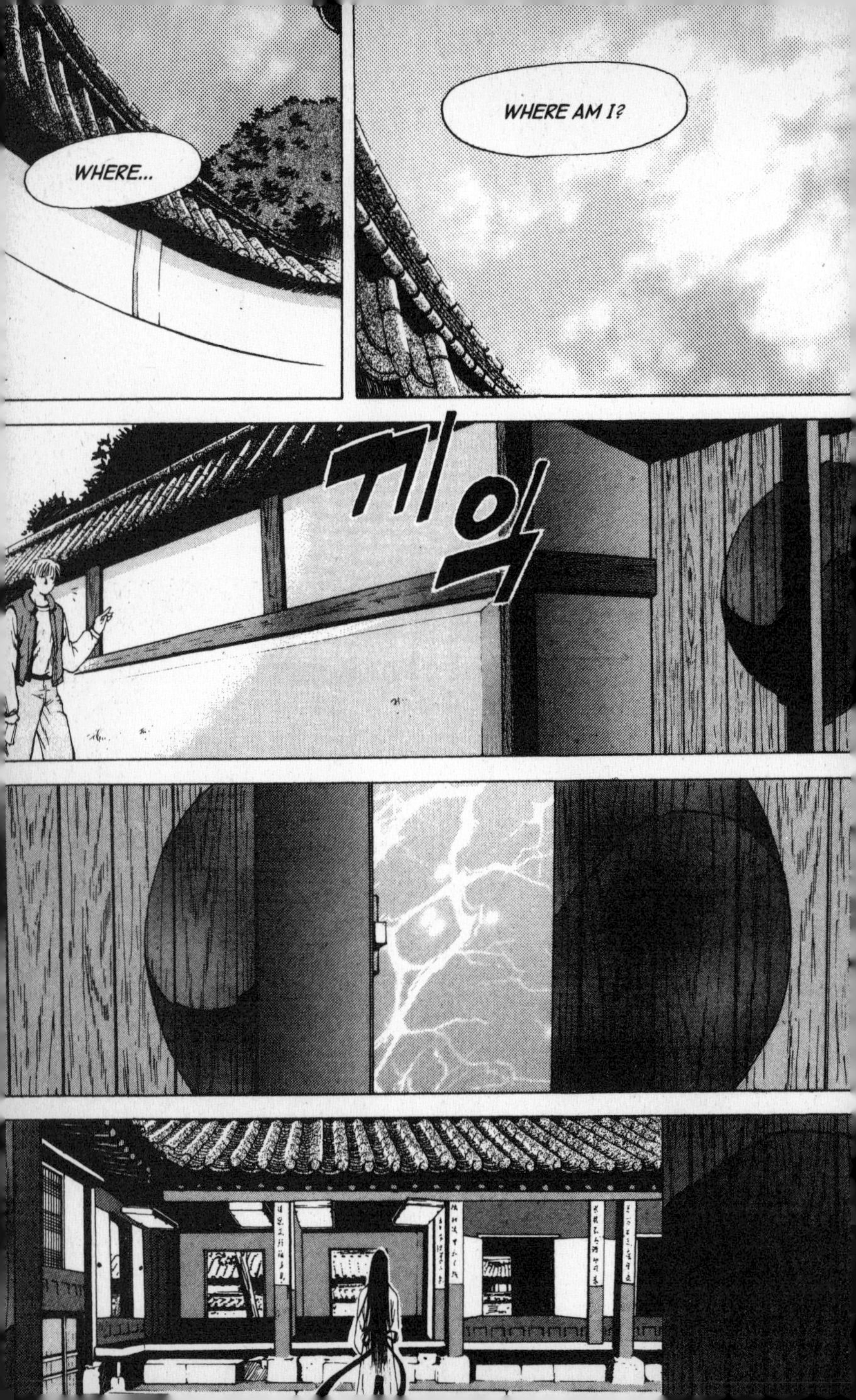
WHERE...
WHERE AM I?
끼익

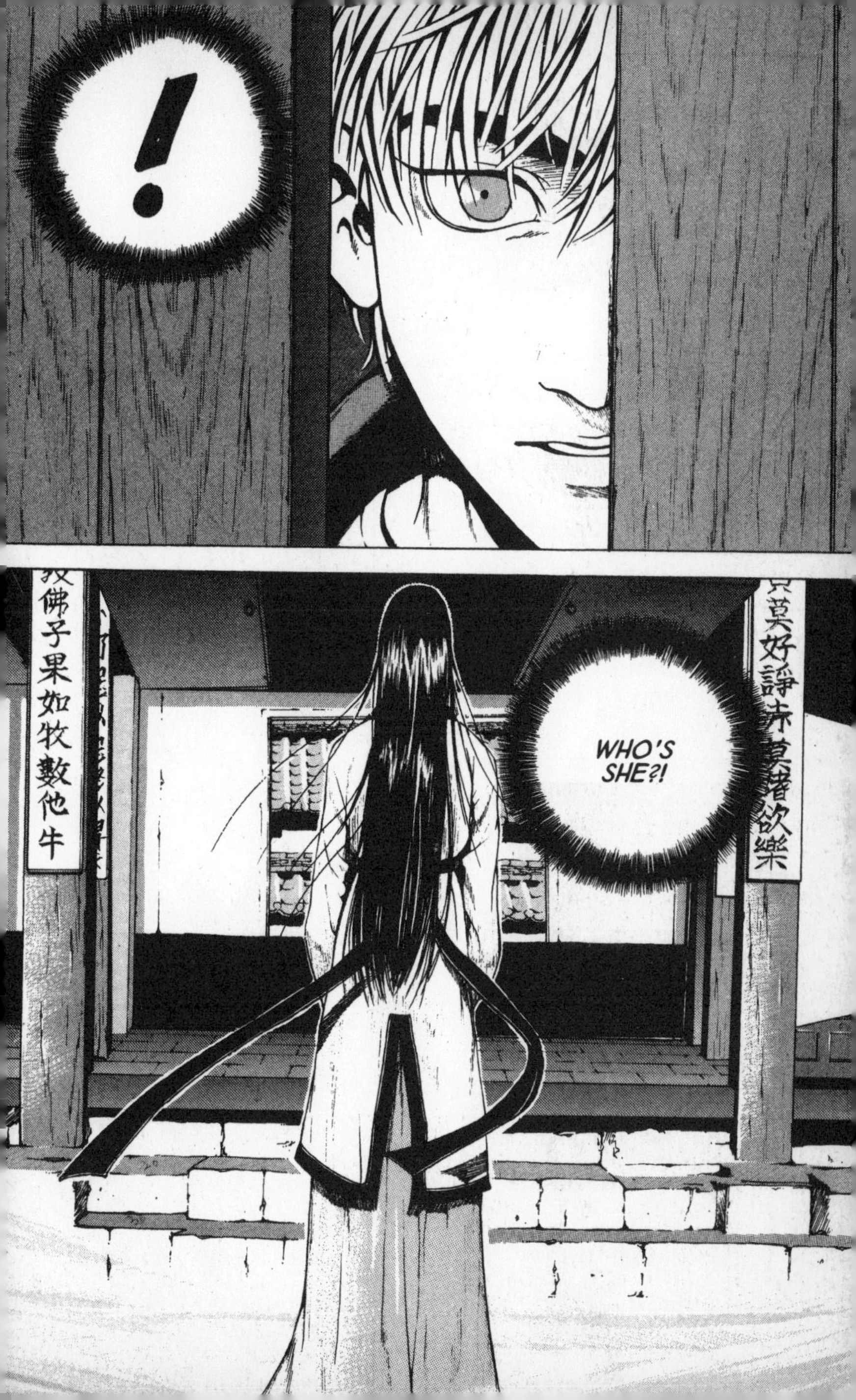
!
佛子果如牧數他牛
WHO'S SHE?!
莫好諍亦莫著欲樂

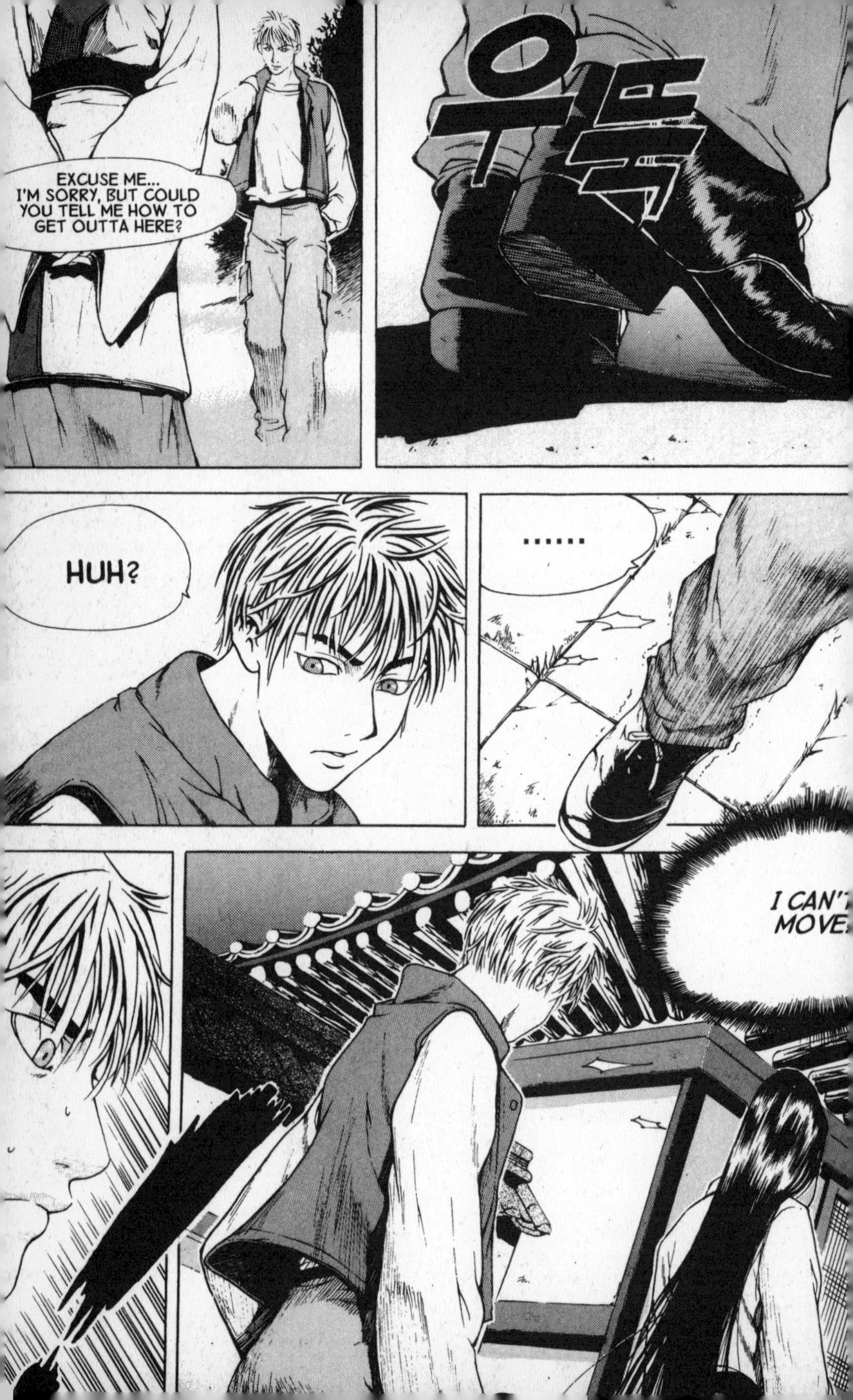
EXCUSE ME... I'M SORRY, BUT COULD YOU TELL ME HOW TO GET OUTTA HERE?
우뚝
HUH?
......
I CAN'T MOVE.

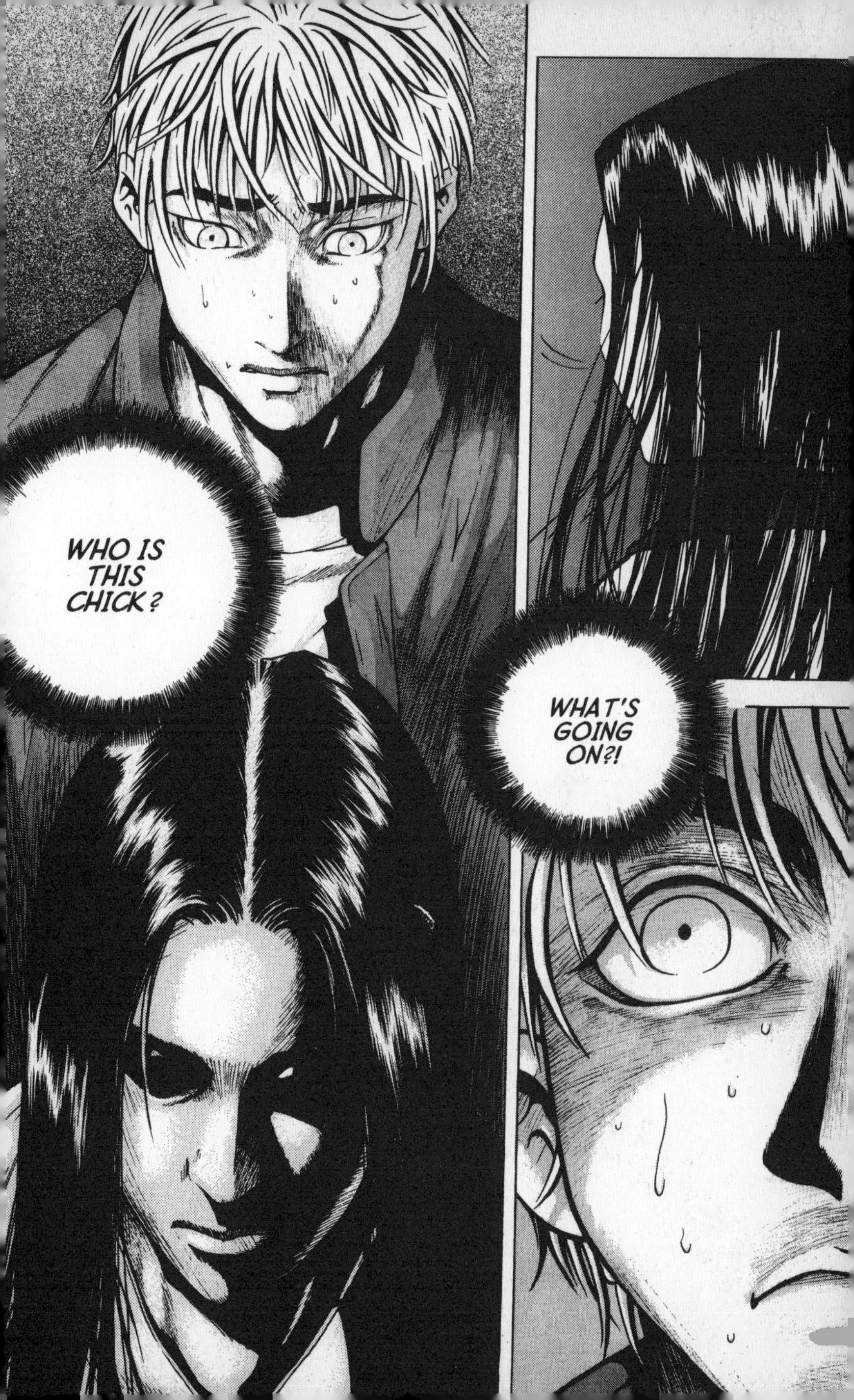
WHO IS THIS CHICK?
WHAT'S GOING ON?!

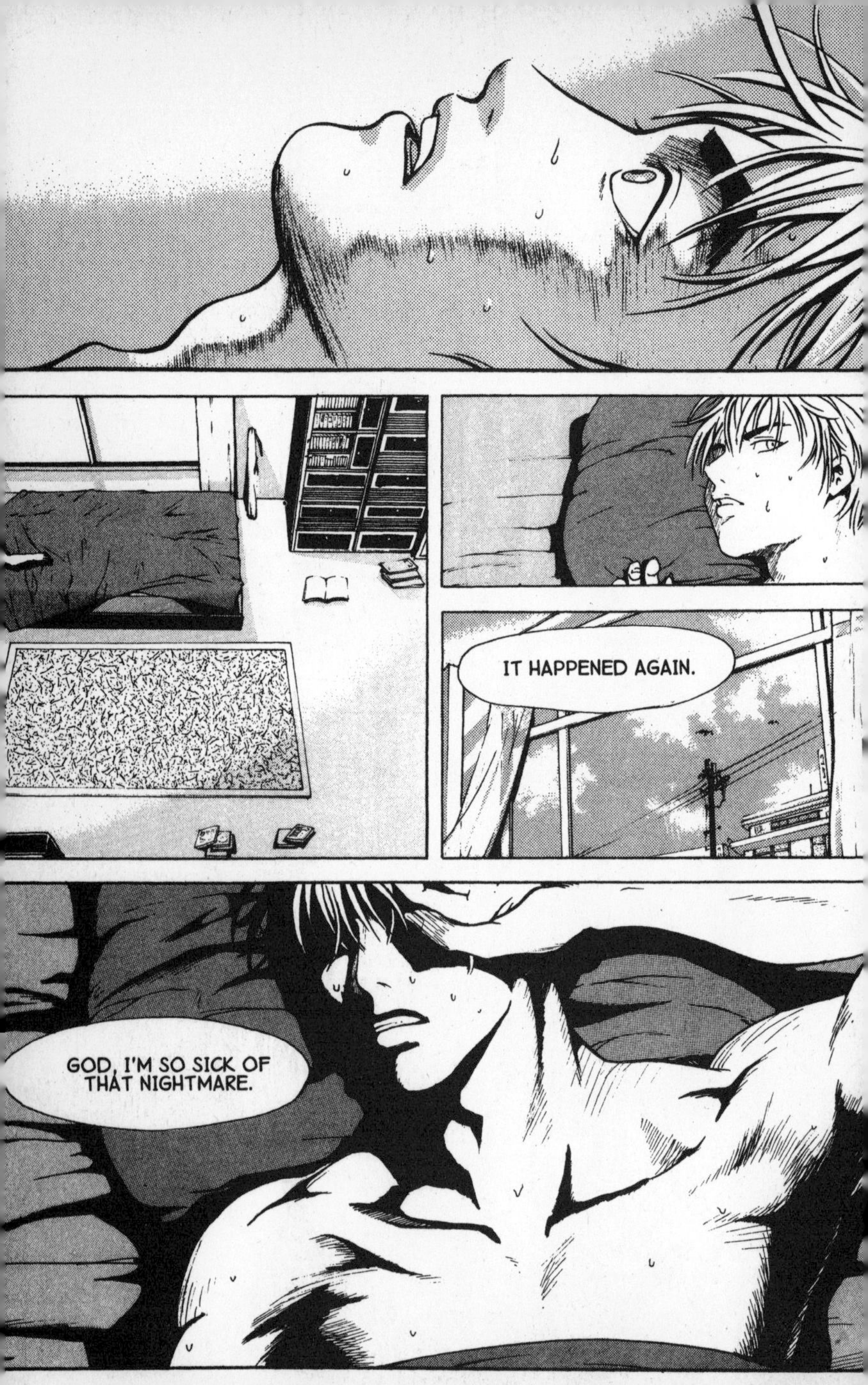
IT HAPPENED AGAIN.
GOD, I'M SO SICK OF THAT NIGHTMARE.

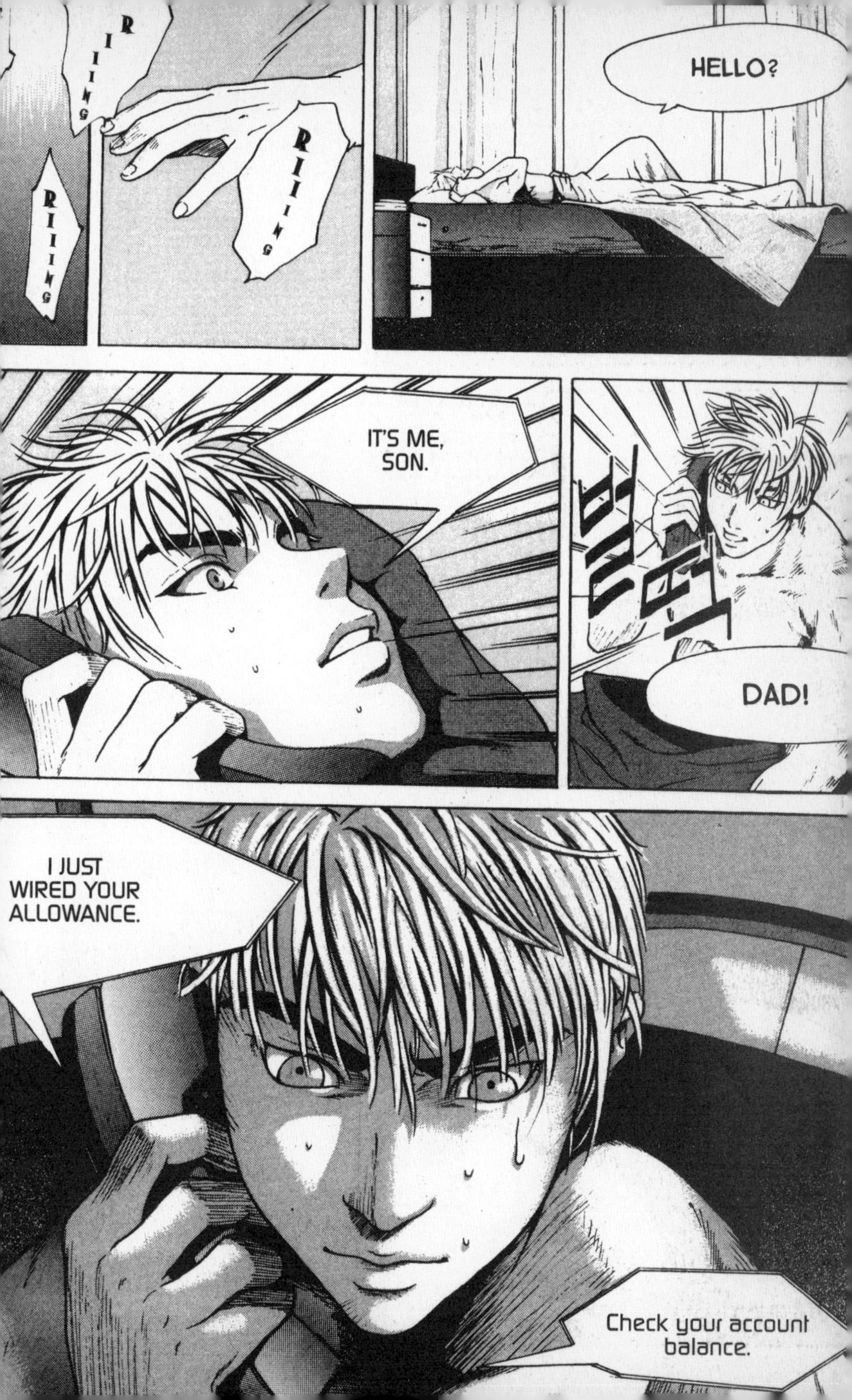

RIIIING
RIIIING
RIIIING
HELLO?
IT'S ME, SON.
DAD!
I JUST WIRED YOUR ALLOWANCE.
Check your account balance.

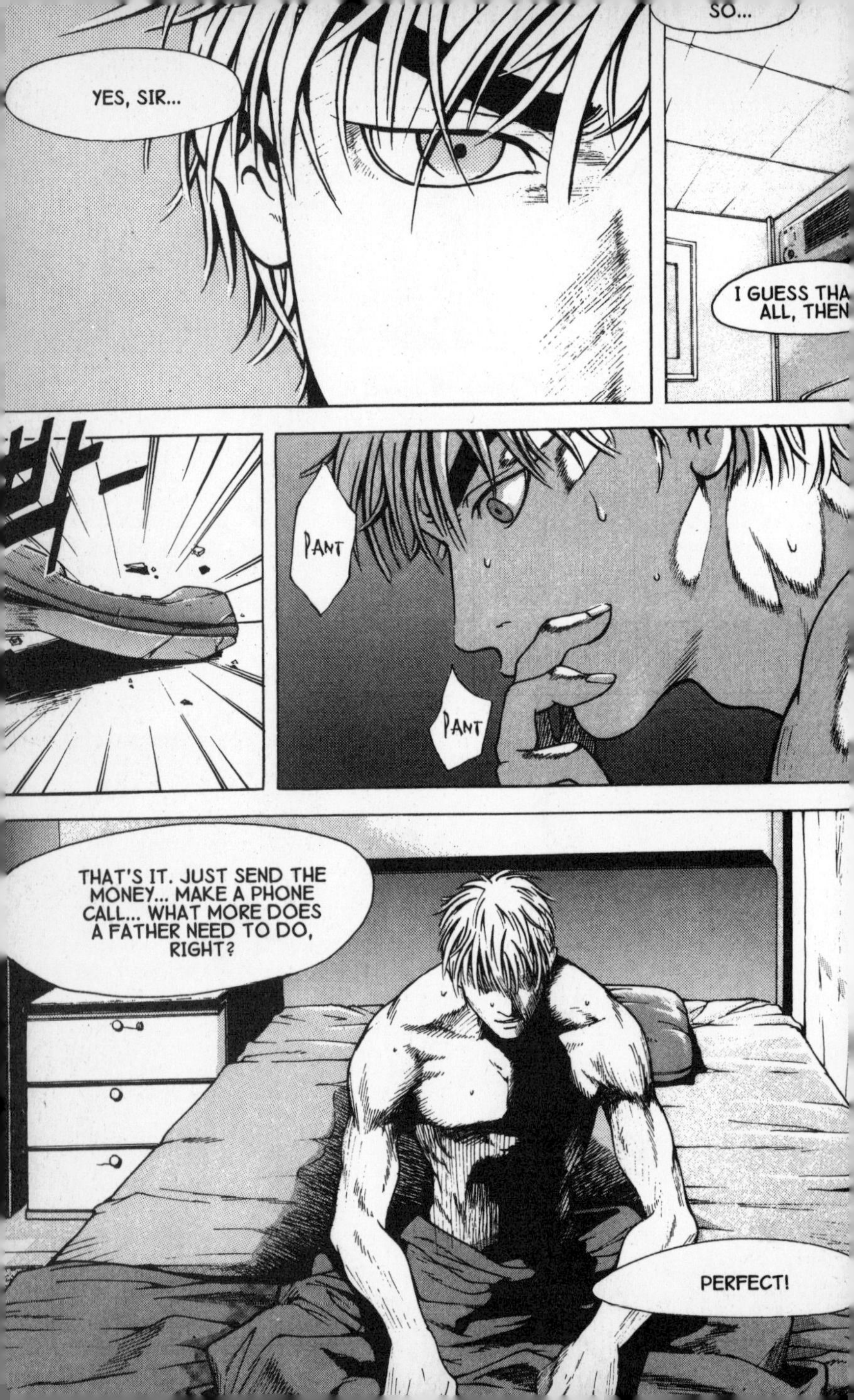

YES, SIR...
SO...
I GUESS THA ALL, THEN
PANT
PANT
THAT'S IT. JUST SEND THE MONEY... MAKE A PHONE CALL... WHAT MORE DOES A FATHER NEED TO DO, RIGHT?
PERFECT!

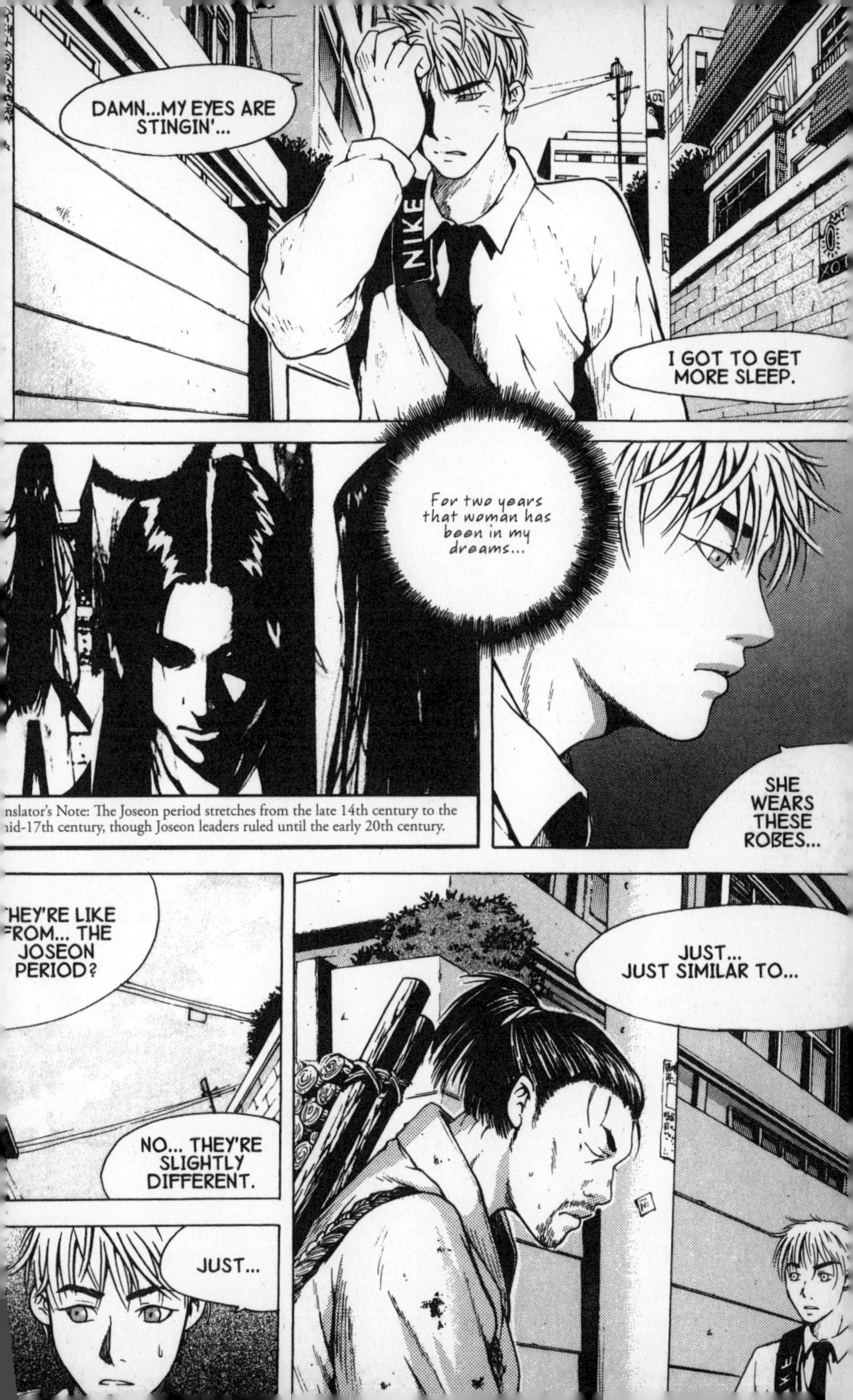
DAMN...MY EYES ARE STINGIN'...
I GOT TO GET MORE SLEEP.
For two years that woman has been in my dreams...
SHE WEARS THESE ROBES...
HEY'RE LIKE FROM... THE JOSEON PERIOD?
NO... THEY'RE SLIGHTLY DIFFERENT.
JUST...
JUST... JUST SIMILAR TO...

nslator's Note: The Joseon period stretches from the late 14th century to the nid-17th century, though Joseon leaders ruled until the early 20th century.

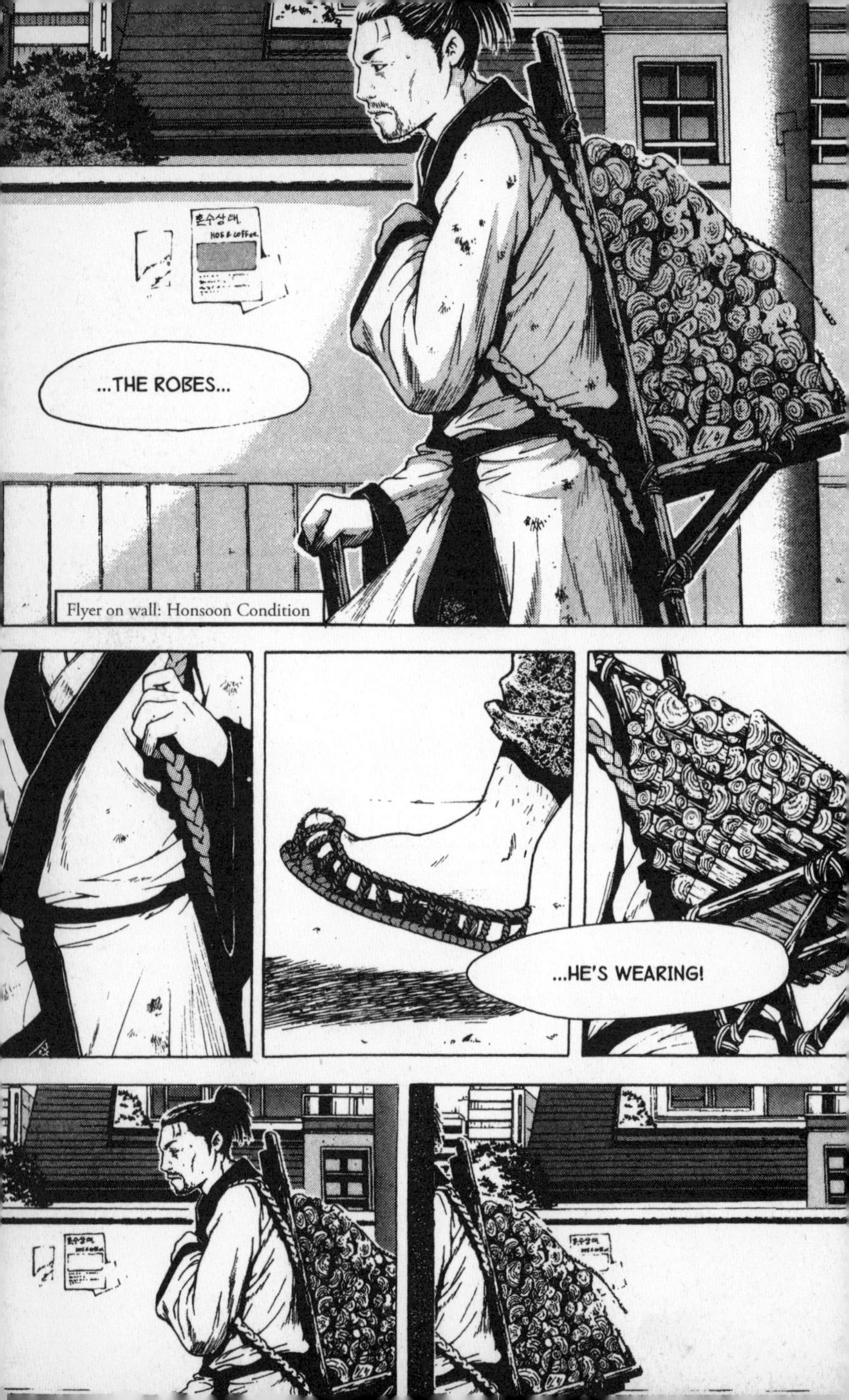
...THE ROBES...
Flyer on wall: Honsoon Condition
...HE'S WEARING!

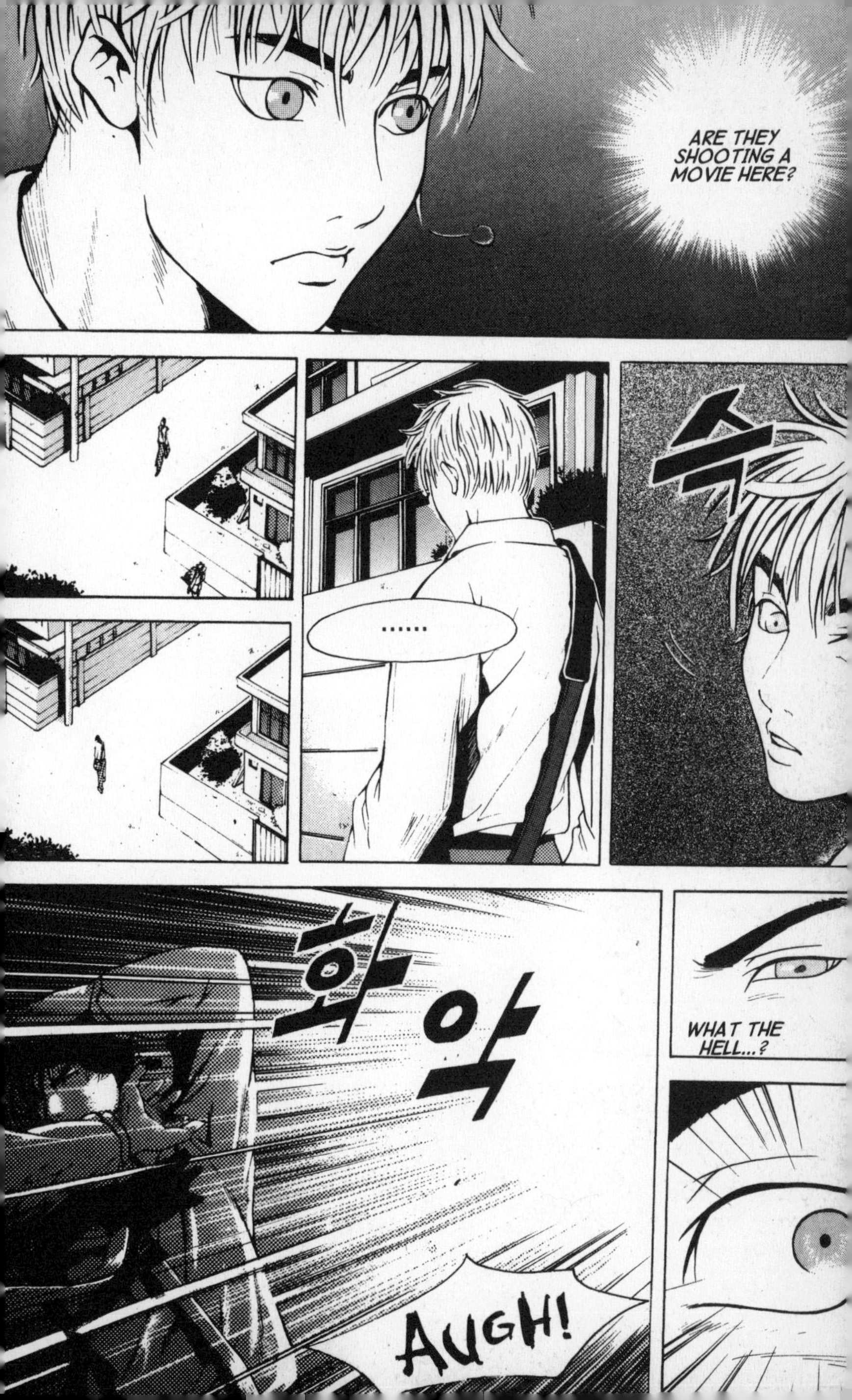
ARE THEY SHOOTING A MOVIE HERE?
......
WHAT THE HELL...?
AUGH!

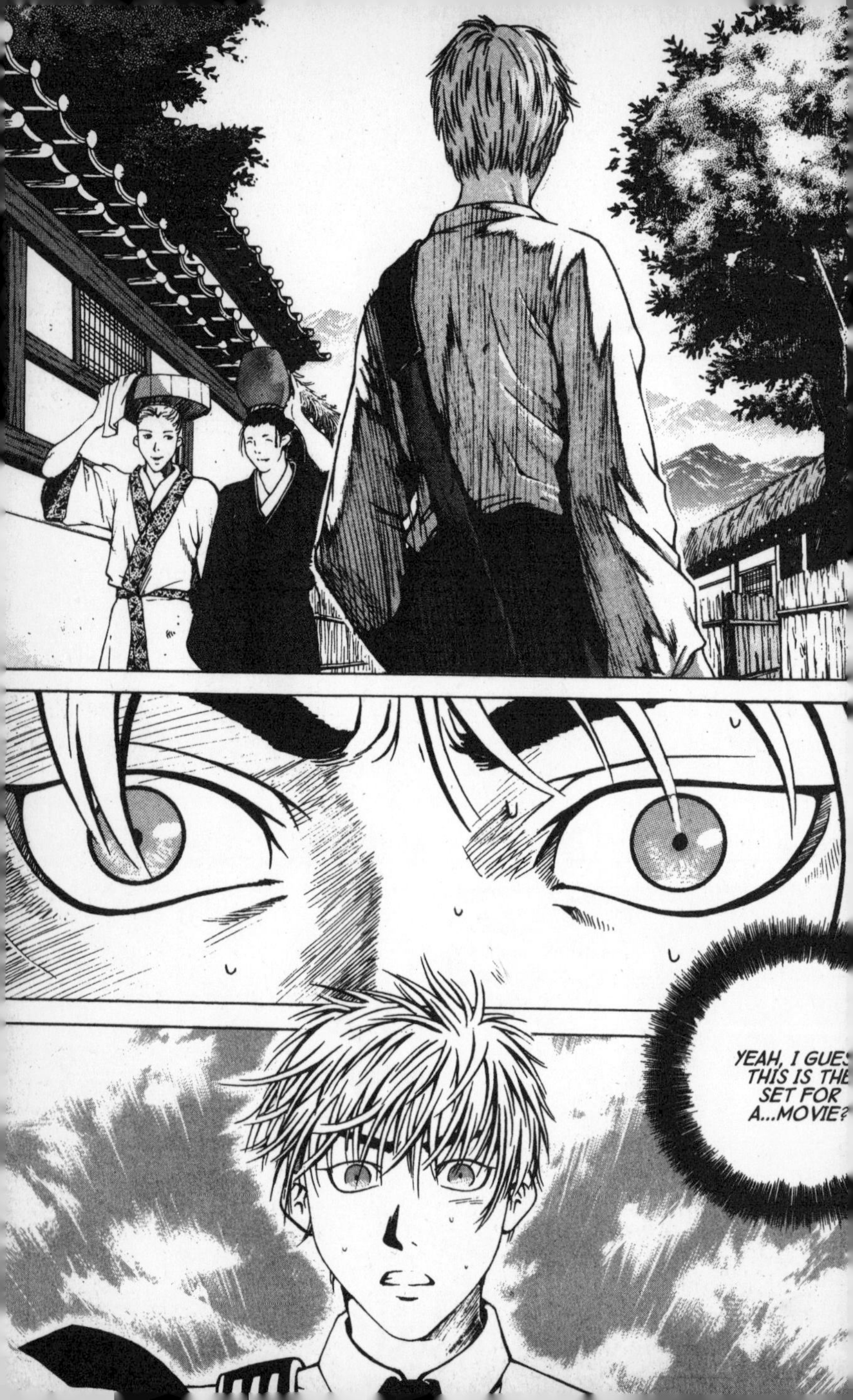
YEAH, I GUES
THIS IS THE
SET FOR
A...MOVIE?

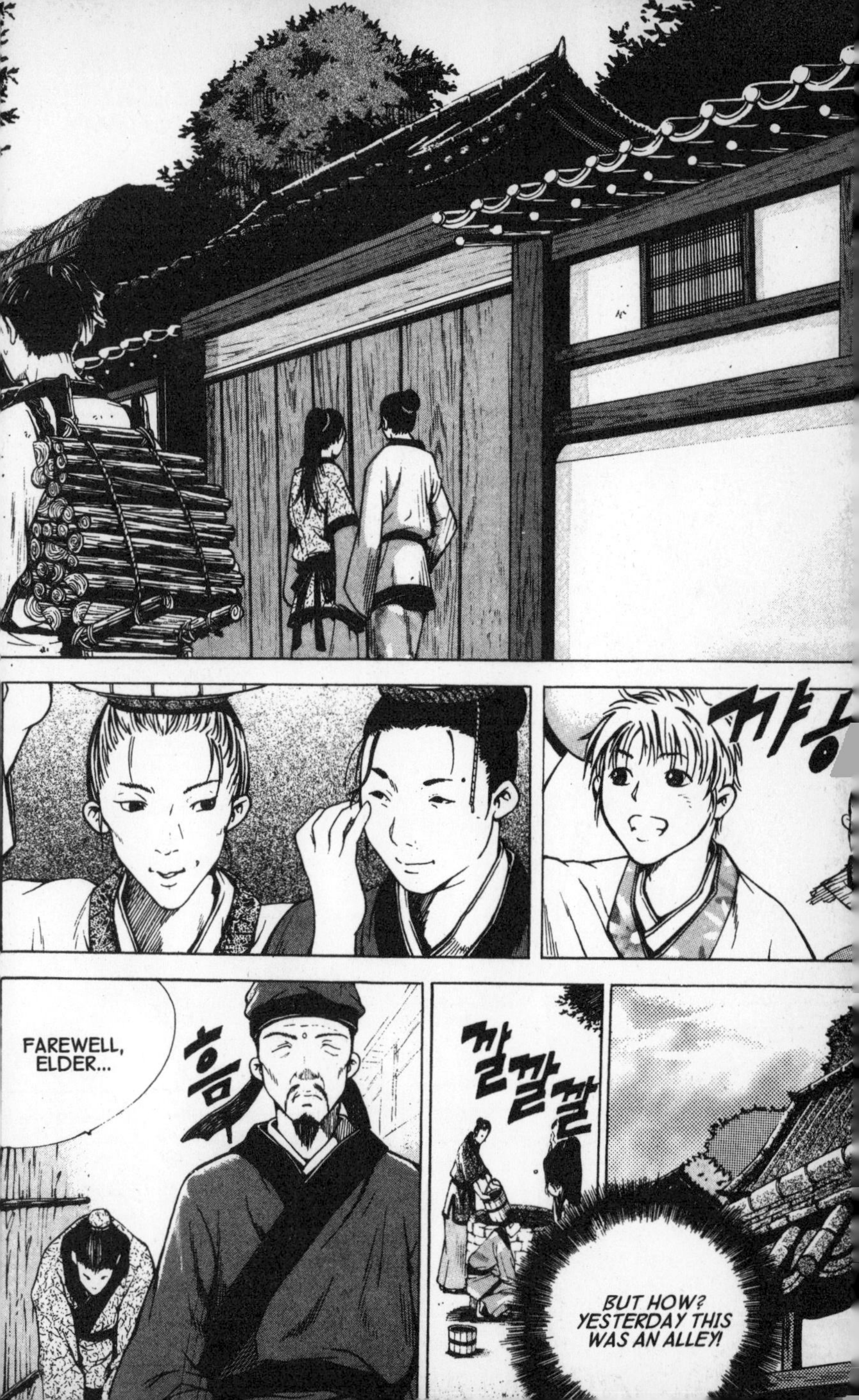

FAREWELL, ELDER...
흠
깔깔깔
BUT HOW? YESTERDAY THIS WAS AN ALLEY!

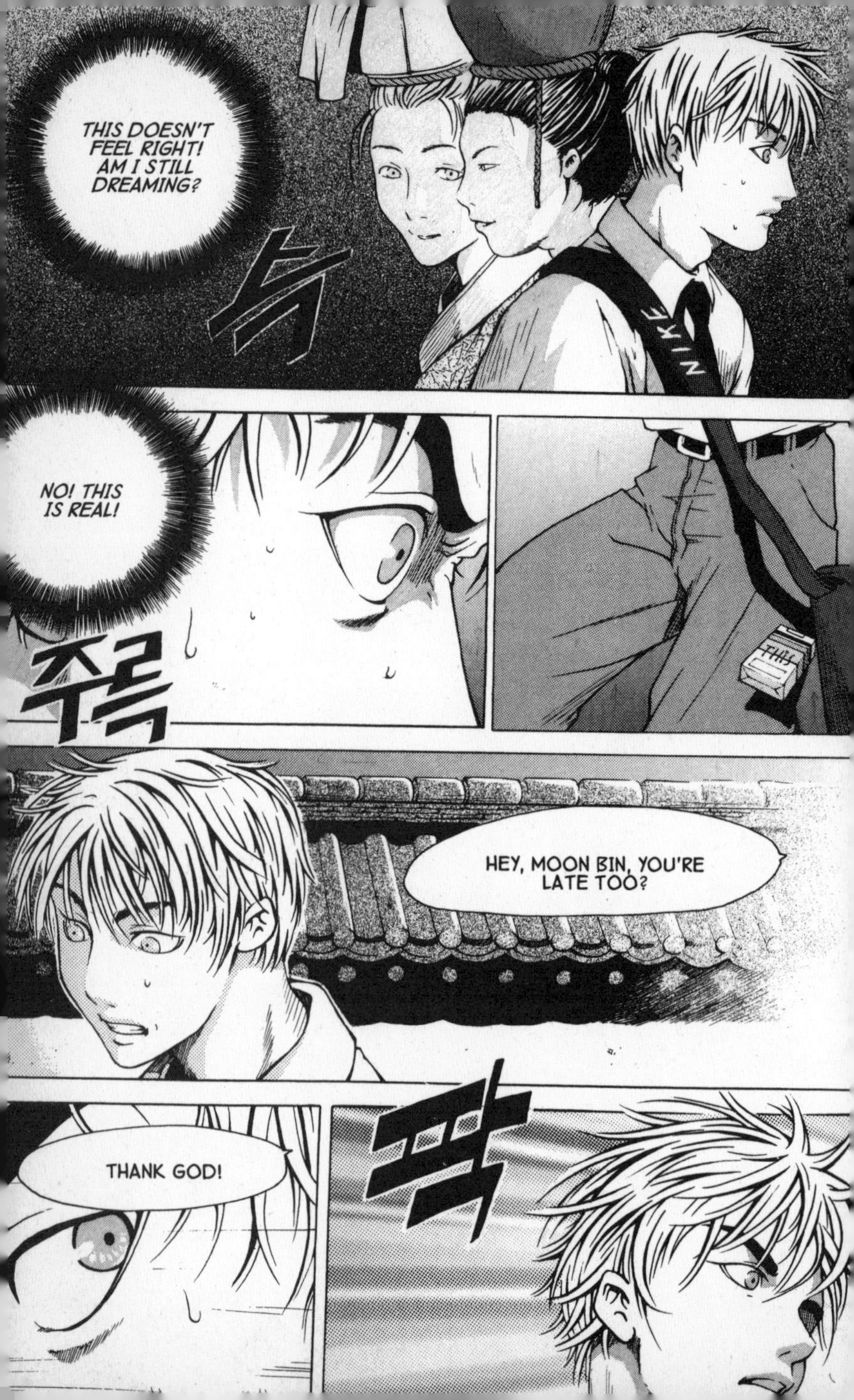
THIS DOESN'T FEEL RIGHT! AM I STILL DREAMING?
슥
NIKE
NO! THIS IS REAL!
주륵
THIS
HEY, MOON BIN, YOU'RE LATE TOO?
THANK GOD!
퍽

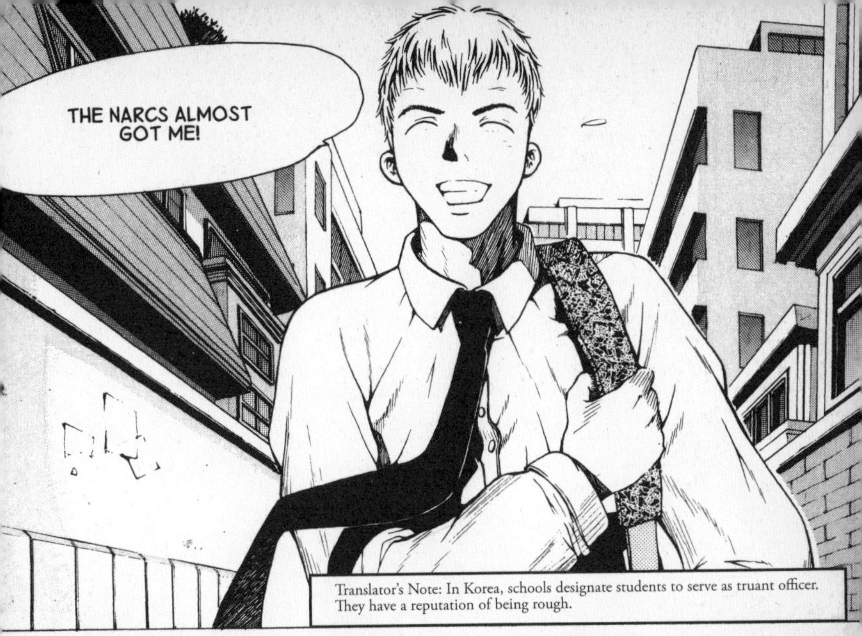
THE NARCS ALMOST GOT ME!

Translator's Note: In Korea, schools designate students to serve as truant officer. They have a reputation of being rough.

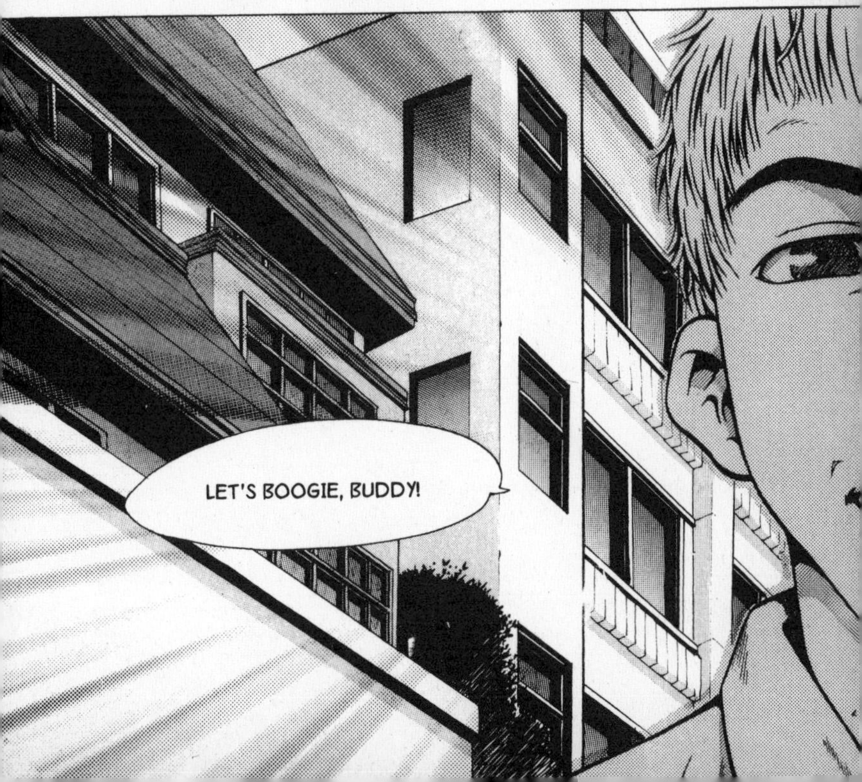
LET'S BOOGIE, BUDDY!

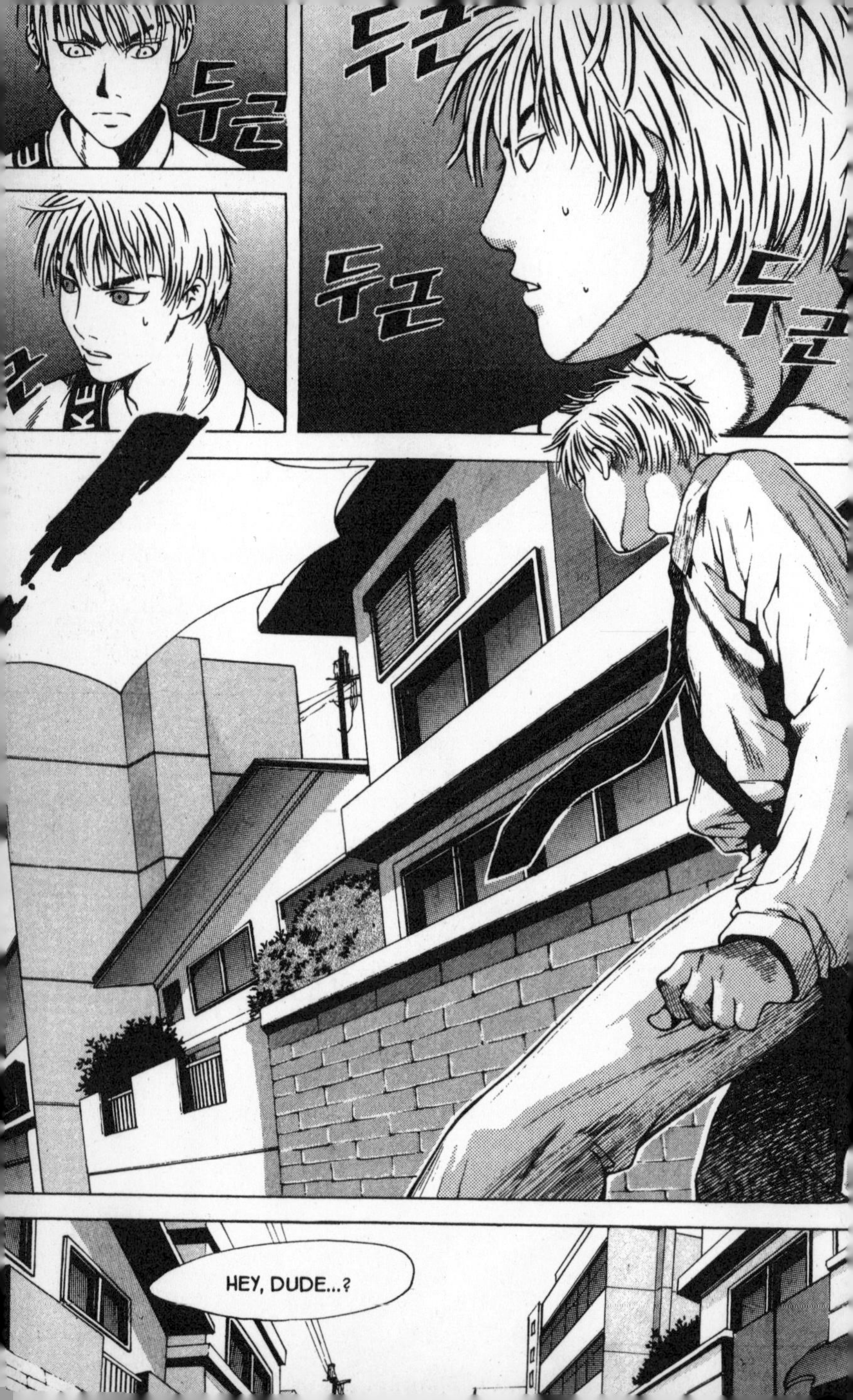
두근
두근
두근
두근
HEY, DUDE...?

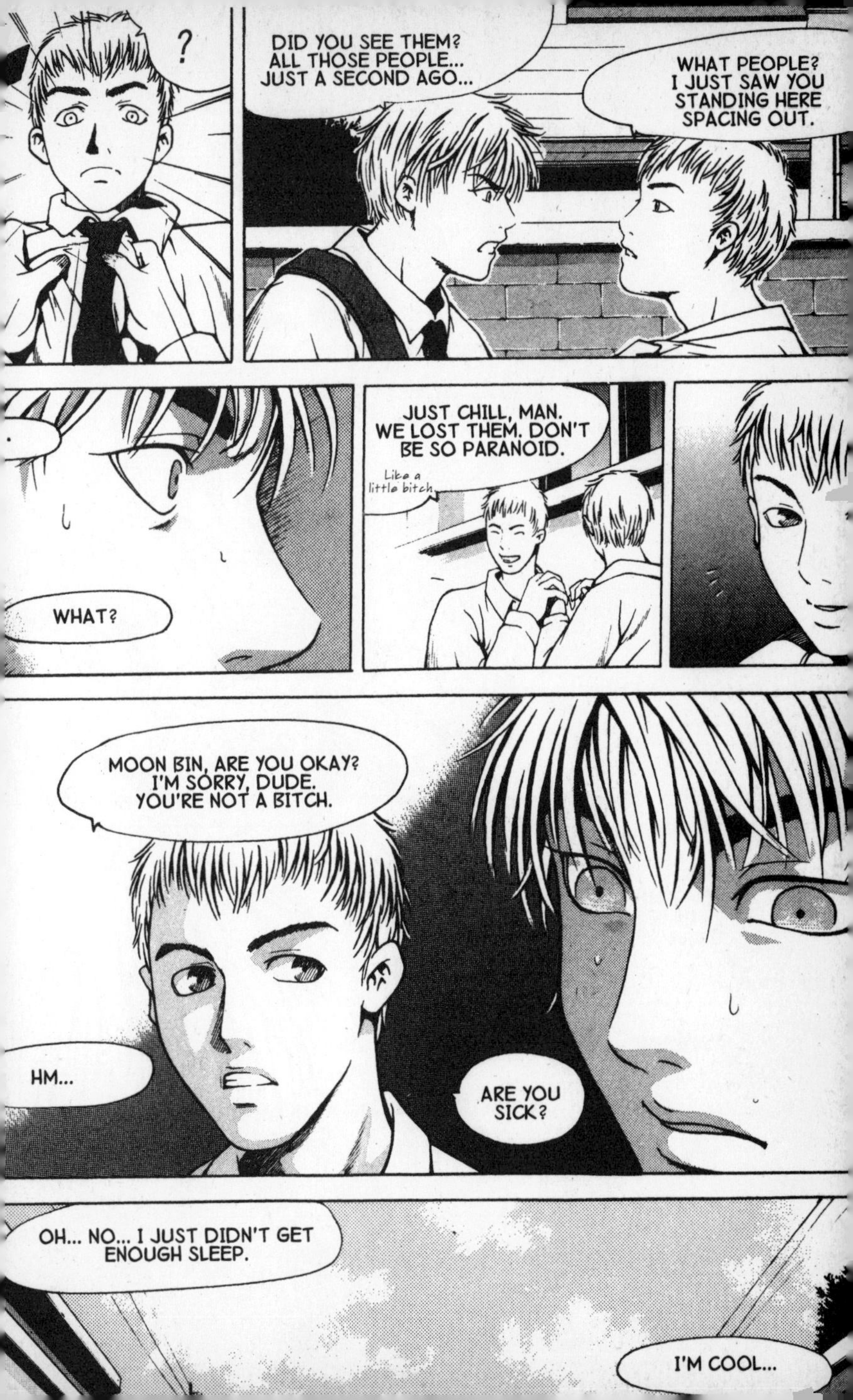
?
DID YOU SEE THEM? ALL THOSE PEOPLE... JUST A SECOND AGO...
WHAT PEOPLE? I JUST SAW YOU STANDING HERE SPACING OUT.
WHAT?
JUST CHILL, MAN. WE LOST THEM. DON'T BE SO PARANOID.
Like a little bitch.
MOON BIN, ARE YOU OKAY? I'M SORRY, DUDE. YOU'RE NOT A BITCH.
HM...
ARE YOU SICK?
OH... NO... I JUST DIDN'T GET ENOUGH SLEEP.
I'M COOL...

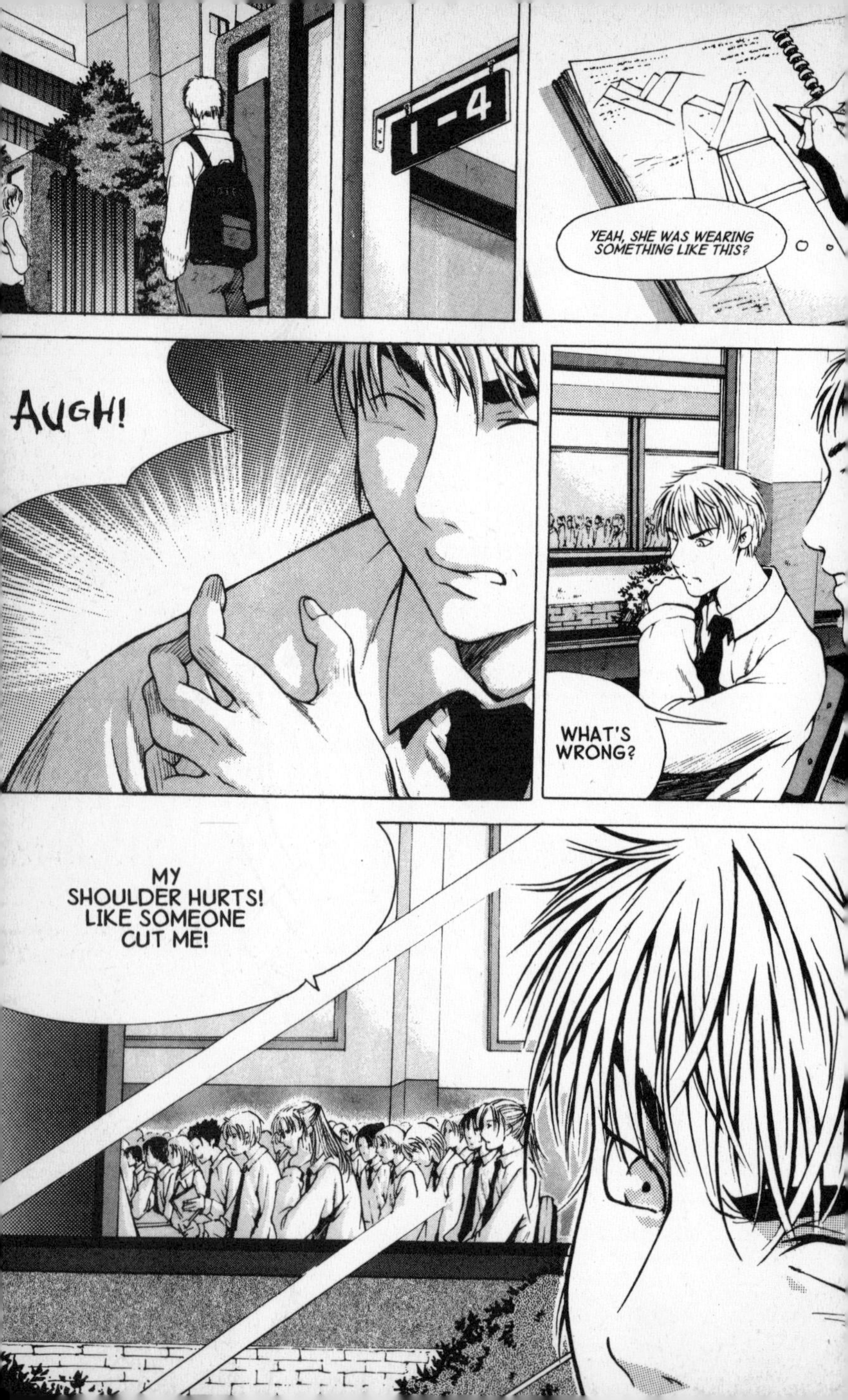
1-4
YEAH, SHE WAS WEARING SOMETHING LIKE THIS?
AUGH!
WHAT'S WRONG?
MY SHOULDER HURTS! LIKE SOMEONE CUT ME!

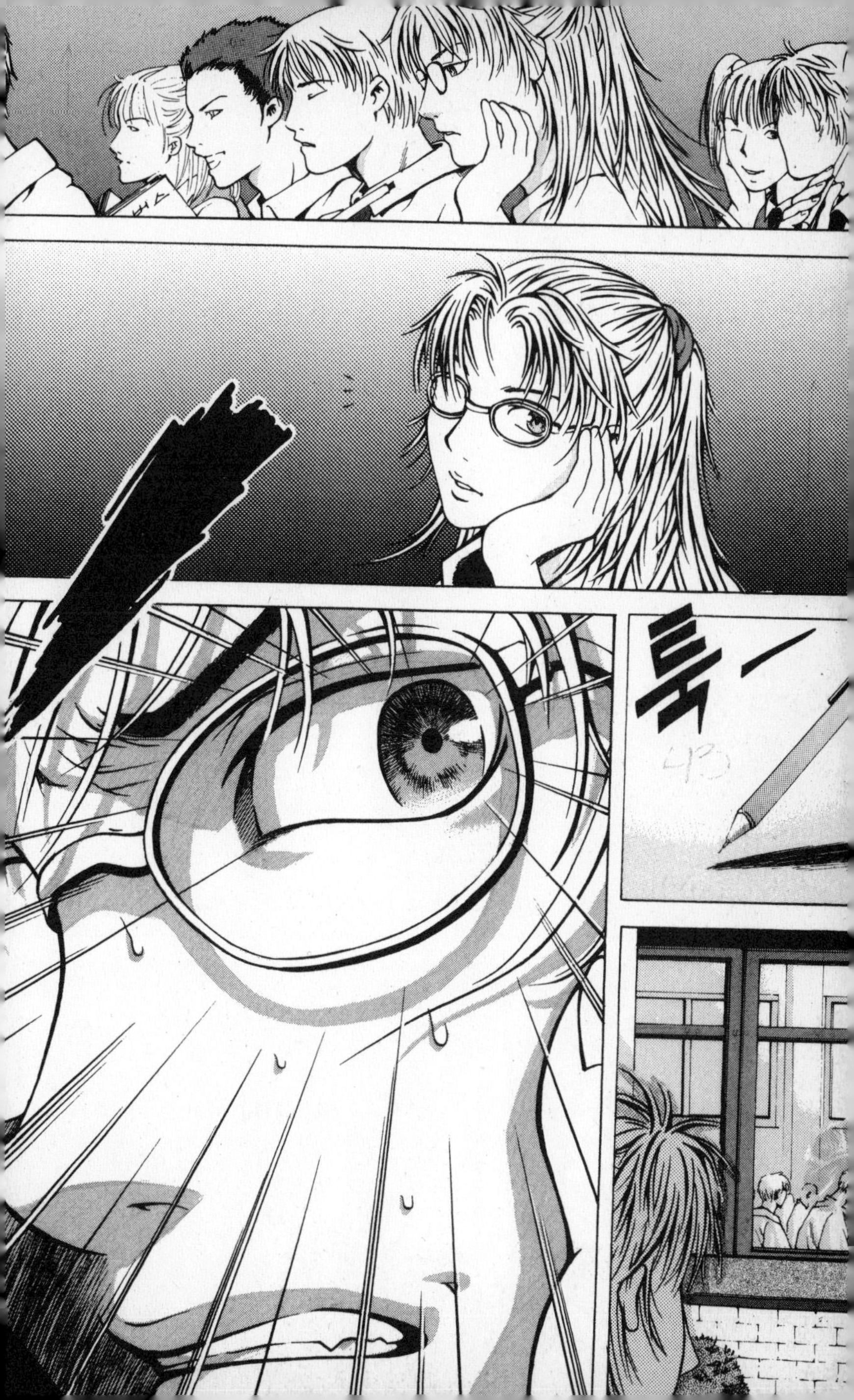
툭—

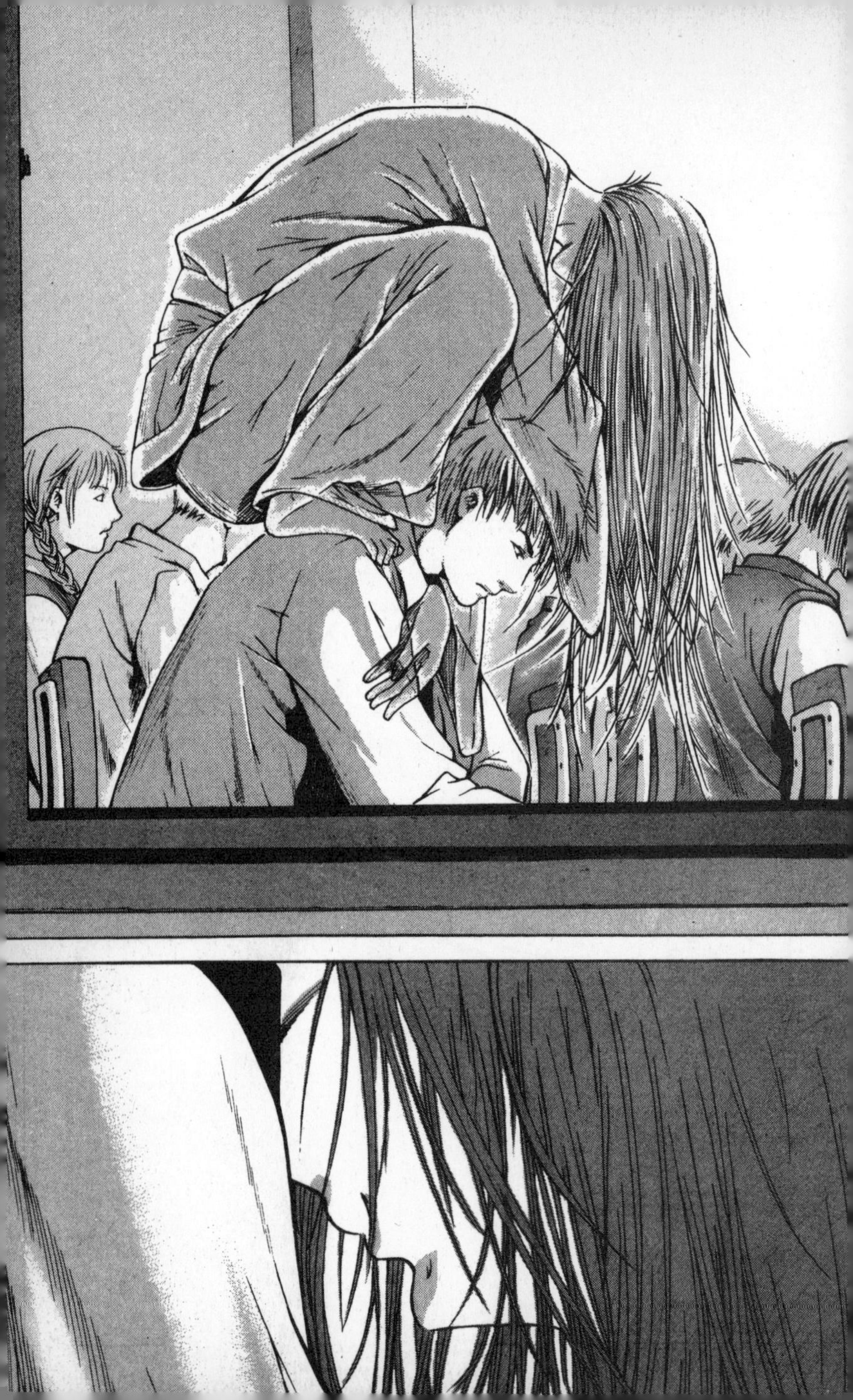

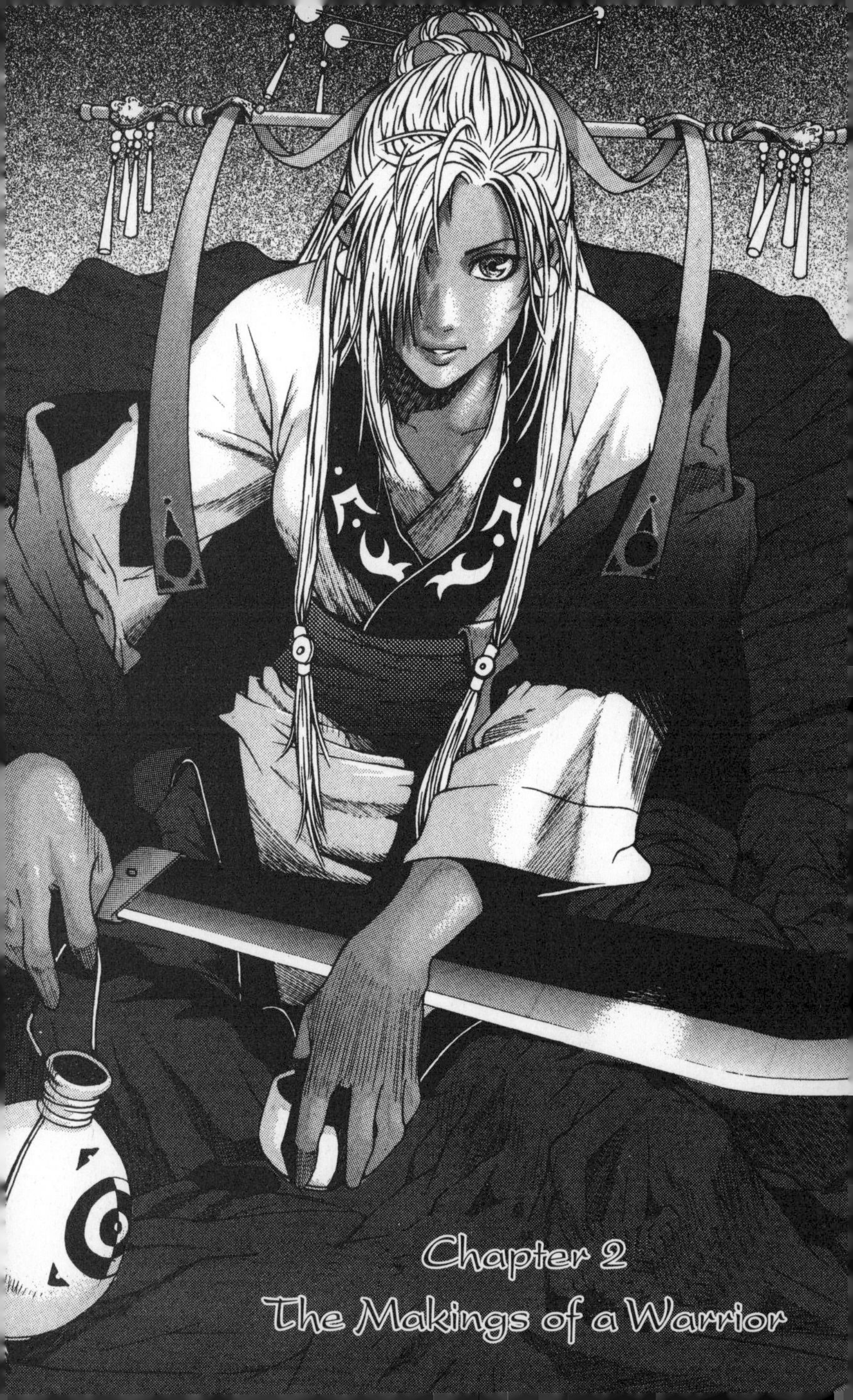
Chapter 2
The Makings of a Warrior

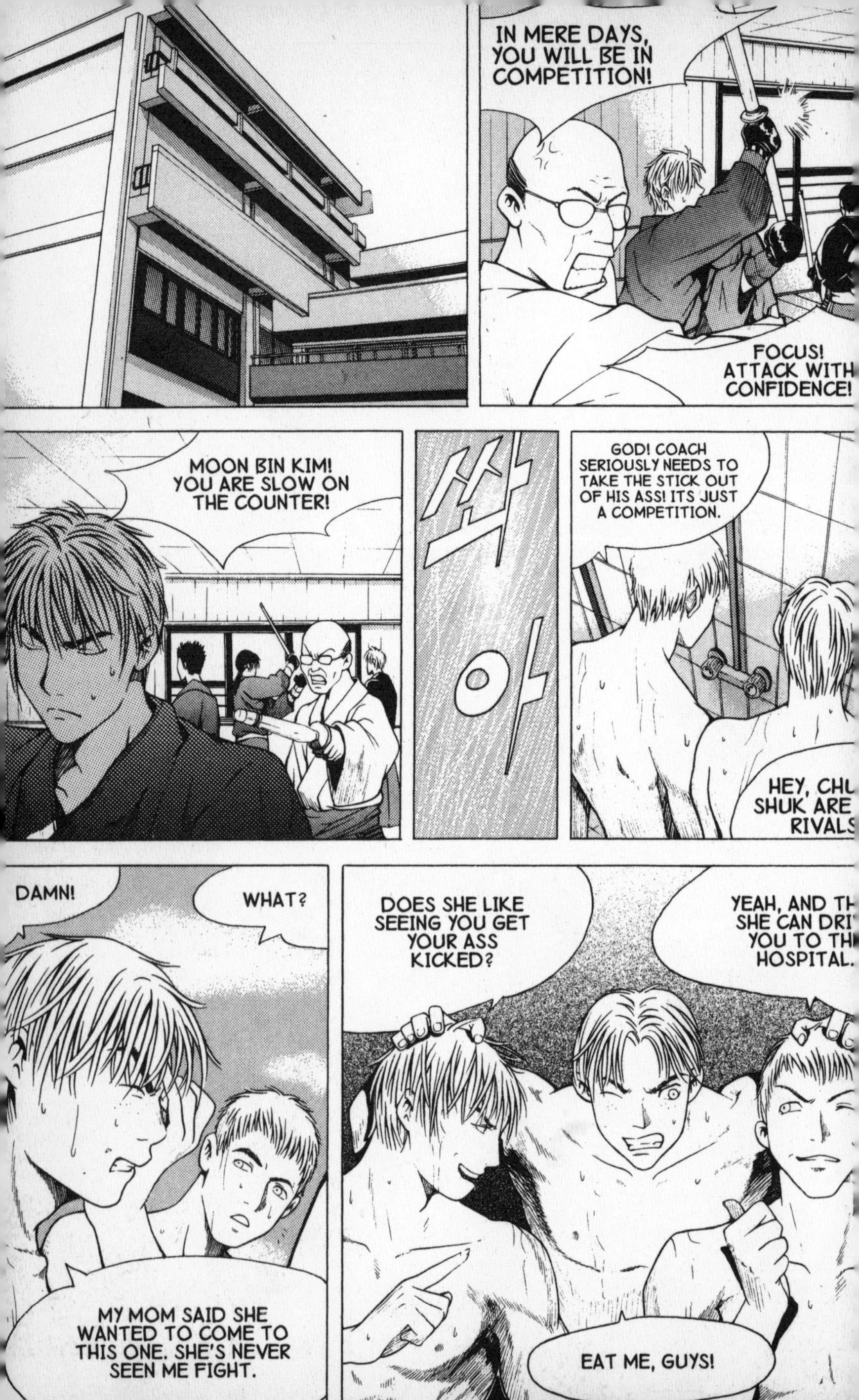
IN MERE DAYS, YOU WILL BE IN COMPETITION!
FOCUS! ATTACK WITH CONFIDENCE!
MOON BIN KIM! YOU ARE SLOW ON THE COUNTER!
쌰아
GOD! COACH SERIOUSLY NEEDS TO TAKE THE STICK OUT OF HIS ASS! ITS JUST A COMPETITION.
HEY, CHU SHUK ARE RIVALS
DAMN!
WHAT?
MY MOM SAID SHE WANTED TO COME TO THIS ONE. SHE'S NEVER SEEN ME FIGHT.
DOES SHE LIKE SEEING YOU GET YOUR ASS KICKED?
YEAH, AND TH SHE CAN DRI YOU TO TH HOSPITAL.
EAT ME, GUYS!

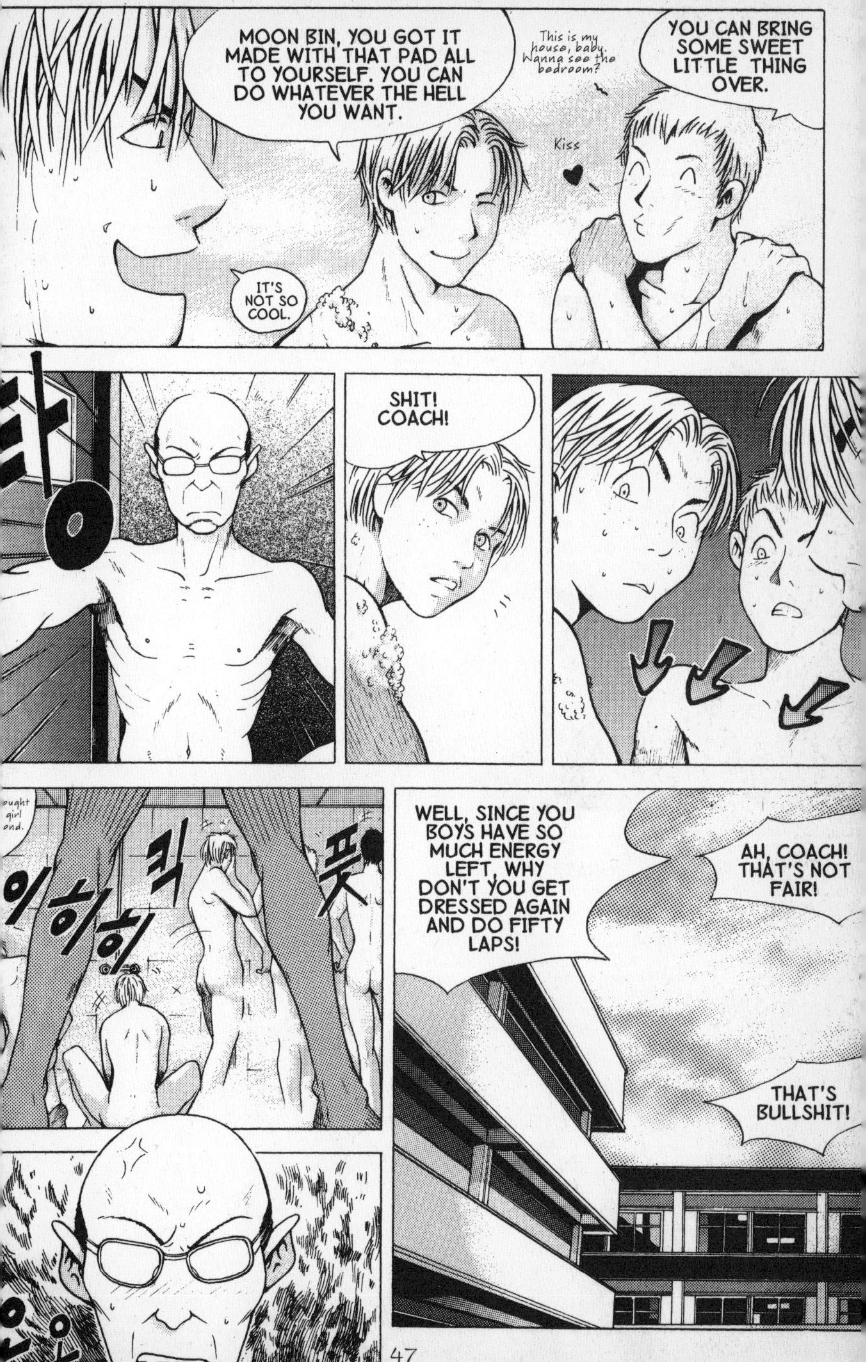
MOON BIN, YOU GOT IT MADE WITH THAT PAD ALL TO YOURSELF. YOU CAN DO WHATEVER THE HELL YOU WANT.
This is my house, baby. Wanna see the bedroom?
YOU CAN BRING SOME SWEET LITTLE THING OVER.
Kiss
IT'S NOT SO COOL.
SHIT! COACH!
이히히
킥
풋
WELL, SINCE YOU BOYS HAVE SO MUCH ENERGY LEFT, WHY DON'T YOU GET DRESSED AGAIN AND DO FIFTY LAPS!
AH, COACH! THAT'S NOT FAIR!
THAT'S BULLSHIT!

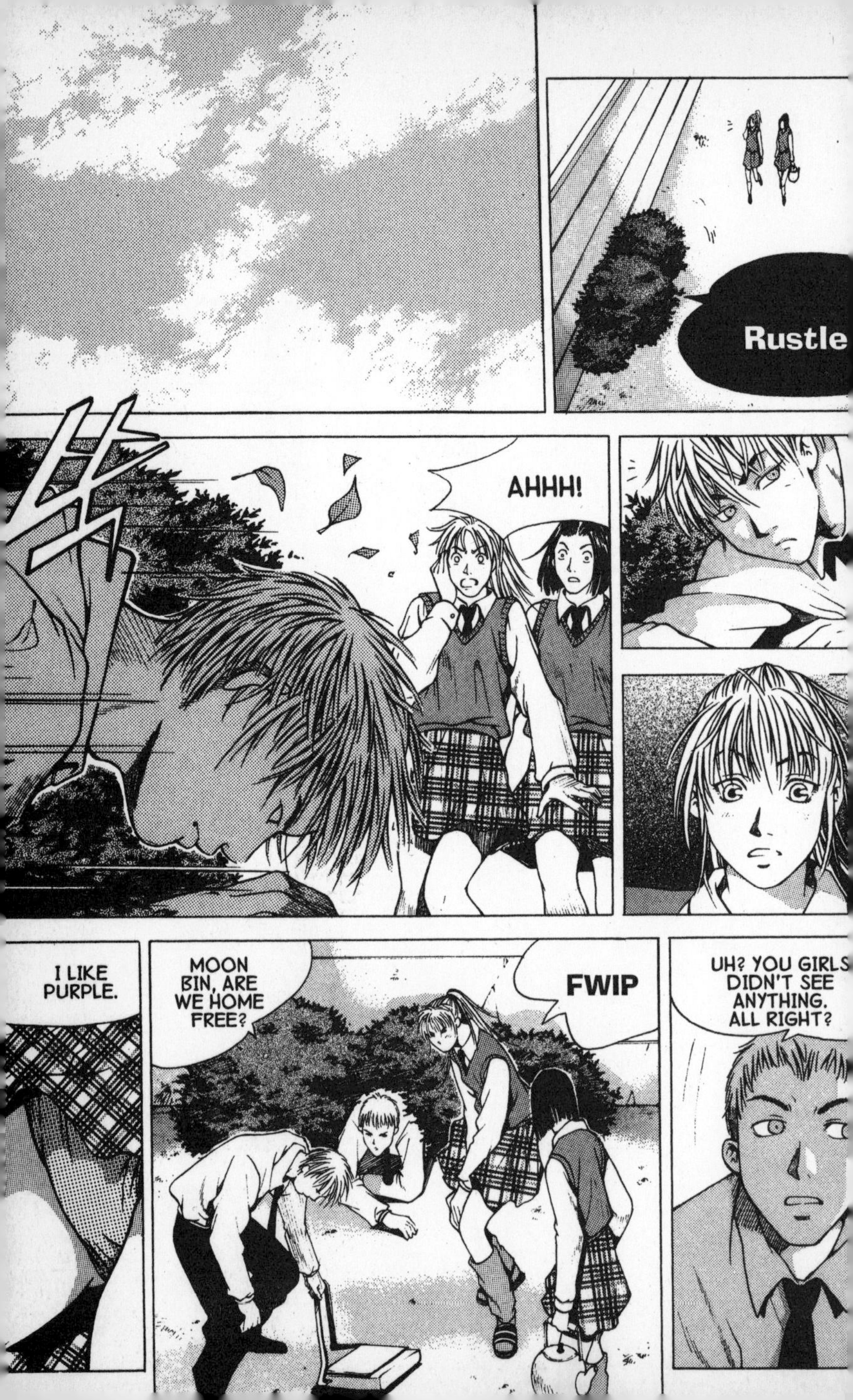
Rustle
AHHH!
I LIKE PURPLE.
MOON BIN, ARE WE HOME FREE?
FWIP
UH? YOU GIRLS DIDN'T SEE ANYTHING. ALL RIGHT?

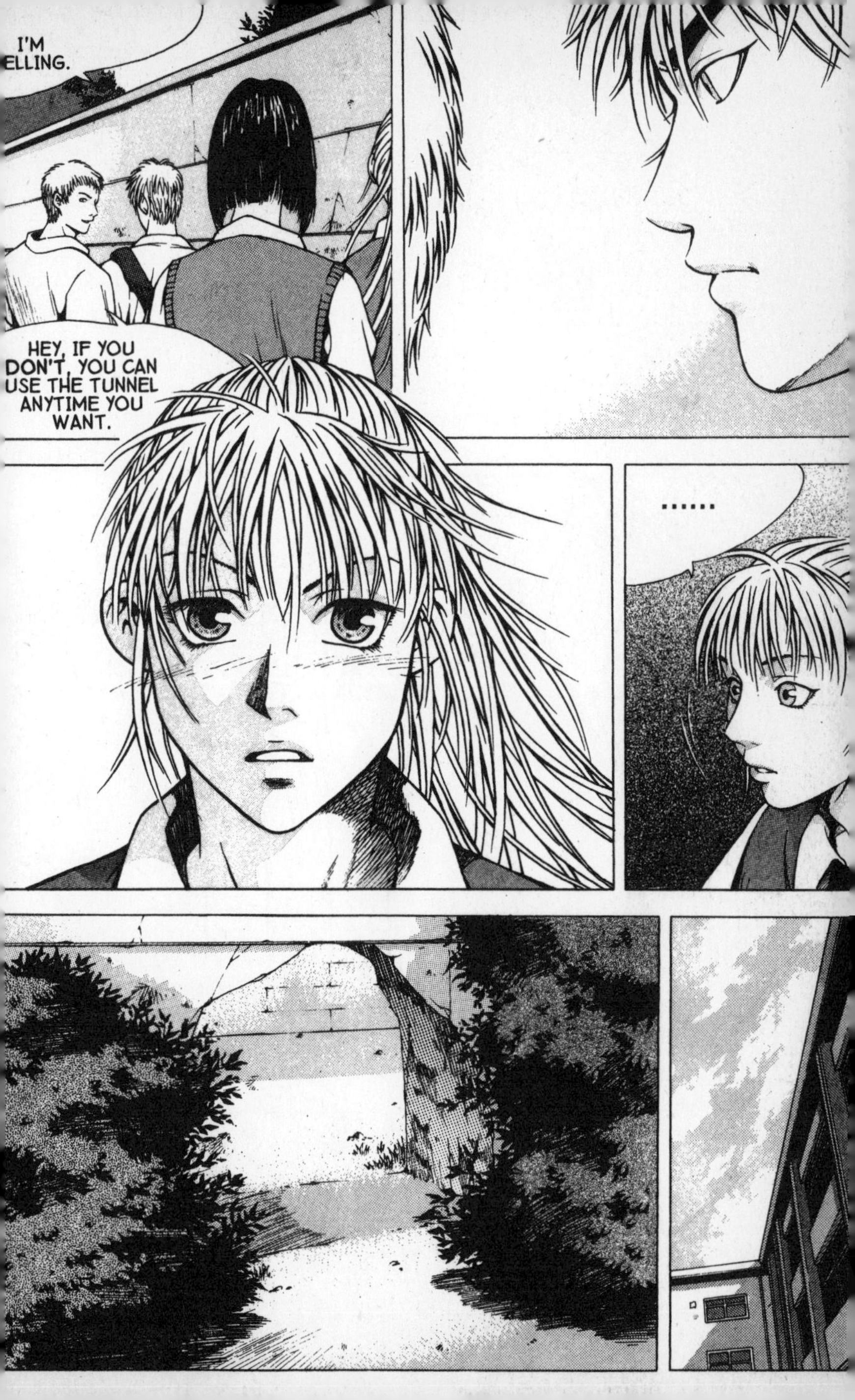
I'M
ELLING.
HEY, IF YOU DON'T, YOU CAN USE THE TUNNEL ANYTIME YOU WANT.
......

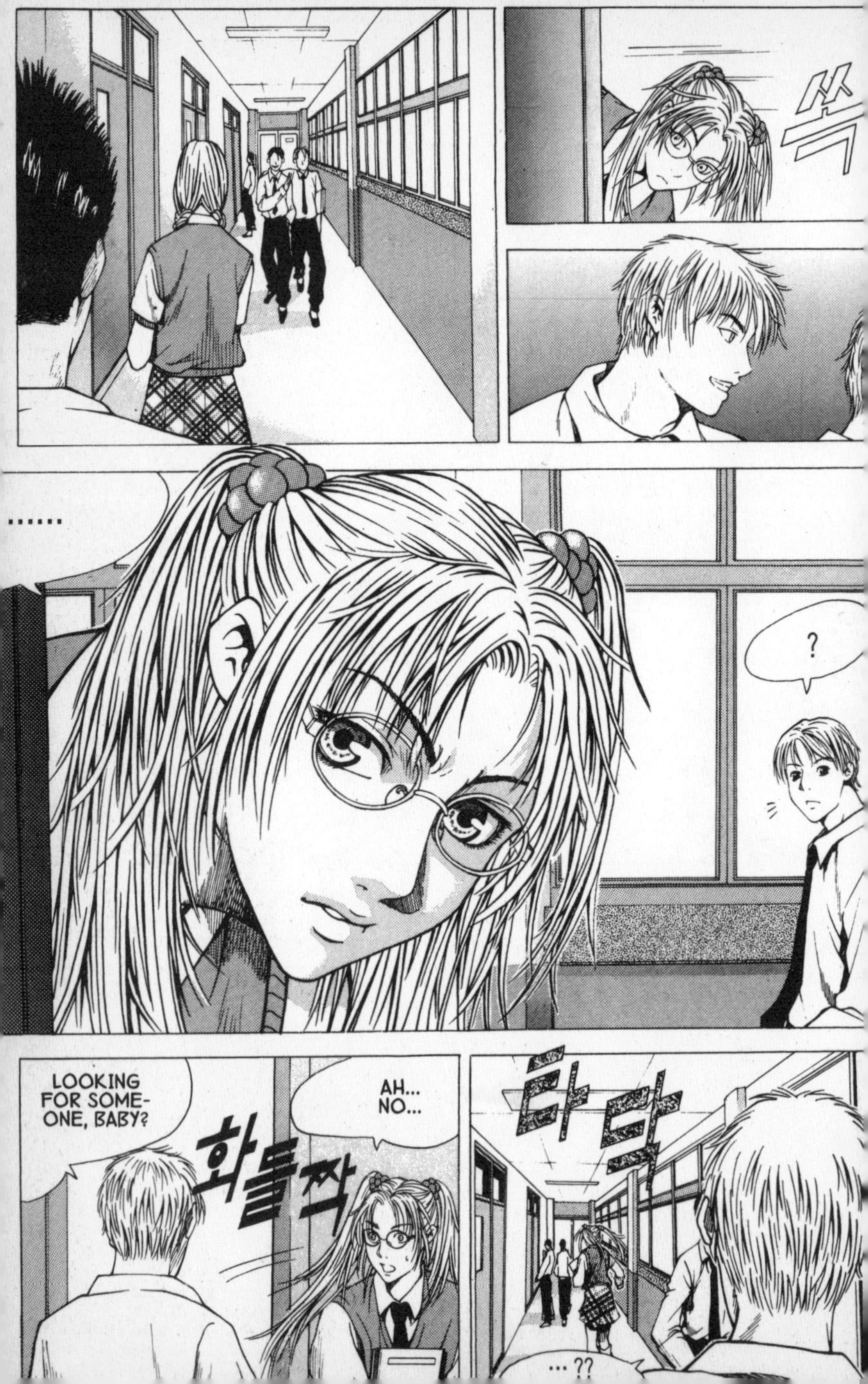
쓰윽
......
?
LOOKING FOR SOME-ONE, BABY?
AH... NO...
화들짝
타닥
...??

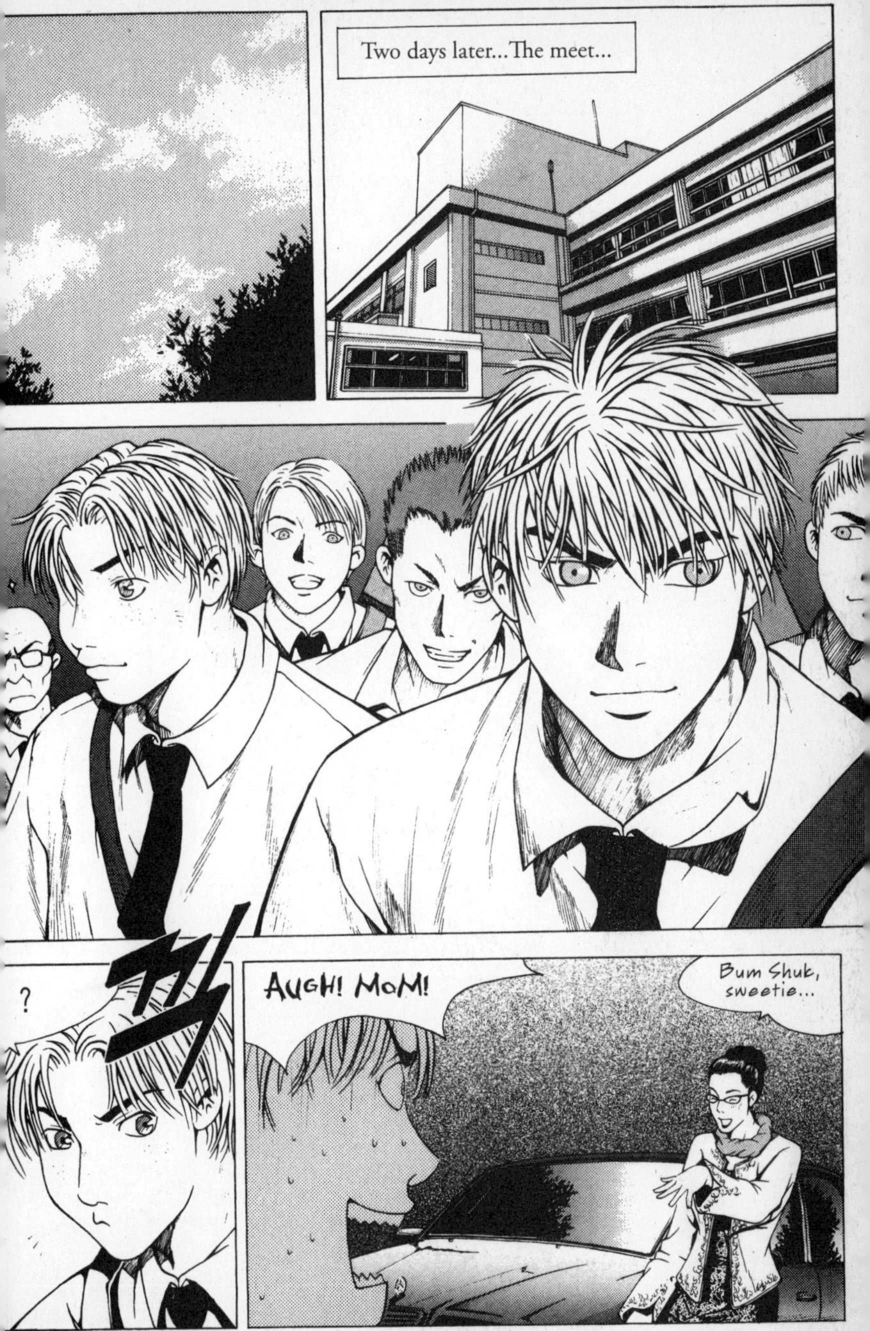
Two days later... The meet...
?
AUGH! MOM!
Bum Shuk, sweetie...

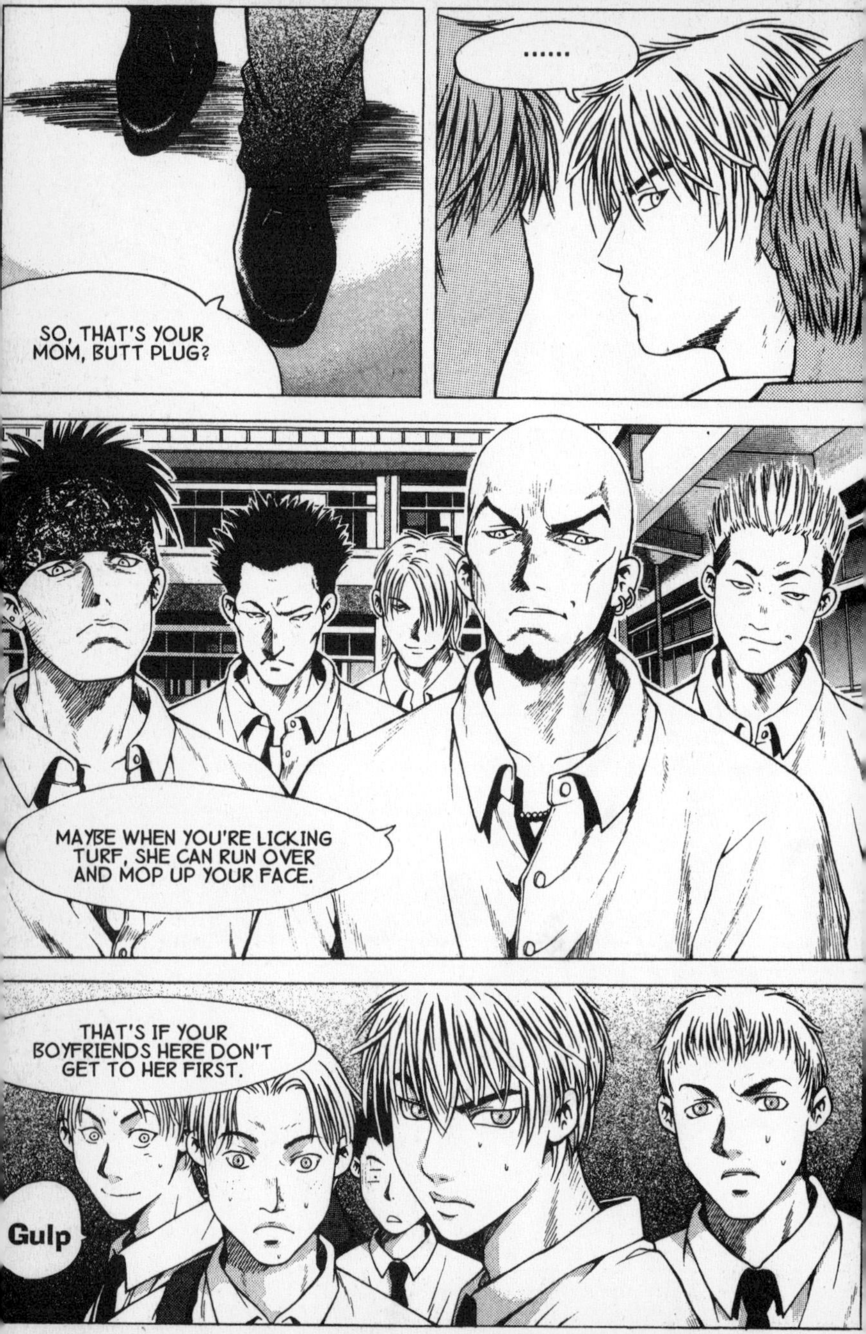
SO, THAT'S YOUR MOM, BUTT PLUG?
......
MAYBE WHEN YOU'RE LICKING TURF, SHE CAN RUN OVER AND MOP UP YOUR FACE.
THAT'S IF YOUR BOYFRIENDS HERE DON'T GET TO HER FIRST.
Gulp

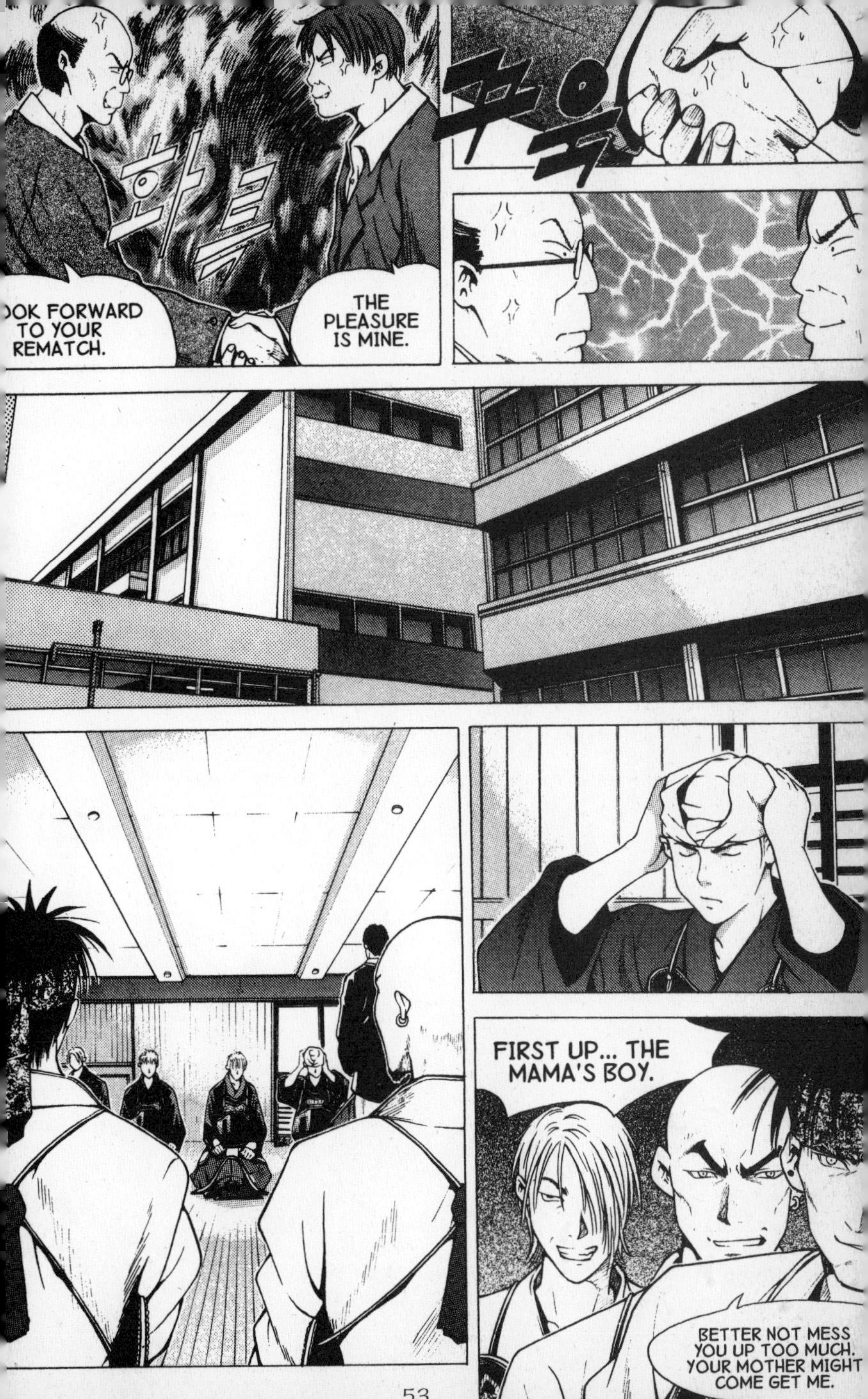

OOK FORWARD TO YOUR REMATCH.
THE PLEASURE IS MINE.
FIRST UP... THE MAMA'S BOY.
BETTER NOT MESS YOU UP TOO MUCH. YOUR MOTHER MIGHT COME GET ME.

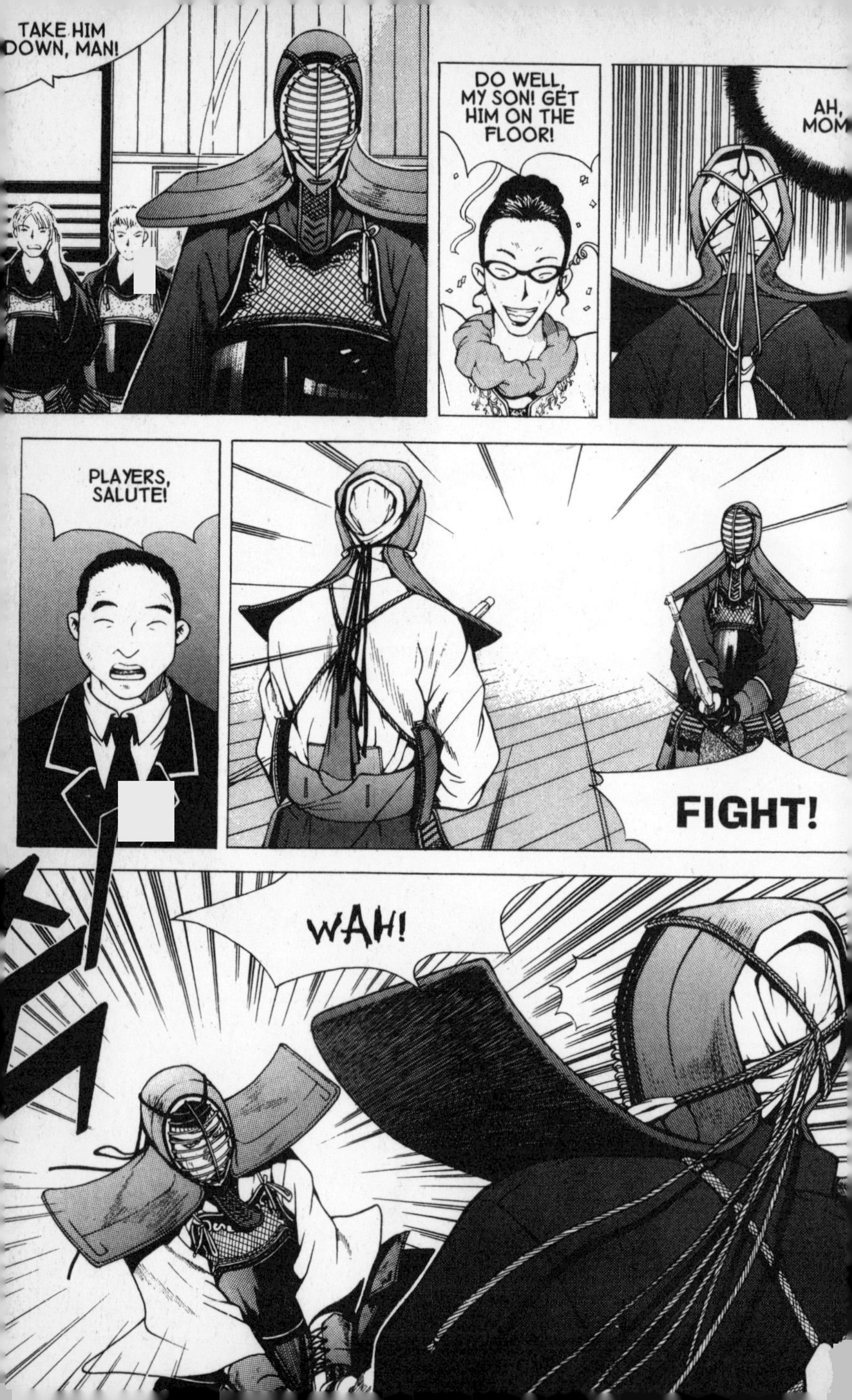
TAKE HIM DOWN, MAN!
DO WELL, MY SON! GET HIM ON THE FLOOR!
AH, MOM
PLAYERS, SALUTE!
FIGHT!
WAH!

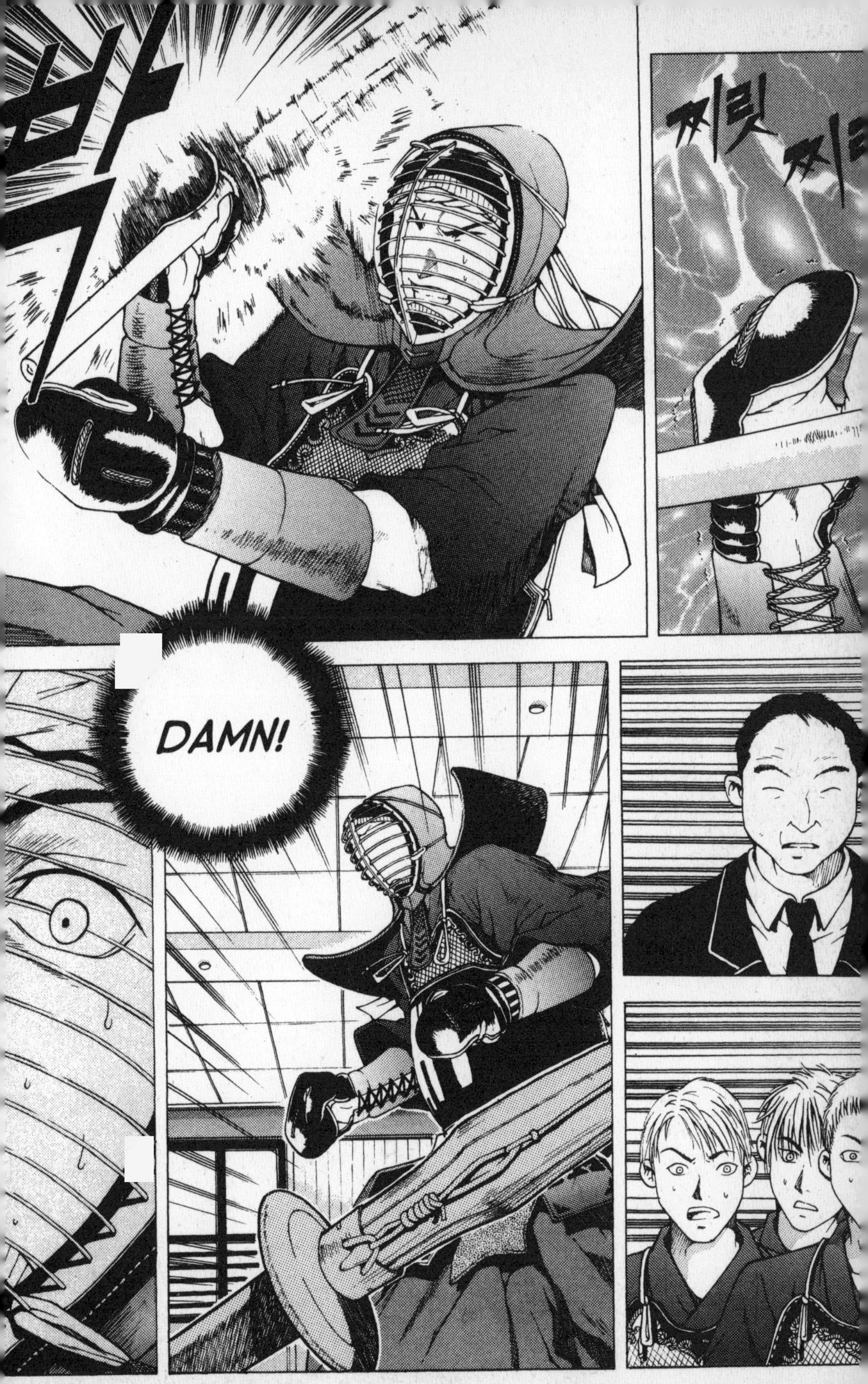

찌릿
DAMN!

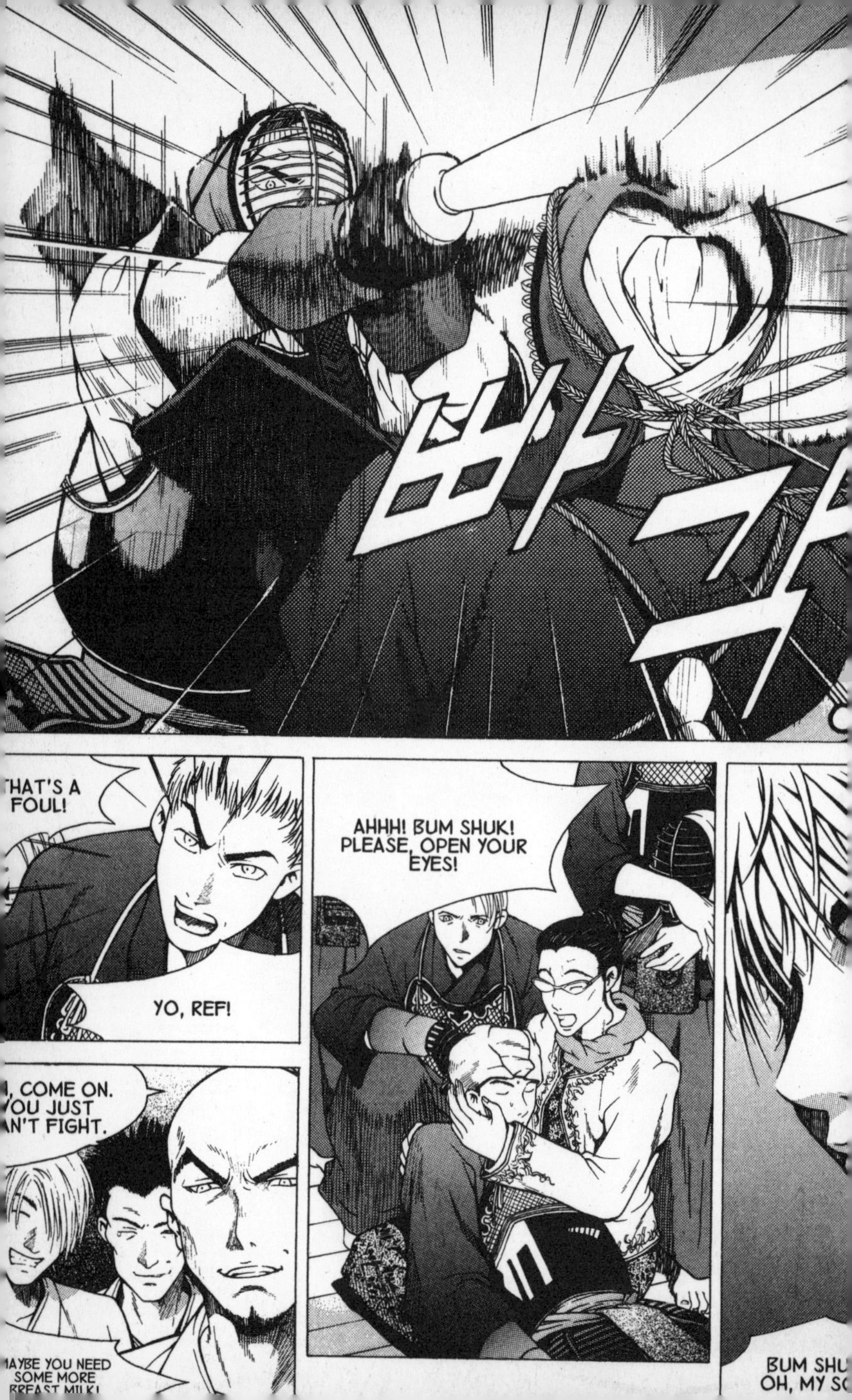
빠
THAT'S A FOUL!
YO, REF!
, COME ON. YOU JUST AN'T FIGHT.
MAYBE YOU NEED SOME MORE BREAST MILK!
AHHH! BUM SHUK! PLEASE, OPEN YOUR EYES!
BUM SHU OH, MY SO

Sign: 40th Annual Sports Festival

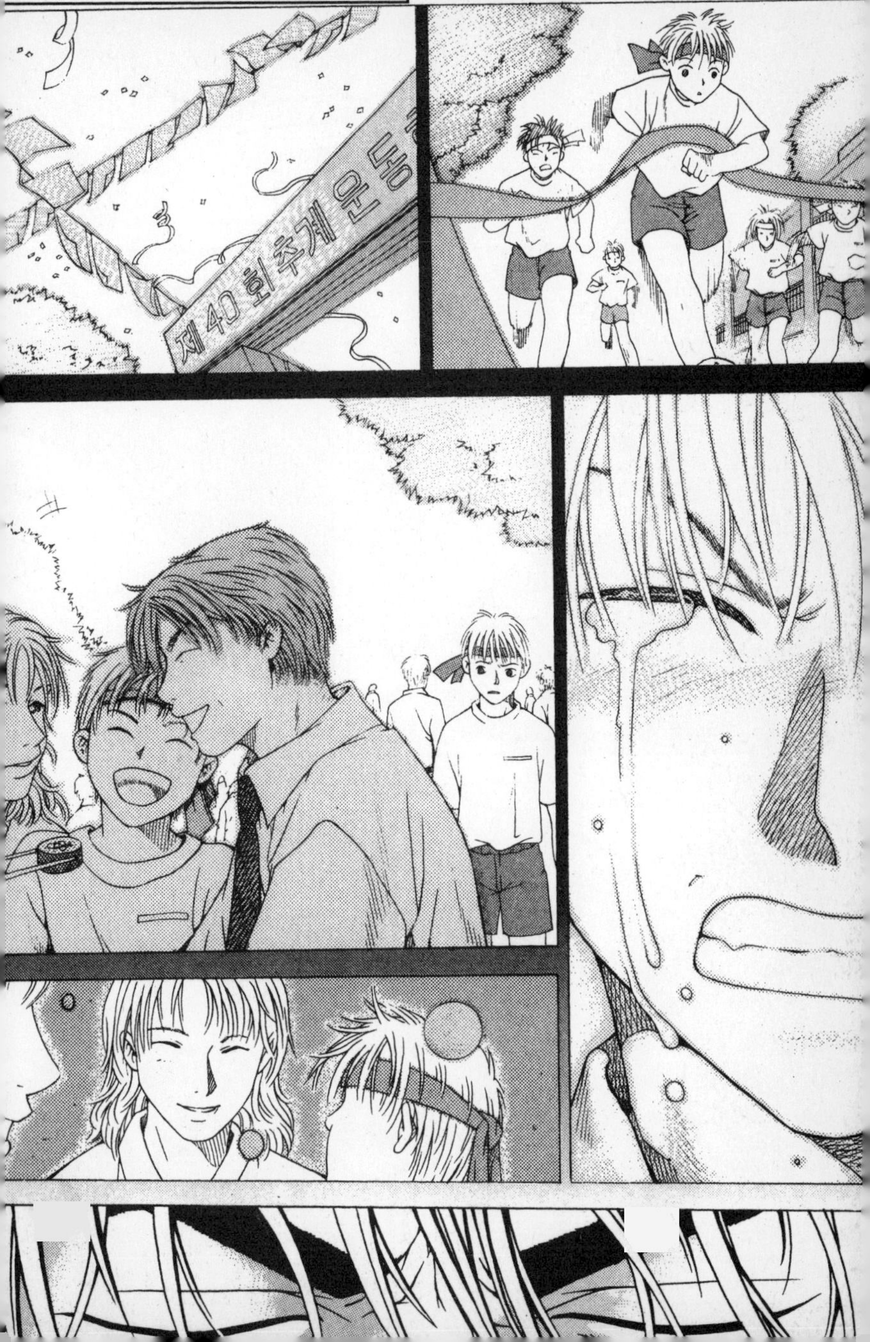
제 40 회 추계 운동

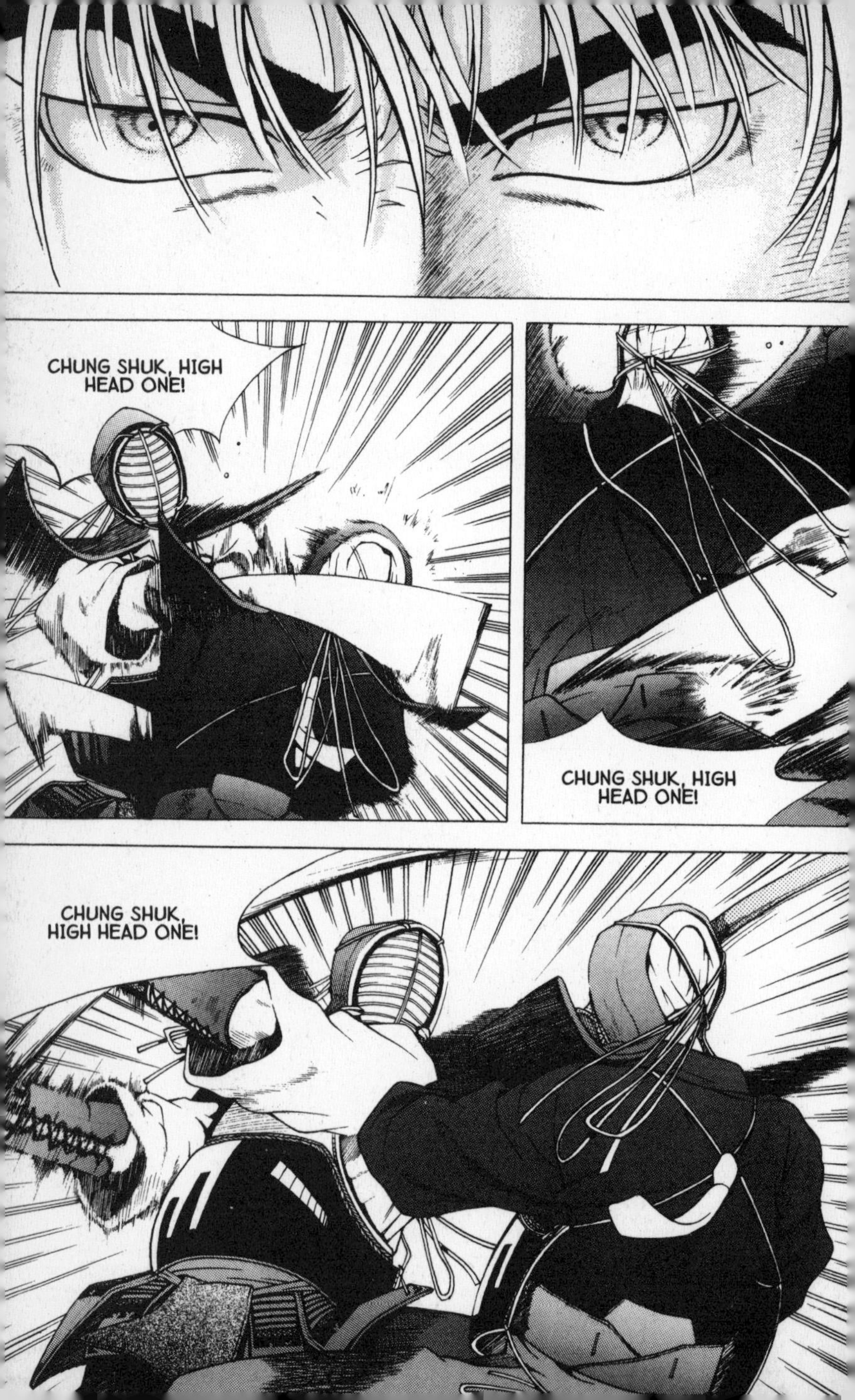
CHUNG SHUK, HIGH HEAD ONE!
CHUNG SHUK, HIGH HEAD ONE!
CHUNG SHUK, HIGH HEAD ONE!

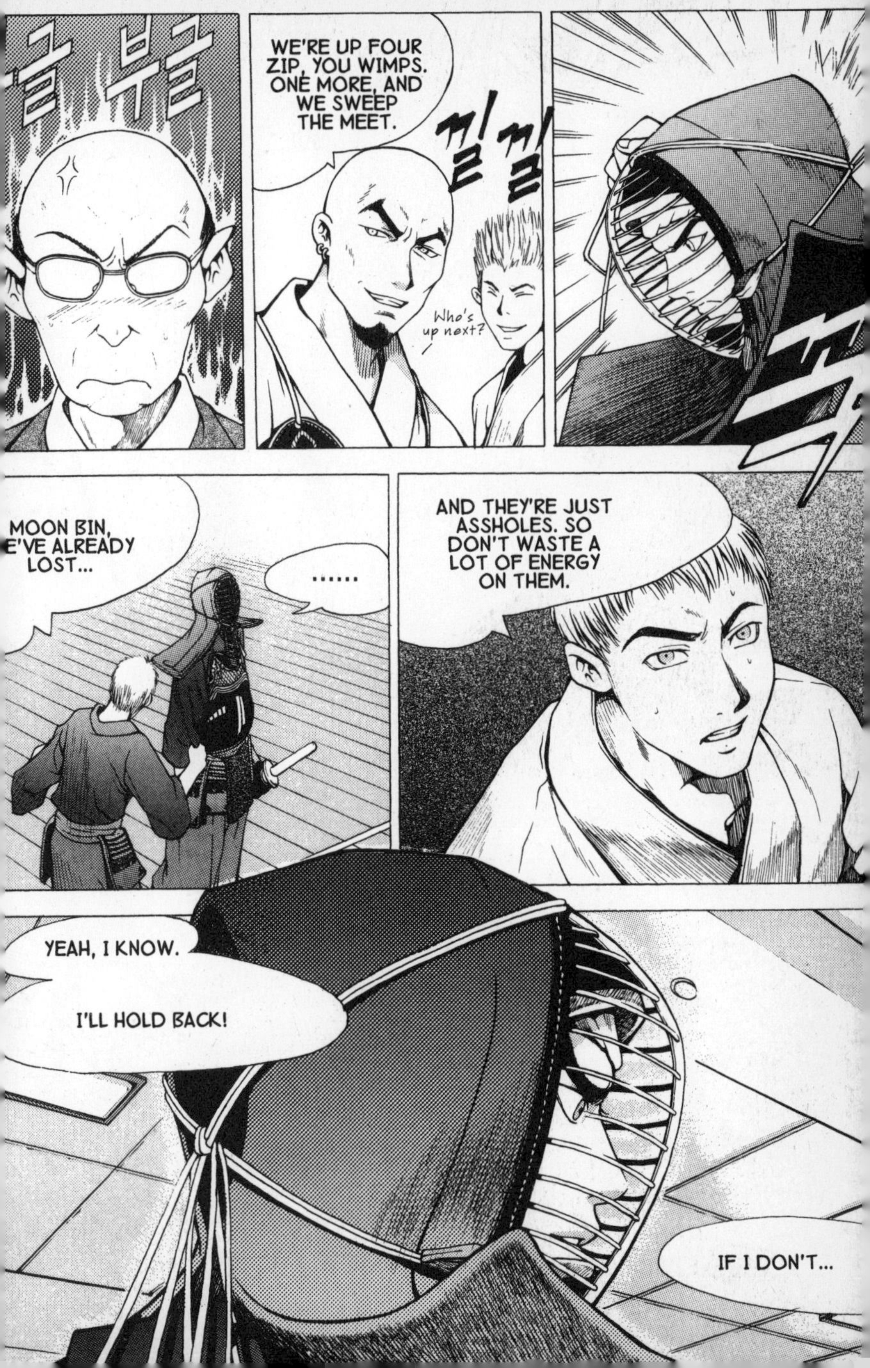
글 부글
WE'RE UP FOUR ZIP, YOU WIMPS. ONE MORE, AND WE SWEEP THE MEET.
낄낄
Who's up next?
MOON BIN, E'VE ALREADY LOST...
......
AND THEY'RE JUST ASSHOLES. SO DON'T WASTE A LOT OF ENERGY ON THEM.
YEAH, I KNOW.
I'LL HOLD BACK!
IF I DON'T...

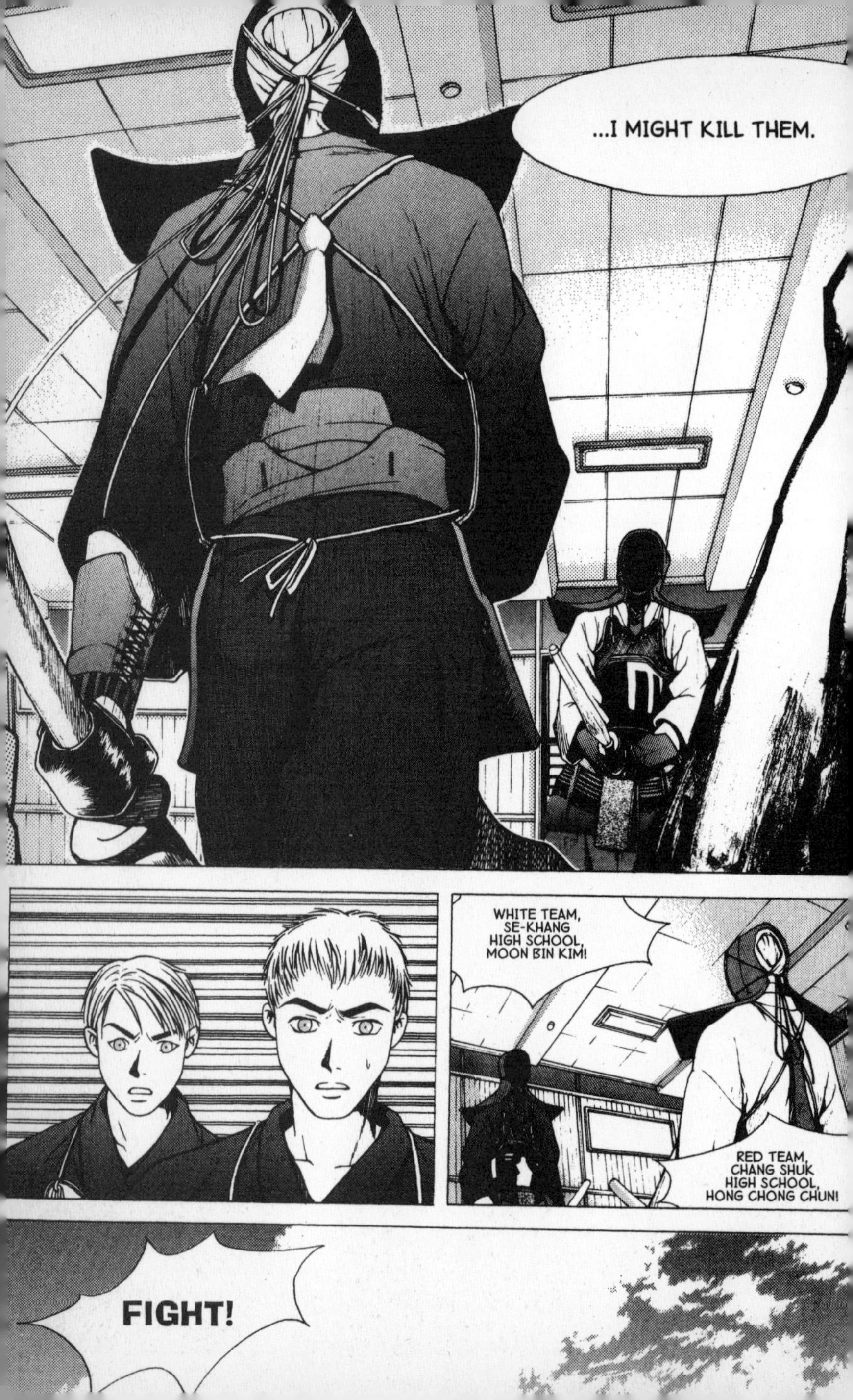

...I MIGHT KILL THEM.
WHITE TEAM, SE-KHANG HIGH SCHOOL, MOON BIN KIM!
RED TEAM, CHANG SHUK HIGH SCHOOL, HONG CHONG CHUN!
FIGHT!

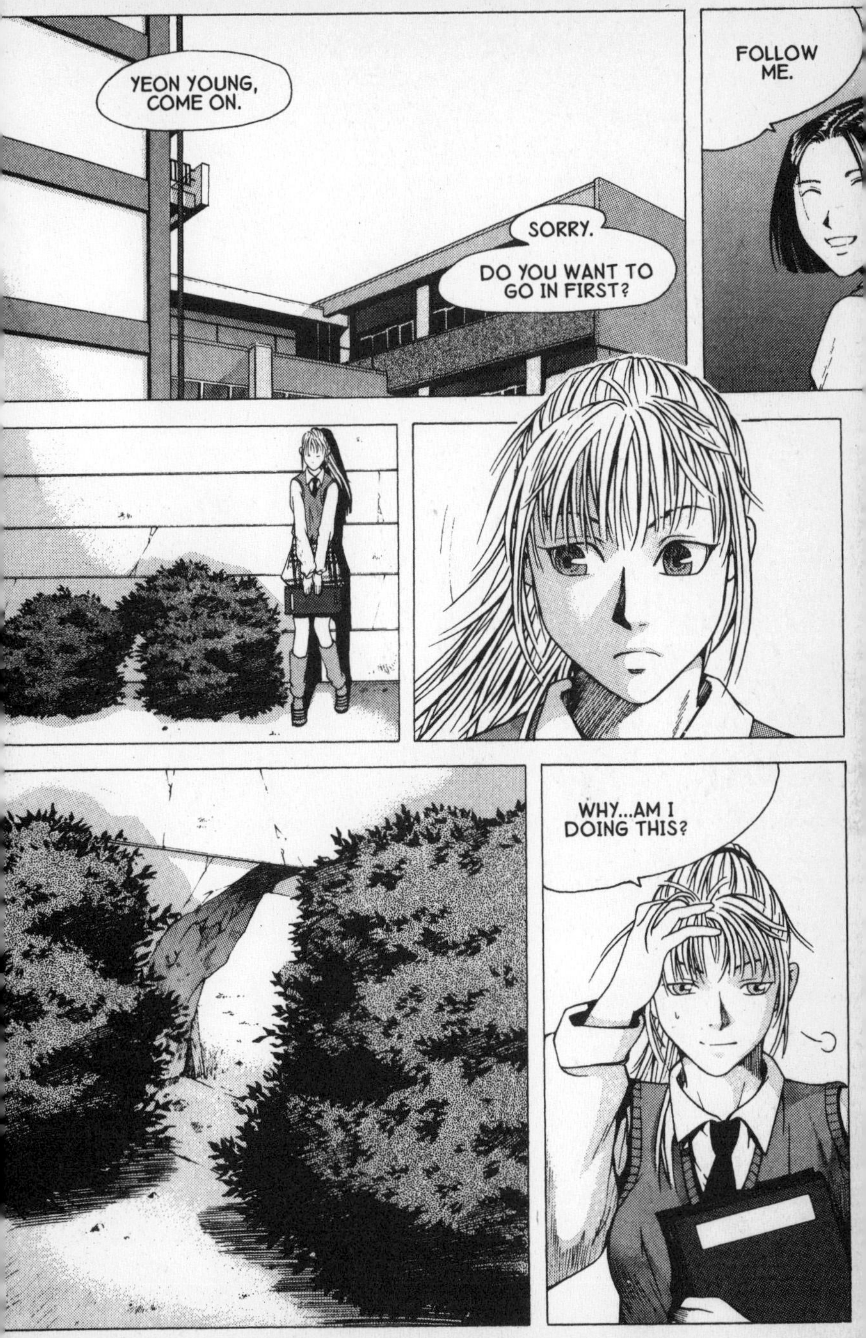

YEON YOUNG, COME ON.
SORRY.
DO YOU WANT TO GO IN FIRST?
FOLLOW ME.
WHY...AM I DOING THIS?

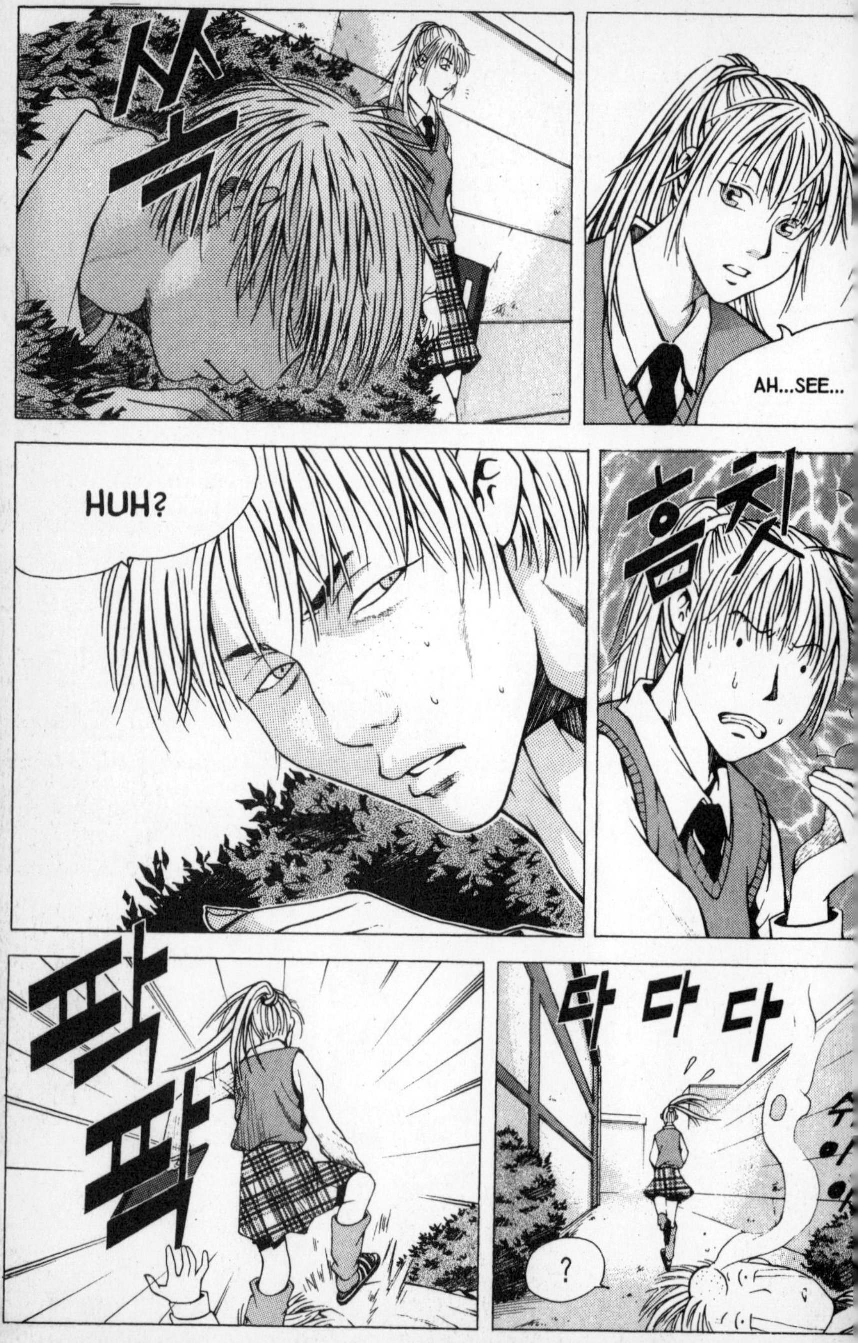
AH...SEE...
HUH?
흠칫
다 다 다 다
?

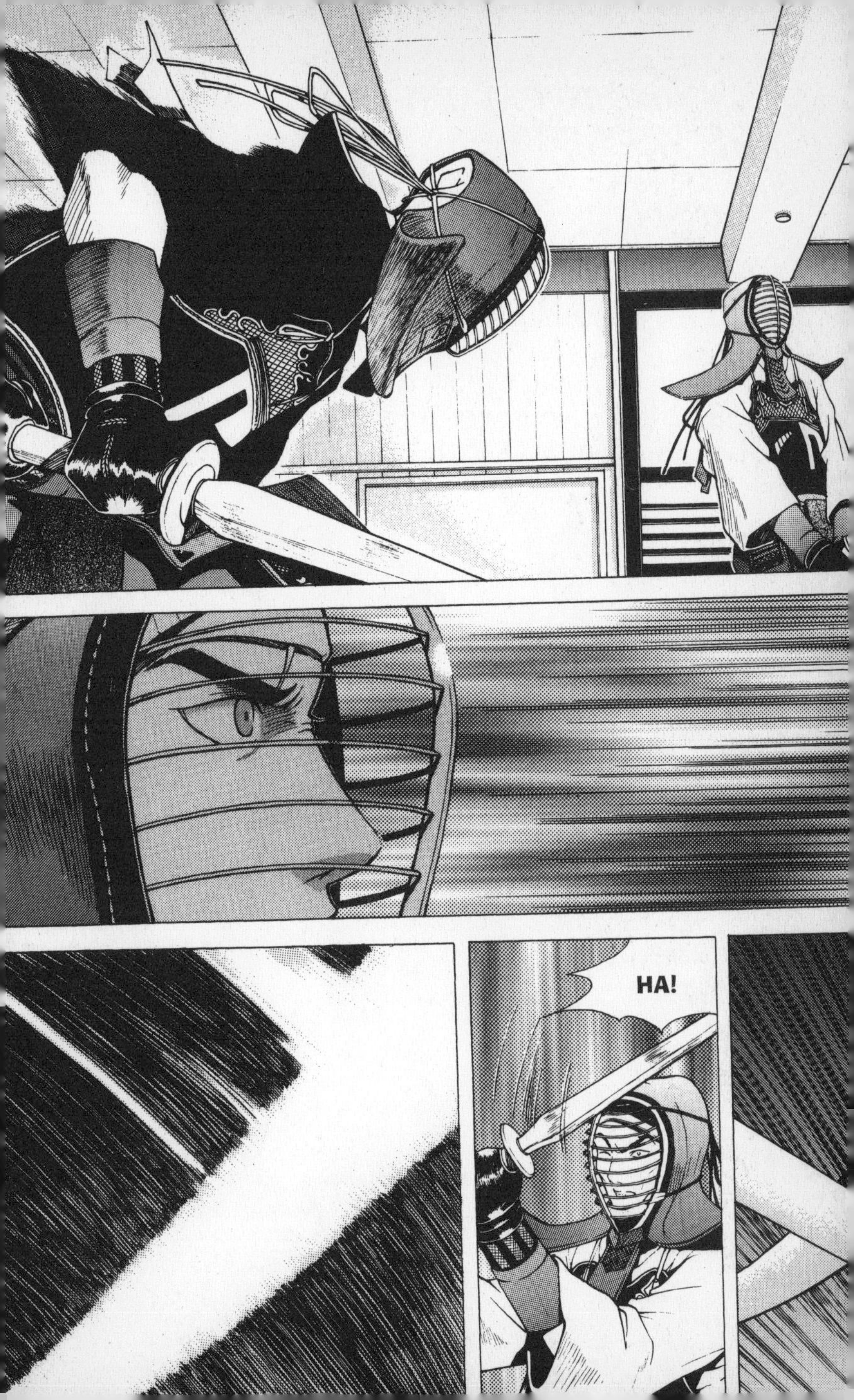
HA!

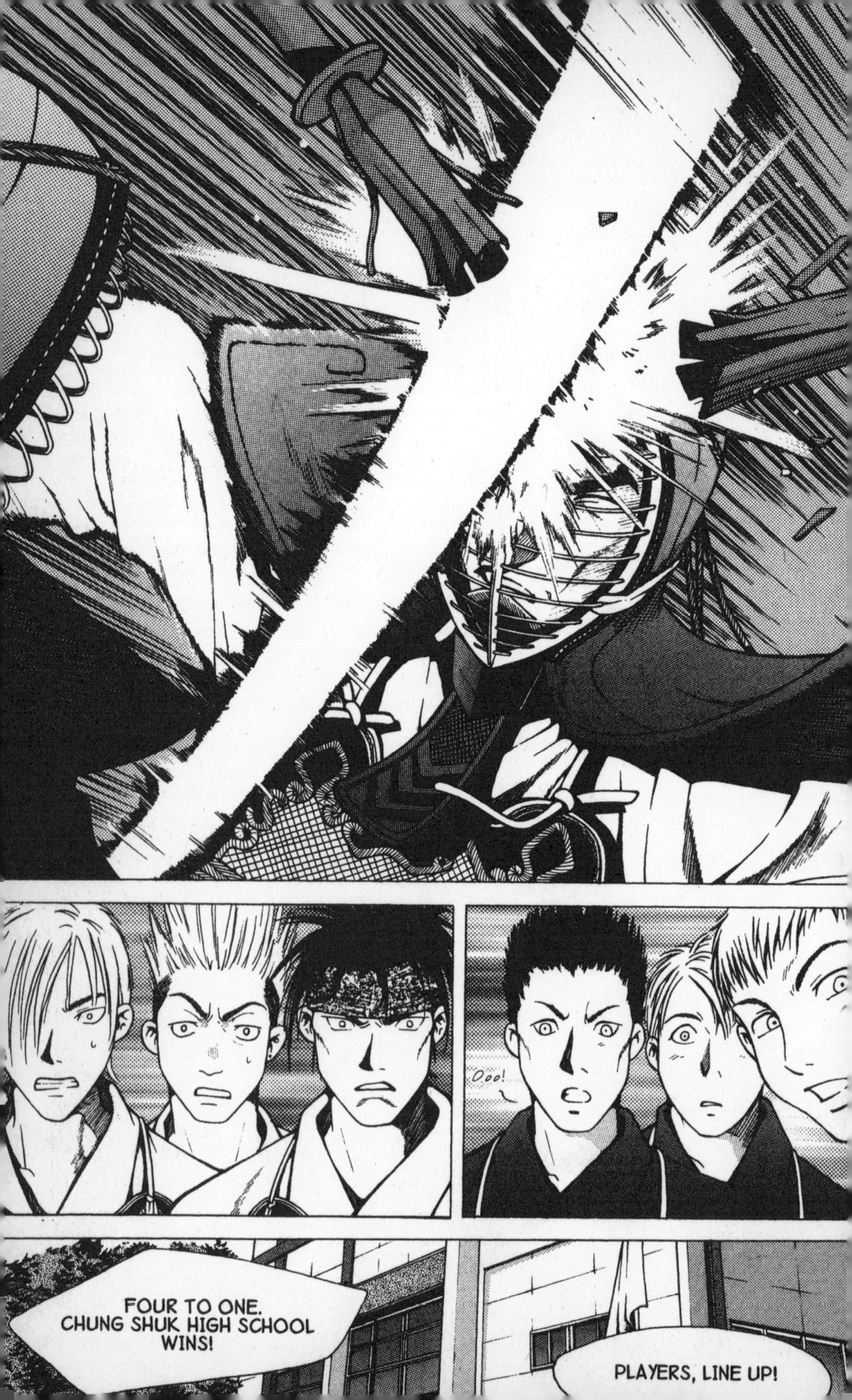
Ooo!
FOUR TO ONE. CHUNG SHUK HIGH SCHOOL WINS!
PLAYERS, LINE UP!

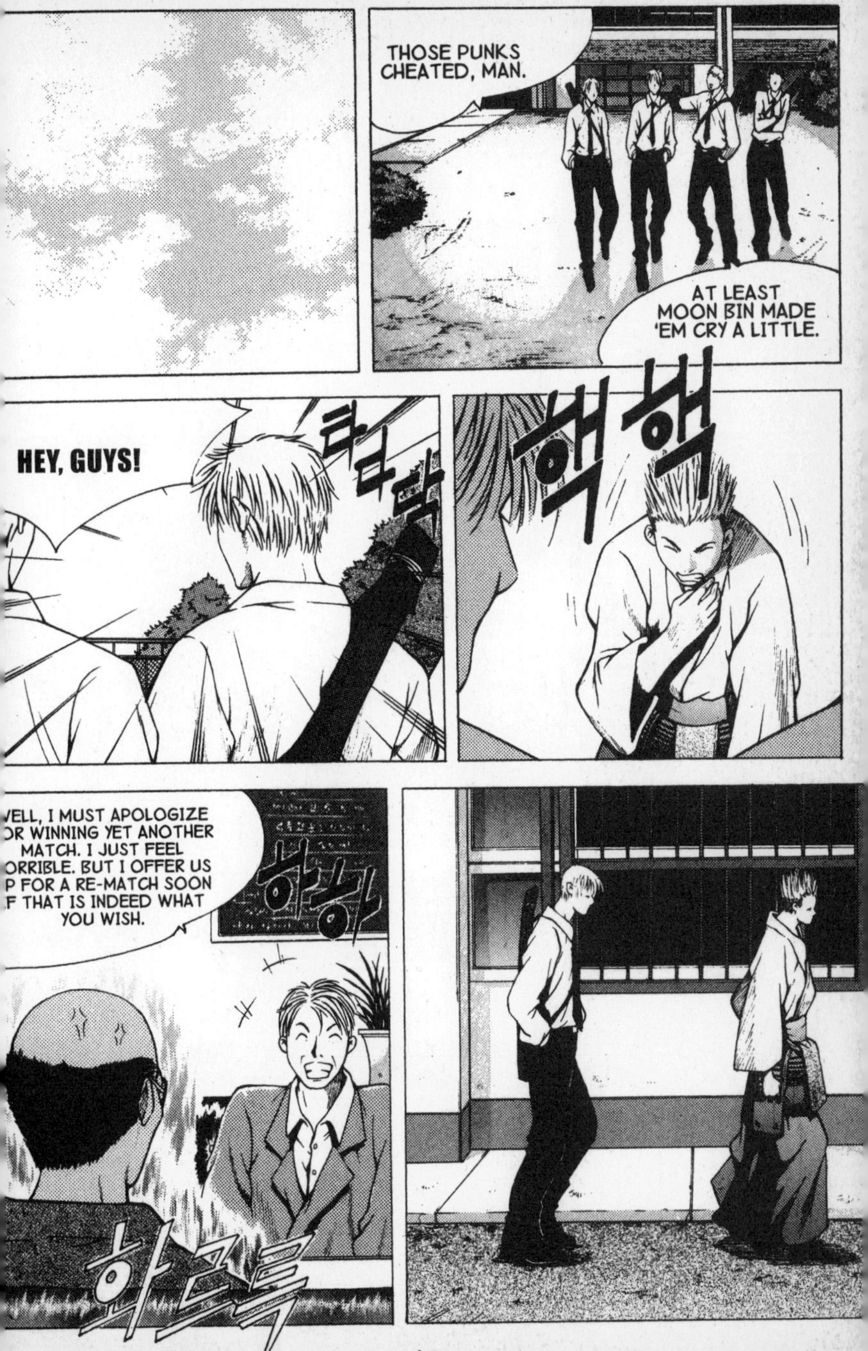
THOSE PUNKS CHEATED, MAN.
AT LEAST MOON BIN MADE 'EM CRY A LITTLE.
HEY, GUYS!
다다닥
헉헉
VELL, I MUST APOLOGIZE OR WINNING YET ANOTHER MATCH. I JUST FEEL ORRIBLE. BUT I OFFER US P FOR A RE-MATCH SOON F THAT IS INDEED WHAT YOU WISH.
하하
화르륵

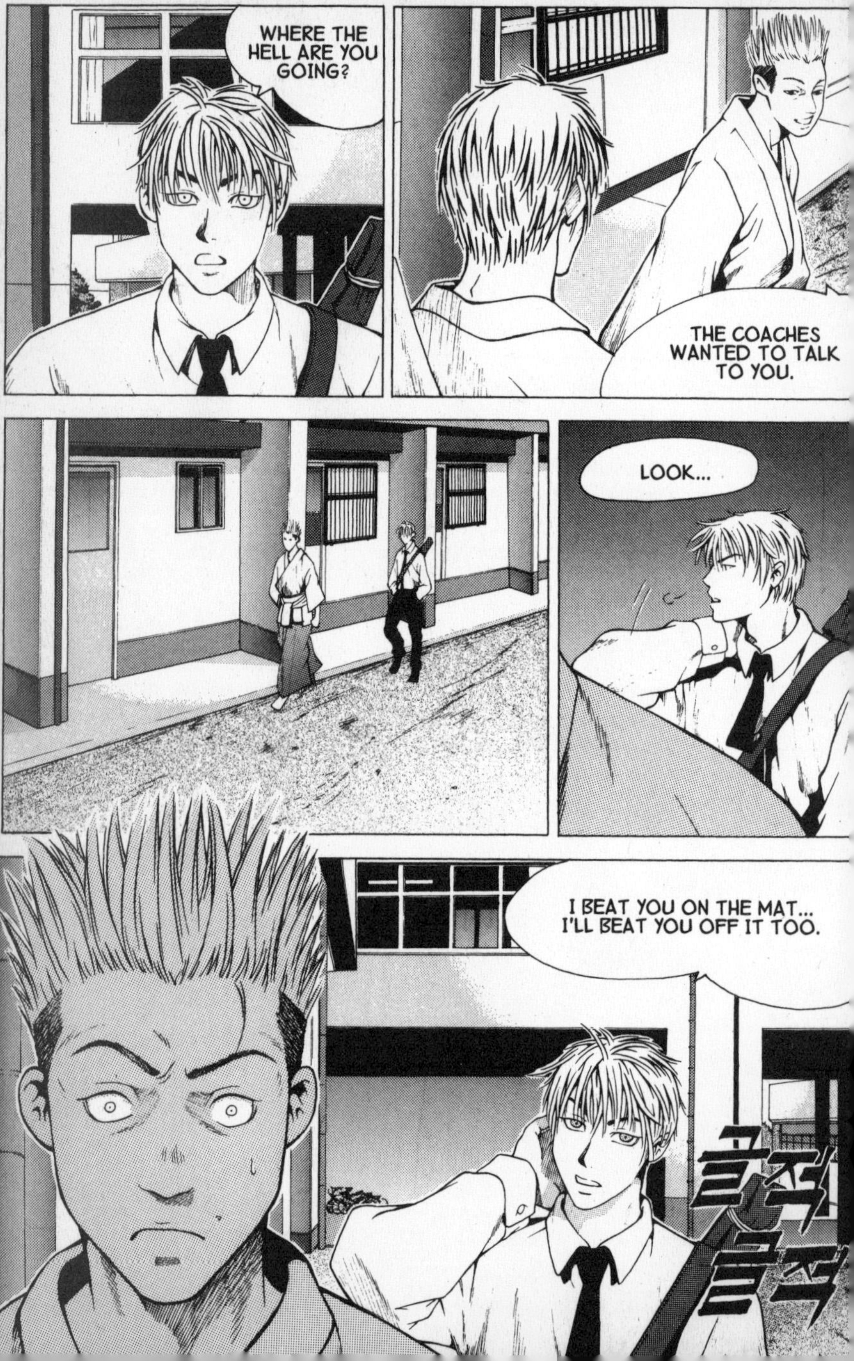
WHERE THE HELL ARE YOU GOING?
THE COACHES WANTED TO TALK TO YOU.
LOOK...
I BEAT YOU ON THE MAT... I'LL BEAT YOU OFF IT TOO.
글적 글적

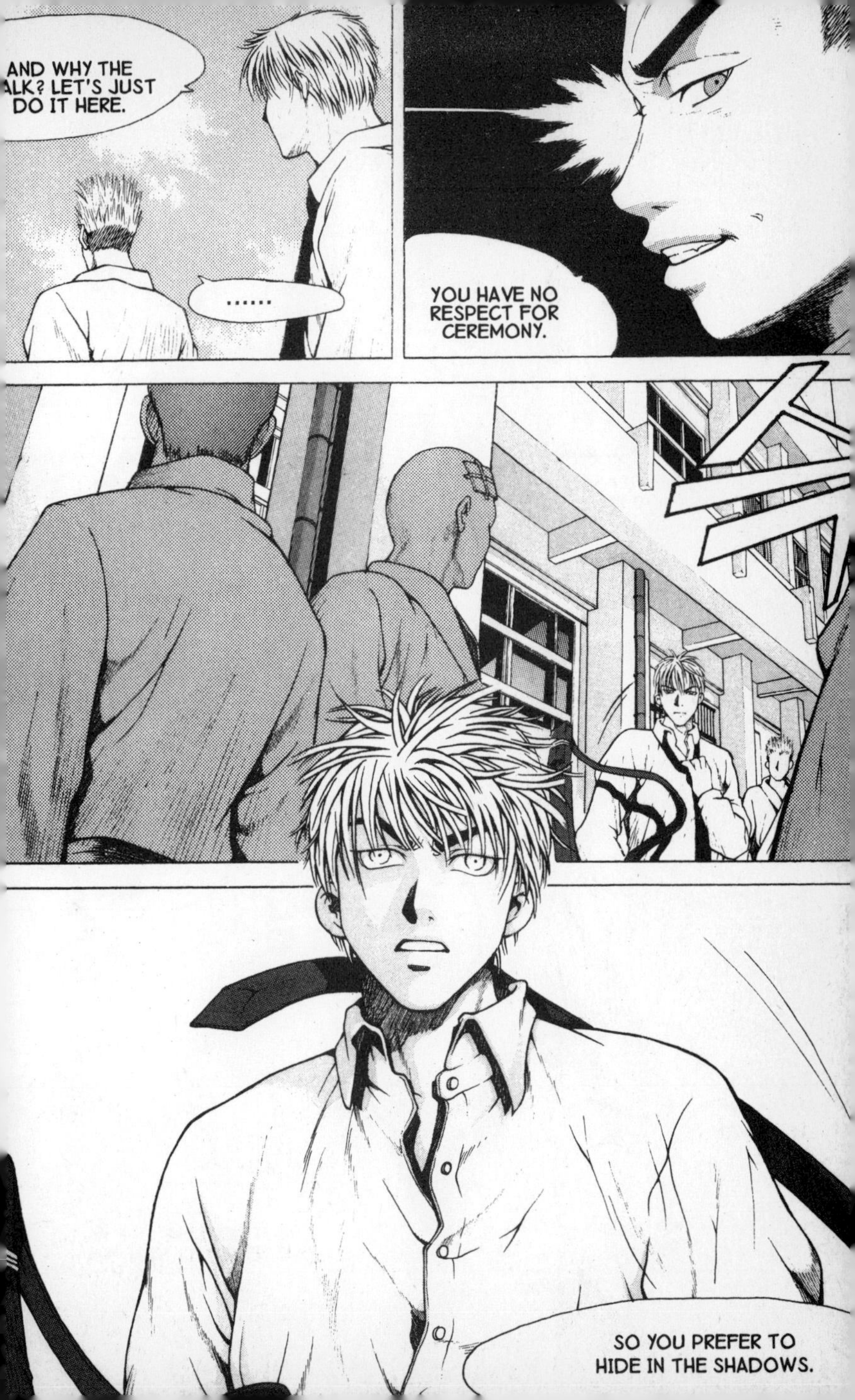
AND WHY THE
ALK? LET'S JUST
DO IT HERE.
......
YOU HAVE NO
RESPECT FOR
CEREMONY.
SO YOU PREFER TO
HIDE IN THE SHADOWS.

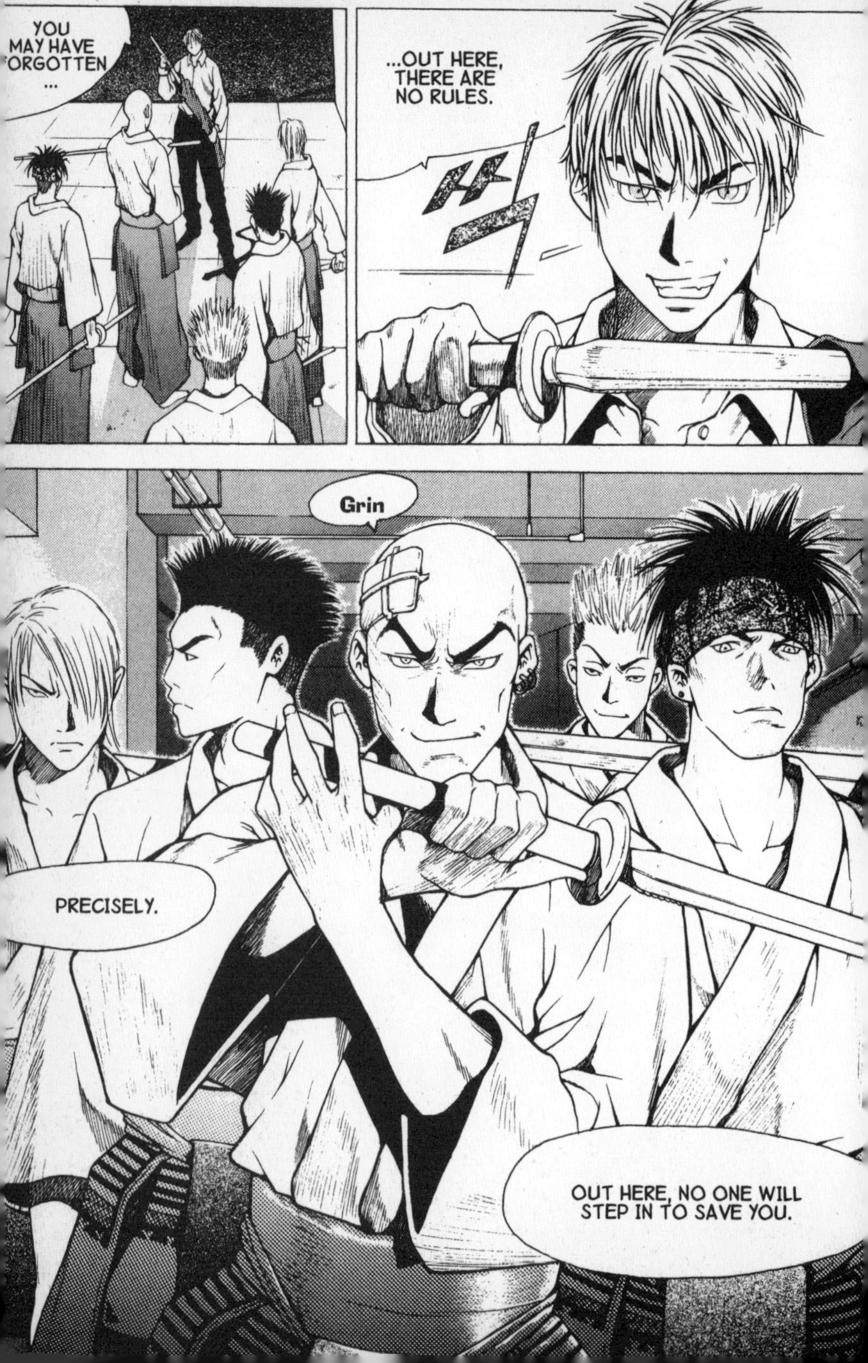
YOU MAY HAVE FORGOTTEN ...
...OUT HERE, THERE ARE NO RULES.
Grin
PRECISELY.
OUT HERE, NO ONE WILL STEP IN TO SAVE YOU.

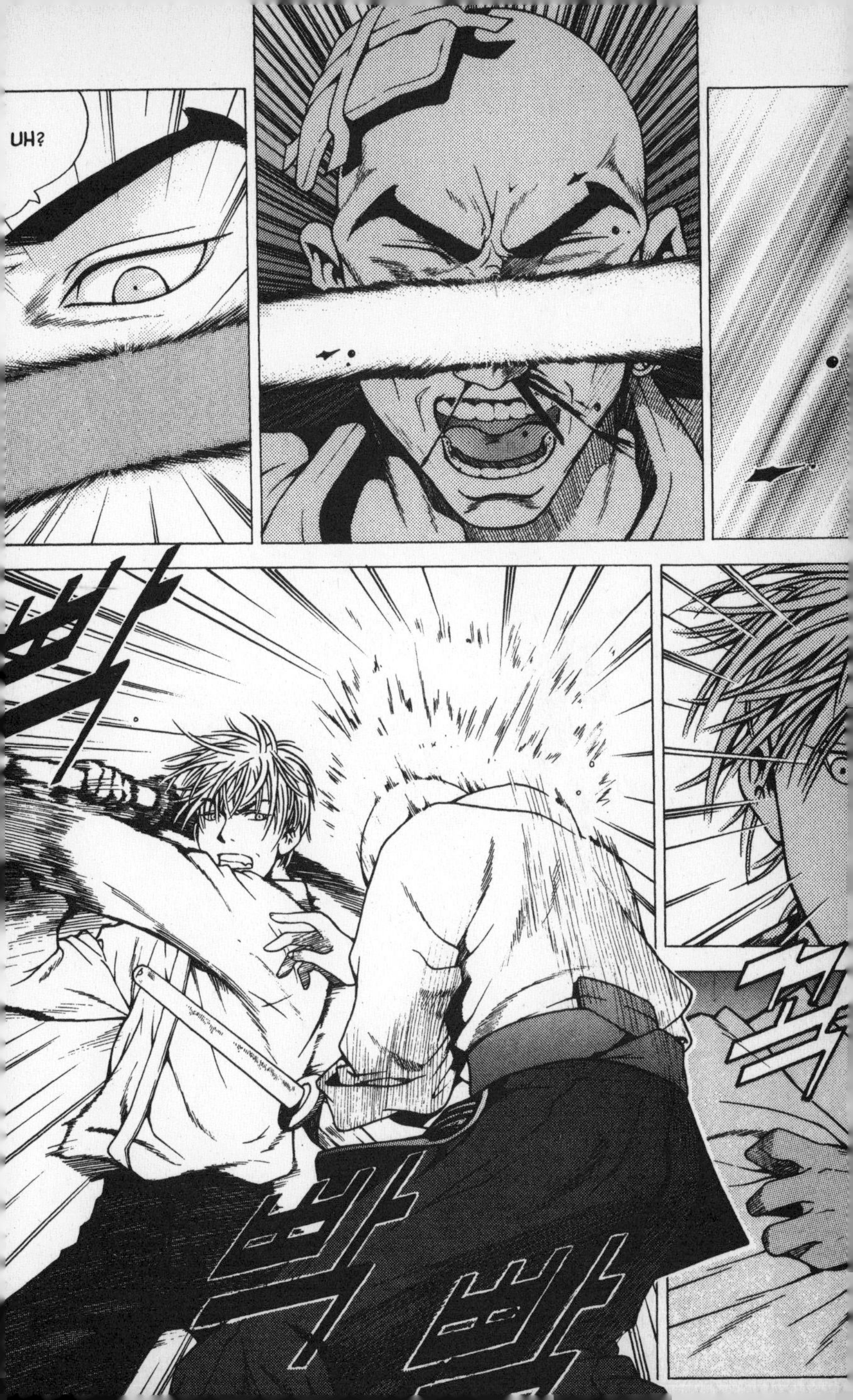
UH?

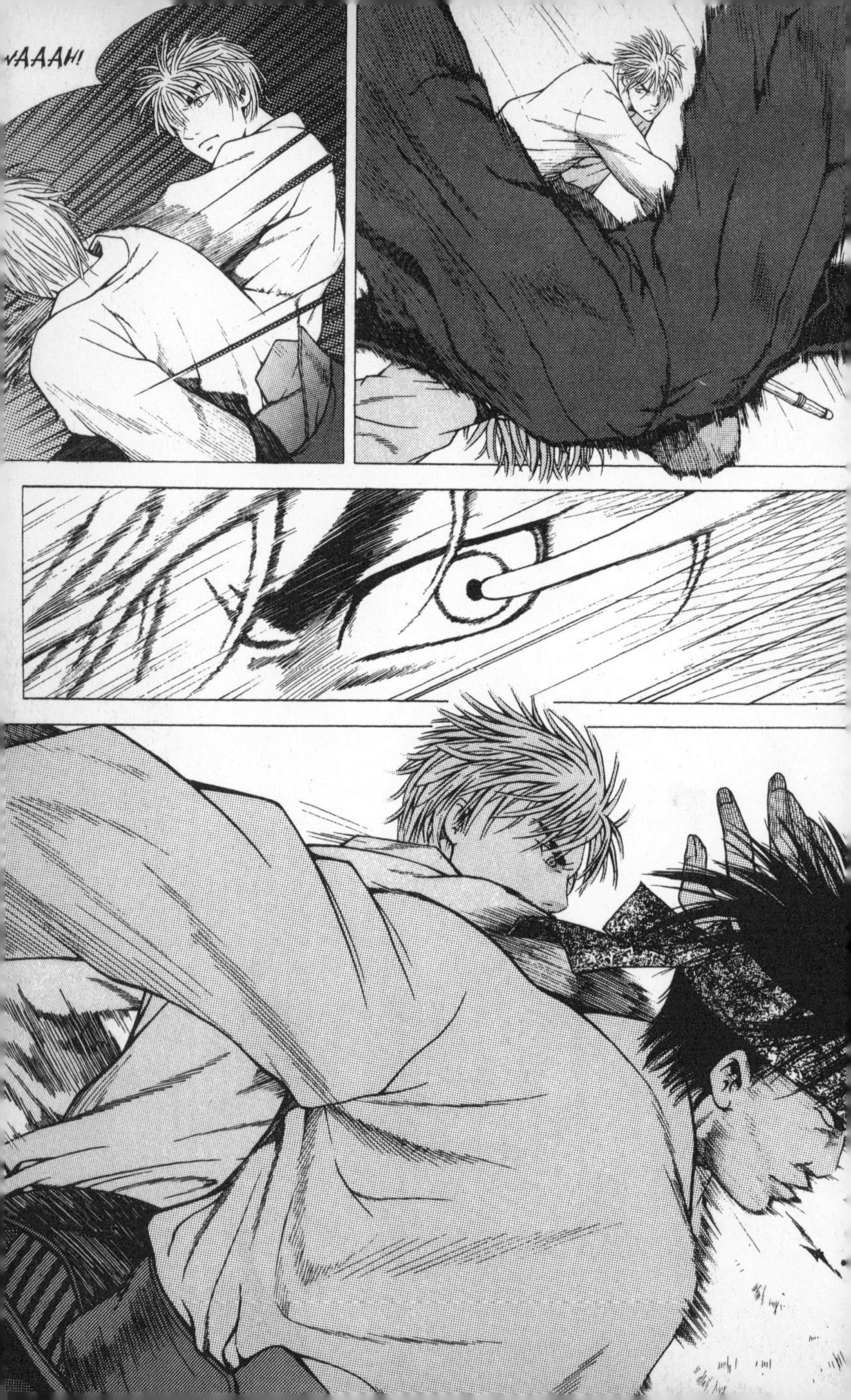
AAAAH!

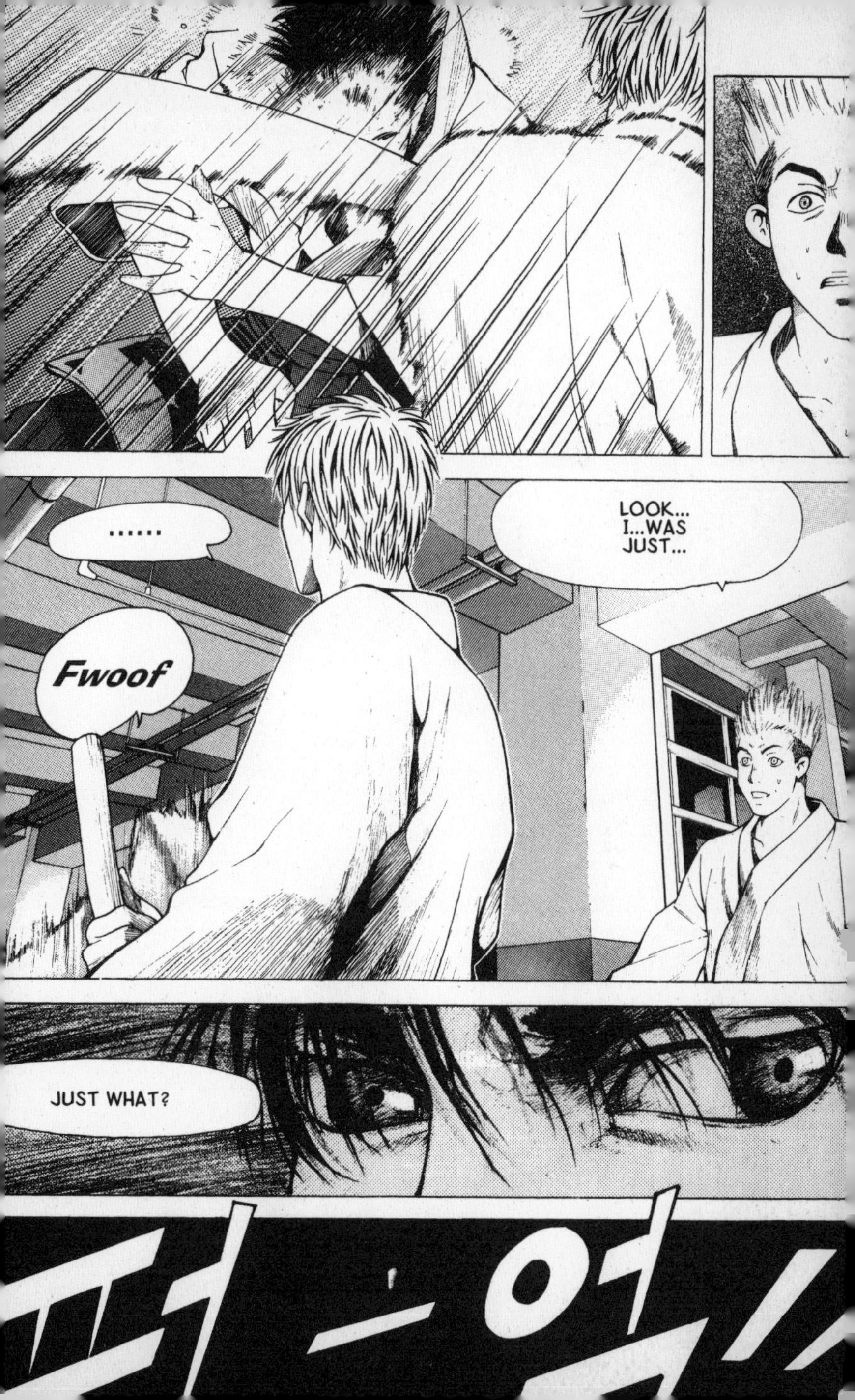
......
LOOK... I...WAS JUST...
Fwoof
JUST WHAT?
퍼-억

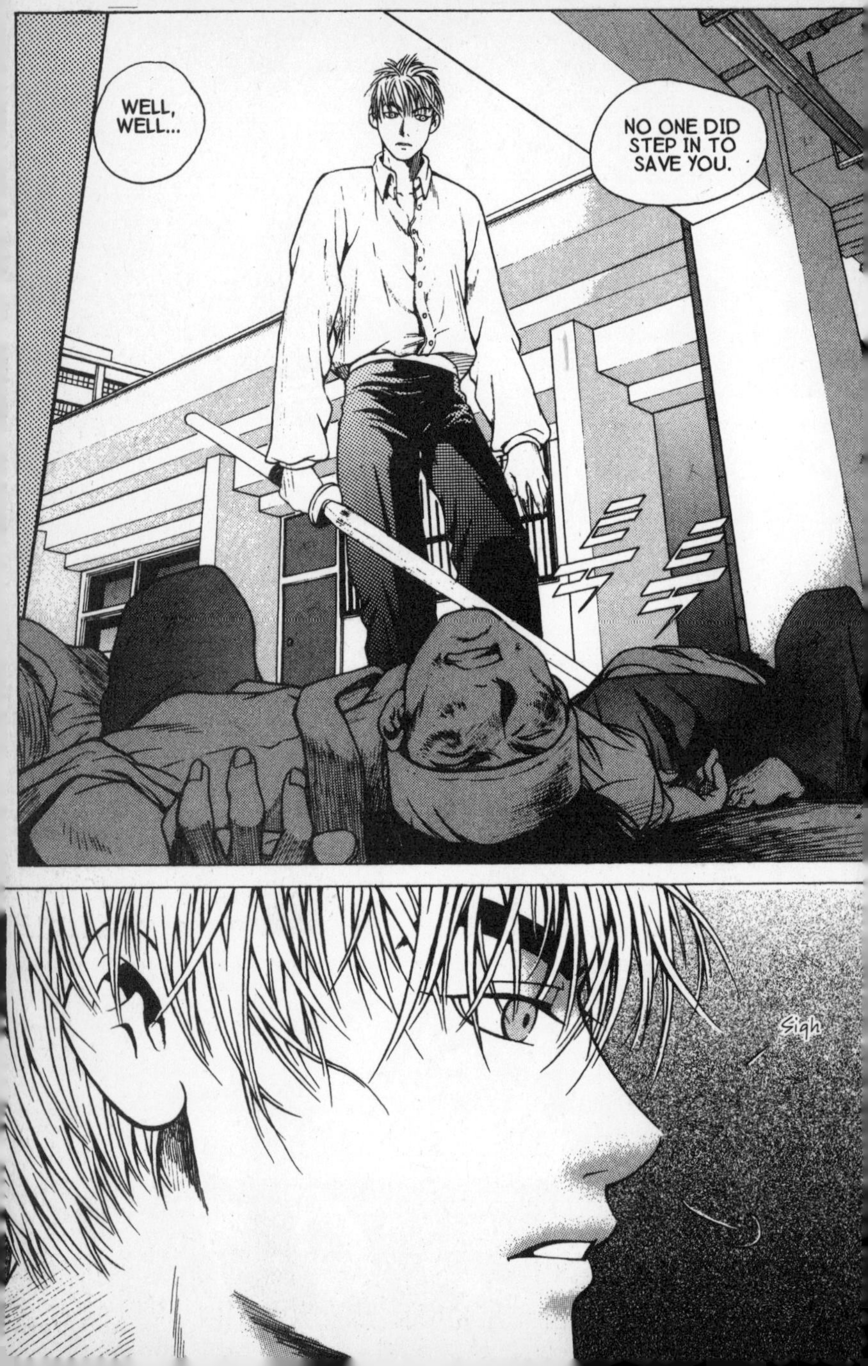
WELL, WELL...
NO ONE DID STEP IN TO SAVE YOU.
Sigh

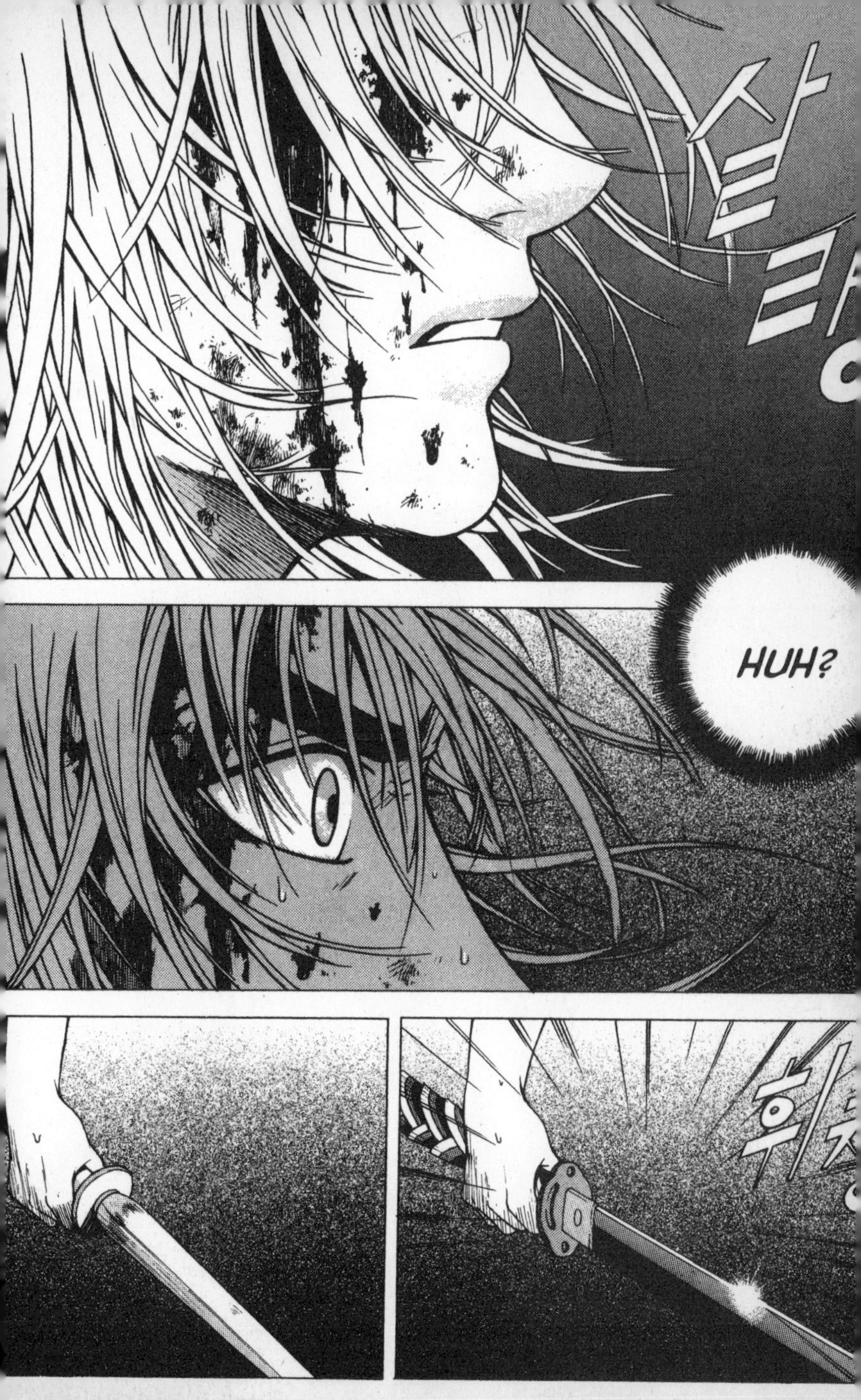
HUH?

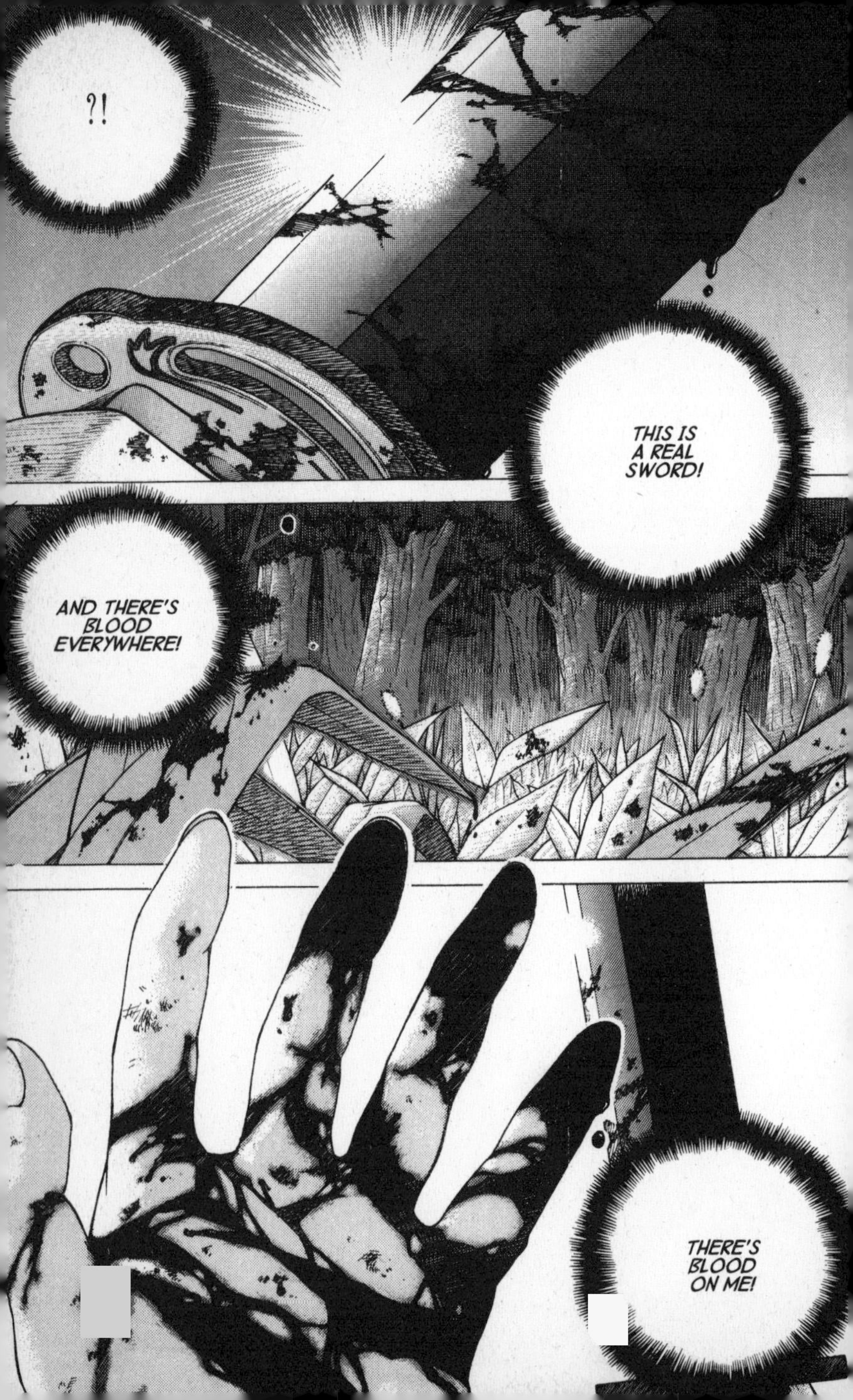
?!
THIS IS A REAL SWORD!
AND THERE'S BLOOD EVERYWHERE!
THERE'S BLOOD ON ME!

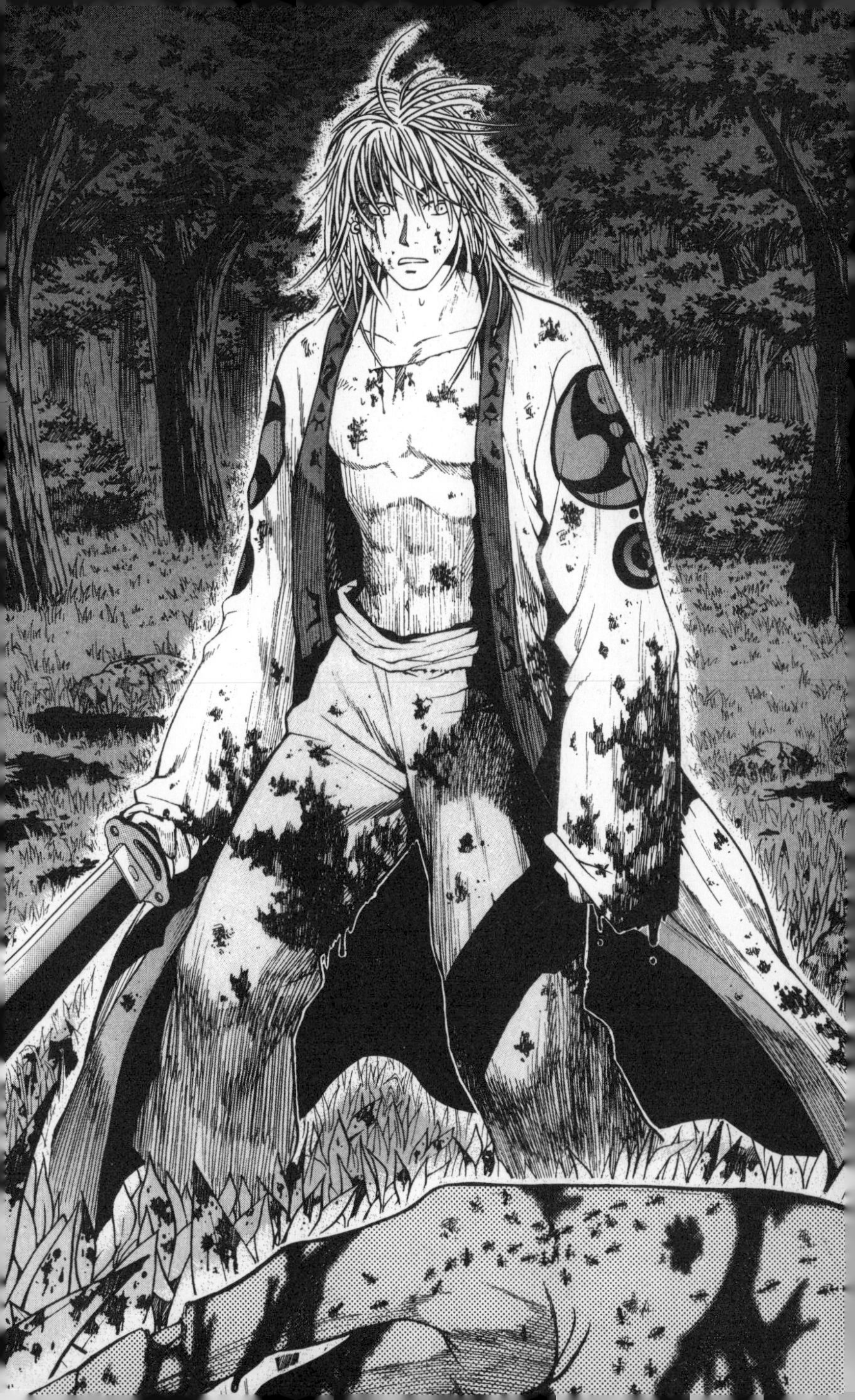

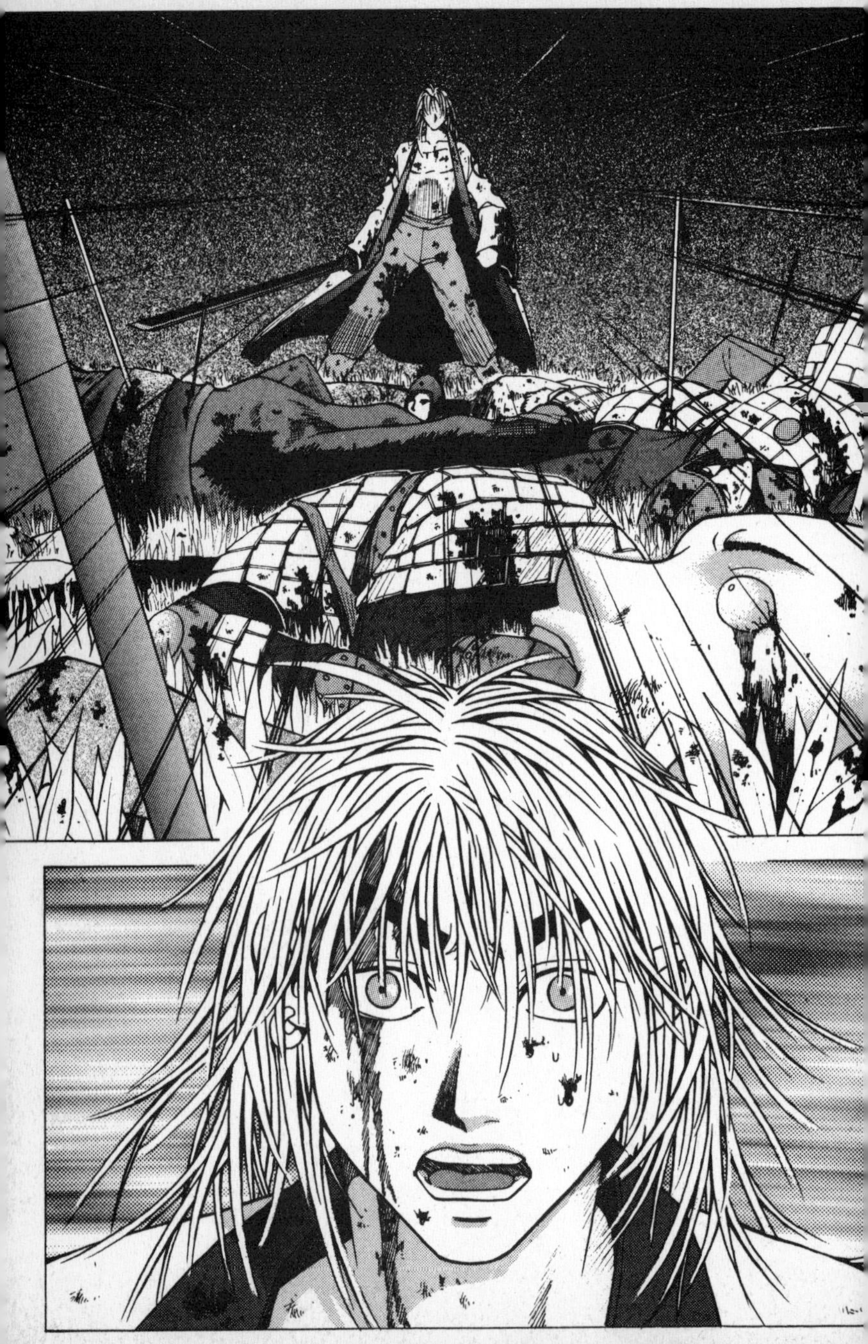

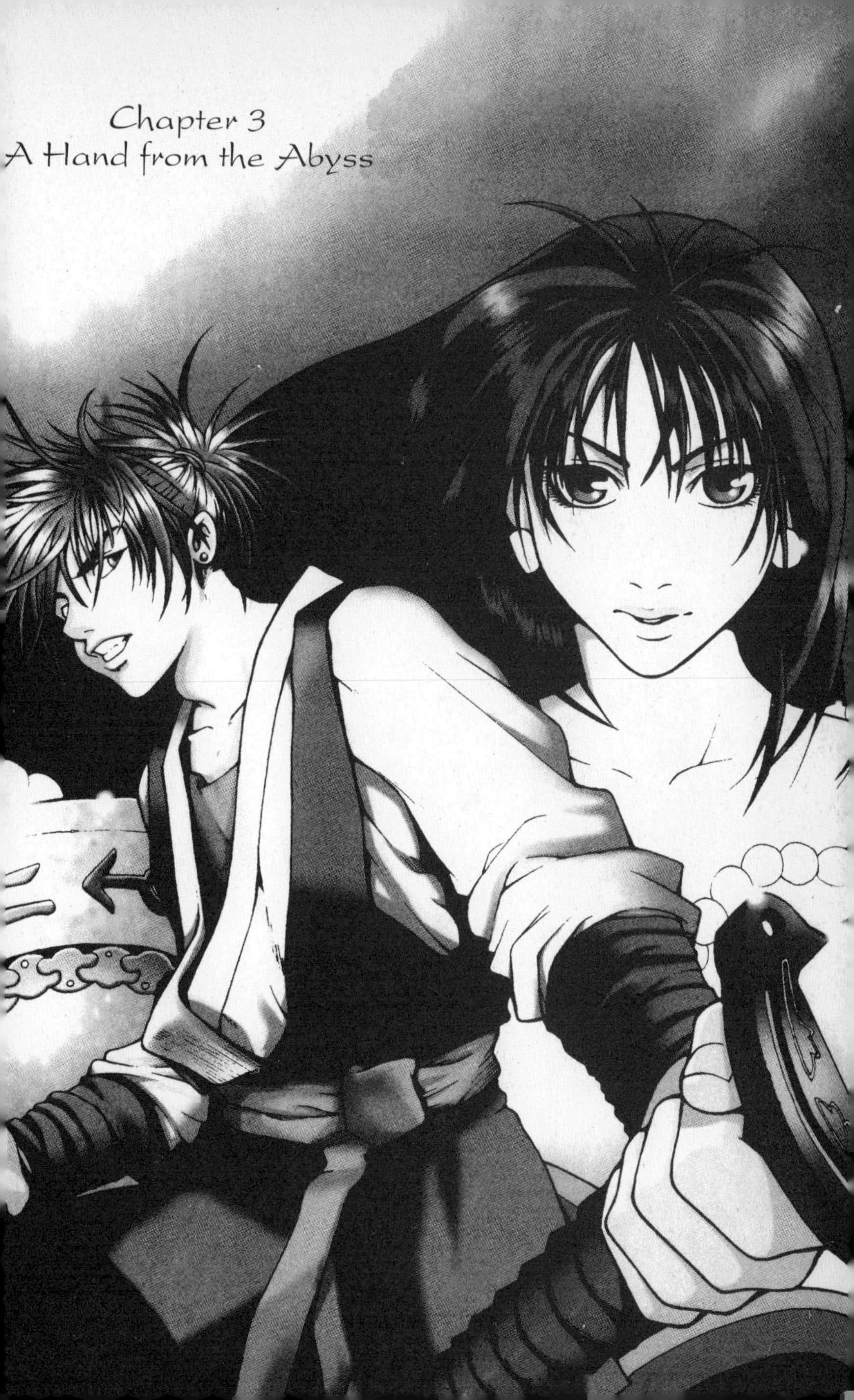
Chapter 3
A Hand from the Abyss

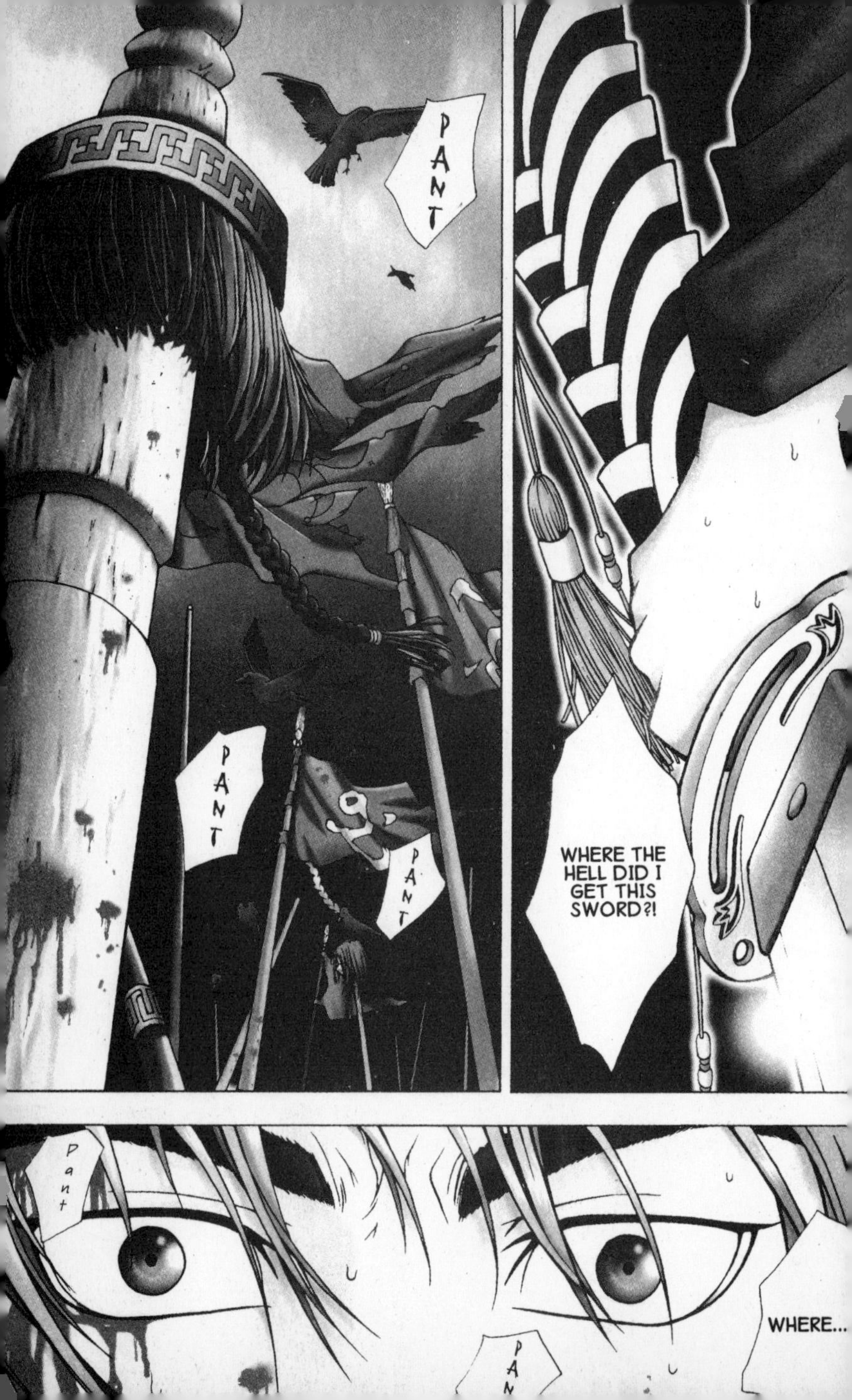
PANT
PANT
PANT
WHERE THE HELL DID I GET THIS SWORD?!
Pant
WHERE...
PAN

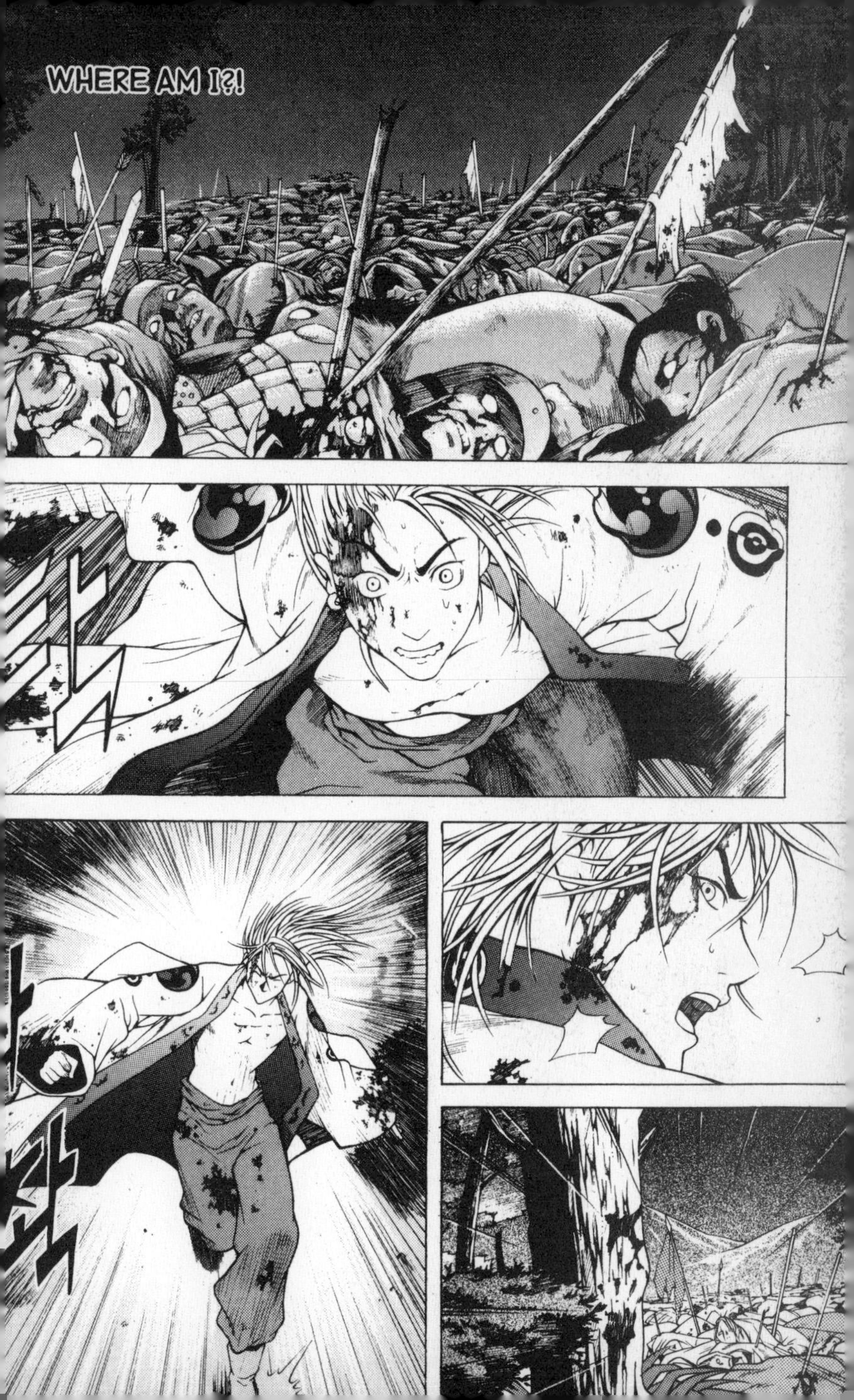
WHERE AM I?!

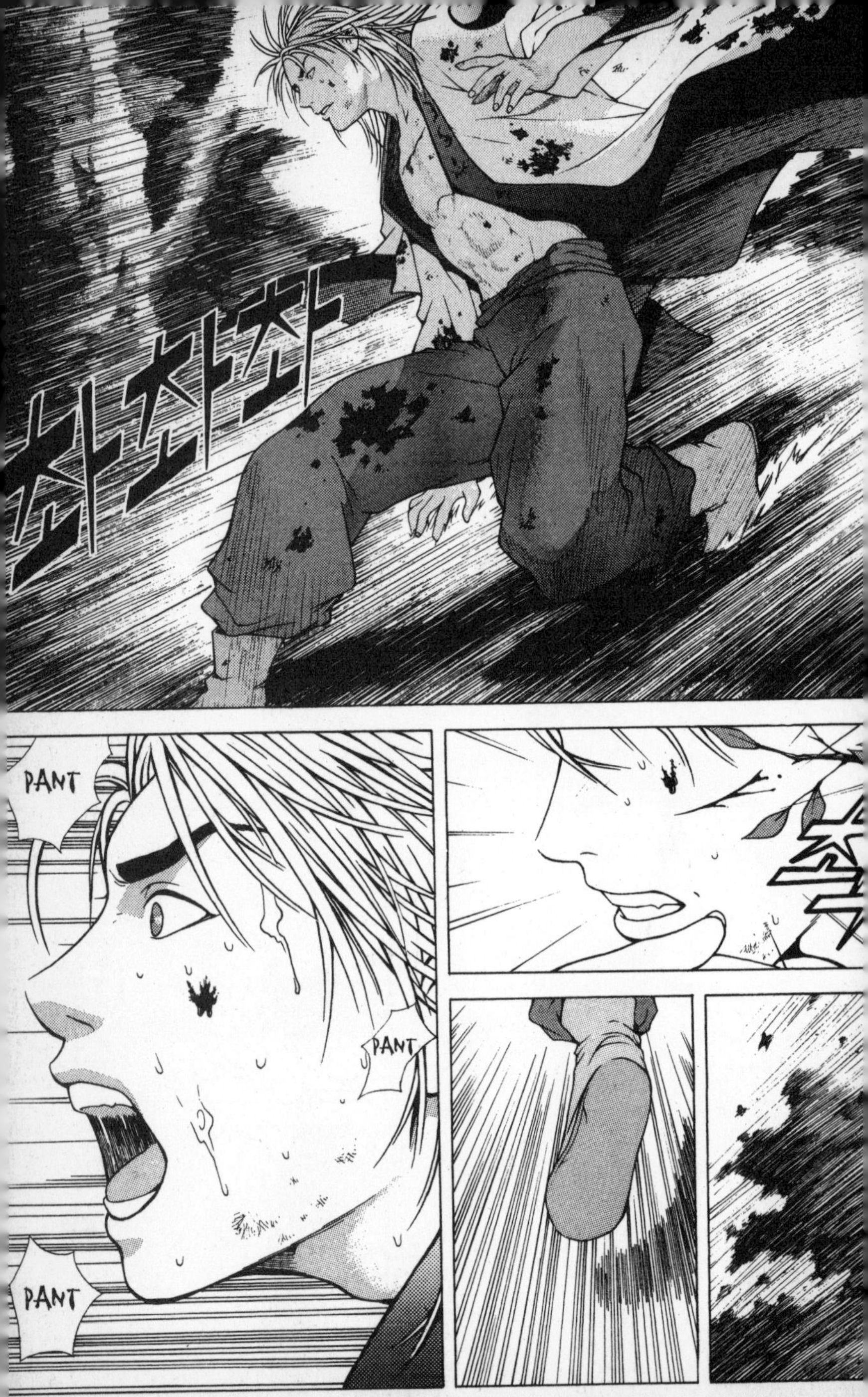
PANT
PANT
PANT

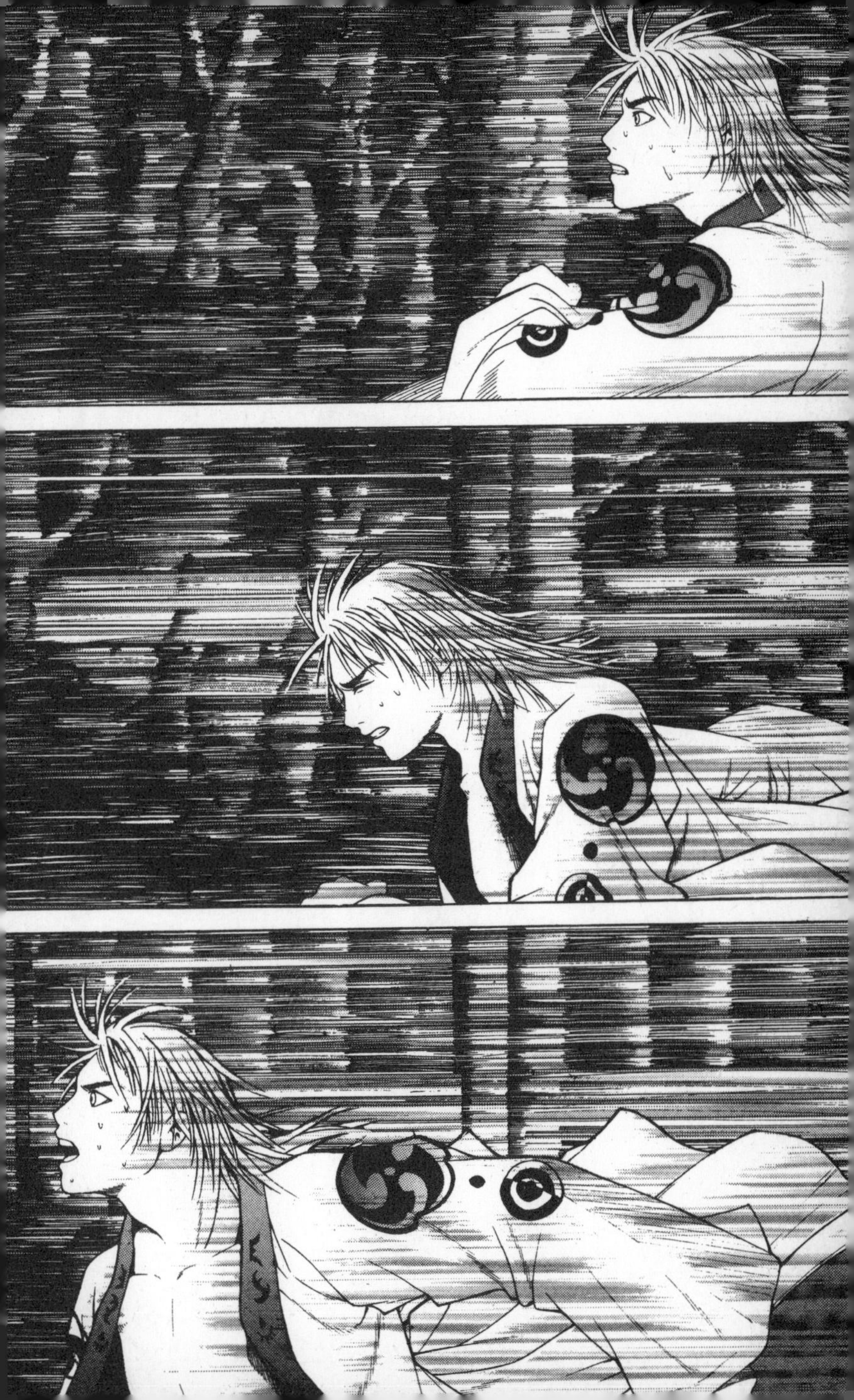

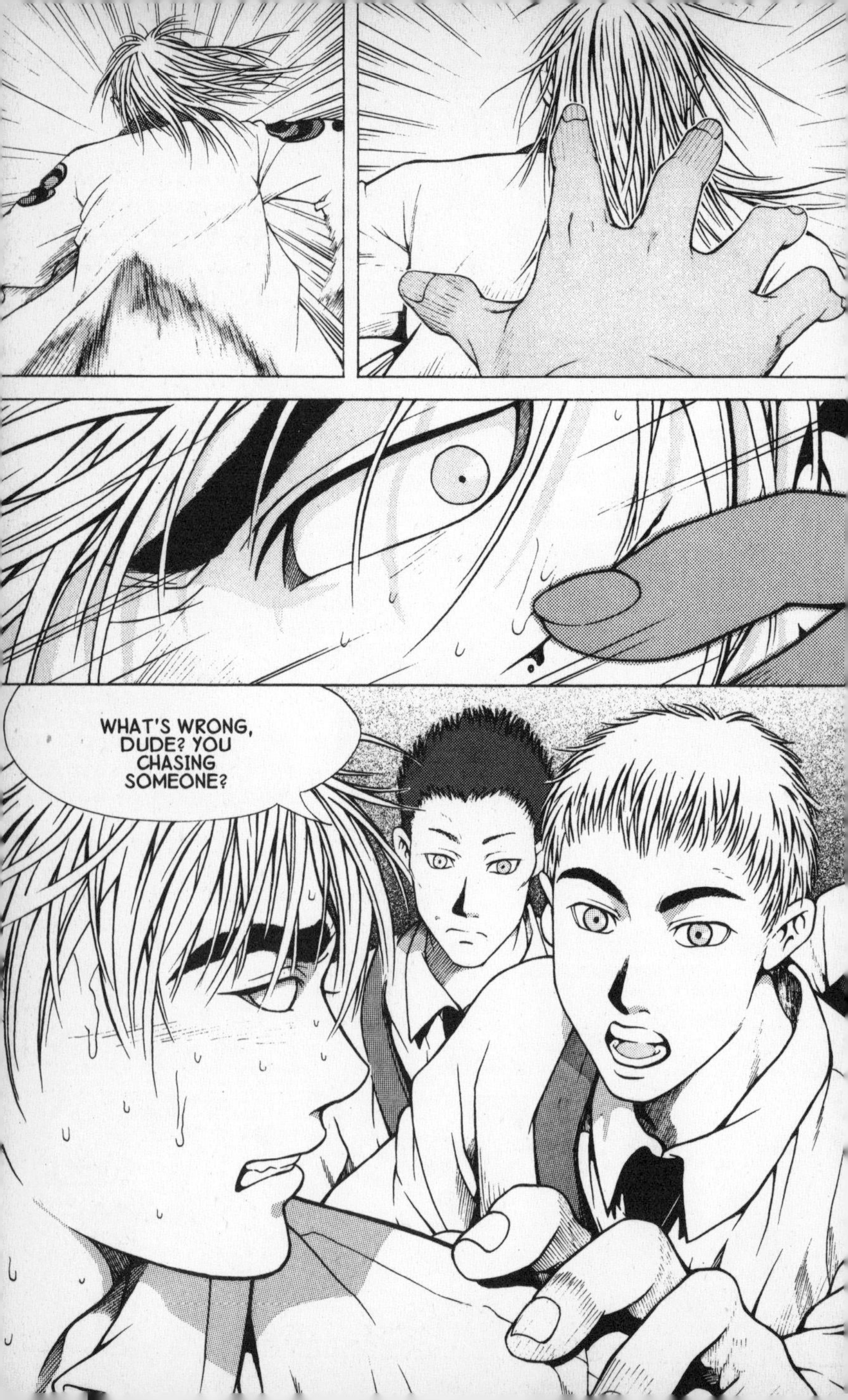
WHAT'S WRONG, DUDE? YOU CHASING SOMEONE?

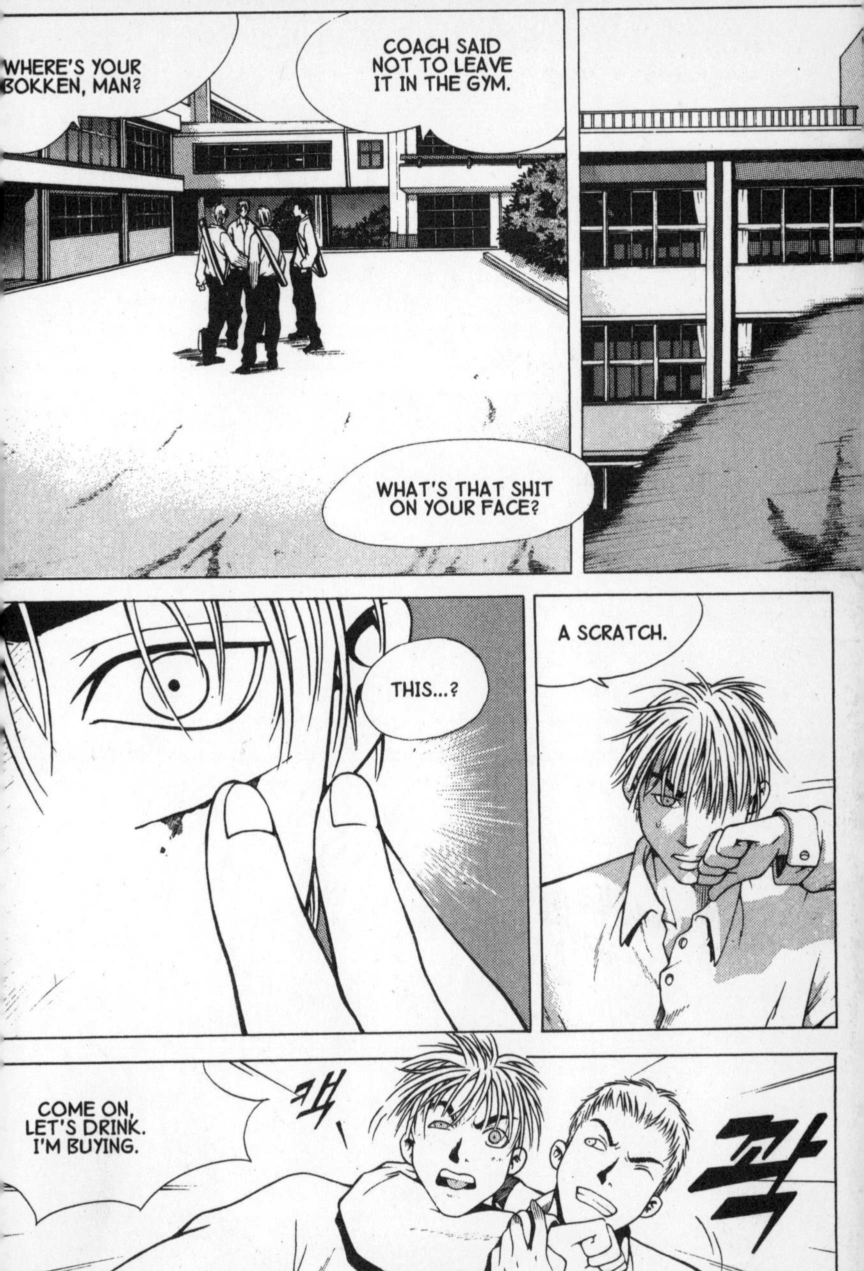
WHERE'S YOUR BOKKEN, MAN?
COACH SAID NOT TO LEAVE IT IN THE GYM.
WHAT'S THAT SHIT ON YOUR FACE?
THIS...?
A SCRATCH.
COME ON, LET'S DRINK. I'M BUYING.
캑
꽉

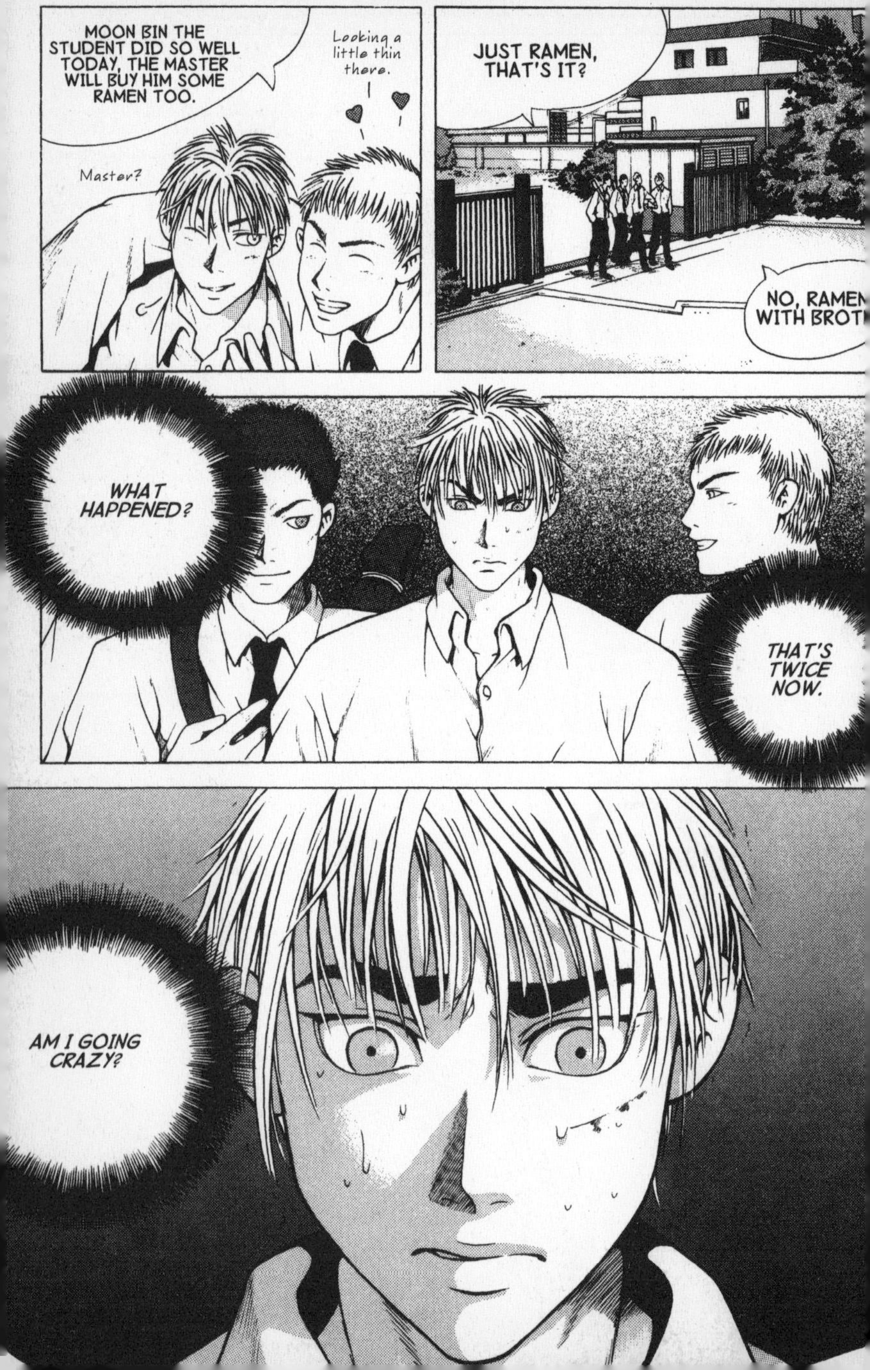
MOON BIN THE STUDENT DID SO WELL TODAY, THE MASTER WILL BUY HIM SOME RAMEN TOO.
Looking a little thin there.
Master?
JUST RAMEN, THAT'S IT?
...
NO, RAMEN WITH BROT
WHAT HAPPENED?
THAT'S TWICE NOW.
AM I GOING CRAZY?

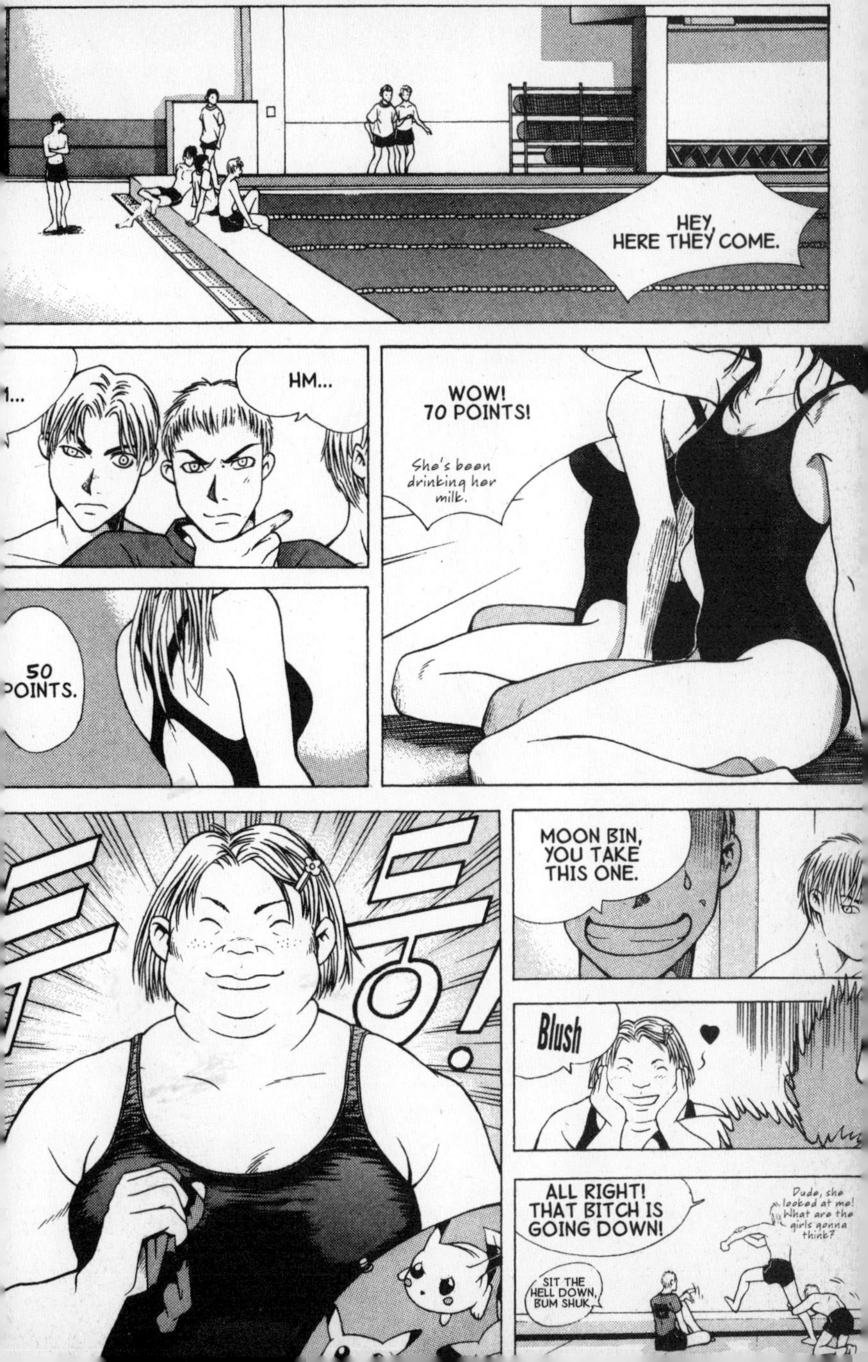
HEY, HERE THEY COME.
HM...
50 POINTS.
WOW! 70 POINTS!
She's been drinking her milk.
MOON BIN, YOU TAKE THIS ONE.
Blush
ALL RIGHT! THAT BITCH IS GOING DOWN!
SIT THE HELL DOWN, BUM SHUK.
Dude, she looked at me! What are the girls gonna think?

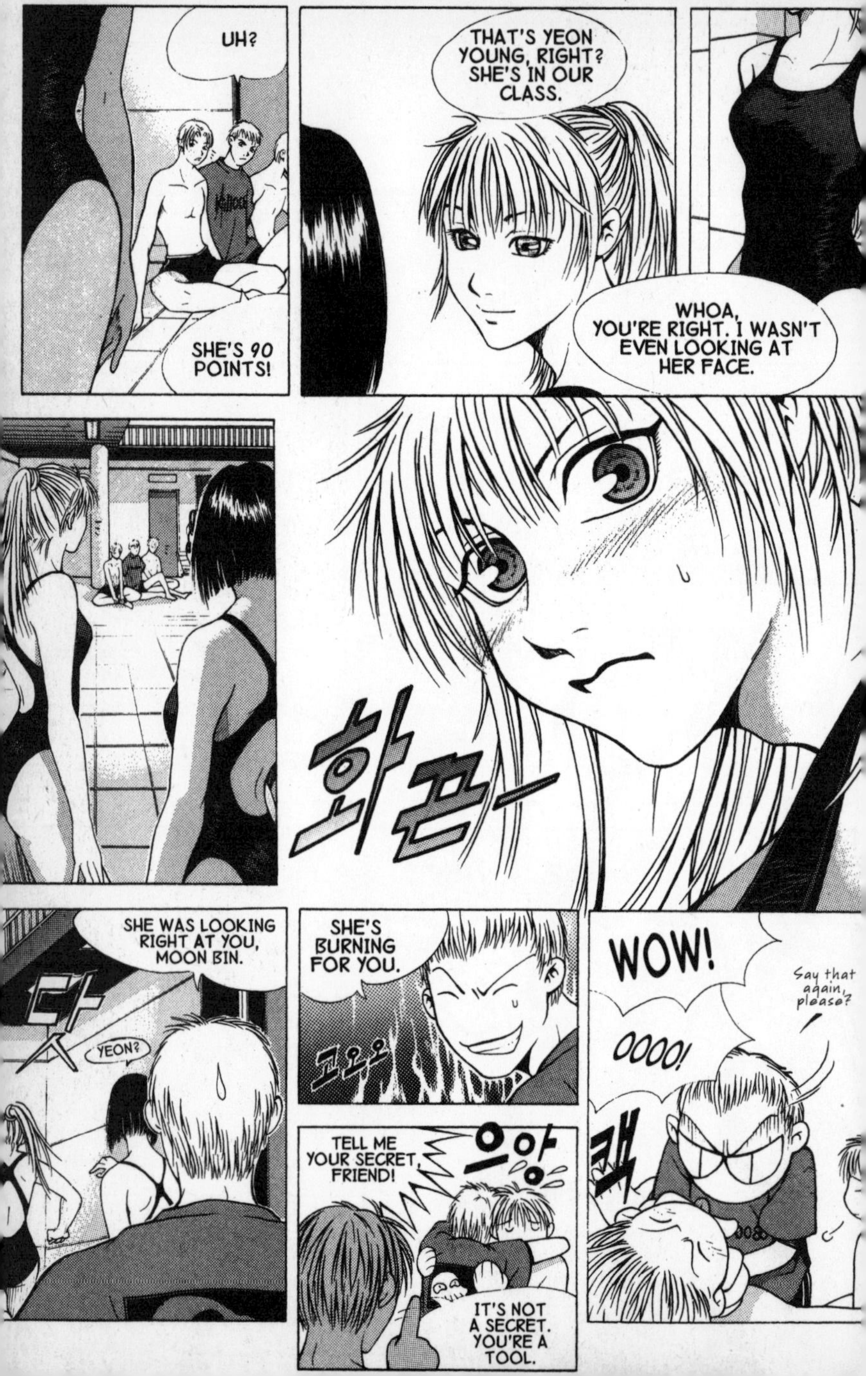
UH?
SHE'S 90 POINTS!
THAT'S YEON YOUNG, RIGHT? SHE'S IN OUR CLASS.
WHOA, YOU'RE RIGHT. I WASN'T EVEN LOOKING AT HER FACE.
화끈—
SHE WAS LOOKING RIGHT AT YOU, MOON BIN.
닷
YEON?
SHE'S BURNING FOR YOU.
고오오
TELL ME YOUR SECRET, FRIEND!
으앙
IT'S NOT A SECRET. YOU'RE A TOOL.
WOW!
Say that again, please?
OOOO!
캑

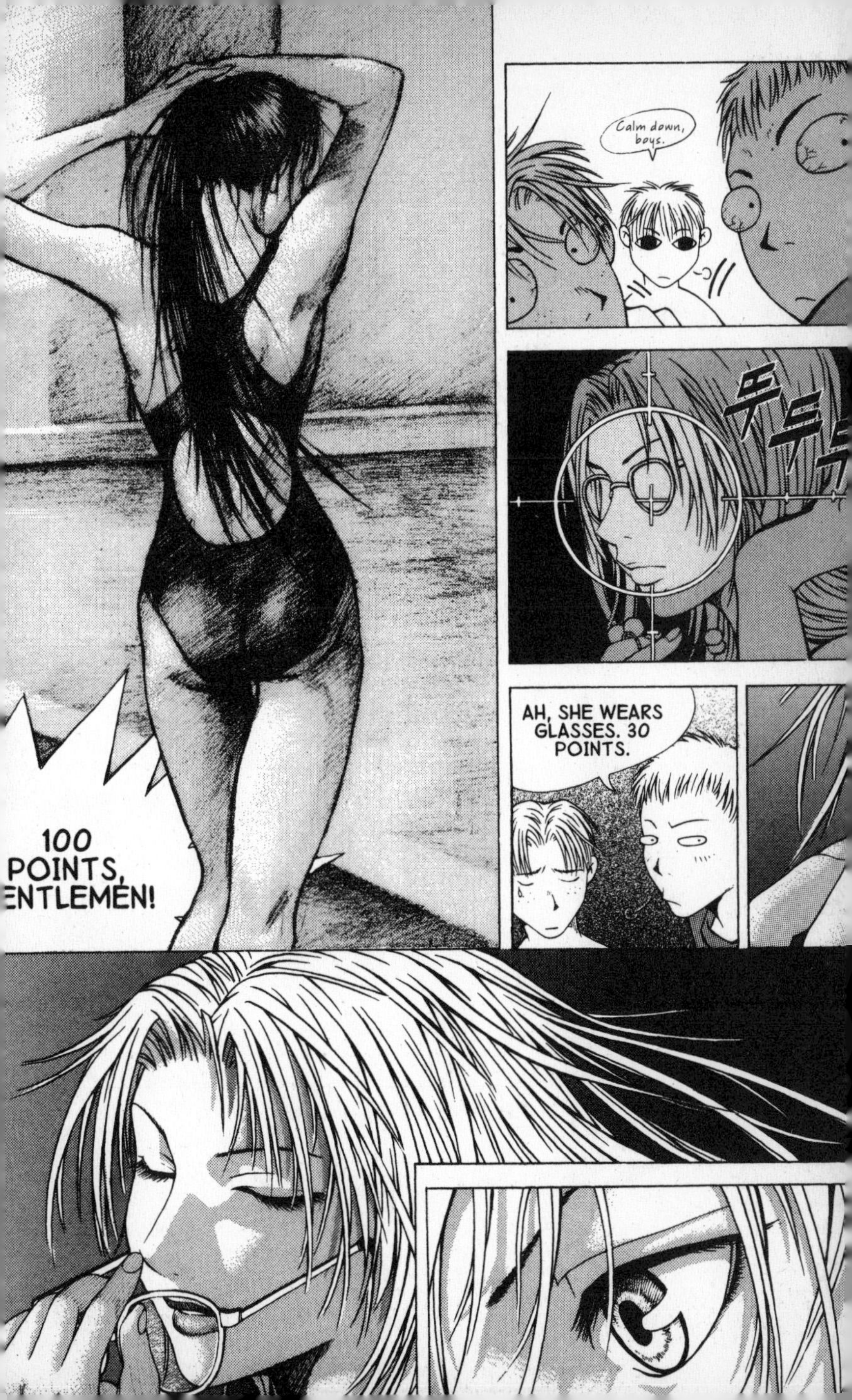

100 POINTS, ENTLEMEN!
Calm down, boys.
AH, SHE WEARS GLASSES. 30 POINTS.

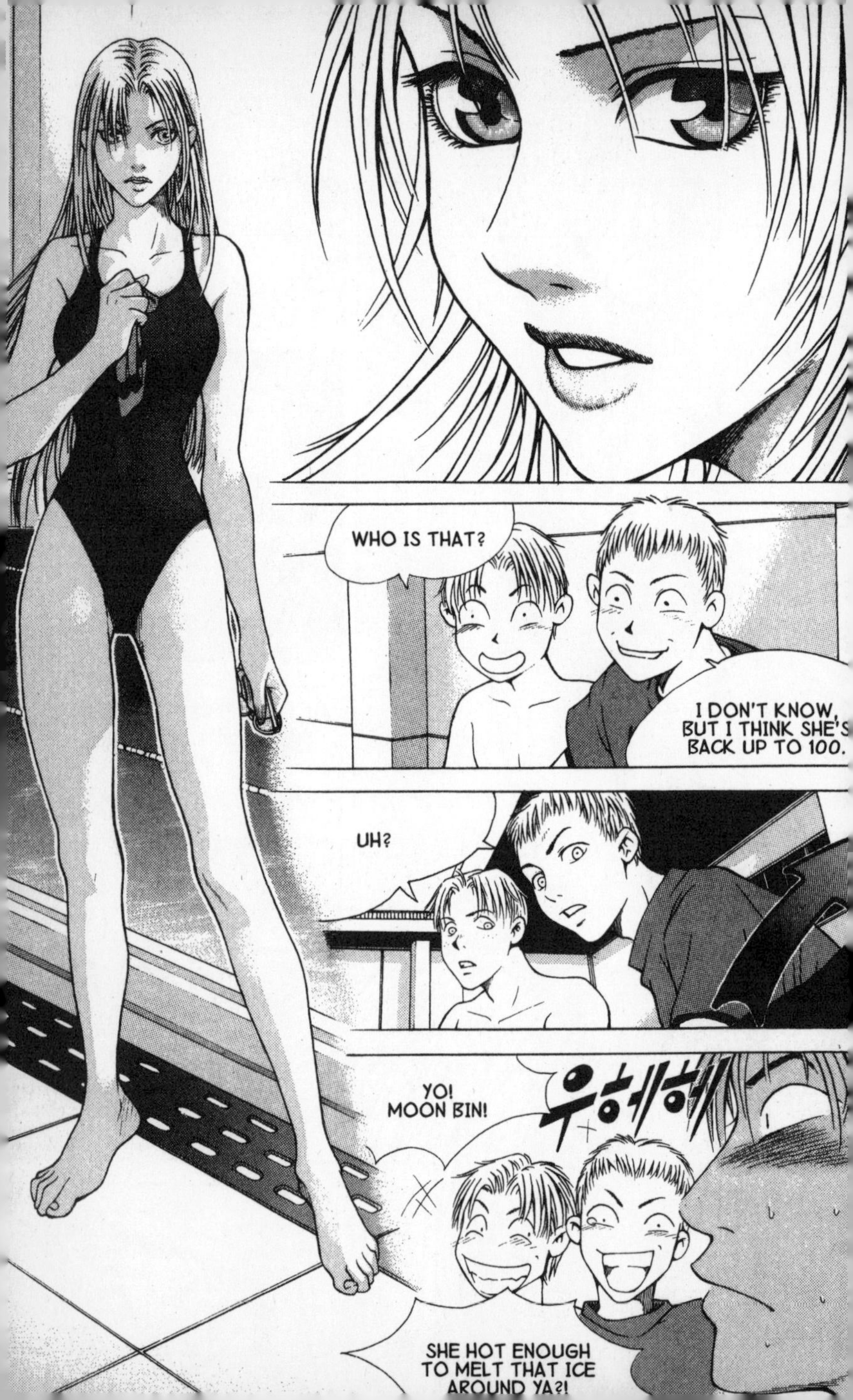
WHO IS THAT?
I DON'T KNOW, BUT I THINK SHE'S BACK UP TO 100.
UH?
YO! MOON BIN!
우헤헤
SHE HOT ENOUGH TO MELT THAT ICE AROUND YA?!

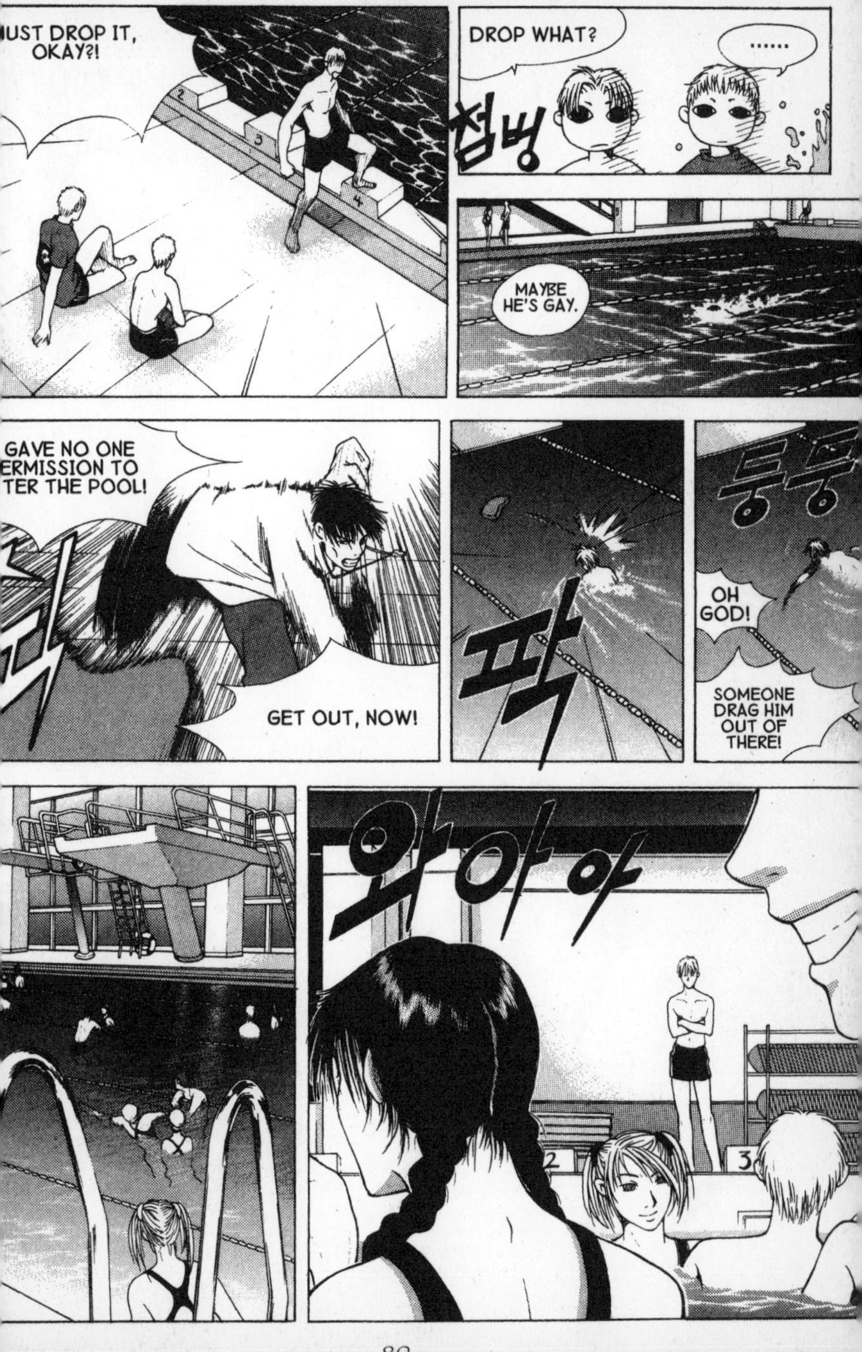
UST DROP IT, OKAY?!
DROP WHAT?
......
첨벙
MAYBE HE'S GAY.
GAVE NO ONE ERMISSION TO TER THE POOL!
GET OUT, NOW!
팍
둥둥
OH GOD!
SOMEONE DRAG HIM OUT OF THERE!
와아아

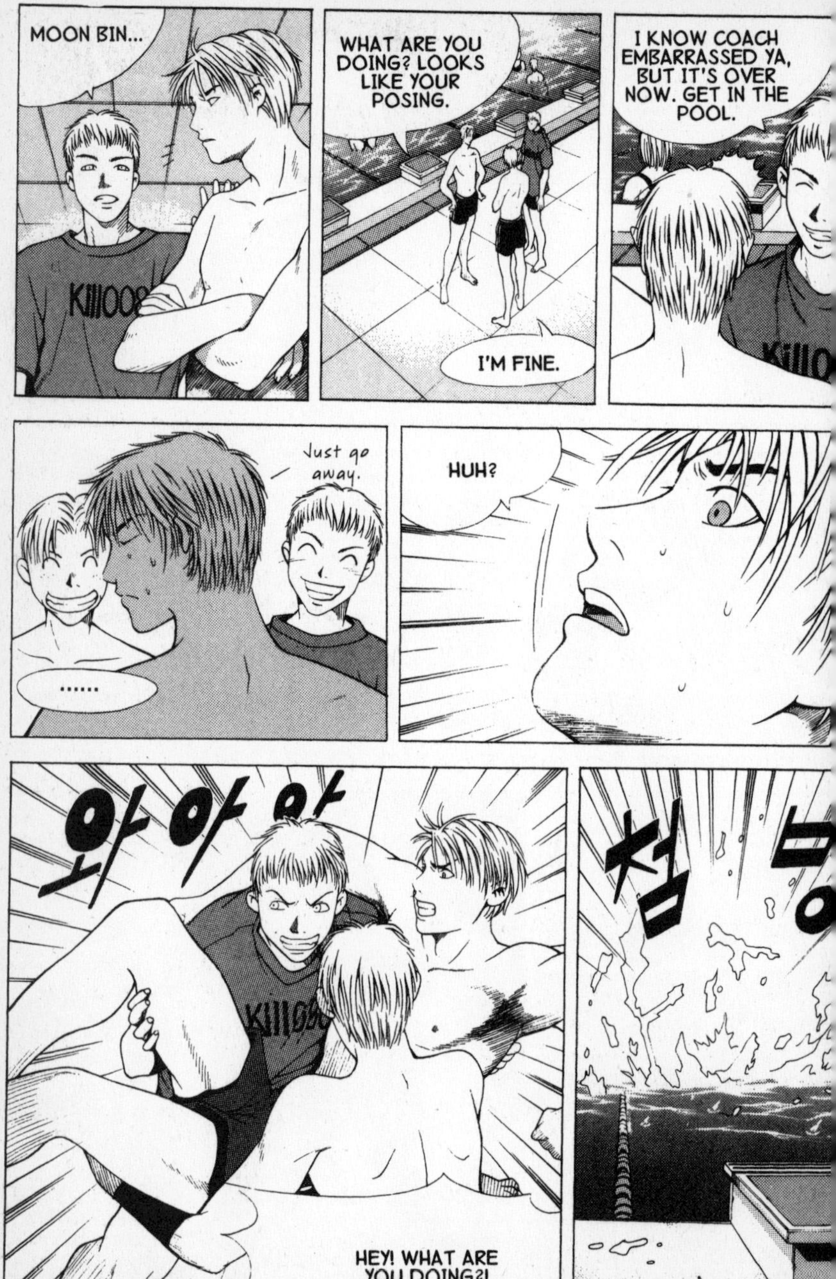
MOON BIN...
WHAT ARE YOU DOING? LOOKS LIKE YOUR POSING.
I'M FINE.
I KNOW COACH EMBARRASSED YA, BUT IT'S OVER NOW. GET IN THE POOL.
Just go away.
......
HUH?
와아아
HEY! WHAT ARE YOU DOING?!
첨벙

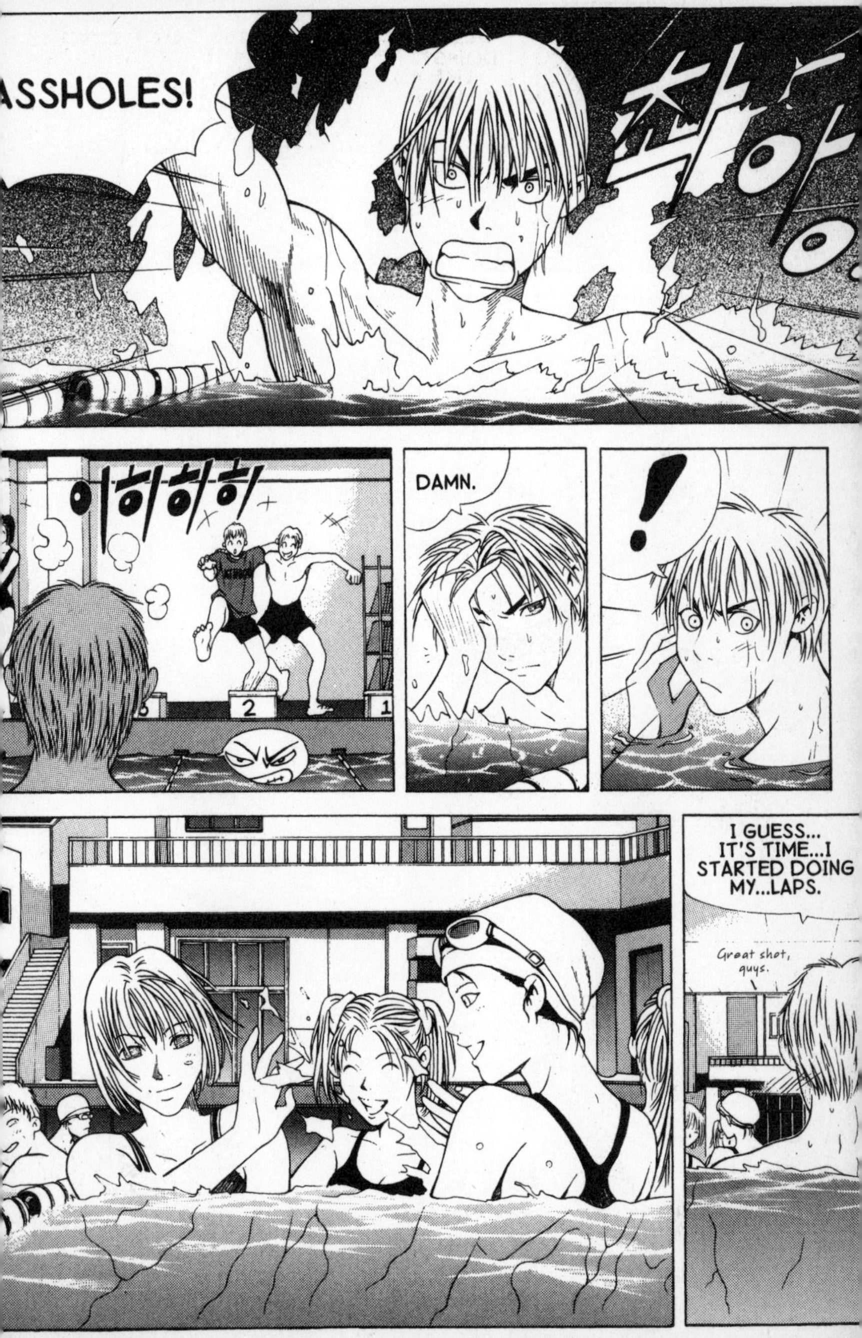

ASSHOLES!
촤아
이히히히
DAMN.
!
I GUESS... IT'S TIME...I STARTED DOING MY...LAPS.
Great shot, guys.

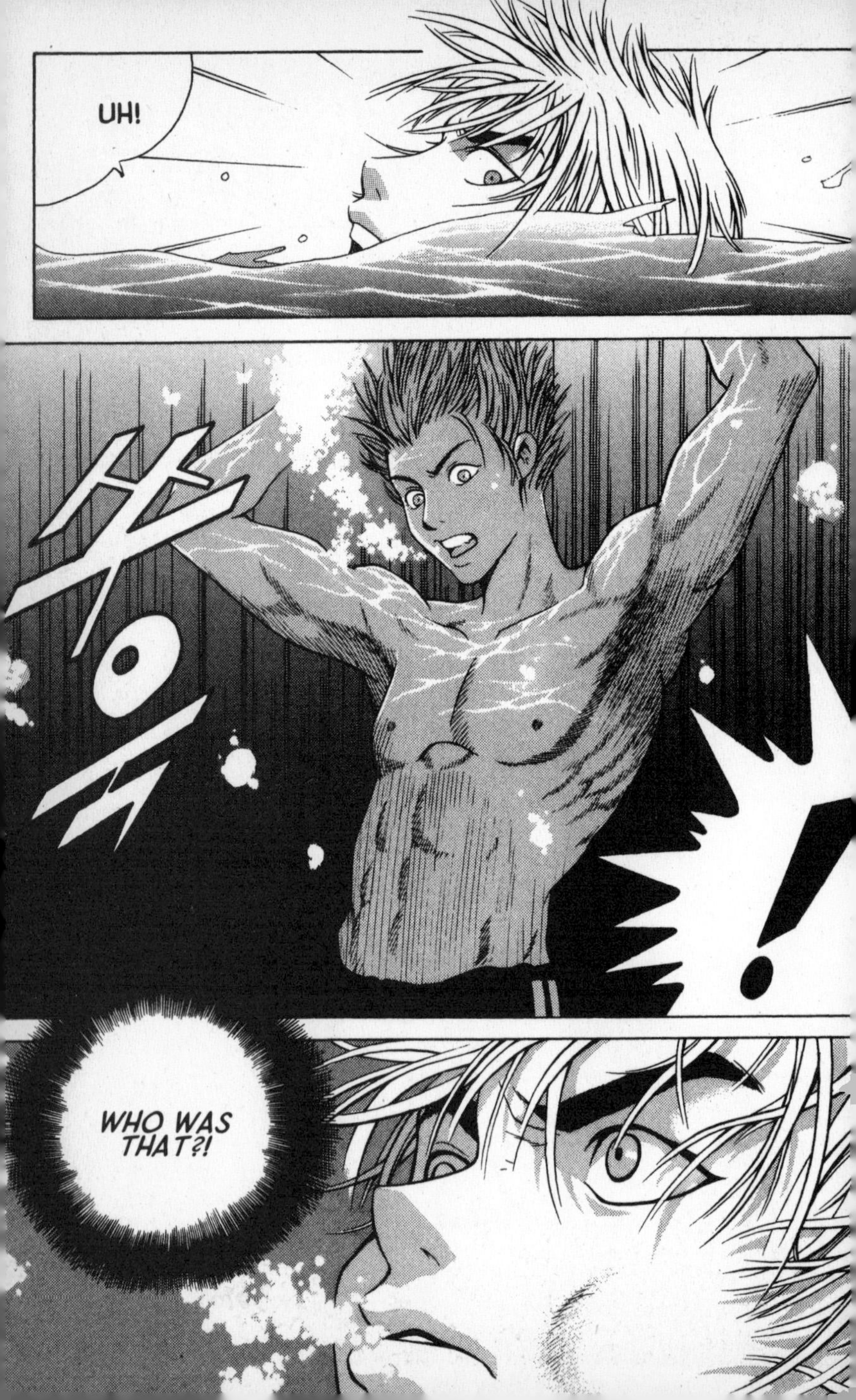
UH!
!
WHO WAS THAT?!

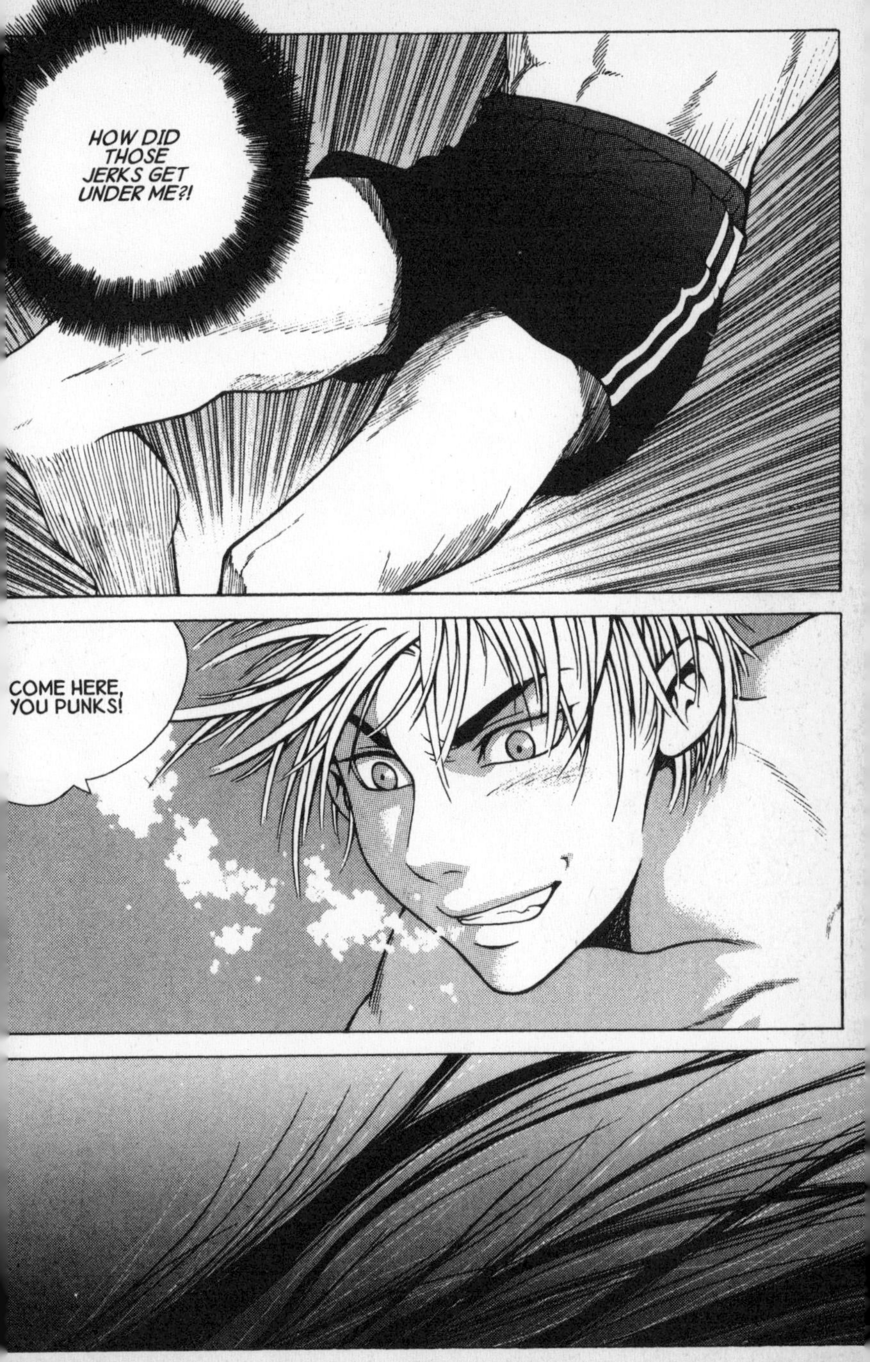
HOW DID THOSE JERKS GET UNDER ME?!
COME HERE, YOU PUNKS!

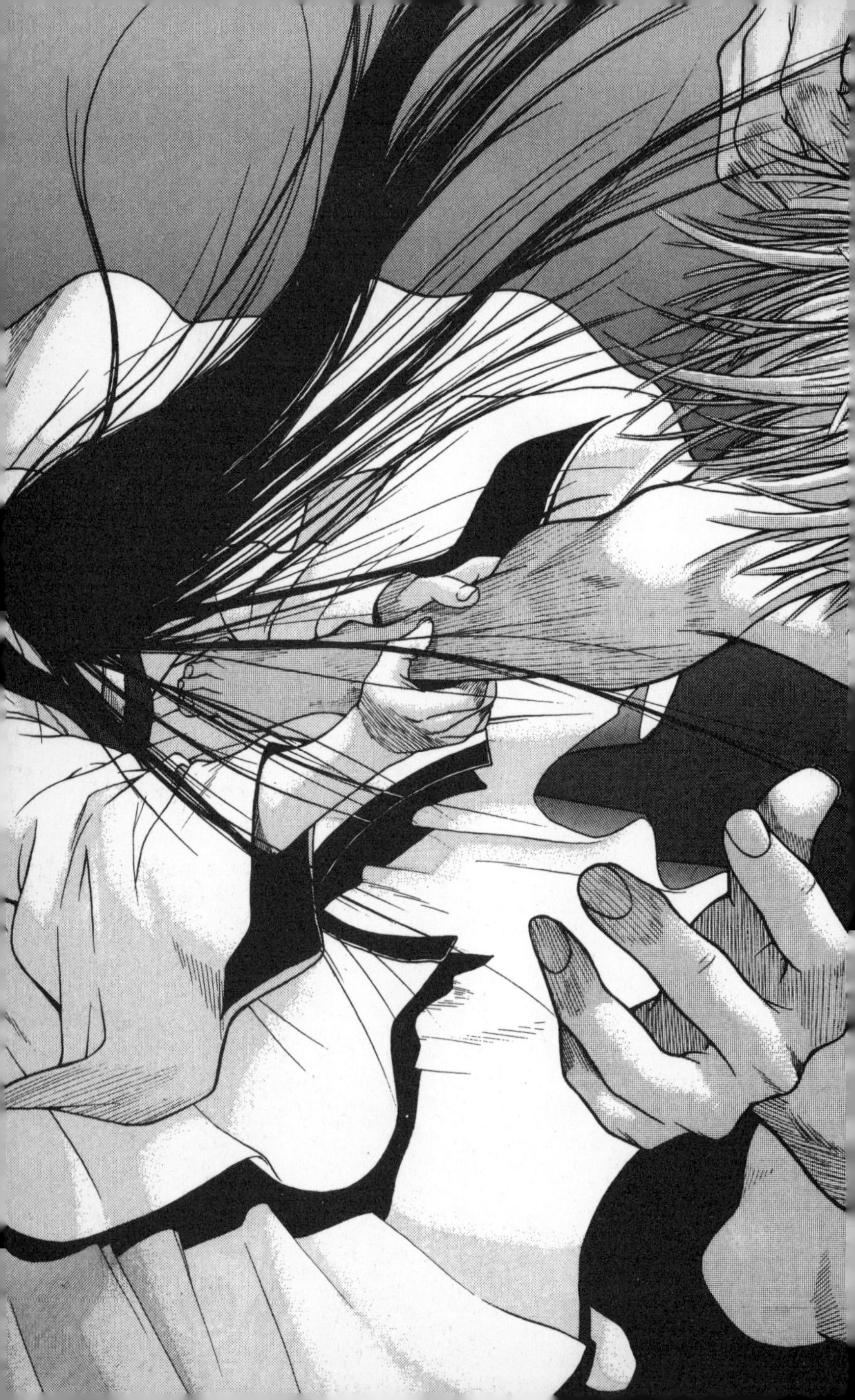

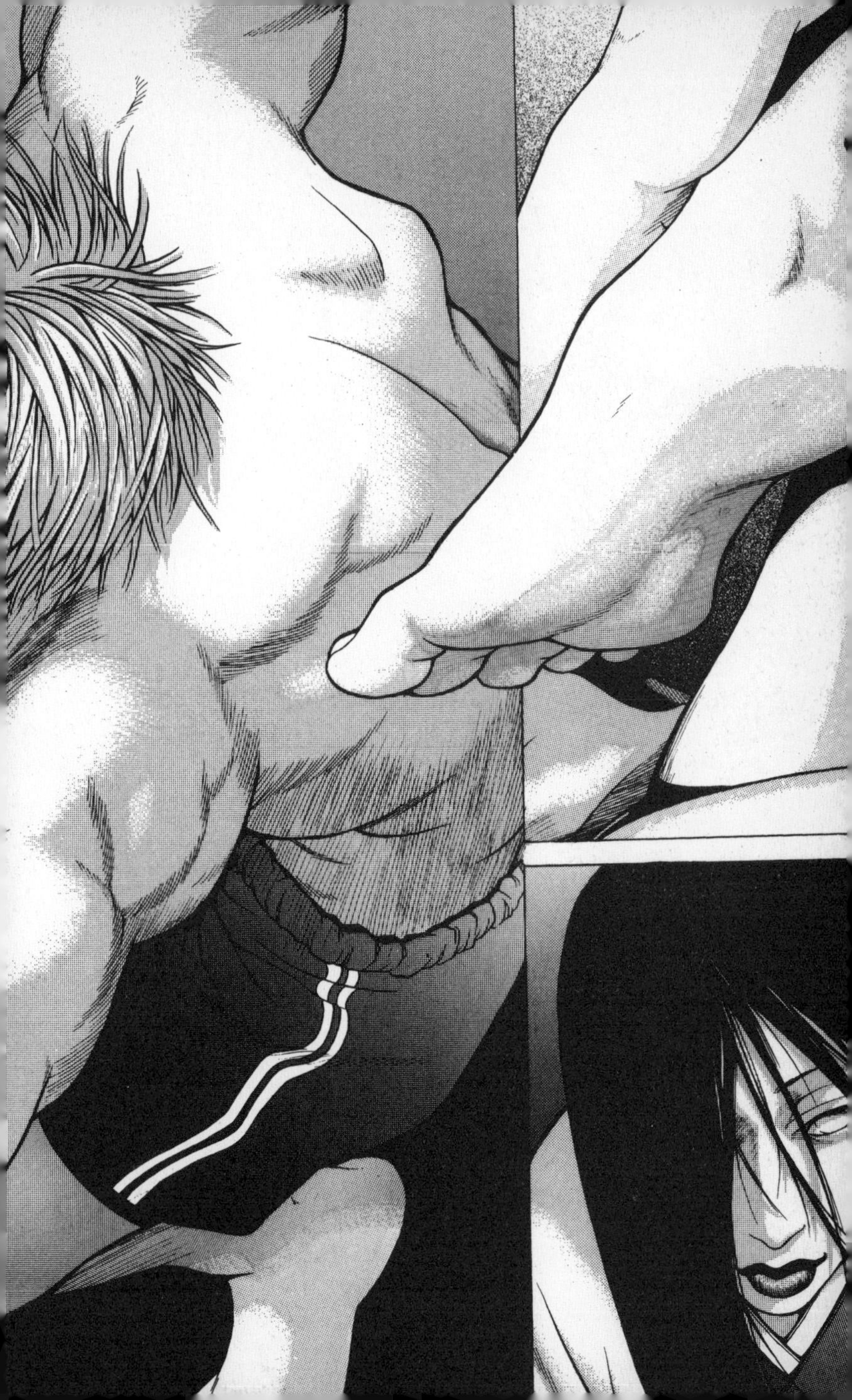

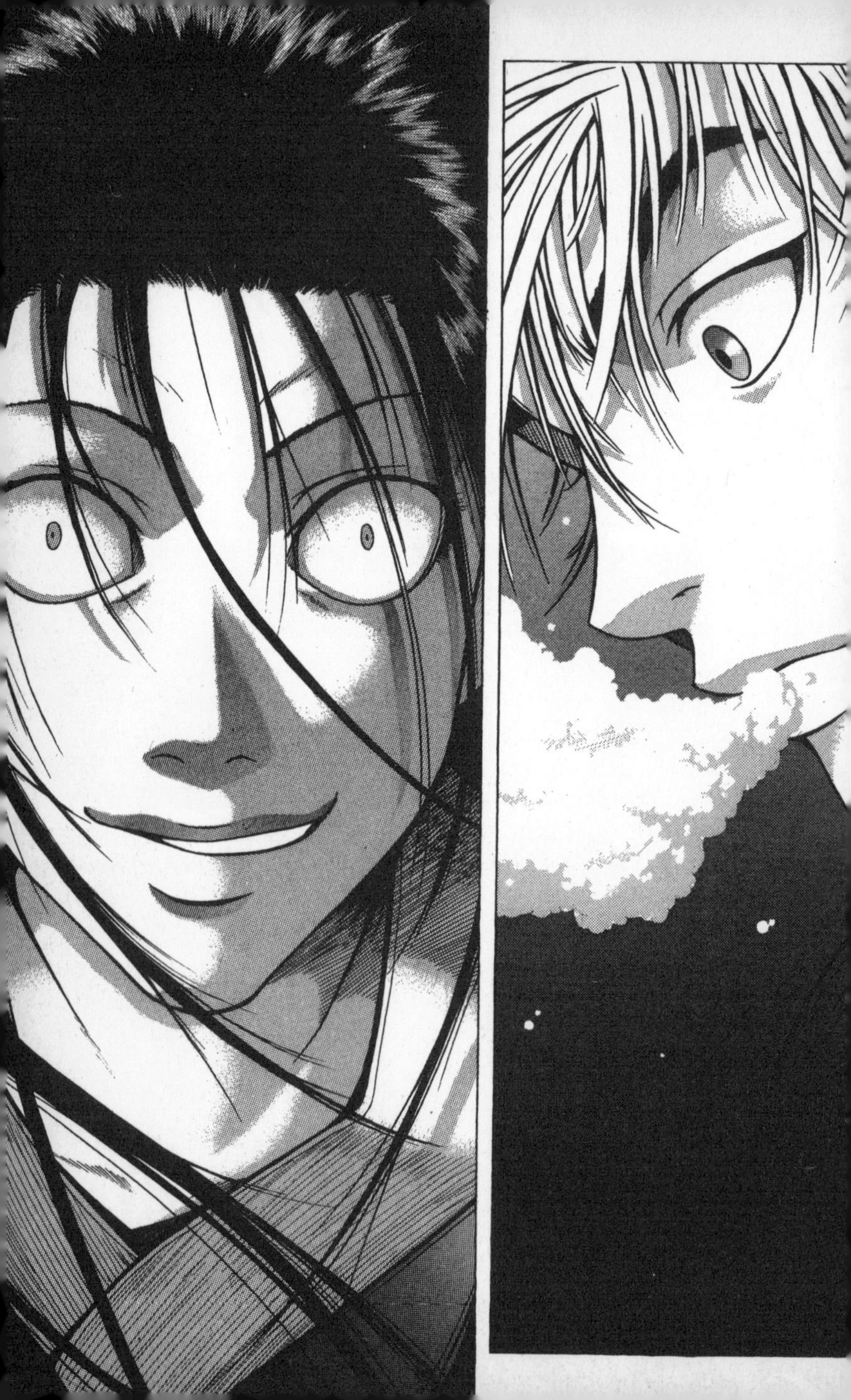

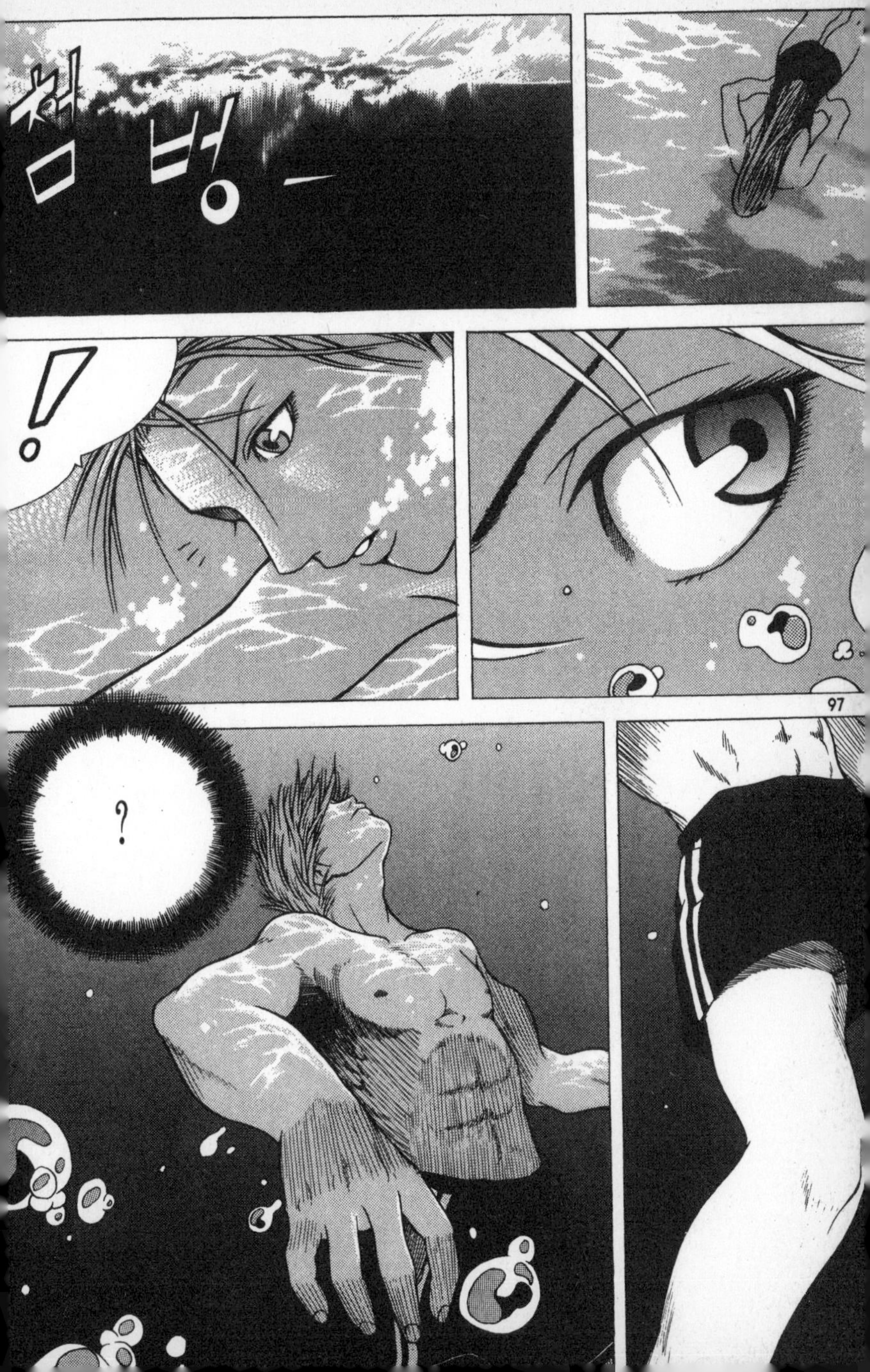
첨벙-
!
?

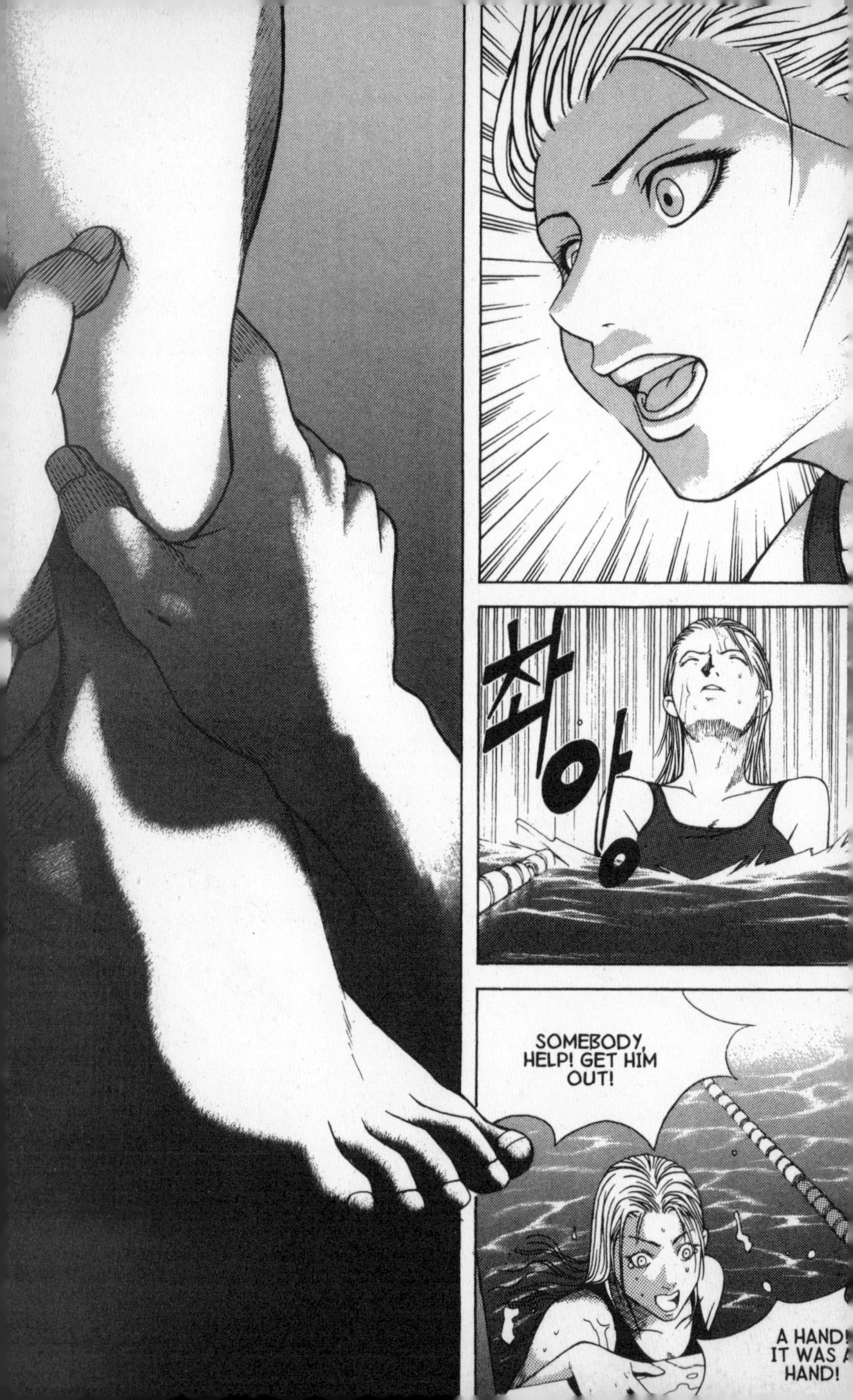
촤아
SOMEBODY, HELP! GET HIM OUT!
A HAND! IT WAS A HAND!

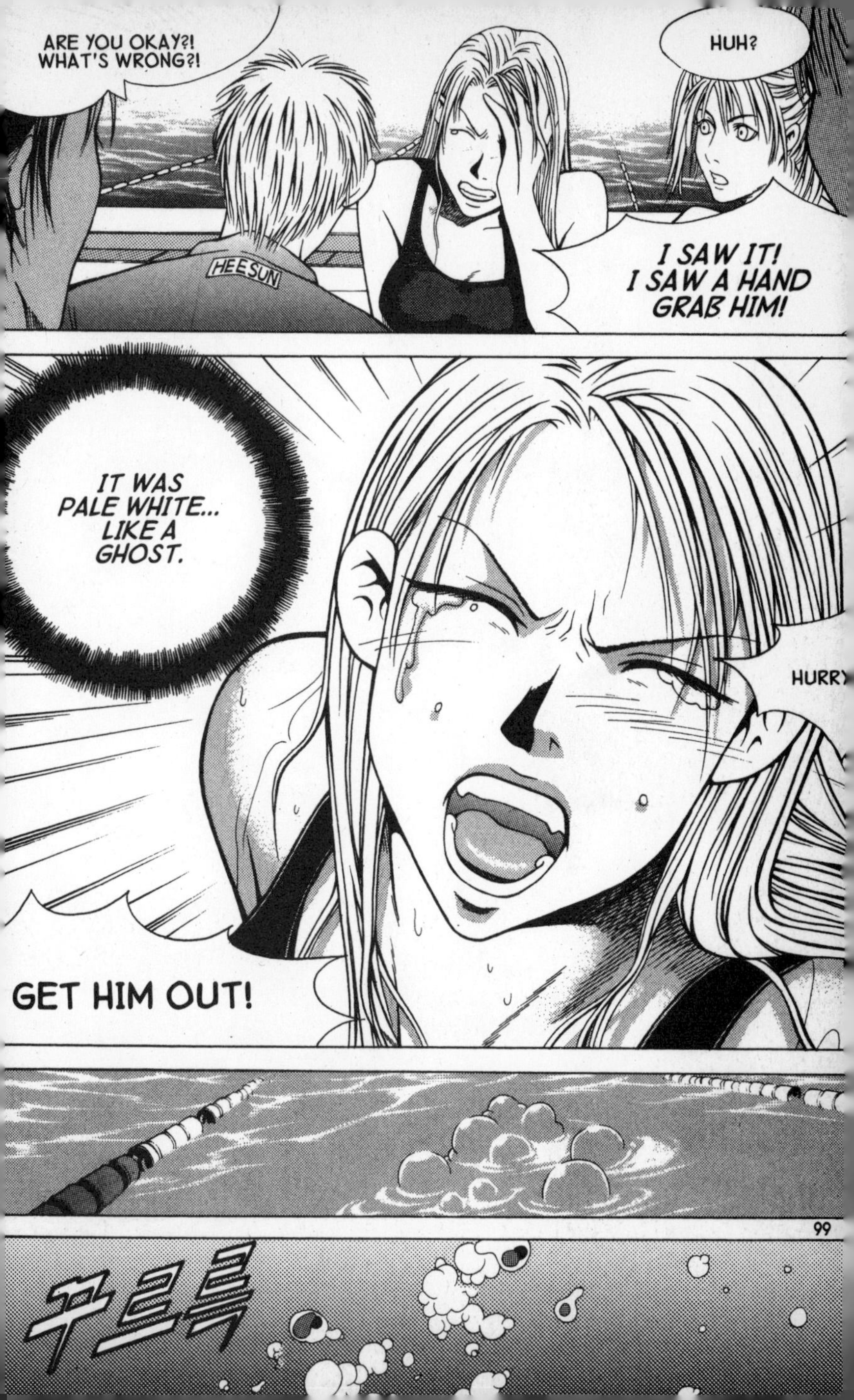
ARE YOU OKAY?! WHAT'S WRONG?!
HUH?
I SAW IT! I SAW A HAND GRAB HIM!
IT WAS PALE WHITE... LIKE A GHOST.
HURRY
GET HIM OUT!
구르륵

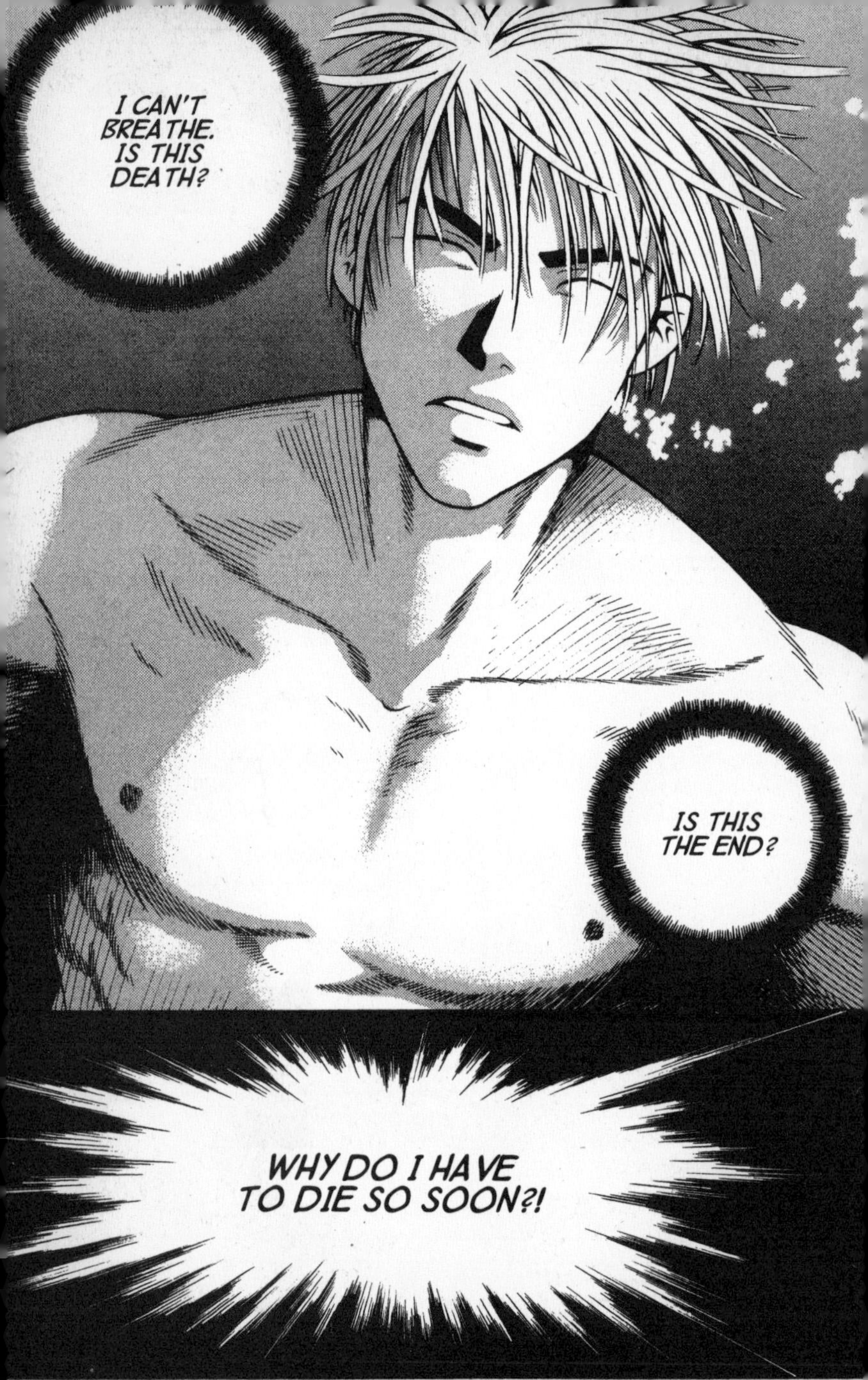
I CAN'T BREATHE. IS THIS DEATH?
IS THIS THE END?
WHY DO I HAVE TO DIE SO SOON?!

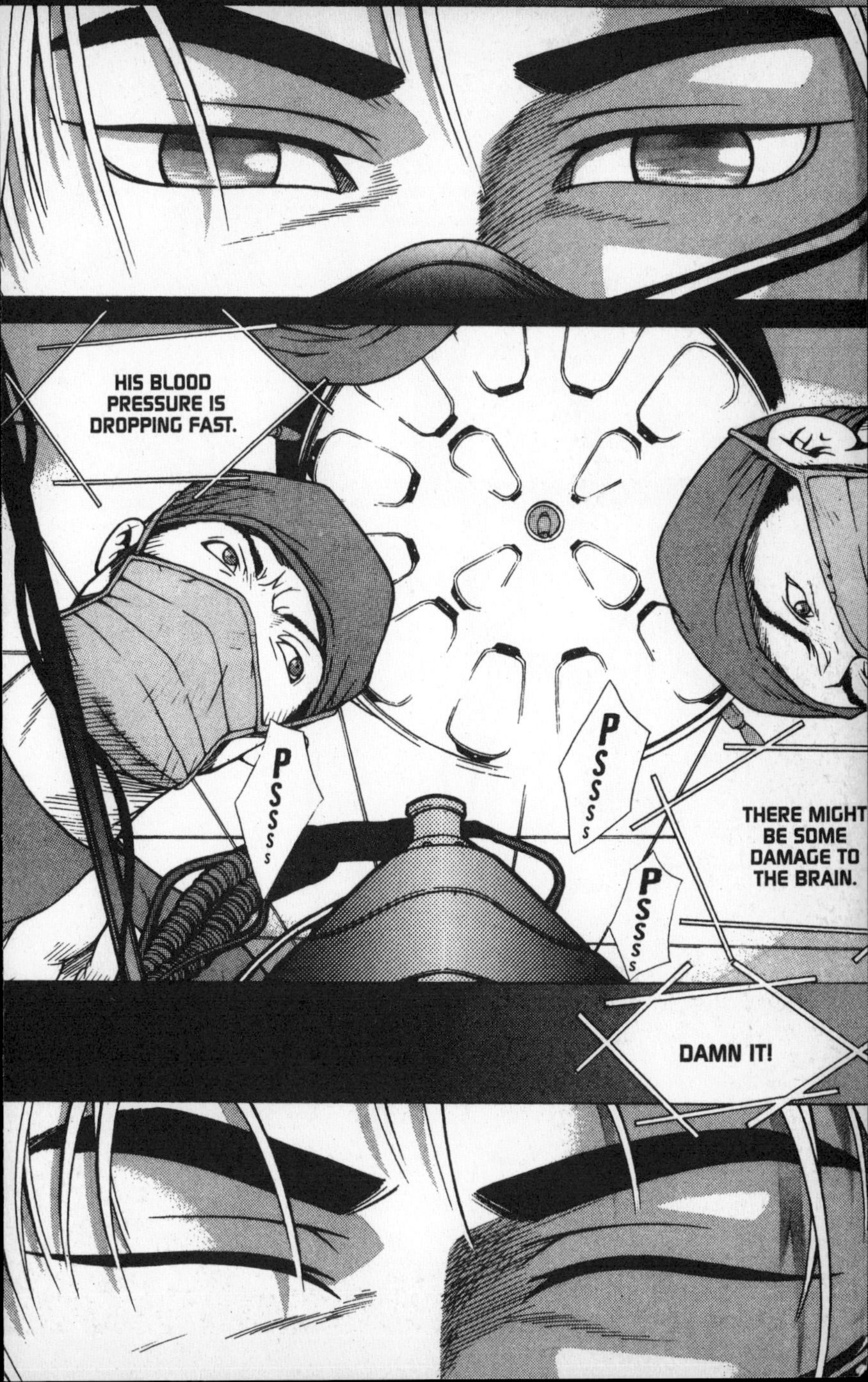
HIS BLOOD PRESSURE IS DROPPING FAST.
PSSSS
PSSSS
PSSSS
THERE MIGHT BE SOME DAMAGE TO THE BRAIN.
DAMN IT!

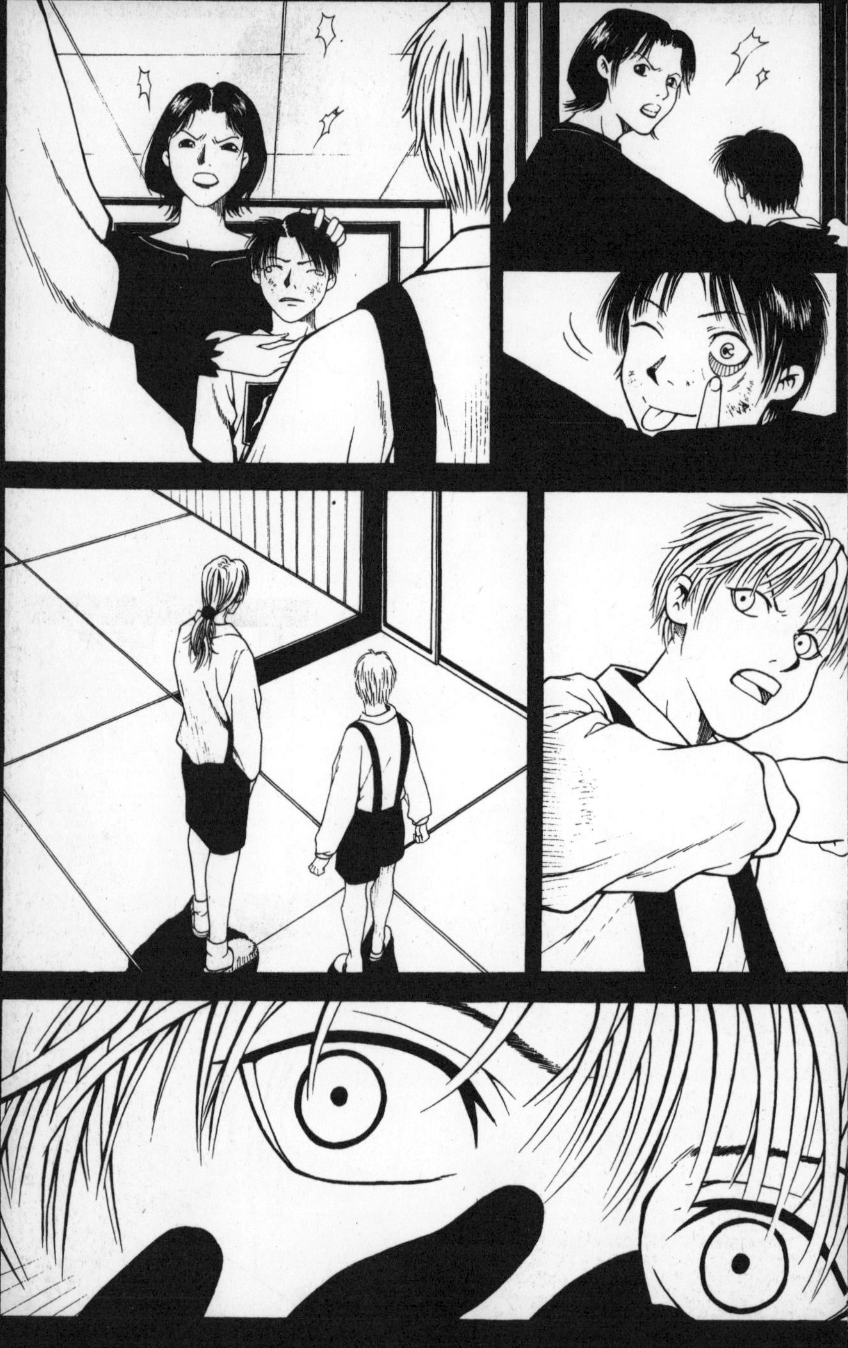

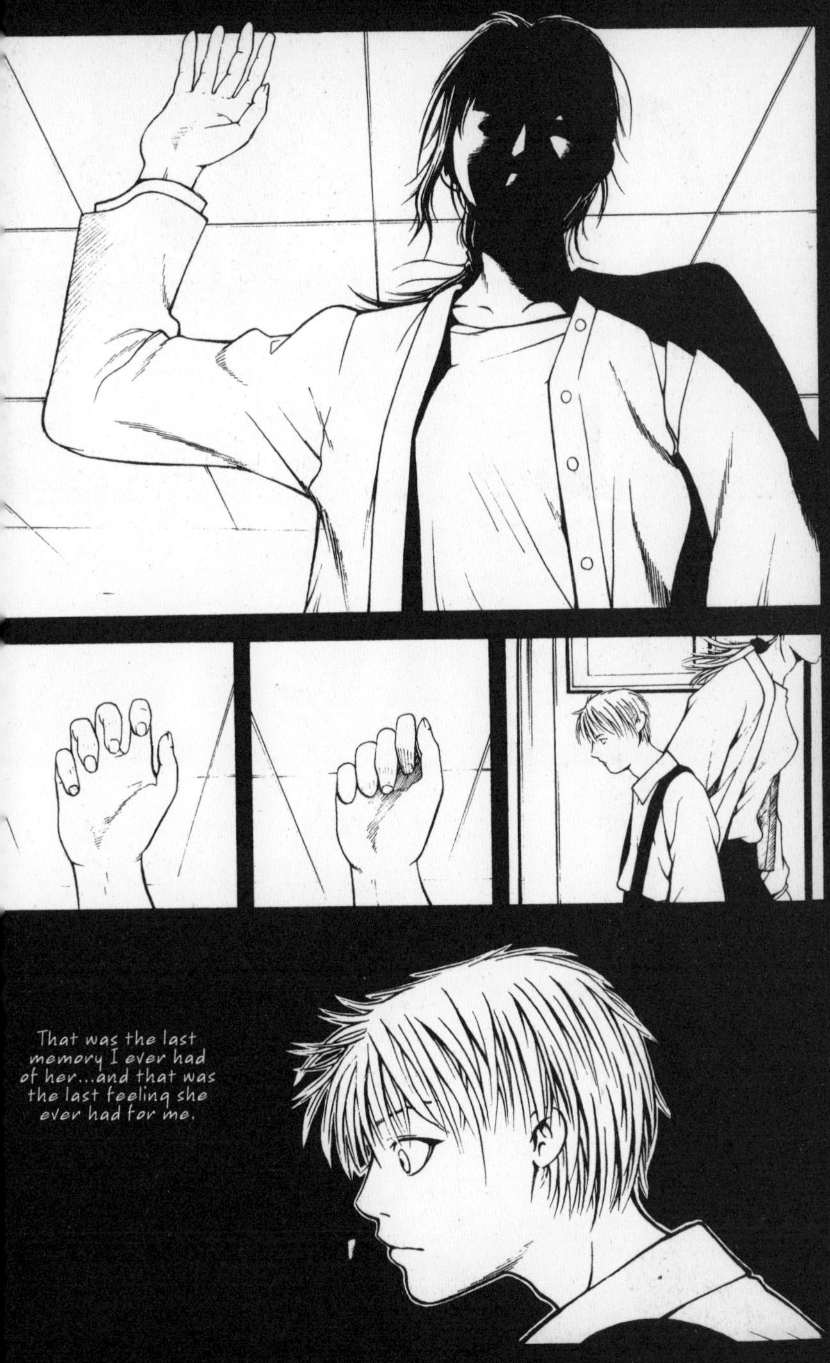
That was the last memory I ever had of her...and that was the last feeling she ever had for me.

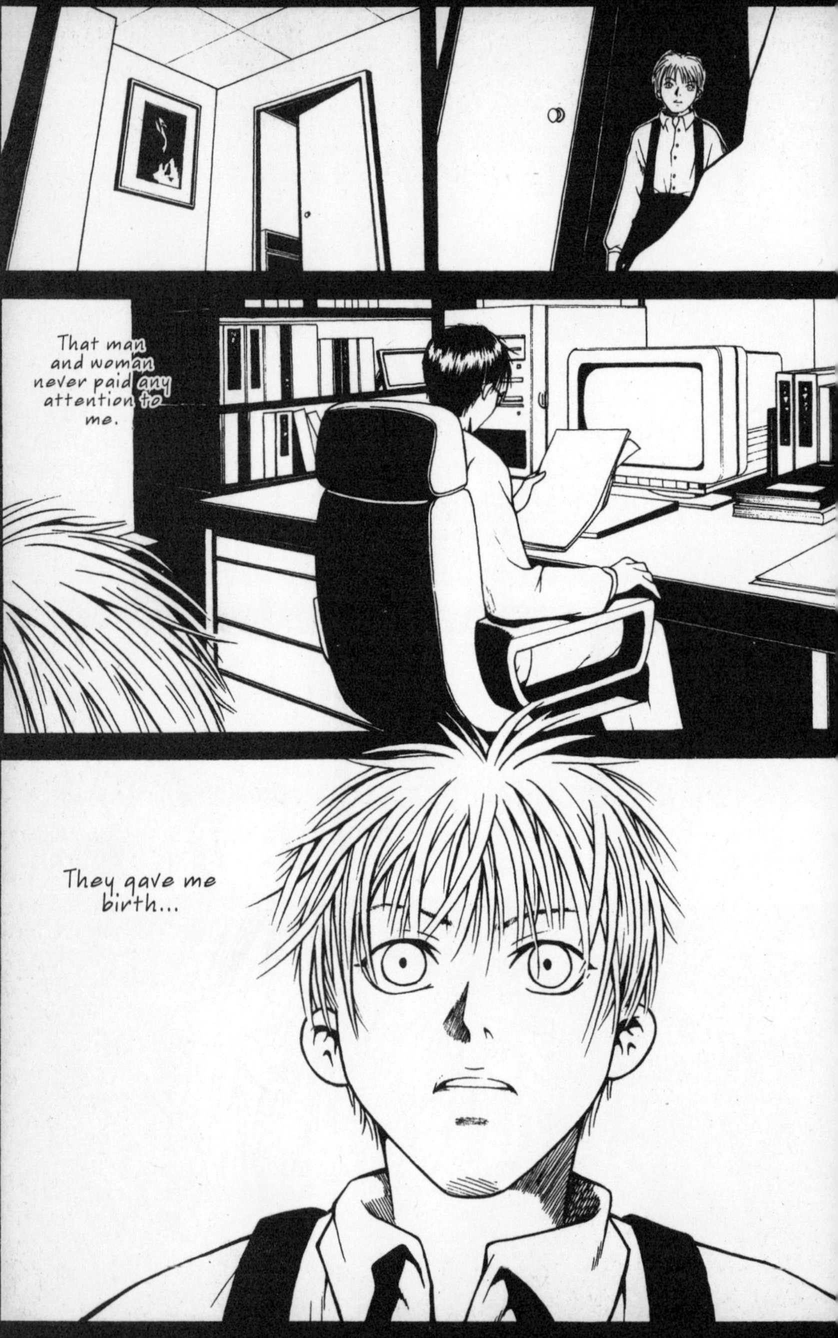
That man and woman never paid any attention to me.
They gave me birth...

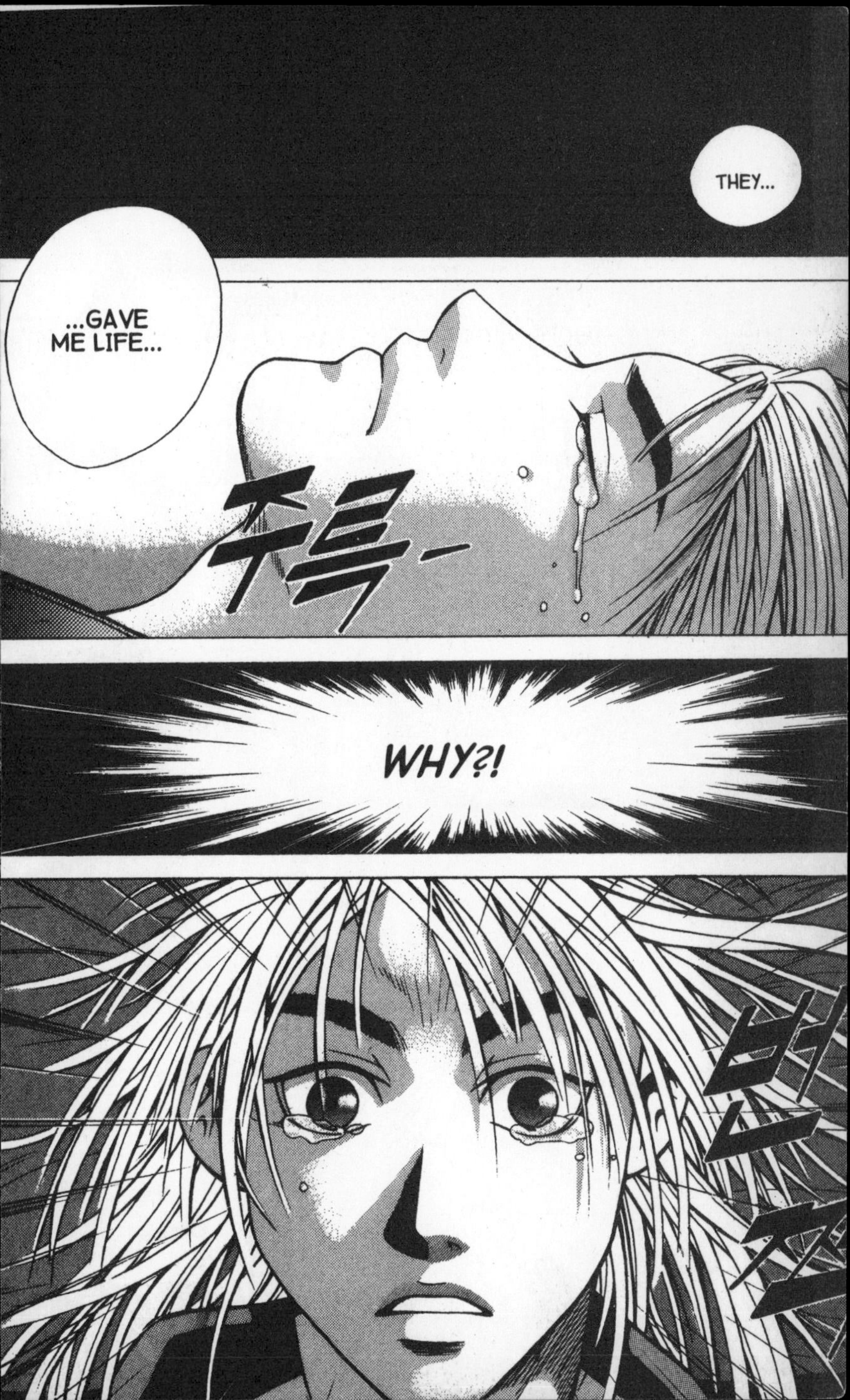
THEY...
...GAVE ME LIFE...
WHY?!

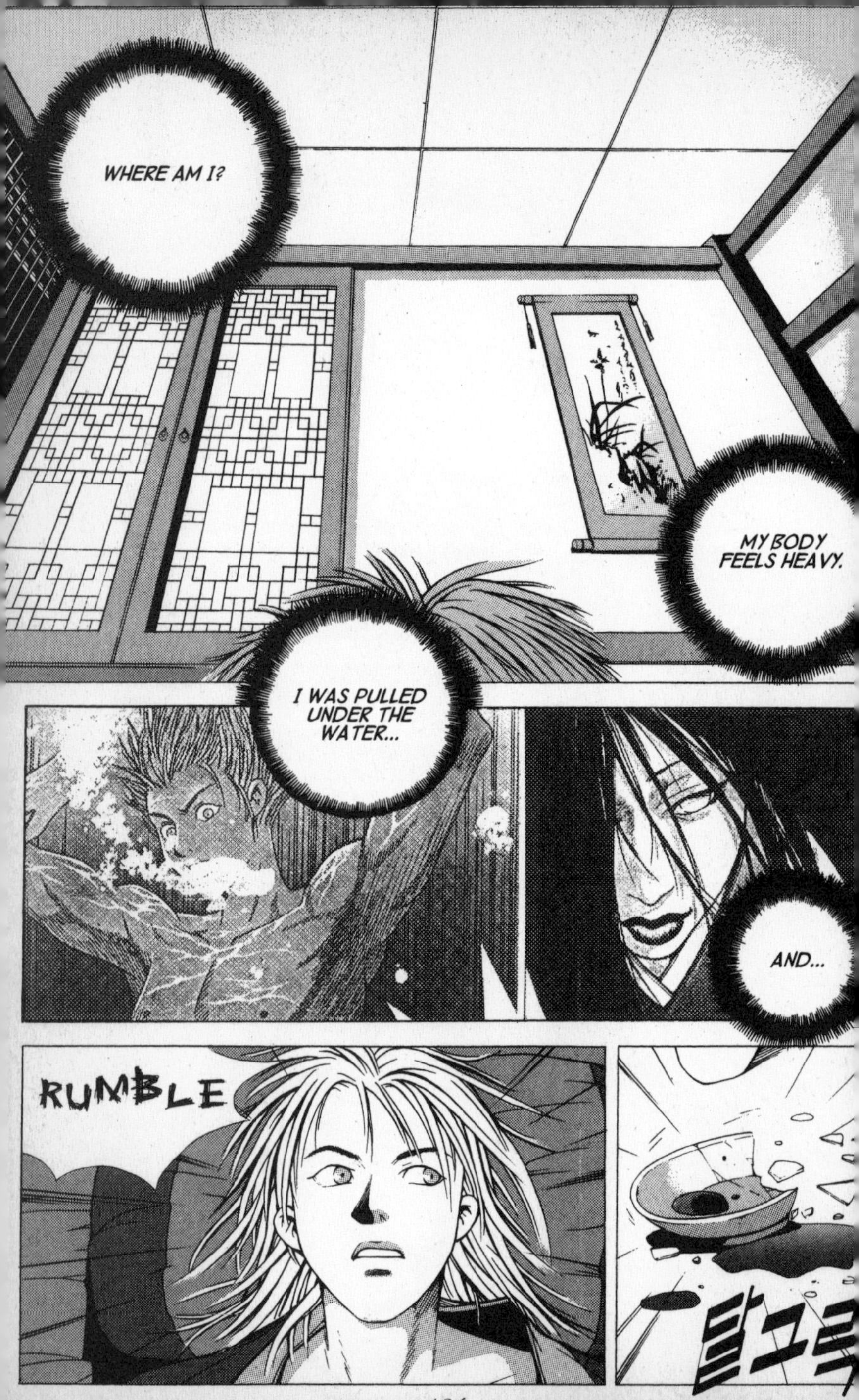
WHERE AM I?
MY BODY FEELS HEAVY.
I WAS PULLED UNDER THE WATER...
AND...
RUMBLE

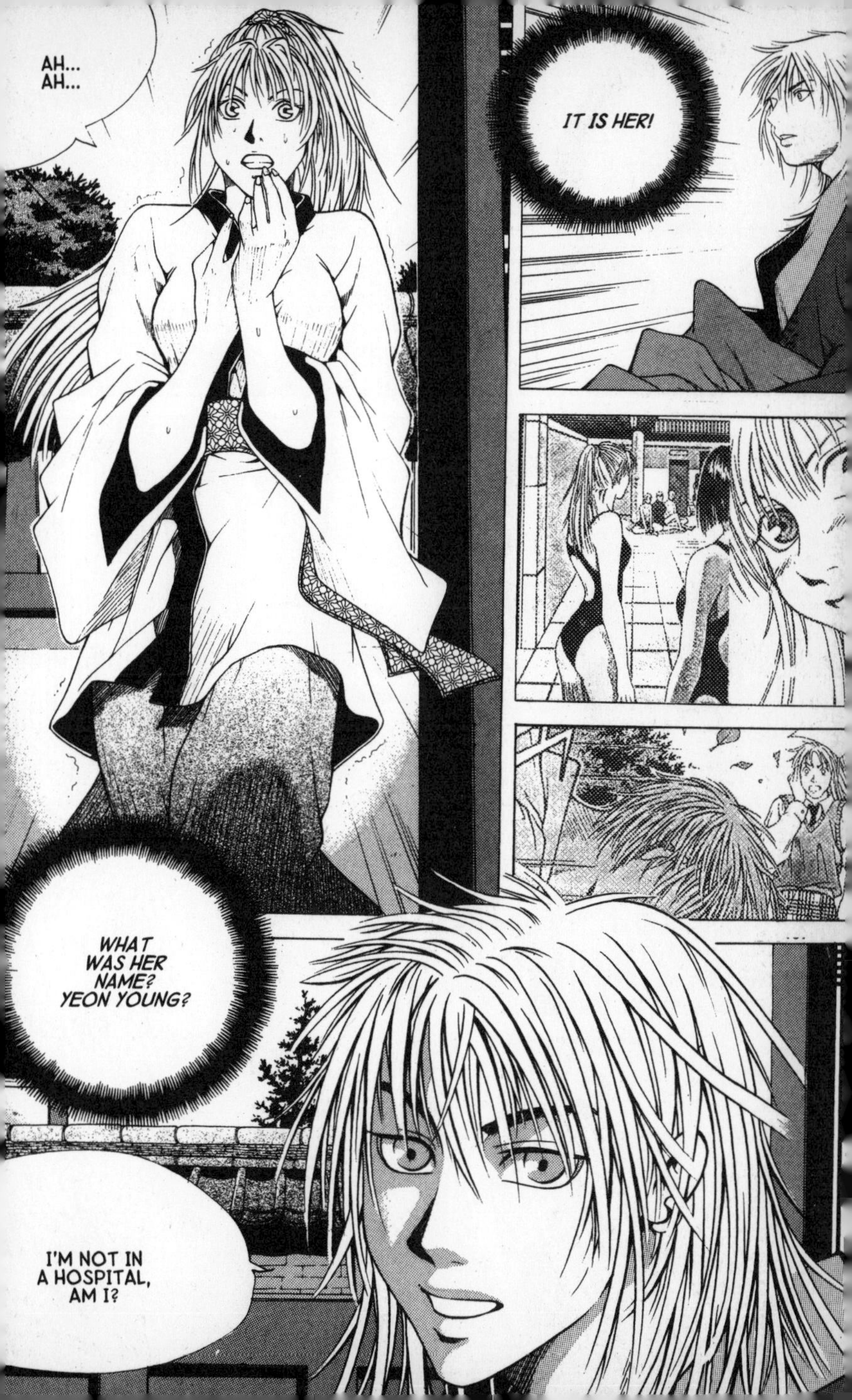
AH... AH...
IT IS HER!
WHAT WAS HER NAME? YEON YOUNG?
I'M NOT IN A HOSPITAL, AM I?

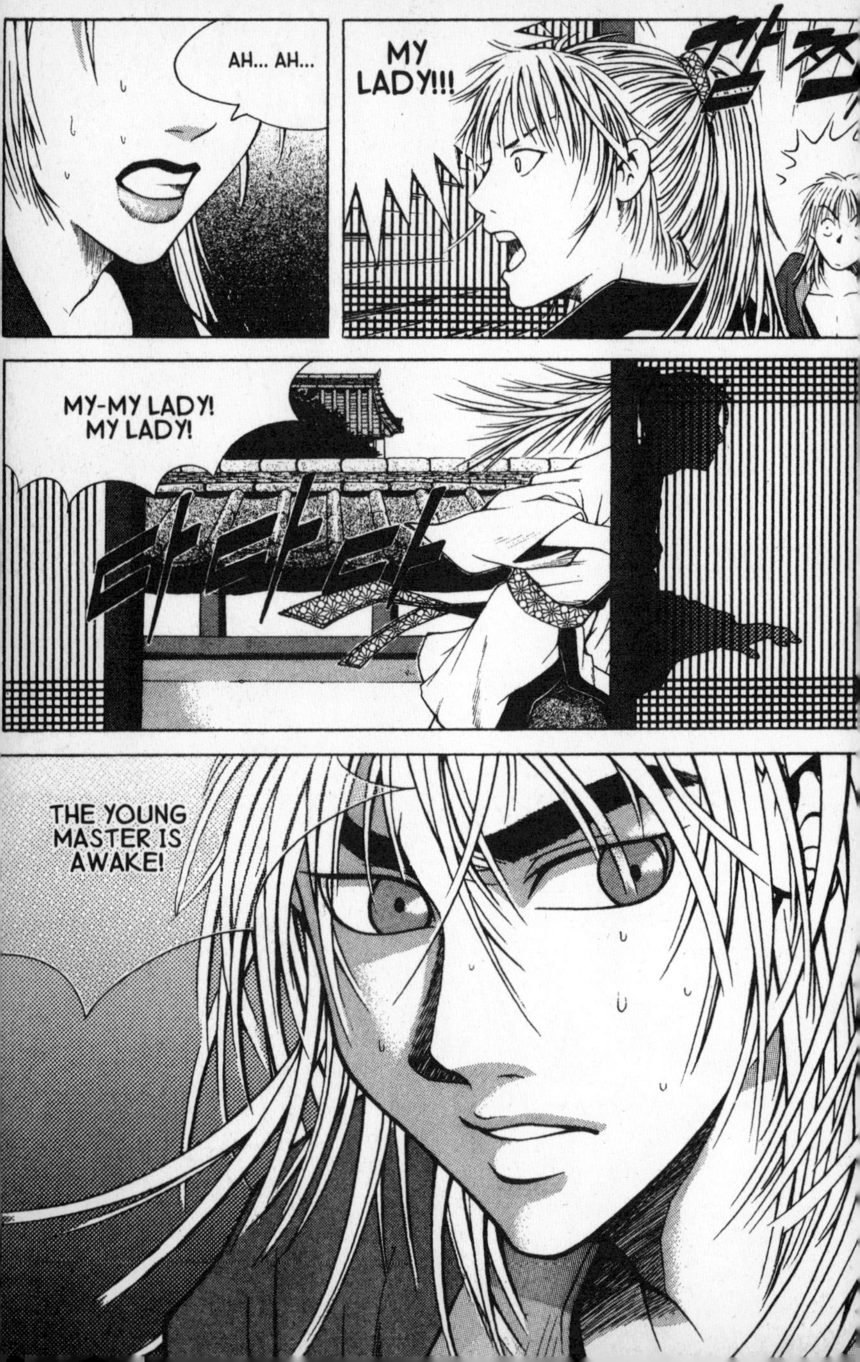
AH... AH...
MY LADY!!!
MY-MY LADY! MY LADY!
THE YOUNG MASTER IS AWAKE!

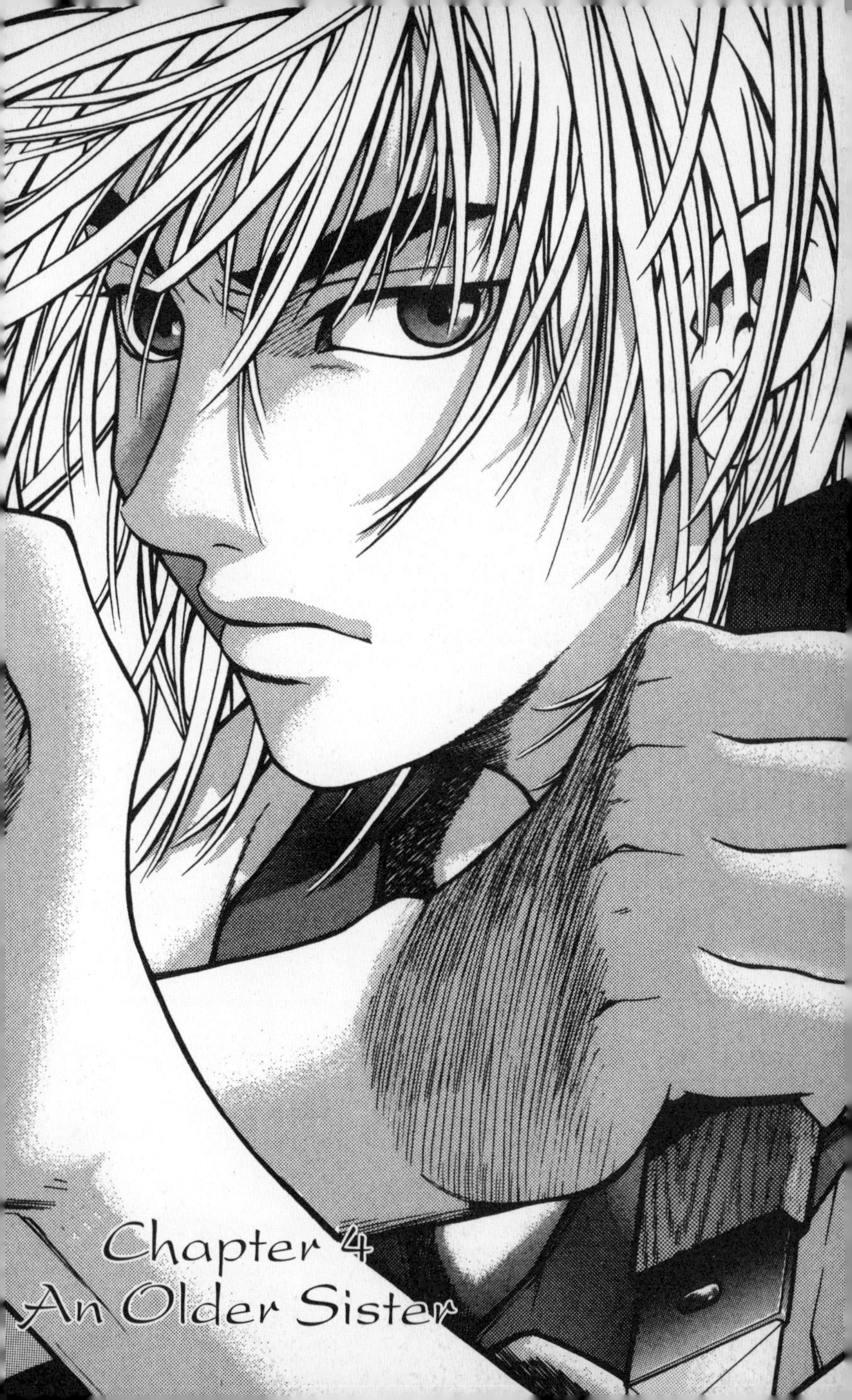
Chapter 4
An Older Sister

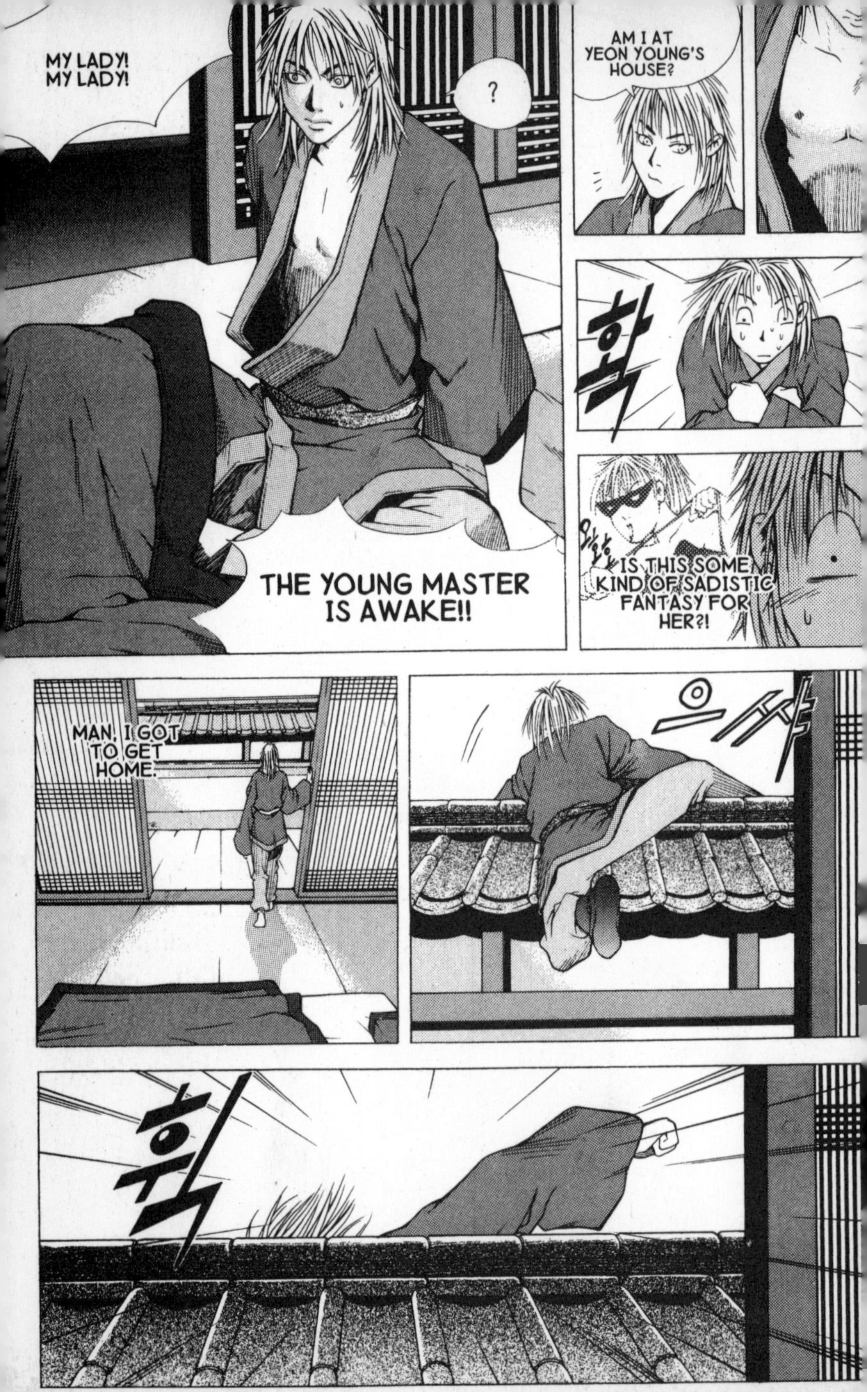
MY LADY! MY LADY!
?
THE YOUNG MASTER IS AWAKE!!
AM I AT YEON YOUNG'S HOUSE?
확
IS THIS SOME KIND OF SADISTIC FANTASY FOR HER?!
MAN, I GOT TO GET HOME.
으쌰

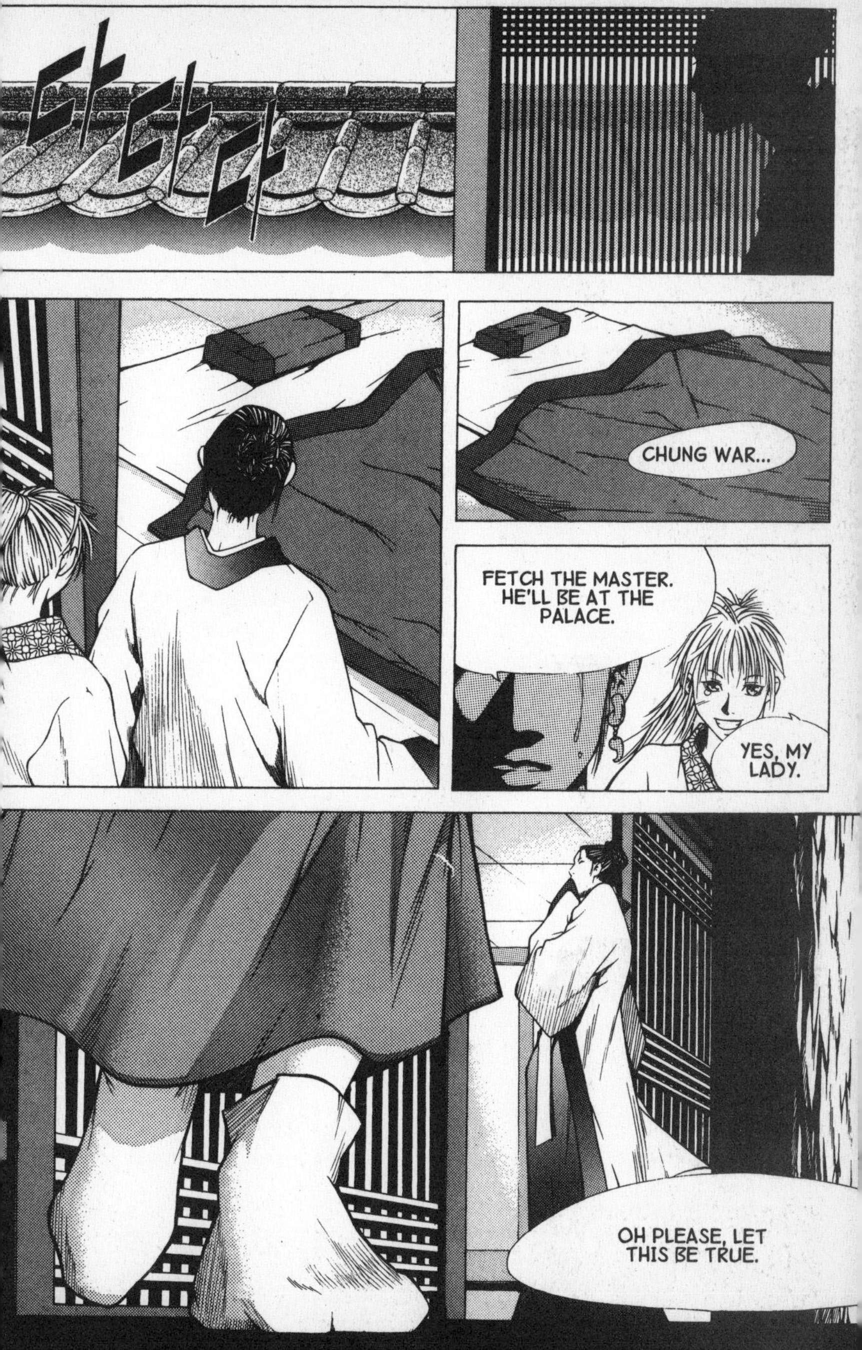
CHUNG WAR...
FETCH THE MASTER. HE'LL BE AT THE PALACE.
YES, MY LADY.
OH PLEASE, LET THIS BE TRUE.

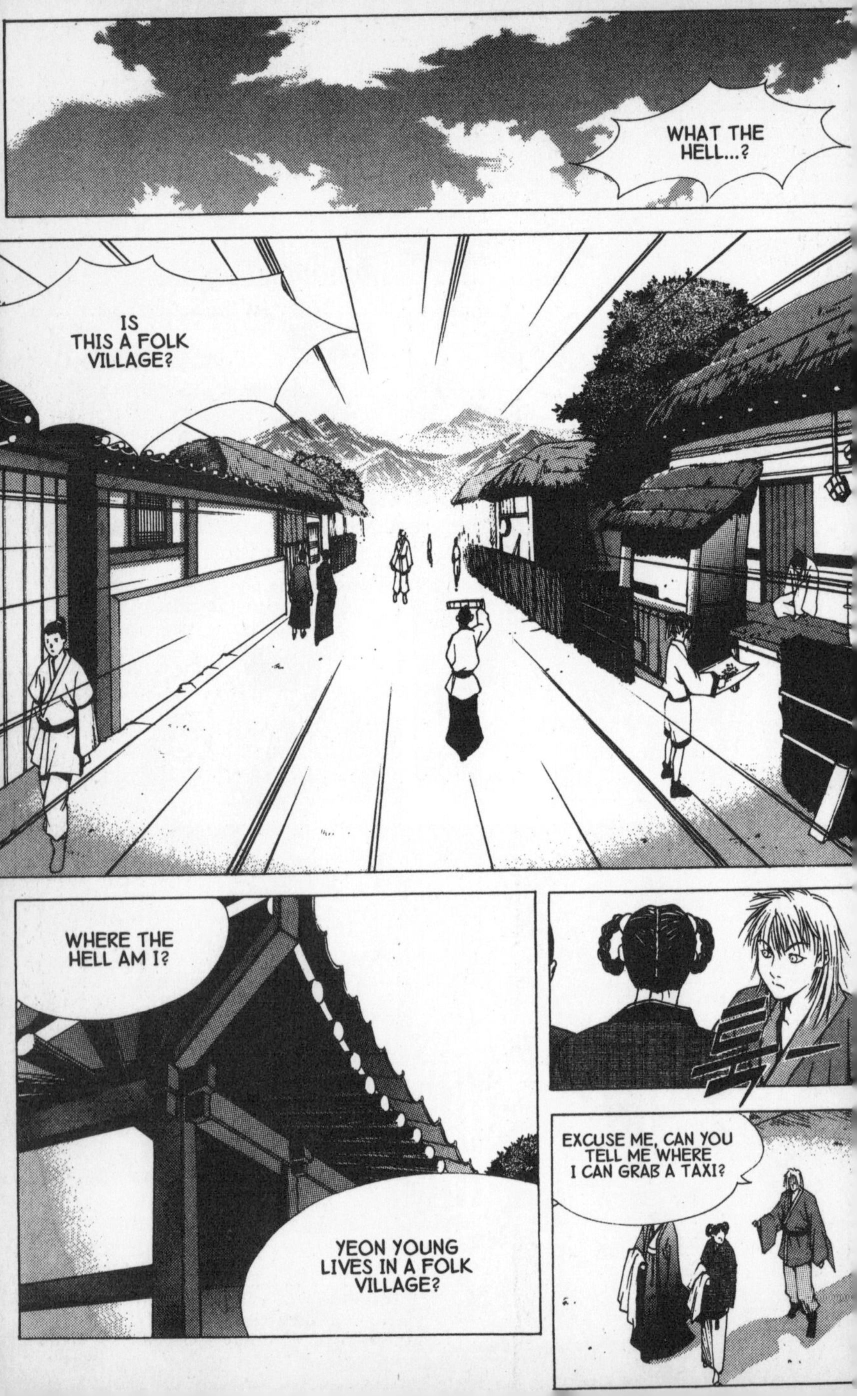
WHAT THE HELL...?
IS THIS A FOLK VILLAGE?
WHERE THE HELL AM I?
YEON YOUNG LIVES IN A FOLK VILLAGE?
EXCUSE ME, CAN YOU TELL ME WHERE I CAN GRAB A TAXI?

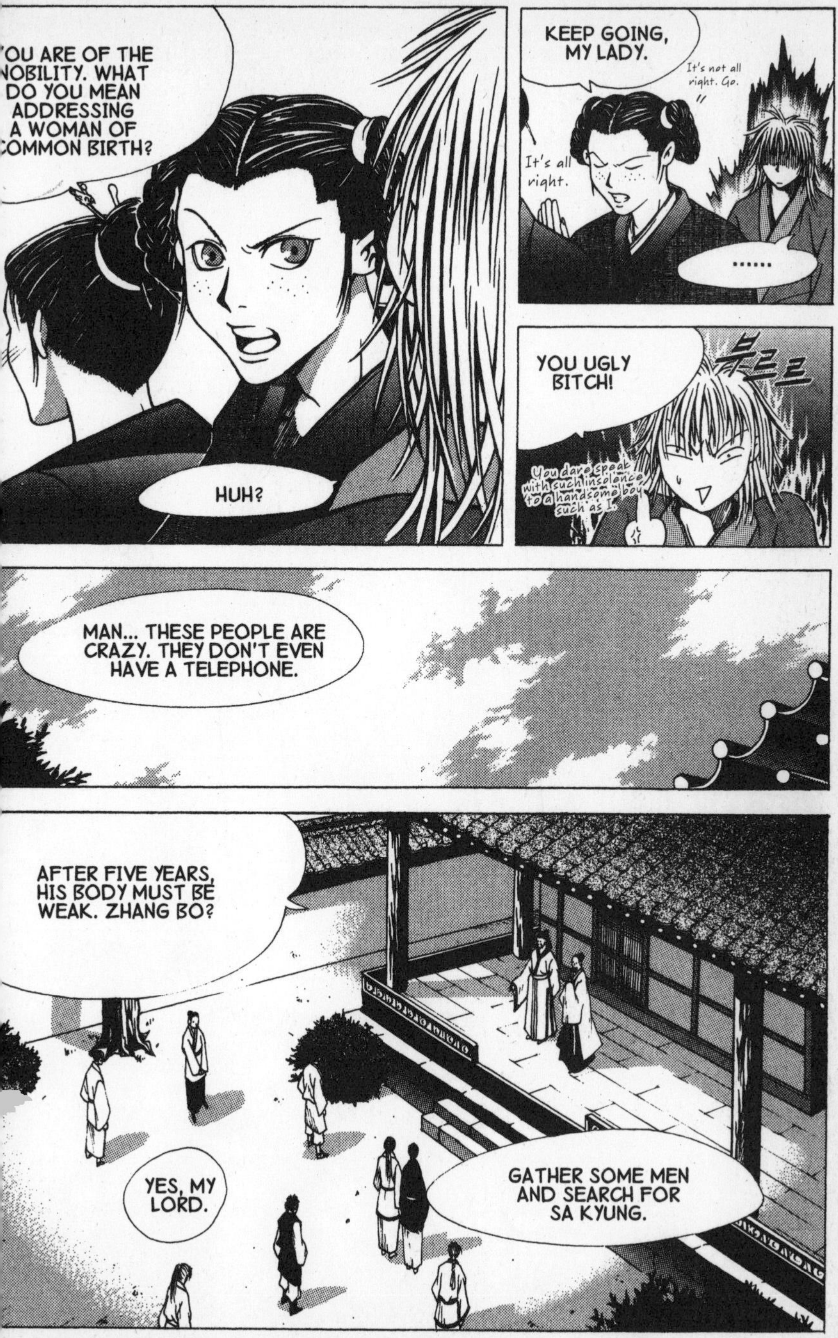

OU ARE OF THE OBILITY. WHAT DO YOU MEAN ADDRESSING A WOMAN OF OMMON BIRTH?
HUH?
KEEP GOING, MY LADY.
It's all right.
It's not all right. Go.
......
YOU UGLY BITCH!
부르르
You dare speak with such insolence to a handsome boy such as I.
MAN... THESE PEOPLE ARE CRAZY. THEY DON'T EVEN HAVE A TELEPHONE.
AFTER FIVE YEARS, HIS BODY MUST BE WEAK. ZHANG BO?
YES, MY LORD.
GATHER SOME MEN AND SEARCH FOR SA KYUNG.

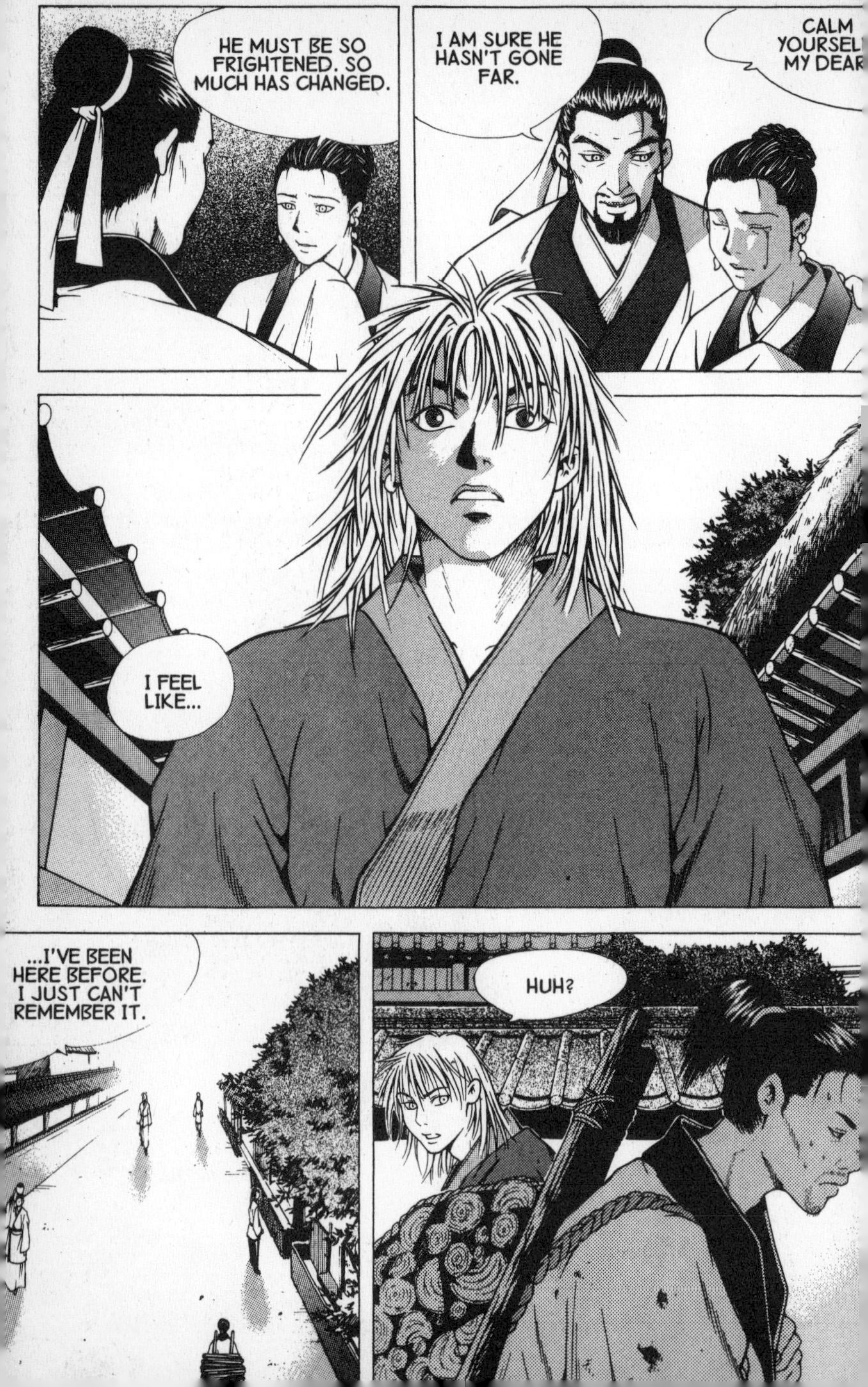
HE MUST BE SO FRIGHTENED. SO MUCH HAS CHANGED.
I AM SURE HE HASN'T GONE FAR.
CALM YOURSELF MY DEAR
I FEEL LIKE...
...I'VE BEEN HERE BEFORE. I JUST CAN'T REMEMBER IT.
HUH?

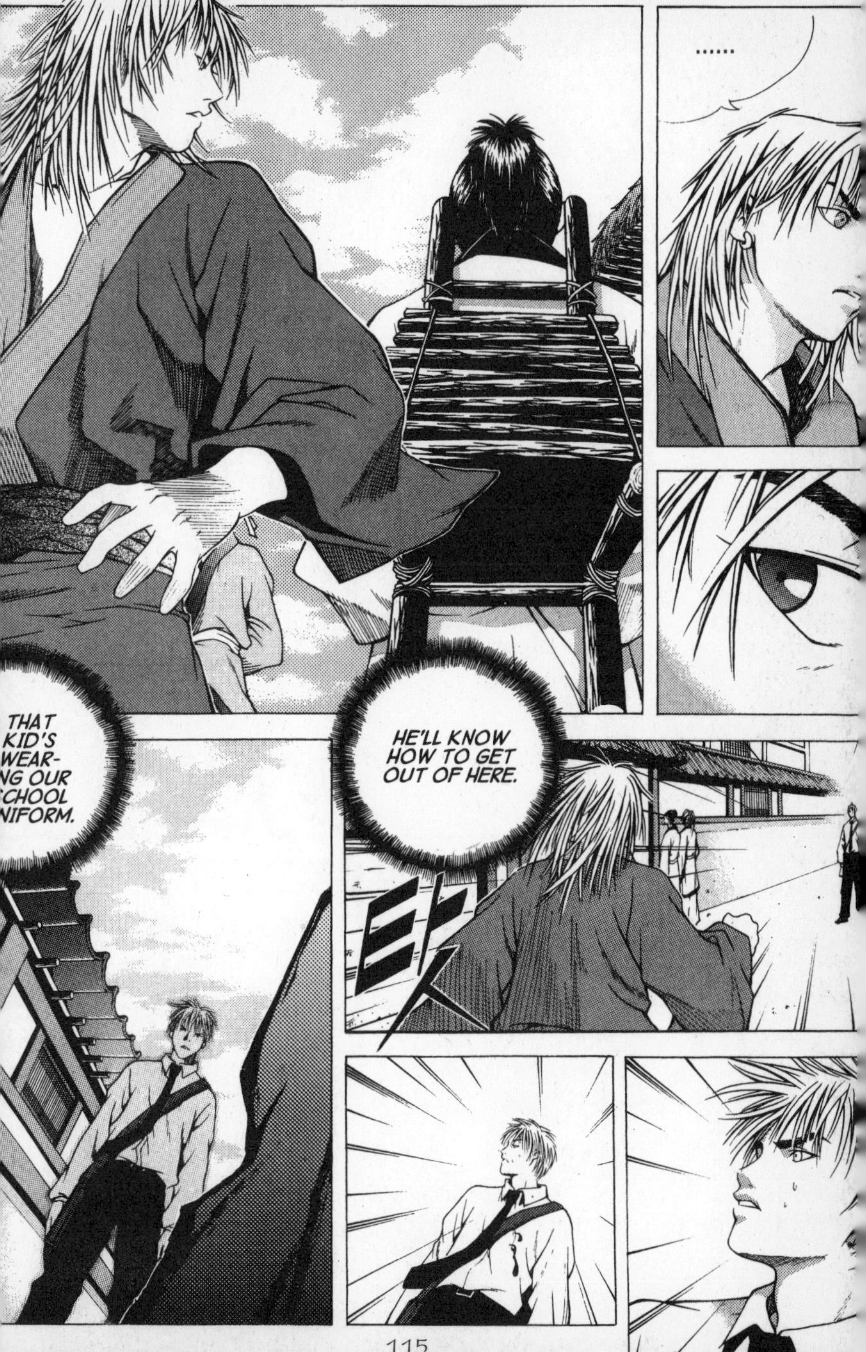
......
THAT KID'S WEAR- NG OUR CHOOL NIFORM.
HE'LL KNOW HOW TO GET OUT OF HERE.

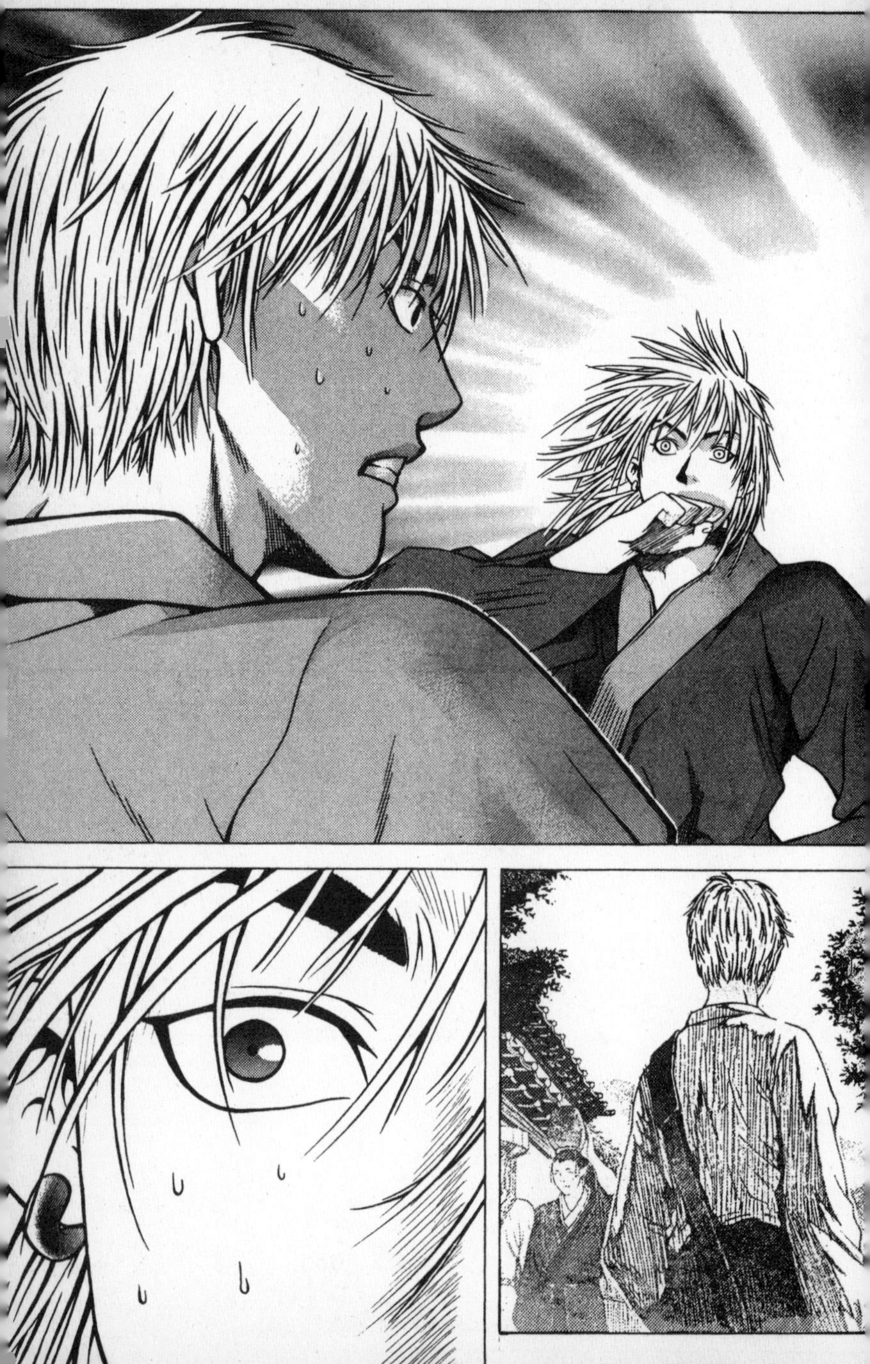

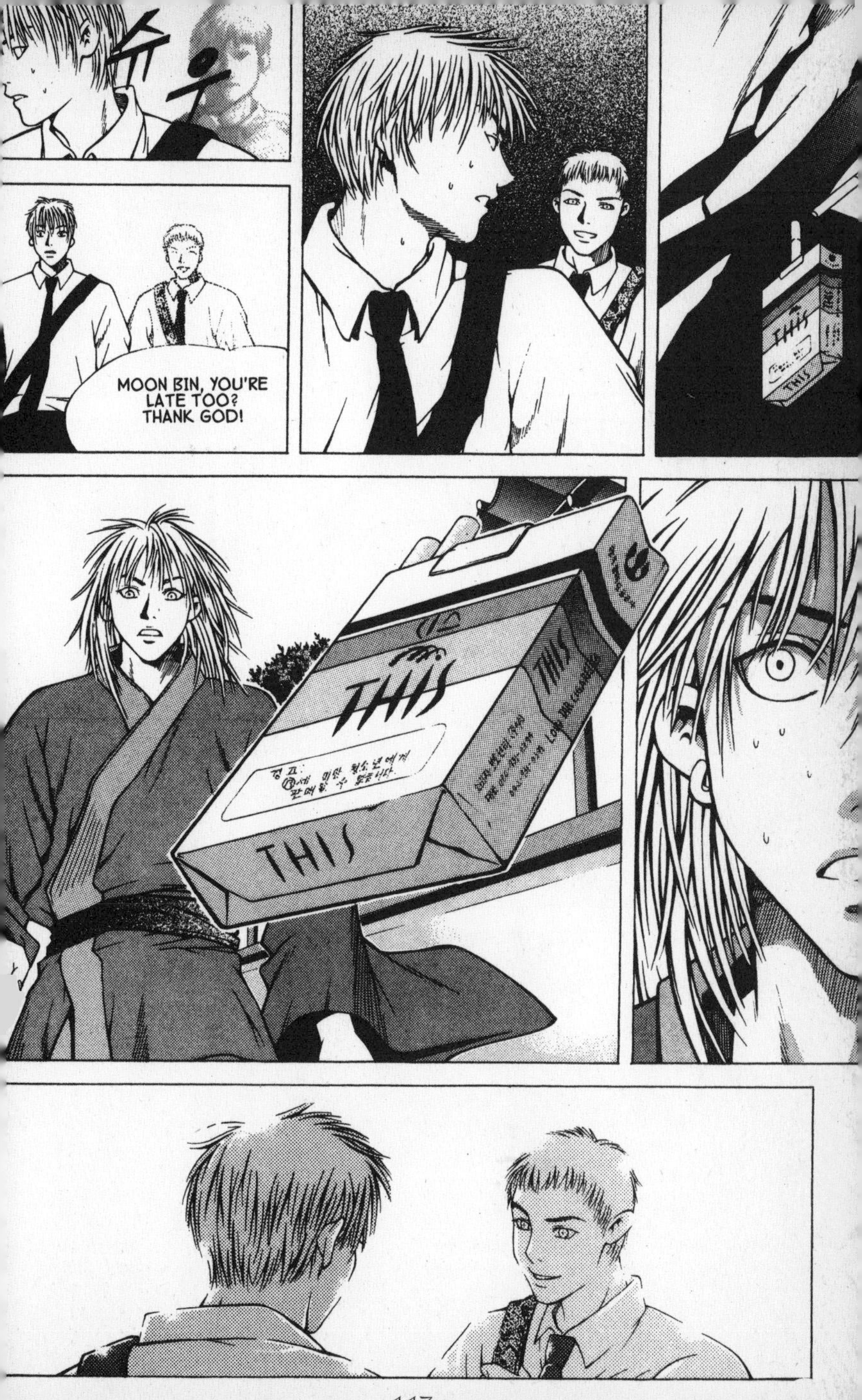

슈우
MOON BIN, YOU'RE LATE TOO? THANK GOD!
THIS
THIS
경고: ⑲세 미만 청소년에게 판매할 수 없습니다.
THIS

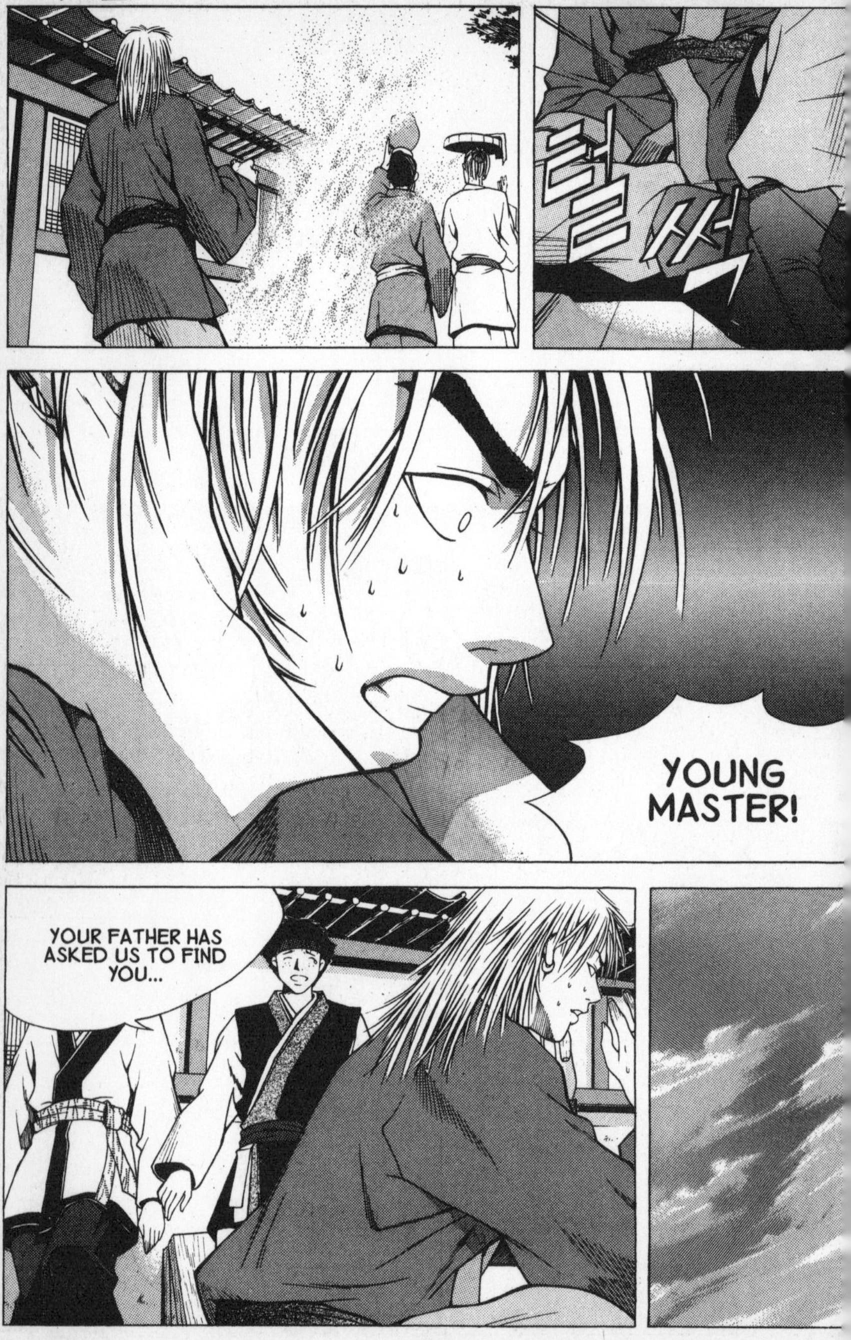

YOUNG MASTER!
YOUR FATHER HAS ASKED US TO FIND YOU...

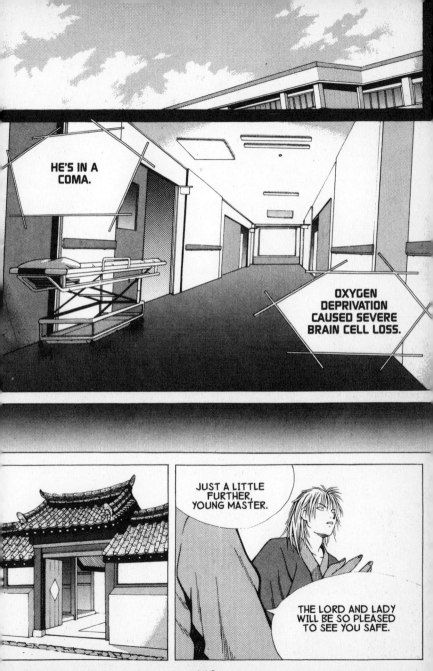

HE'S IN A COMA.

OXYGEN DEPRIVATION CAUSED SEVERE BRAIN CELL LOSS.

JUST A LITTLE FURTHER, YOUNG MASTER.

THE LORD AND LADY WILL BE SO PLEASED TO SEE YOU SAFE.

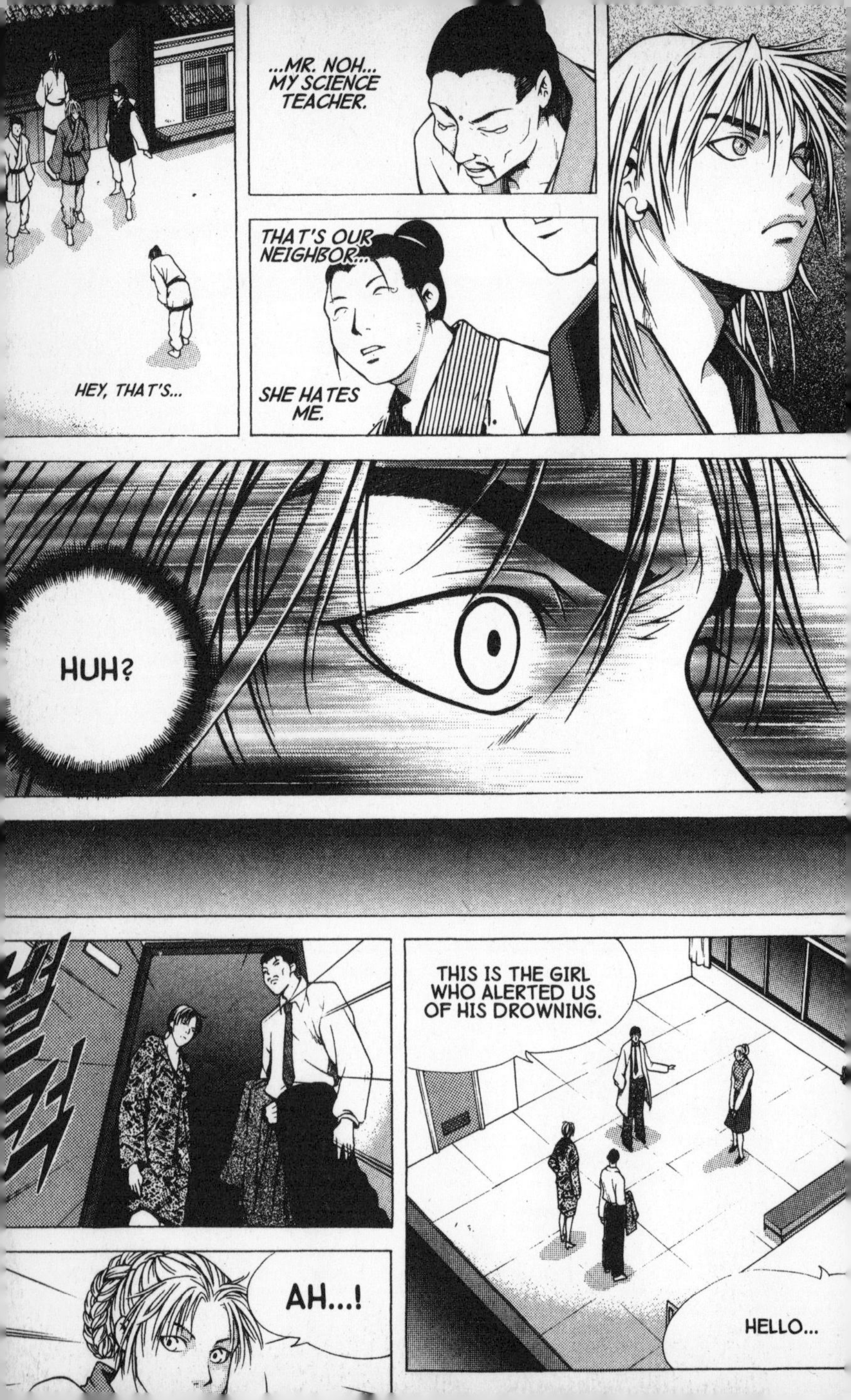
HEY, THAT'S...
...MR. NOH... MY SCIENCE TEACHER.
THAT'S OUR NEIGHBOR...
SHE HATES ME.
HUH?
THIS IS THE GIRL WHO ALERTED US OF HIS DROWNING.
AH...!
HELLO...

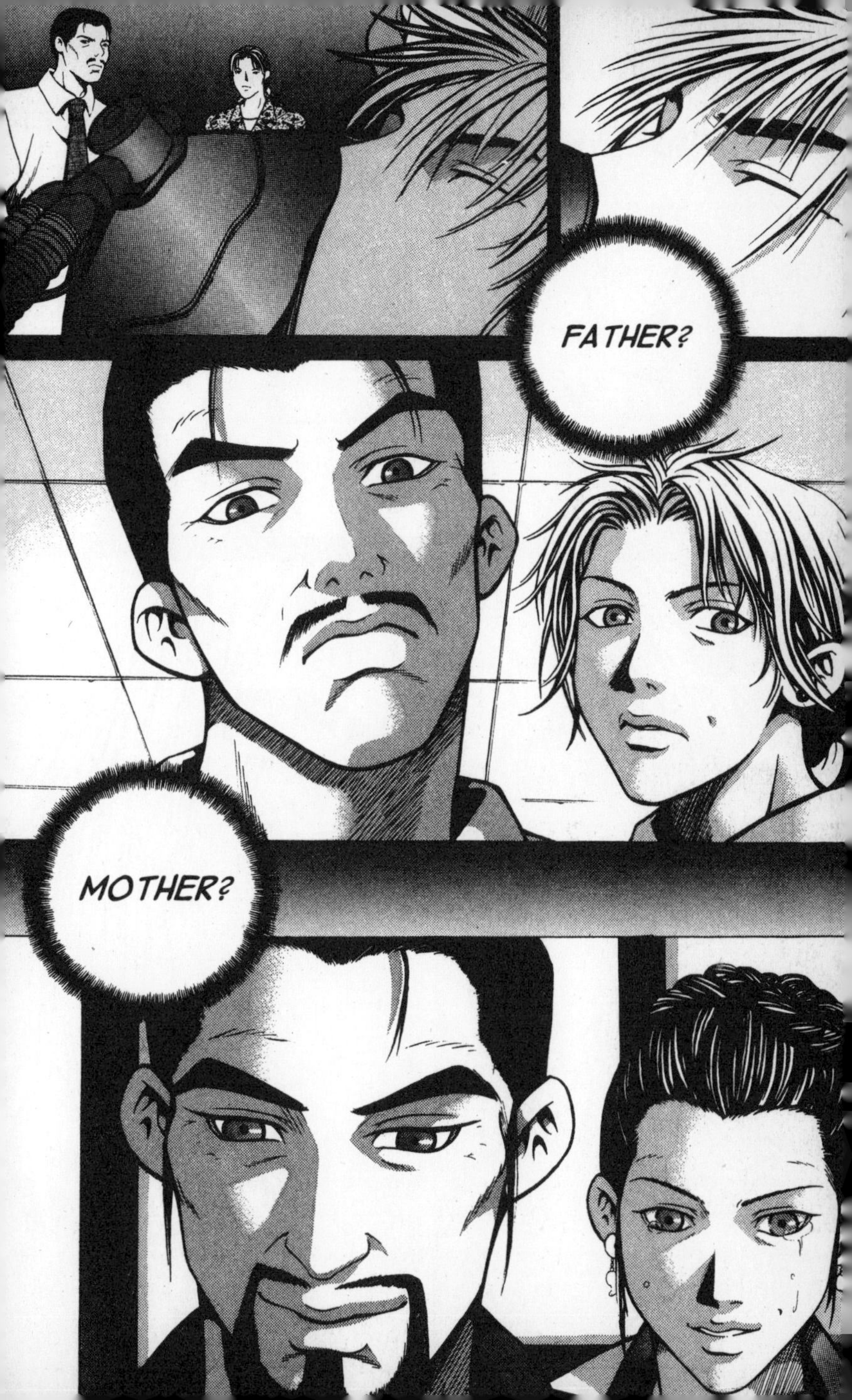
FATHER?
MOTHER?

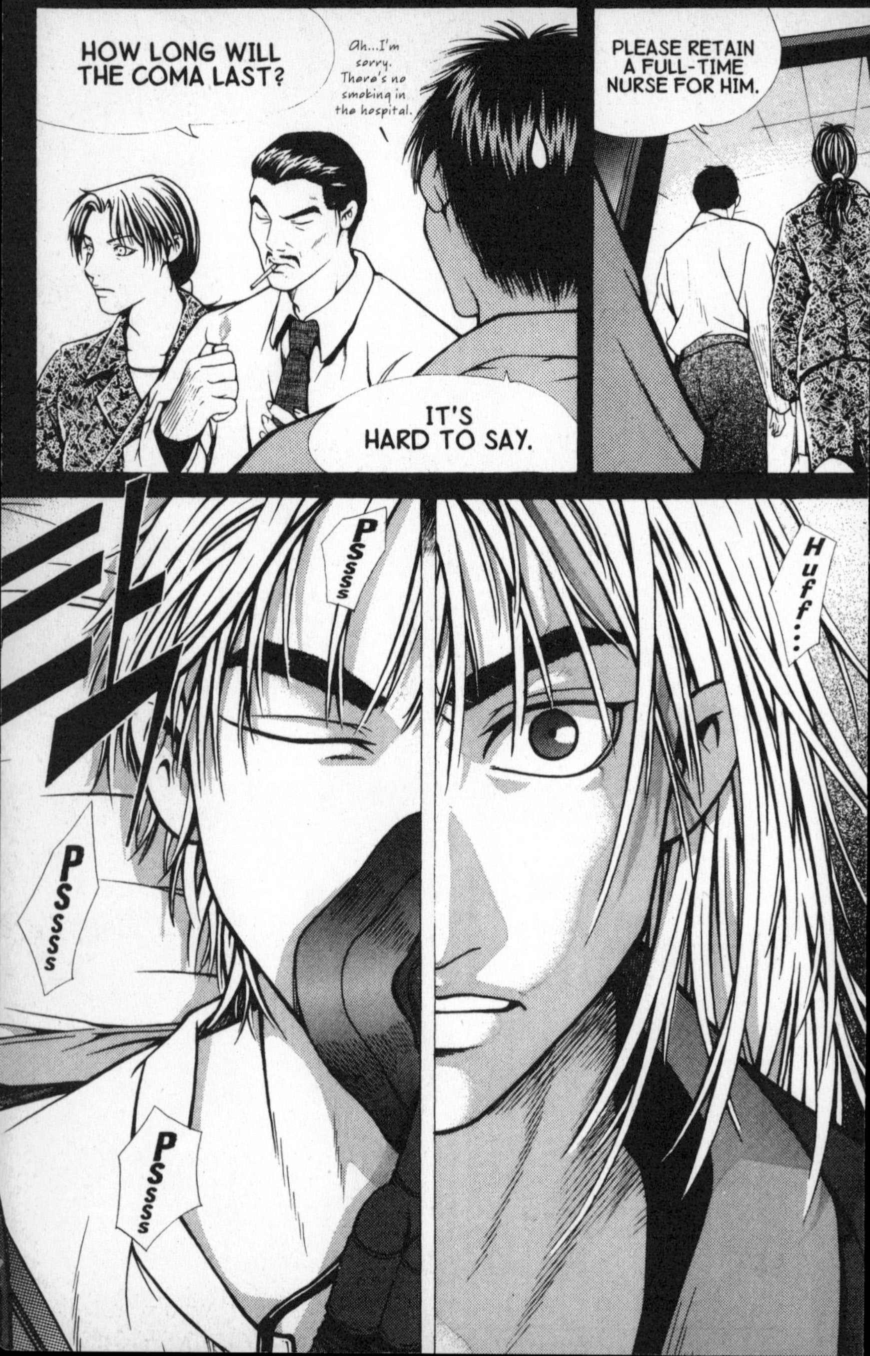
HOW LONG WILL THE COMA LAST?
Ah...I'm sorry. There's no smoking in the hospital.
IT'S HARD TO SAY.
PLEASE RETAIN A FULL-TIME NURSE FOR HIM.
Pssss
Huff...
Pssss
Pssss

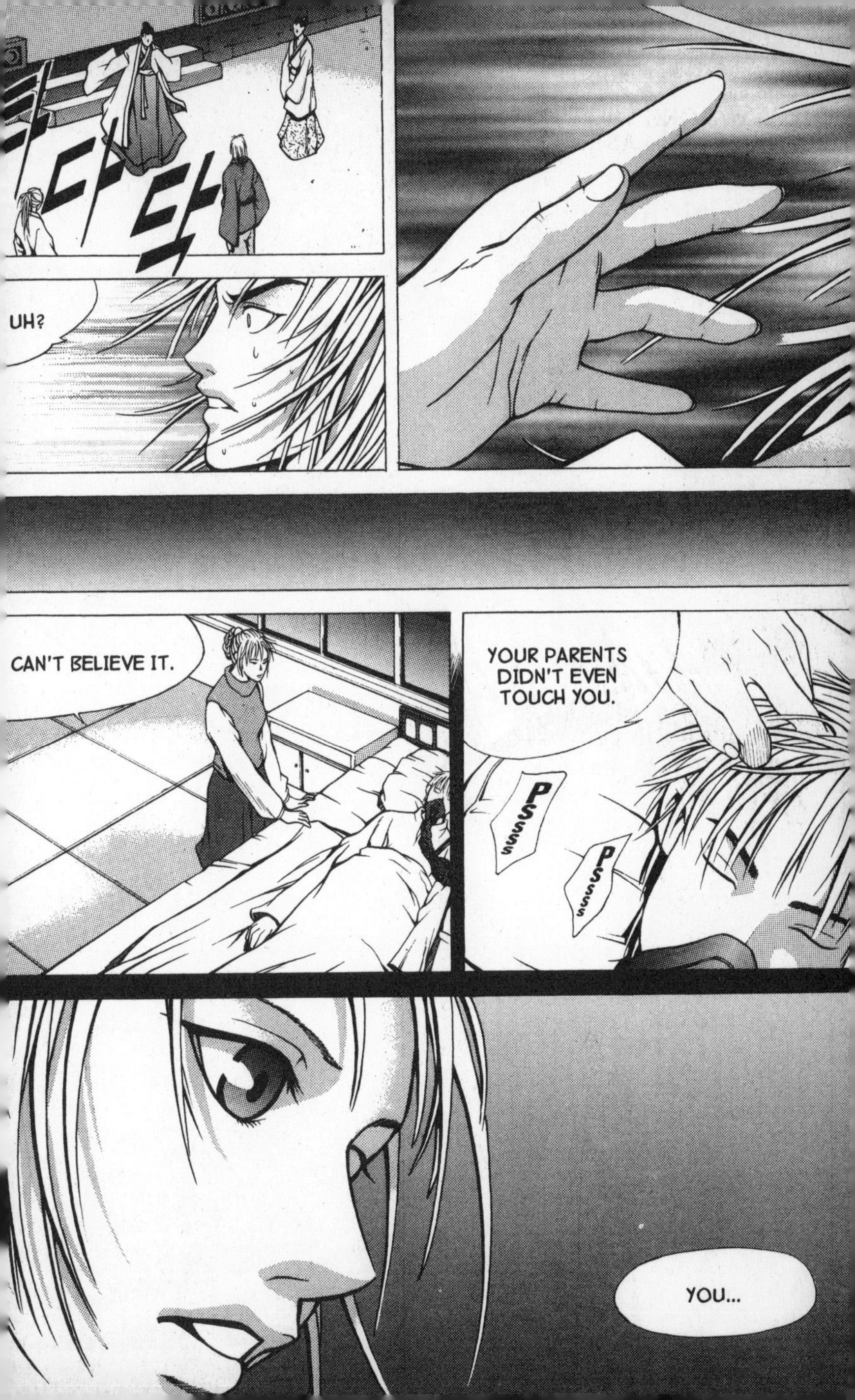
UH?
CAN'T BELIEVE IT.
YOUR PARENTS DIDN'T EVEN TOUCH YOU.
PSSSSS
PSSSSS
YOU...

WHAT ARE YOU DREAMING ABOUT?

MY SON...

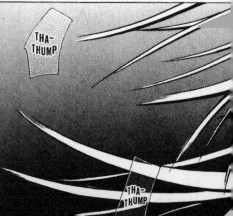

THA-THUMP

THA-THUMP

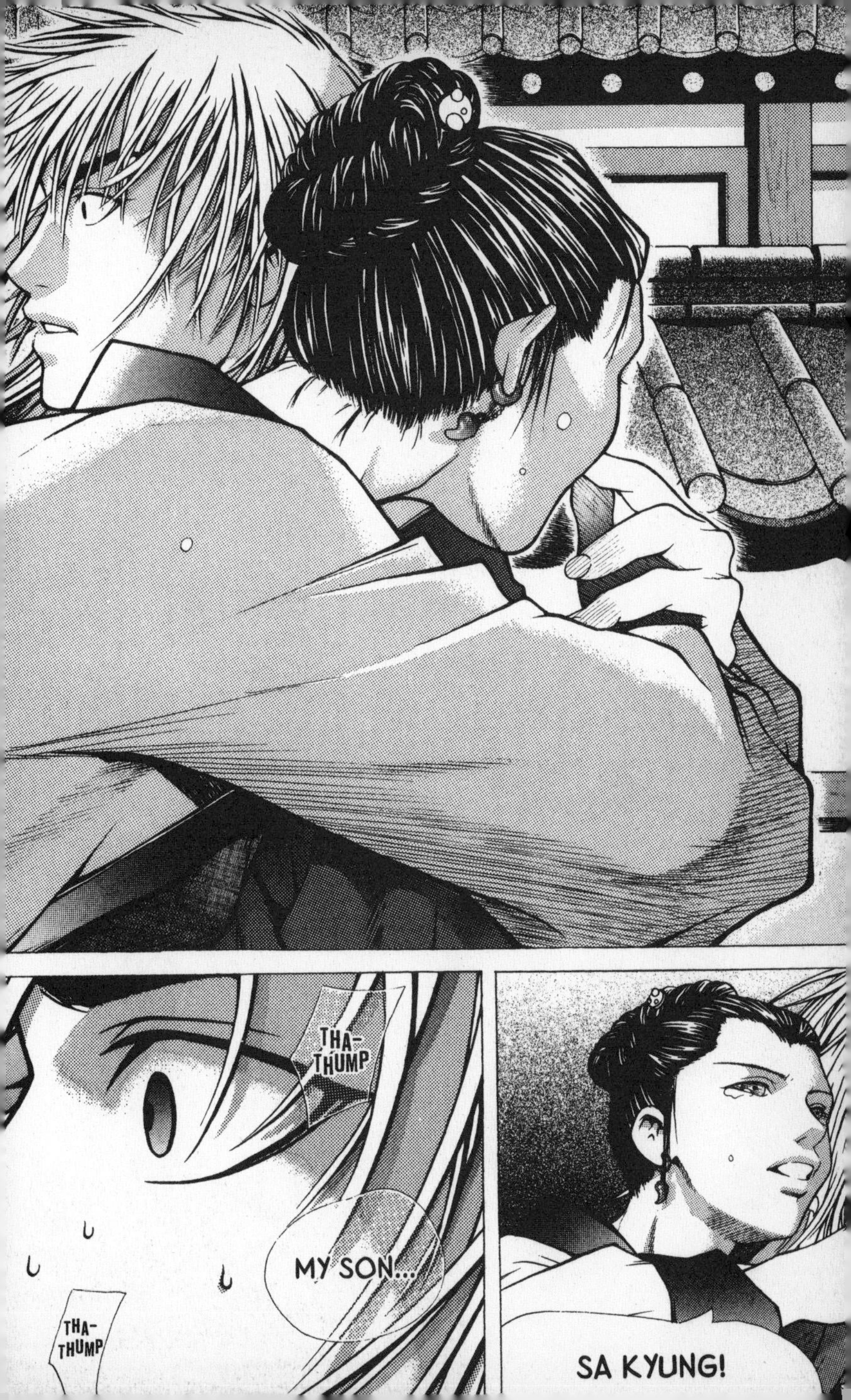
THA-THUMP
MY SON...
THA-THUMP
SA KYUNG!

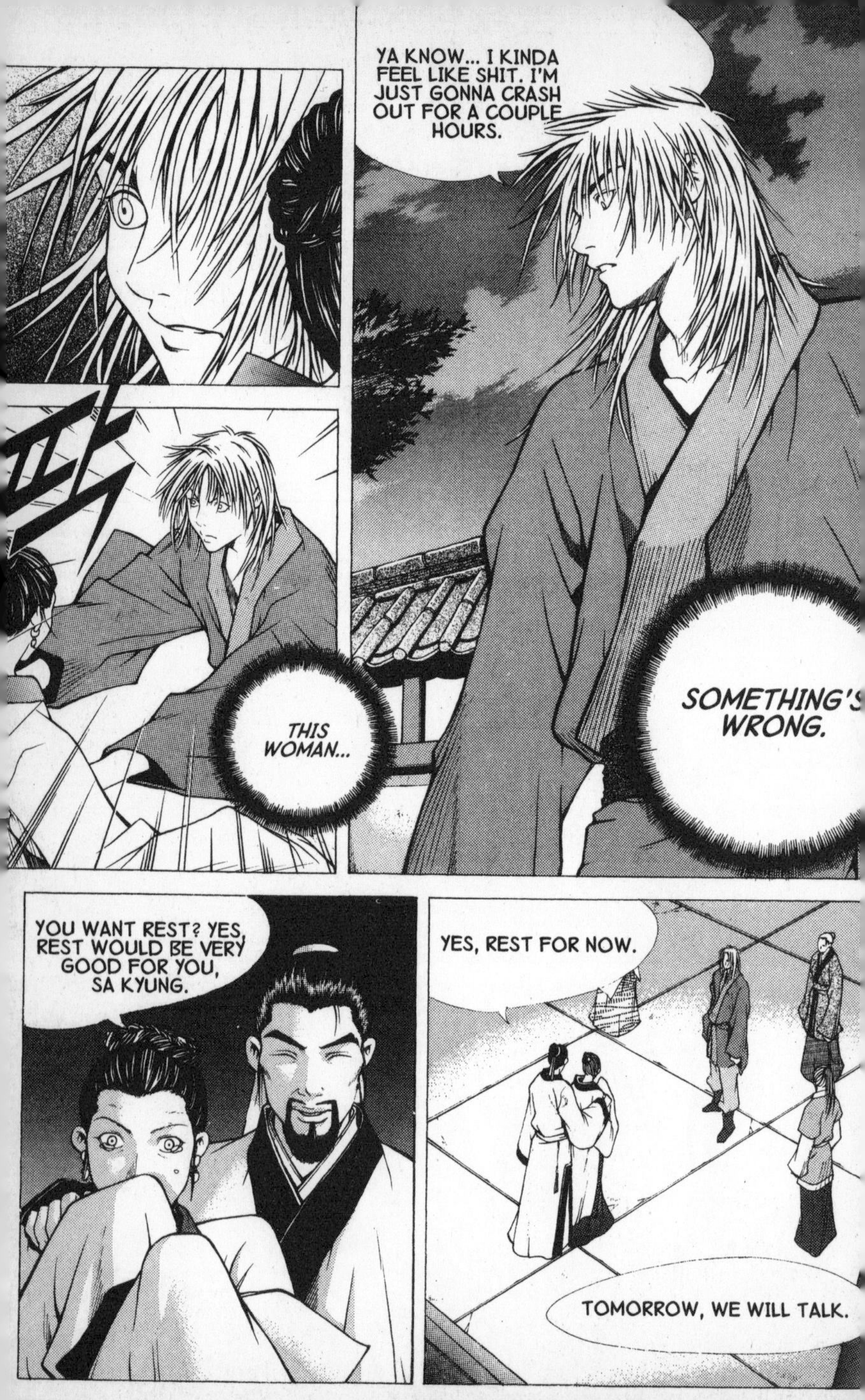
YA KNOW... I KINDA FEEL LIKE SHIT. I'M JUST GONNA CRASH OUT FOR A COUPLE HOURS.
THIS WOMAN...
SOMETHING'S WRONG.
YOU WANT REST? YES, REST WOULD BE VERY GOOD FOR YOU, SA KYUNG.
YES, REST FOR NOW.
TOMORROW, WE WILL TALK.

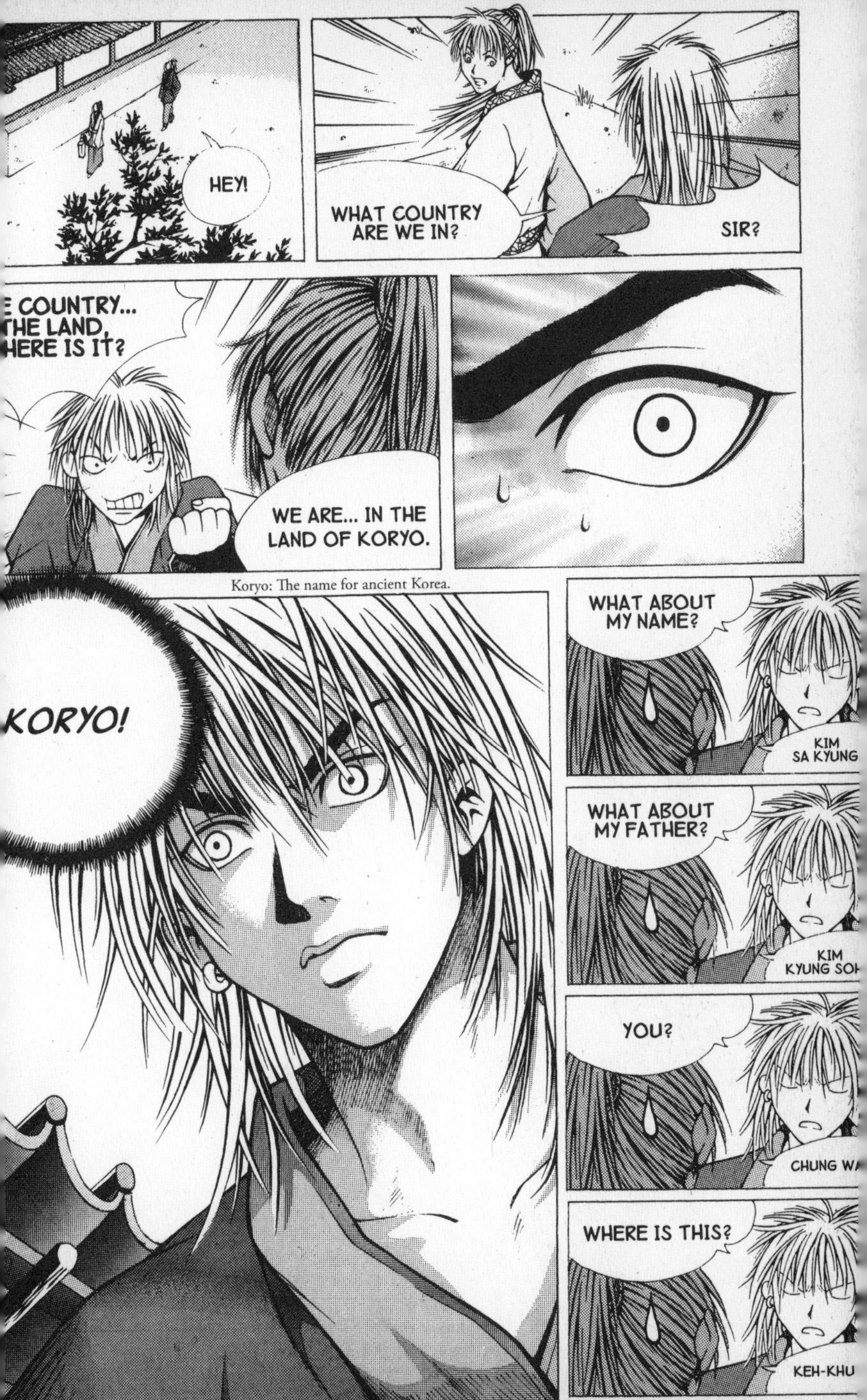

HEY!
WHAT COUNTRY ARE WE IN?
SIR?
E COUNTRY... THE LAND, HERE IS IT?
WE ARE... IN THE LAND OF KORYO.
KORYO!
WHAT ABOUT MY NAME?
KIM SA KYUNG
WHAT ABOUT MY FATHER?
KIM KYUNG SOH
YOU?
CHUNG WA
WHERE IS THIS?
KEH-KHU

Koryo: The name for ancient Korea.

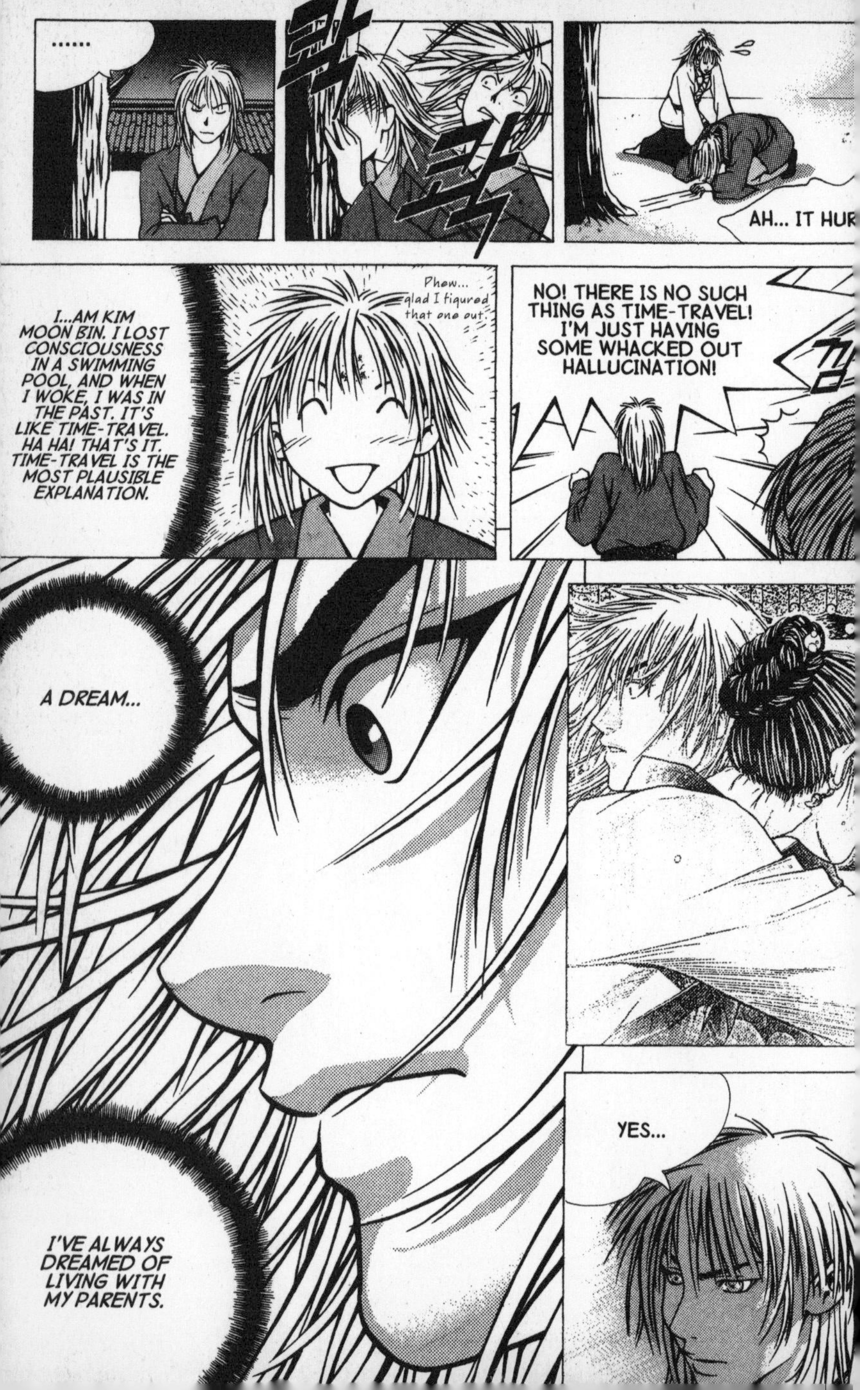
......
AH... IT HUR
I...AM KIM MOON BIN. I LOST CONSCIOUSNESS IN A SWIMMING POOL, AND WHEN I WOKE, I WAS IN THE PAST. IT'S LIKE TIME-TRAVEL. HA HA! THAT'S IT. TIME-TRAVEL IS THE MOST PLAUSIBLE EXPLANATION.
Phew... glad I figured that one out.
NO! THERE IS NO SUCH THING AS TIME-TRAVEL! I'M JUST HAVING SOME WHACKED OUT HALLUCINATION!
A DREAM...
I'VE ALWAYS DREAMED OF LIVING WITH MY PARENTS.
YES...

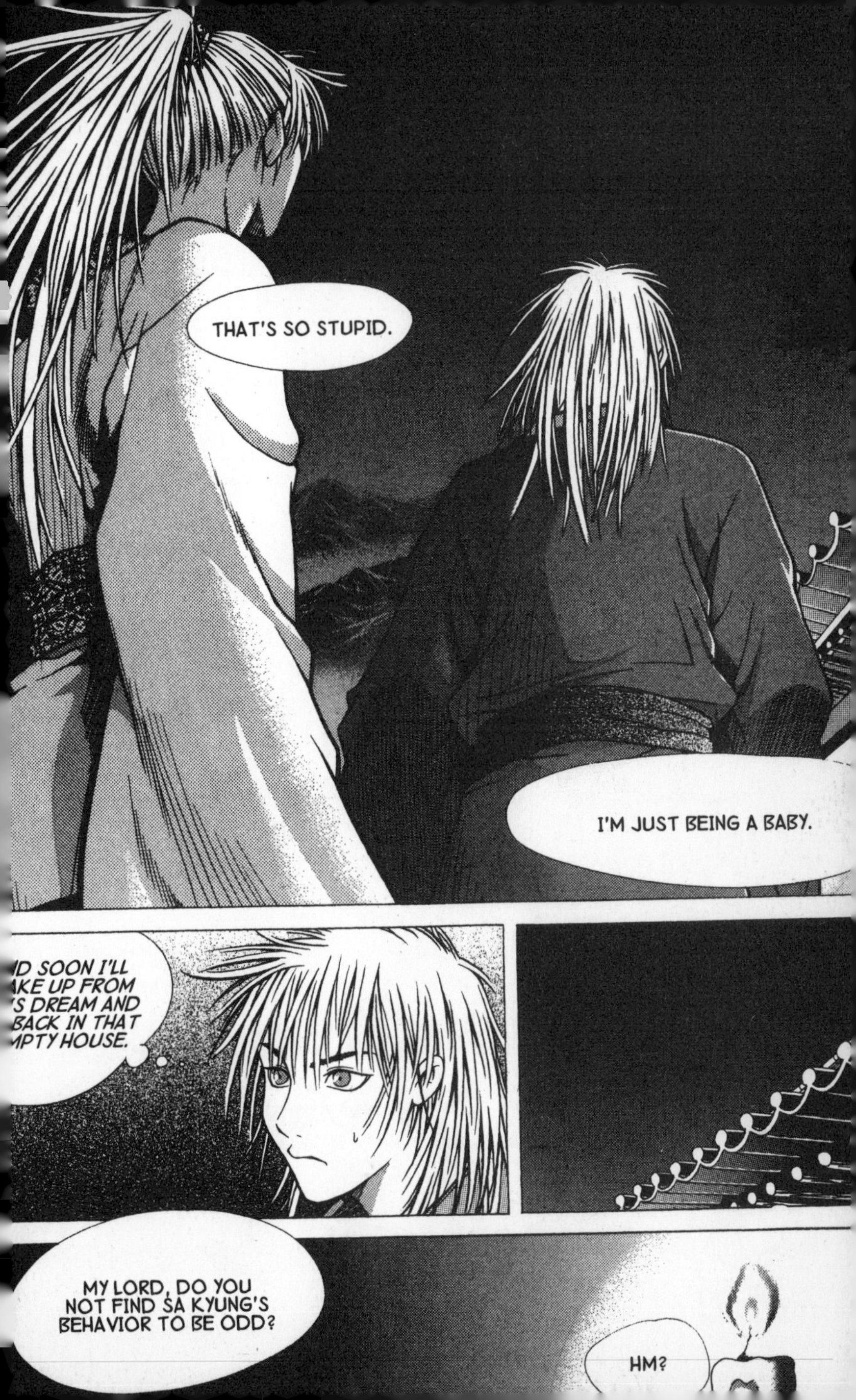
THAT'S SO STUPID.
I'M JUST BEING A BABY.
ID SOON I'LL AKE UP FROM 'S DREAM AND BACK IN THAT MPTY HOUSE.
MY LORD, DO YOU NOT FIND SA KYUNG'S BEHAVIOR TO BE ODD?
HM?

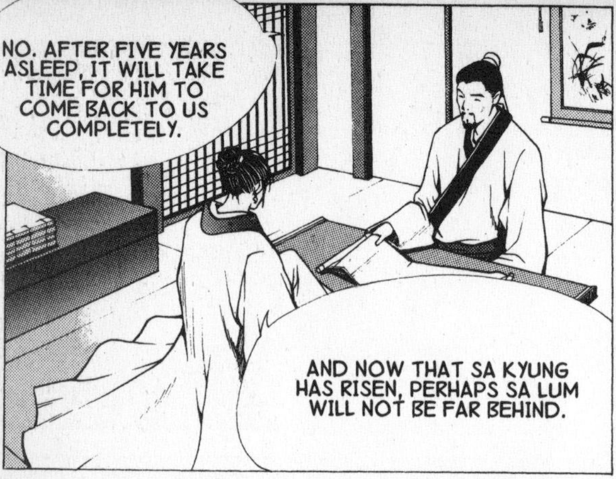
NO. AFTER FIVE YEARS ASLEEP, IT WILL TAKE TIME FOR HIM TO COME BACK TO US COMPLETELY.
AND NOW THAT SA KYUNG HAS RISEN, PERHAPS SA LUM WILL NOT BE FAR BEHIND.

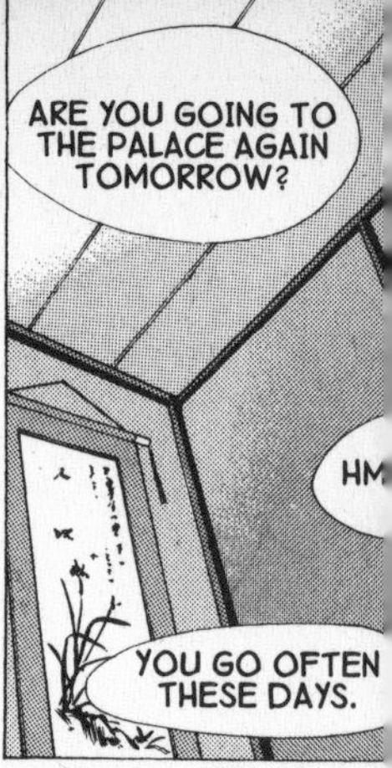
ARE YOU GOING TO THE PALACE AGAIN TOMORROW?
HM
YOU GO OFTEN THESE DAYS.

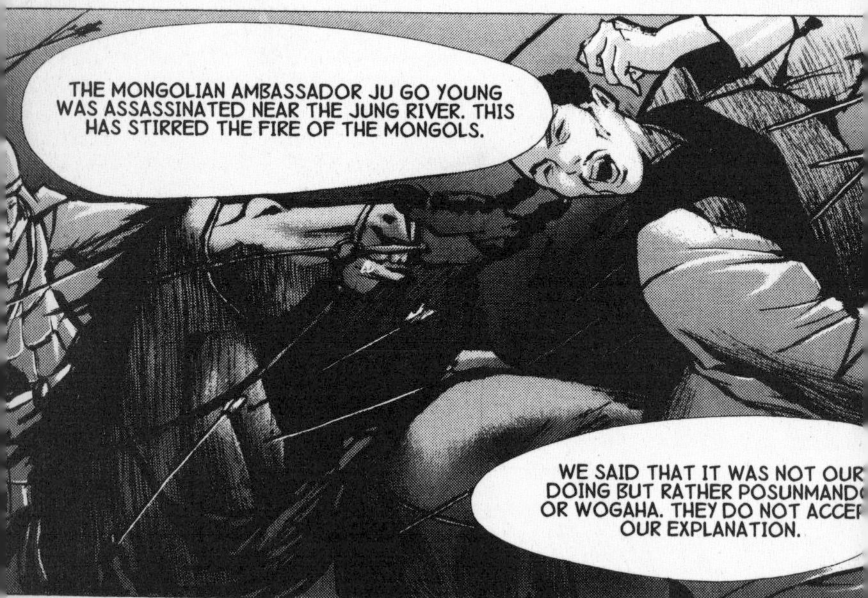
THE MONGOLIAN AMBASSADOR JU GO YOUNG WAS ASSASSINATED NEAR THE JUNG RIVER. THIS HAS STIRRED THE FIRE OF THE MONGOLS.
WE SAID THAT IT WAS NOT OUR DOING BUT RATHER POSUNMAND OR WOGAHA. THEY DO NOT ACCE OUR EXPLANATION.

Go Young: In 1225, an assassin wearing a Koryo uniform killed Ju Go Young. Genghis Khan, in a mpaign to conquer Horazeem, vowed that he would soon turn his sights on Hanam and Koryo.

Posunmando: Person from Dozing
Wogaha: Gold Country General

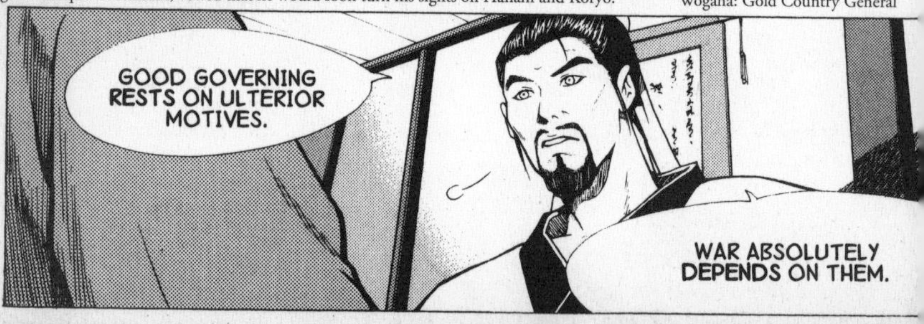
GOOD GOVERNING RESTS ON ULTERIOR MOTIVES.
WAR ABSOLUTELY DEPENDS ON THEM.

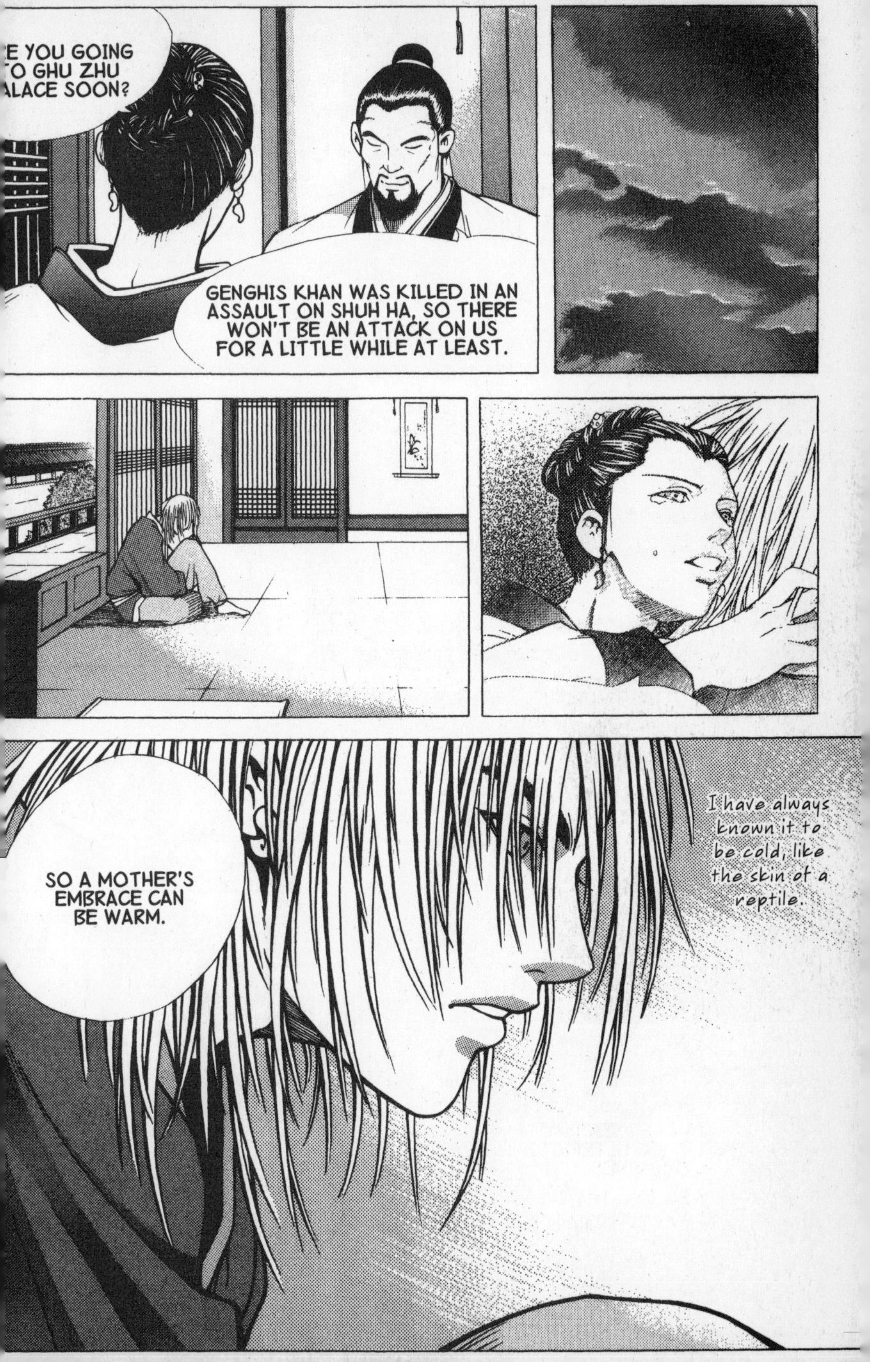
E YOU GOING
O GHU ZHU
ALACE SOON?
GENGHIS KHAN WAS KILLED IN AN ASSAULT ON SHUH HA, SO THERE WON'T BE AN ATTACK ON US FOR A LITTLE WHILE AT LEAST.
SO A MOTHER'S EMBRACE CAN BE WARM.
I have always known it to be cold, like the skin of a reptile.

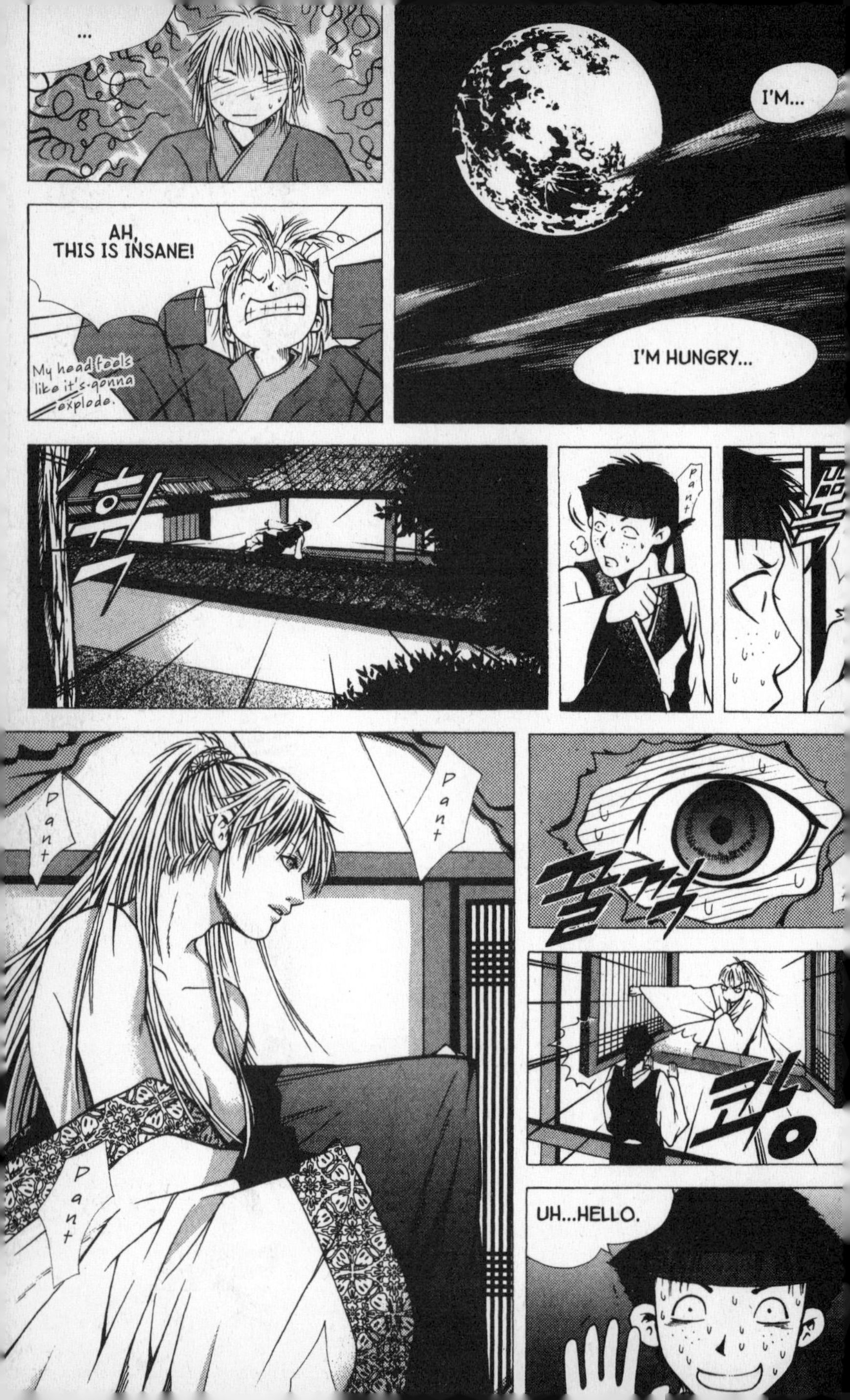
...
AH, THIS IS INSANE!
My head feels like it's gonna explode.
I'M...
I'M HUNGRY...
Pant
Pant
Pant
Pant
꿀꺽
쾅
UH...HELLO.

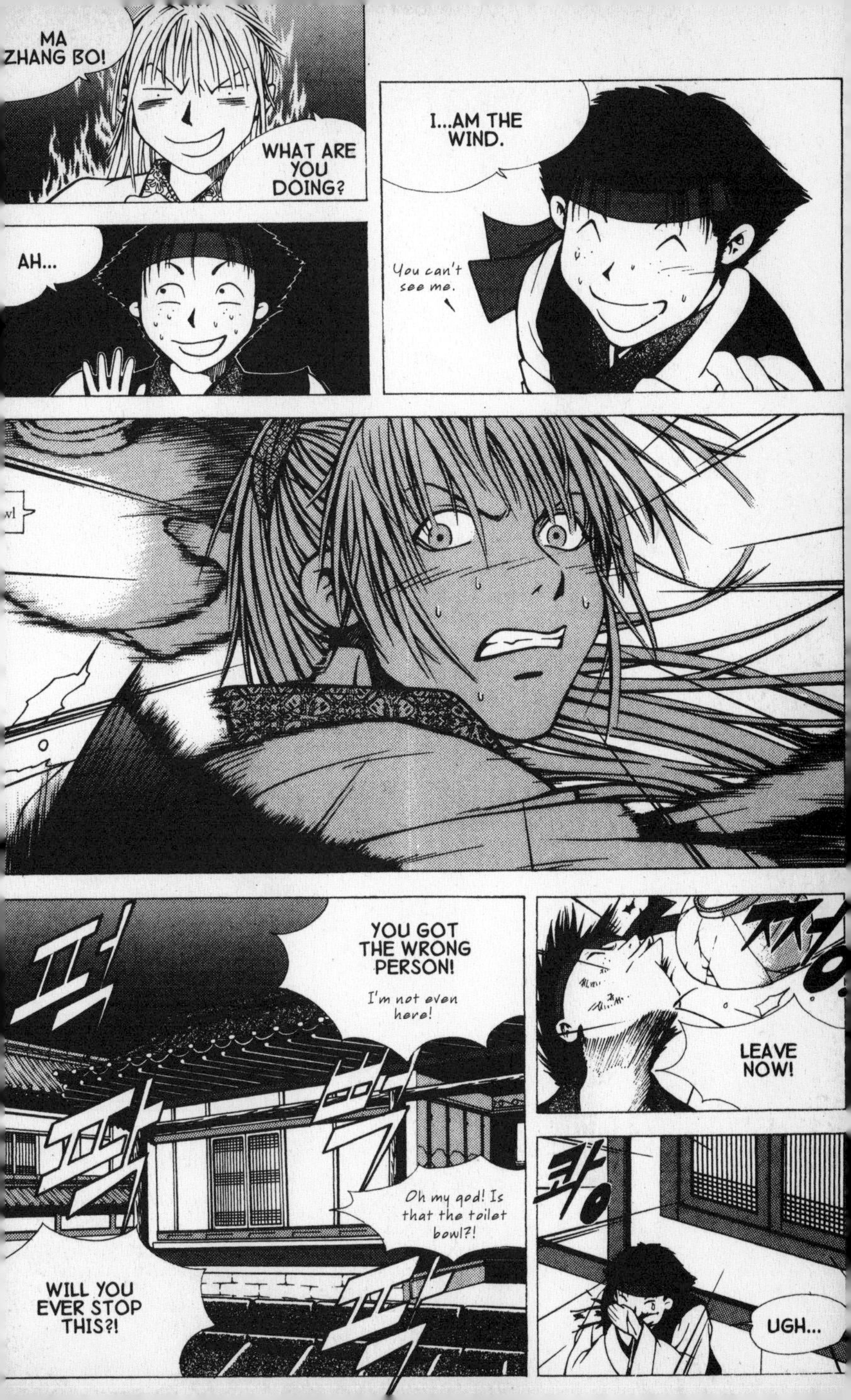
MA ZHANG BO!
WHAT ARE YOU DOING?
AH...
I...AM THE WIND.
You can't see me.
YOU GOT THE WRONG PERSON!
I'm not even here!
Oh my god! Is that the toilet bowl?!
WILL YOU EVER STOP THIS?!
LEAVE NOW!
UGH...

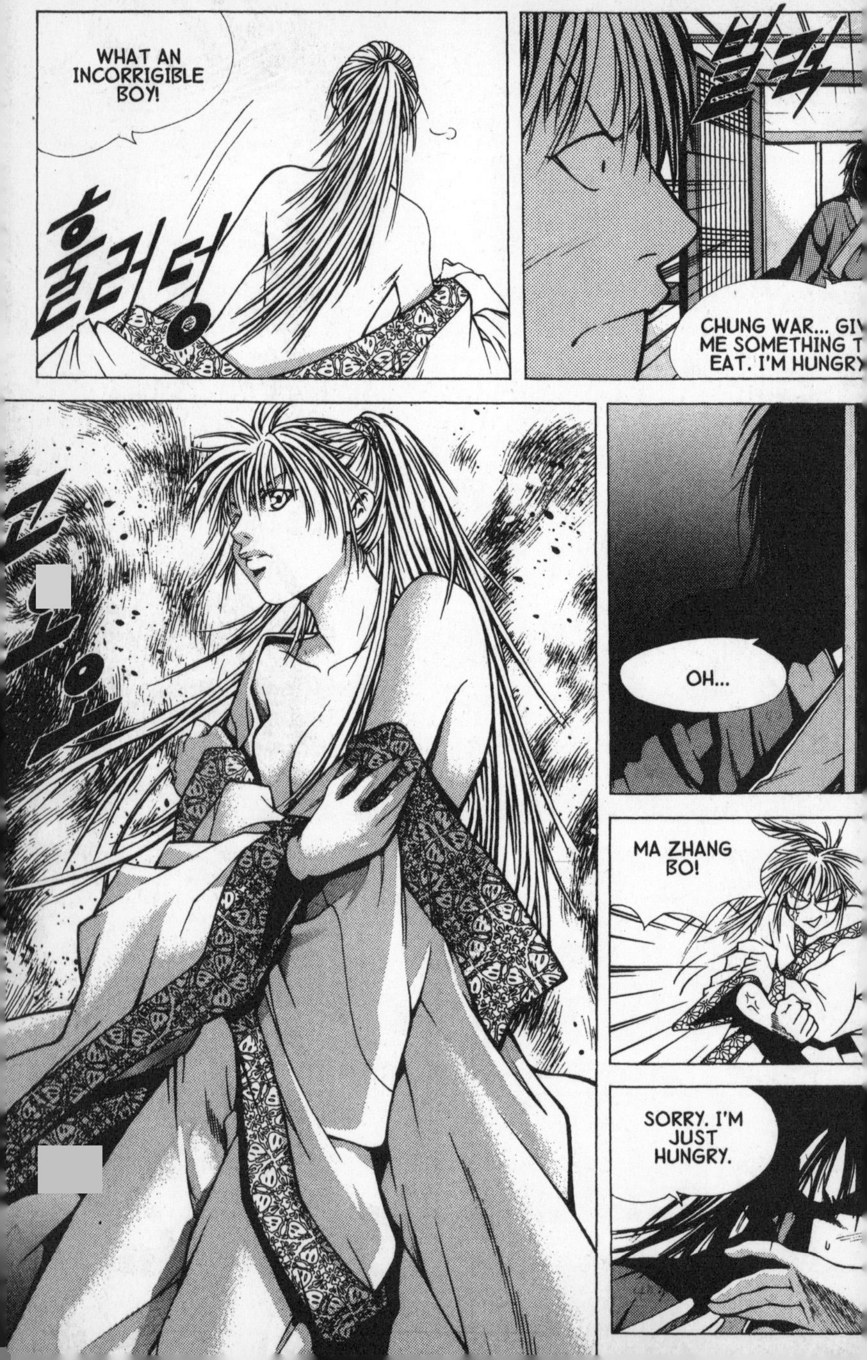
WHAT AN INCORRIGIBLE BOY!
훌러덩
벌컥
CHUNG WAR... GIV ME SOMETHING T EAT. I'M HUNGRY
OH...
MA ZHANG BO!
SORRY. I'M JUST HUNGRY.

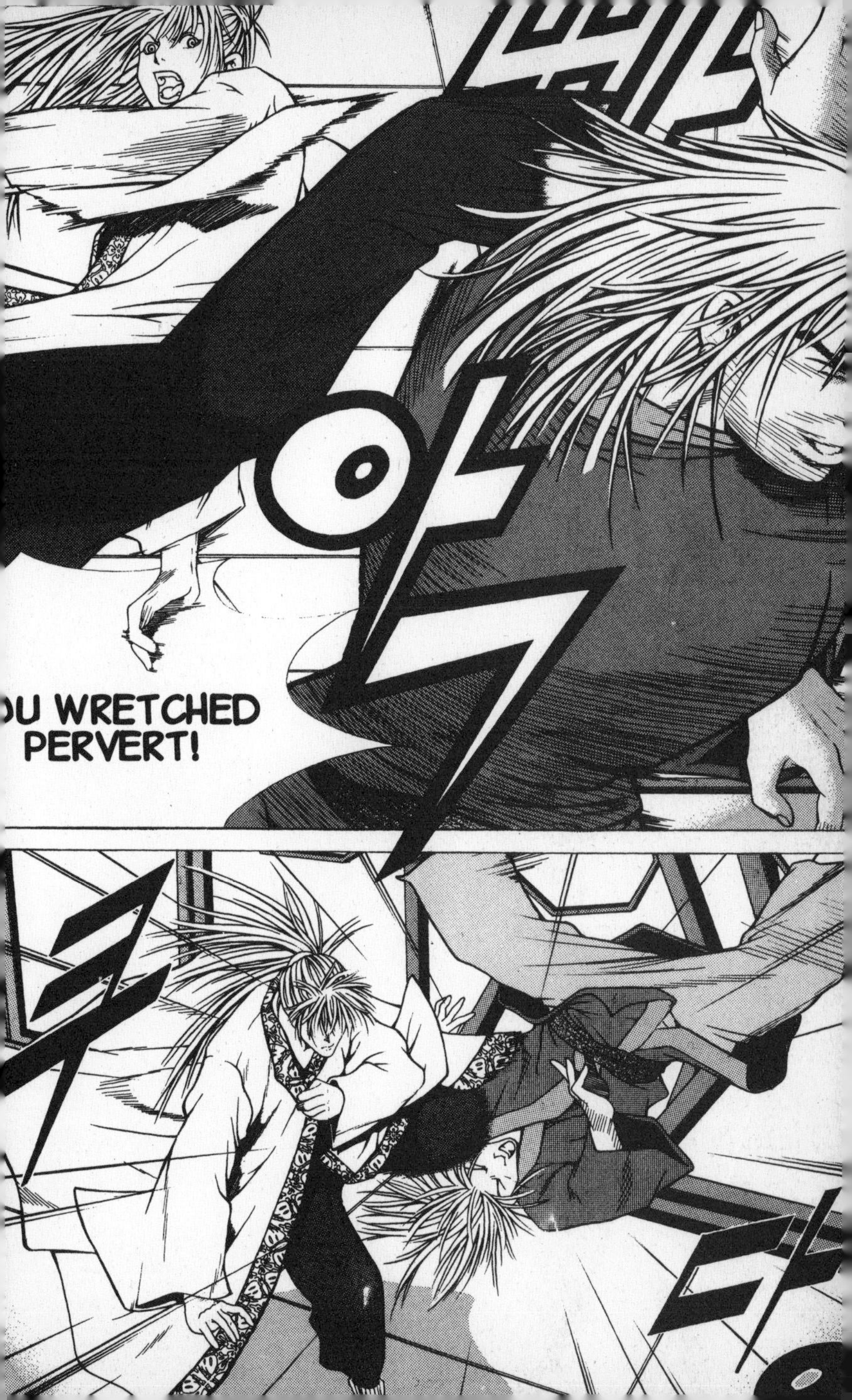
OU WRETCHED PERVERT!

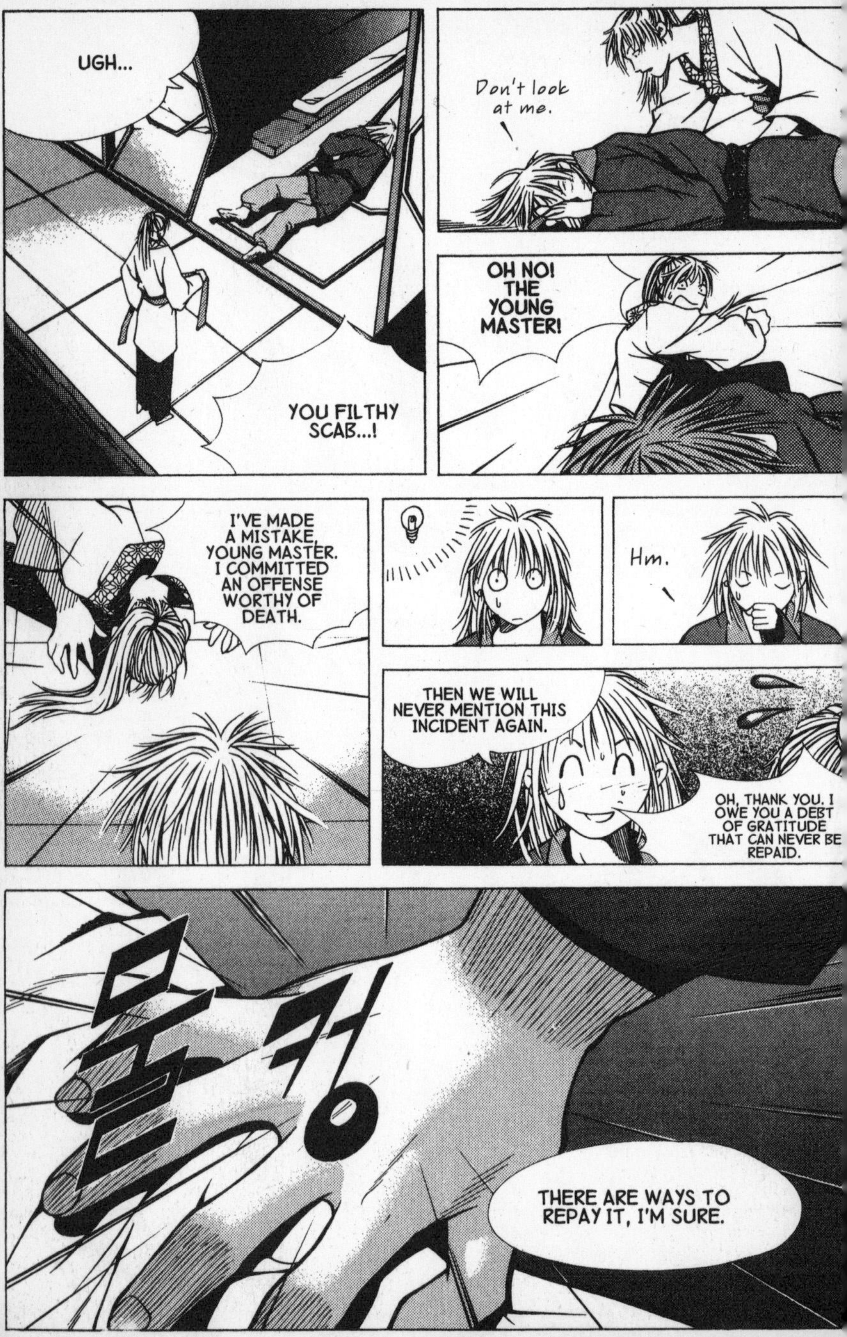
UGH...
YOU FILTHY SCAB...!
Don't look at me.
OH NO! THE YOUNG MASTER!
I'VE MADE A MISTAKE, YOUNG MASTER. I COMMITTED AN OFFENSE WORTHY OF DEATH.
Hm.
THEN WE WILL NEVER MENTION THIS INCIDENT AGAIN.
OH, THANK YOU. I OWE YOU A DEBT OF GRATITUDE THAT CAN NEVER BE REPAID.
THERE ARE WAYS TO REPAY IT, I'M SURE.

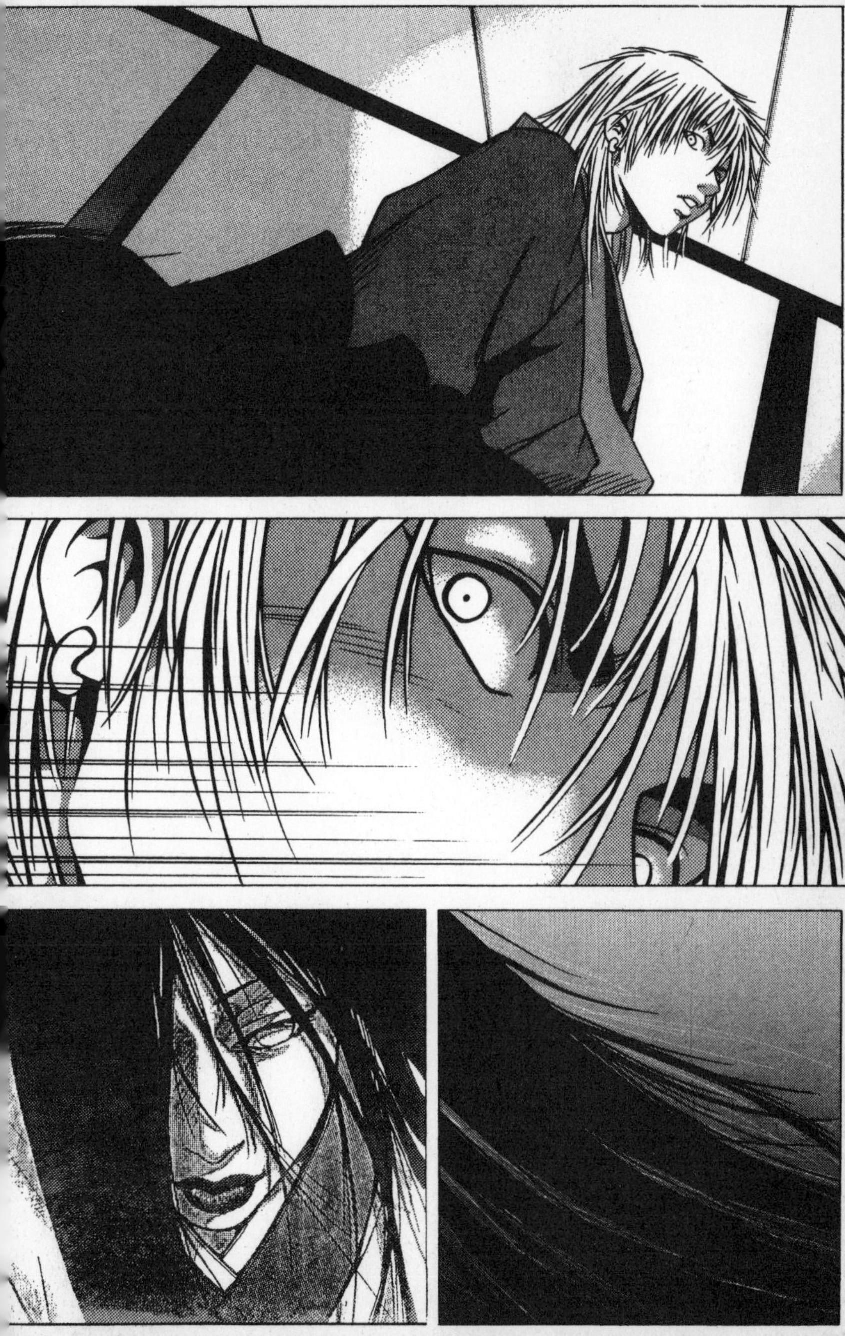

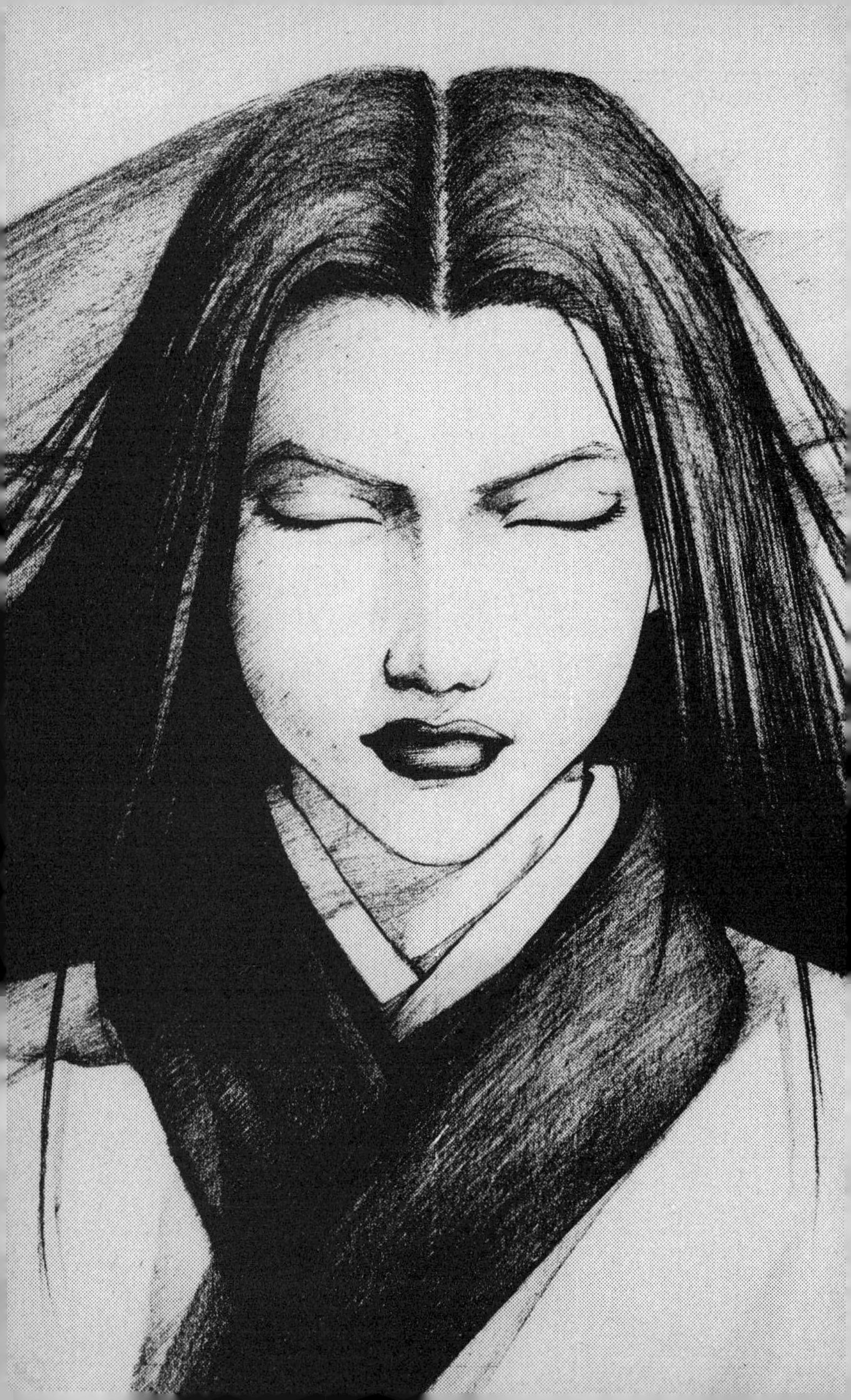

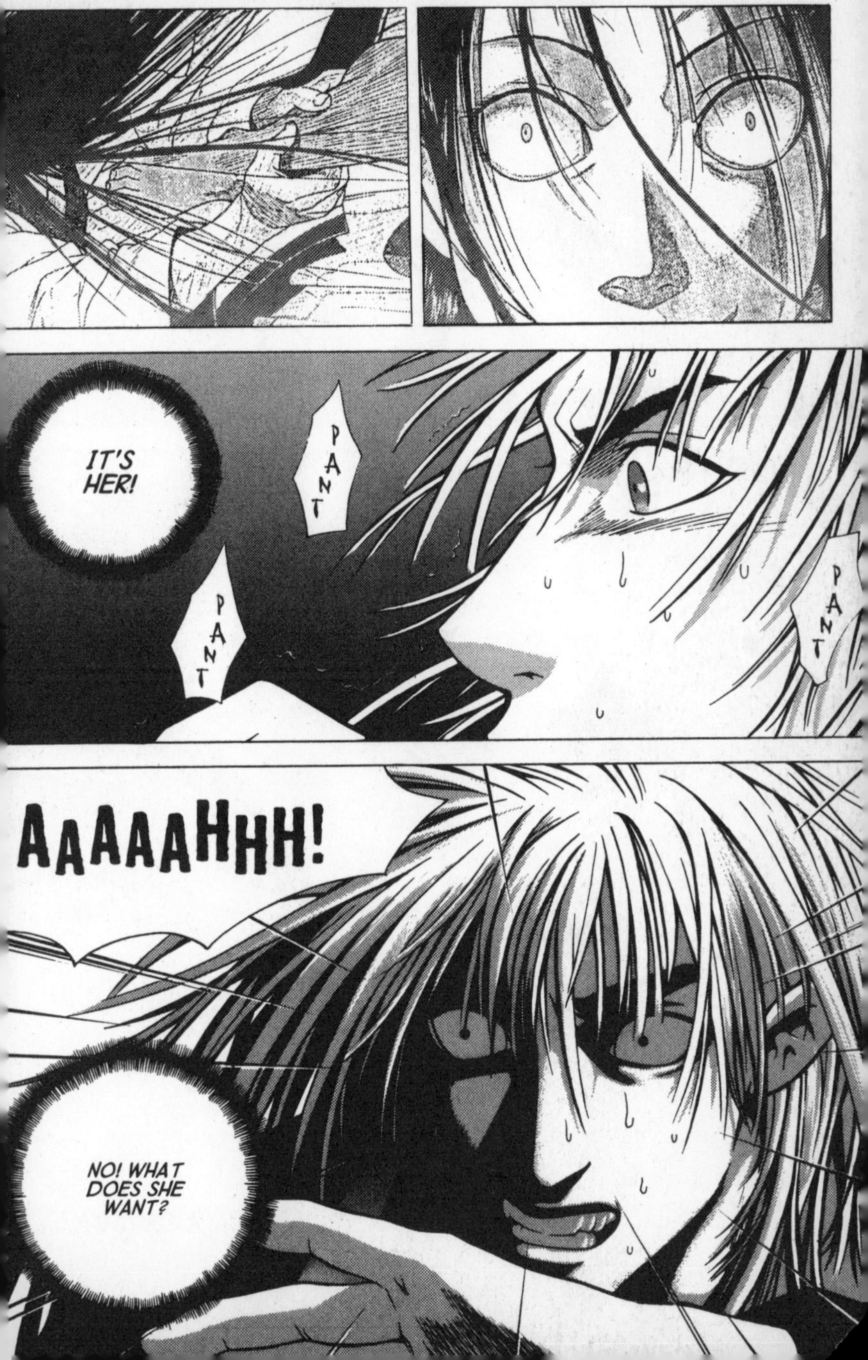
IT'S HER!
PANT
PANT
PANT
AAAAAHHH!
NO! WHAT DOES SHE WANT?

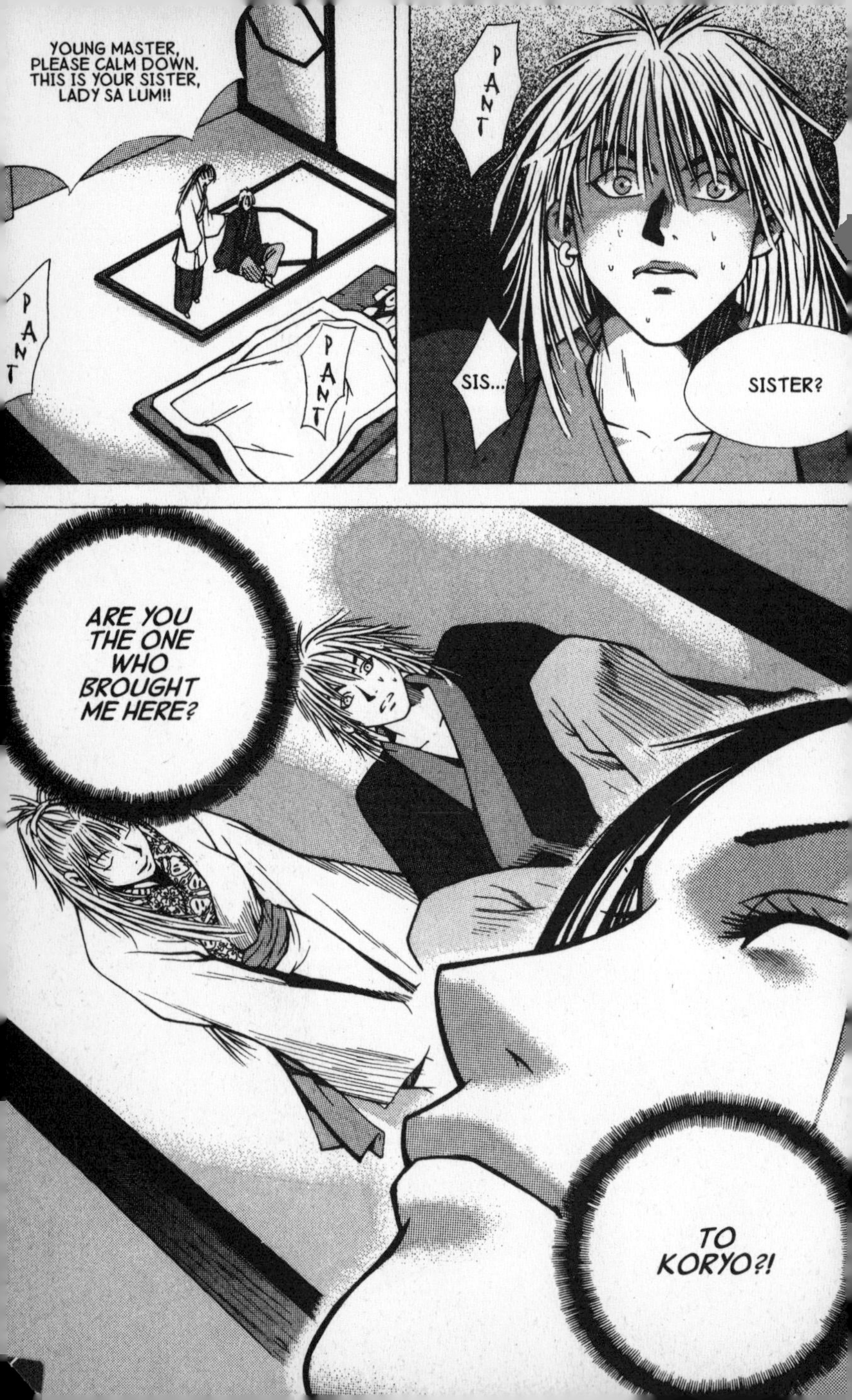
YOUNG MASTER, PLEASE CALM DOWN. THIS IS YOUR SISTER, LADY SA LUM!!
PANT
PANT
PANT
SIS...
SISTER?
ARE YOU THE ONE WHO BROUGHT ME HERE?
TO KORYO?!

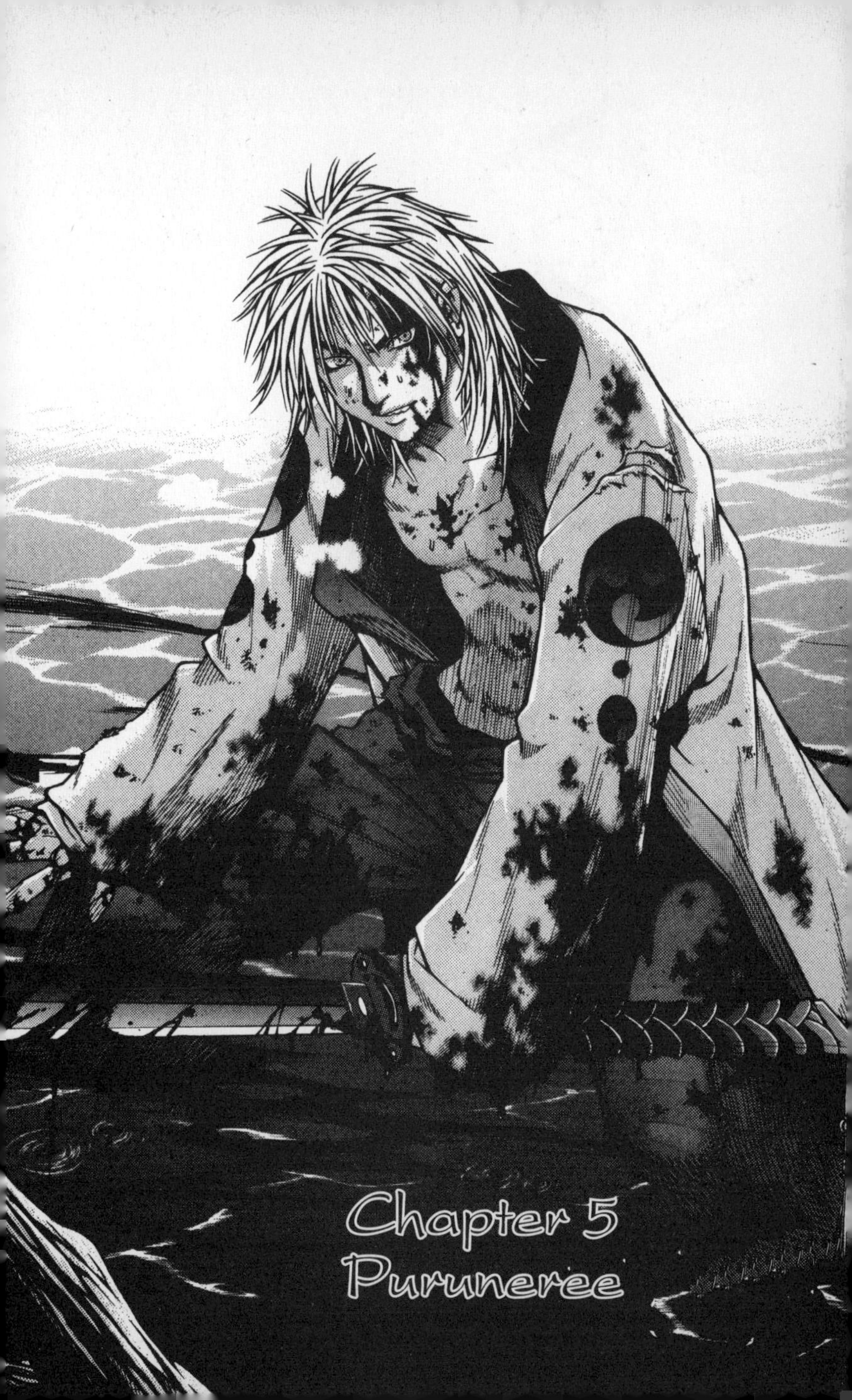
Chapter 5
Puruneree

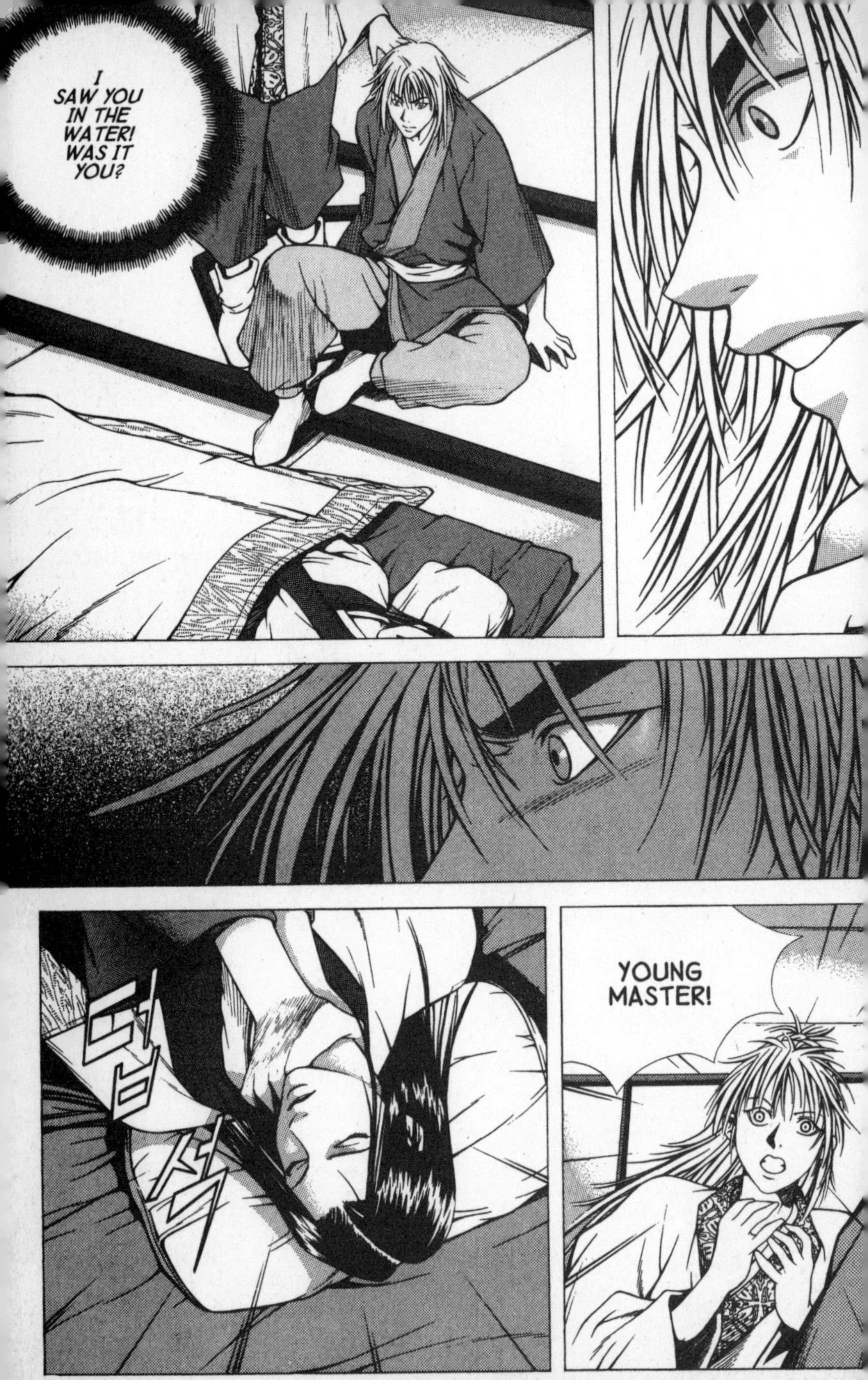
I SAW YOU IN THE WATER! WAS IT YOU?
YOUNG MASTER!

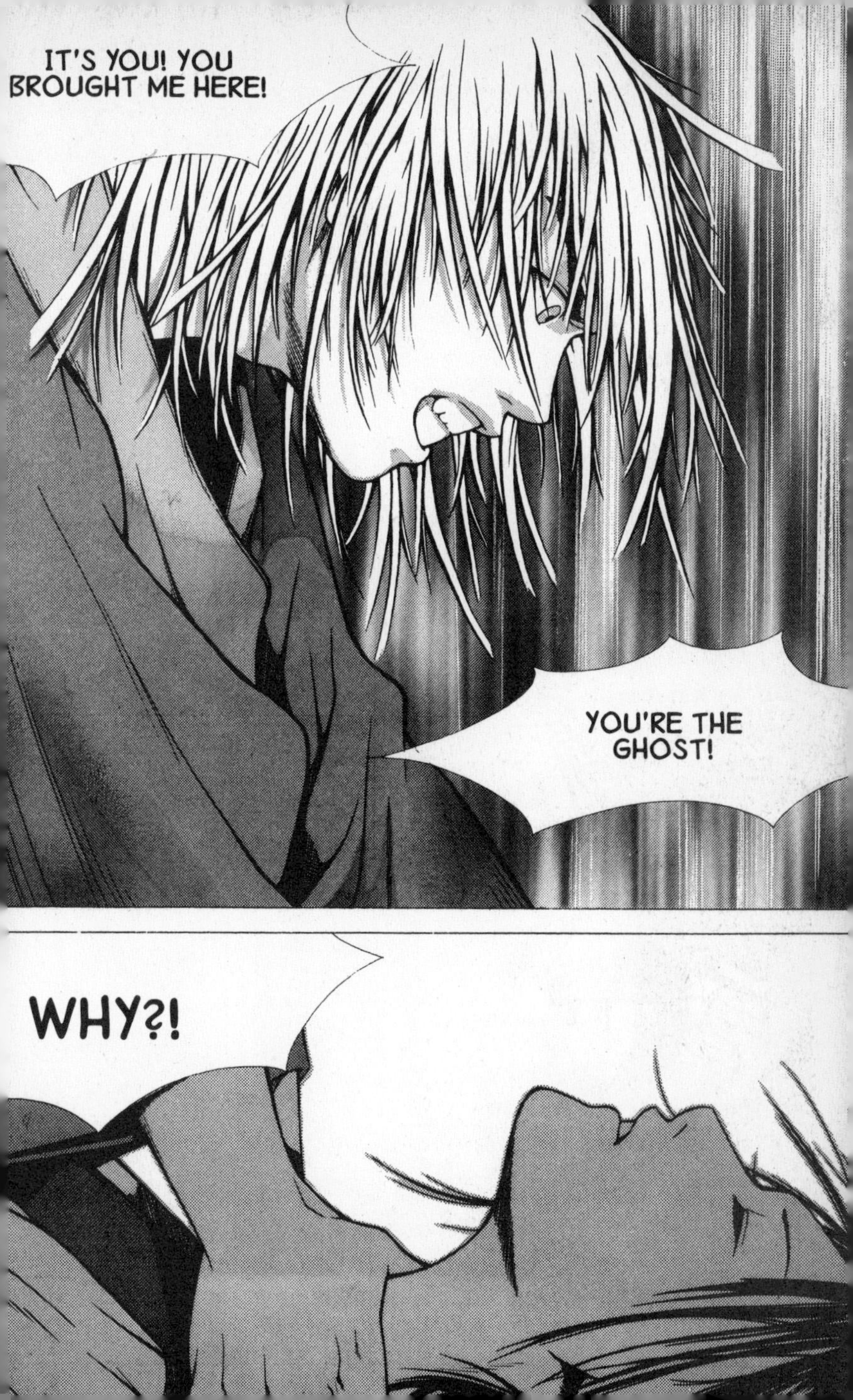
IT'S YOU! YOU BROUGHT ME HERE!
YOU'RE THE GHOST!
WHY?!

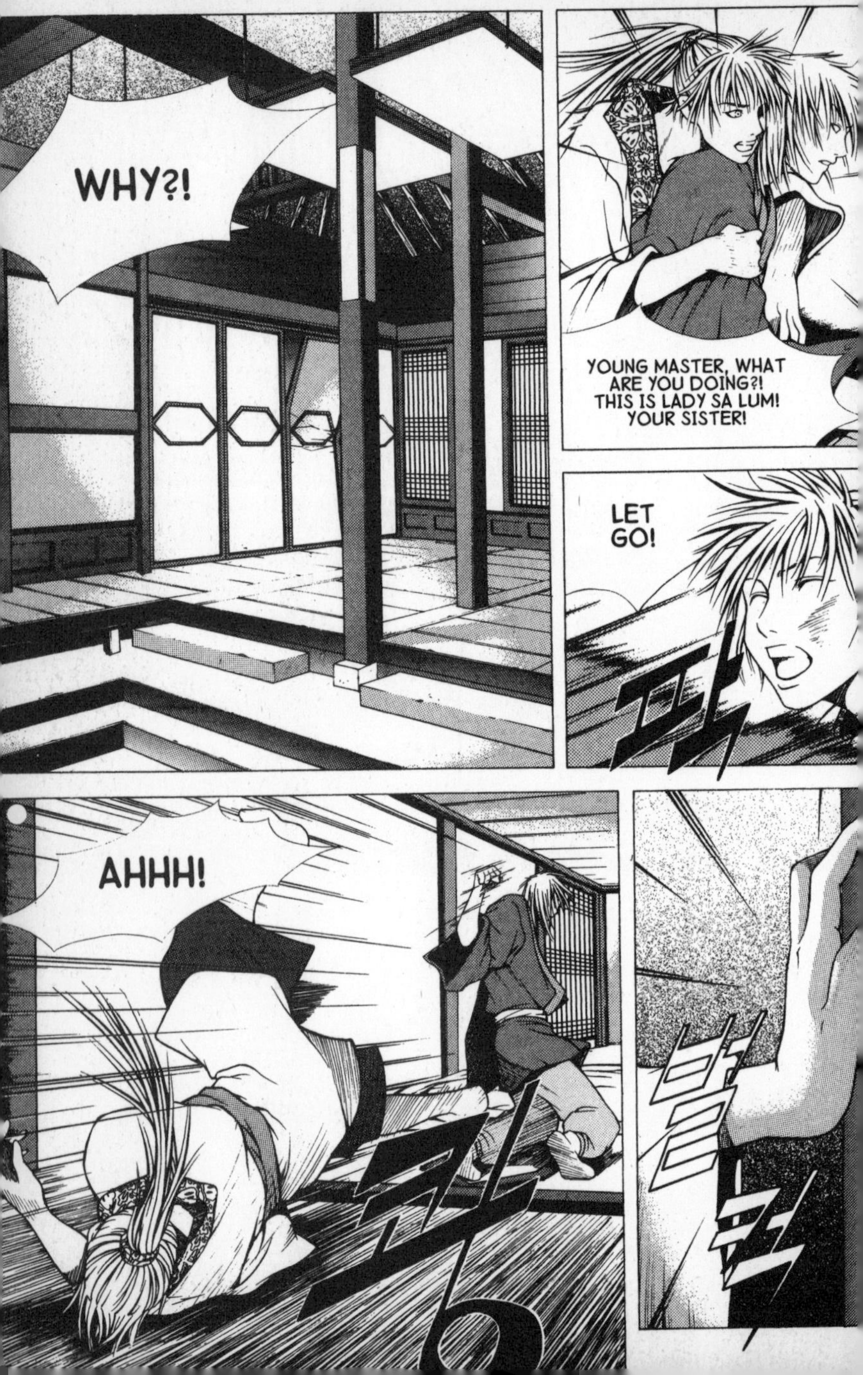
WHY?!
YOUNG MASTER, WHAT ARE YOU DOING?! THIS IS LADY SA LUM! YOUR SISTER!
LET GO!
AHHH!

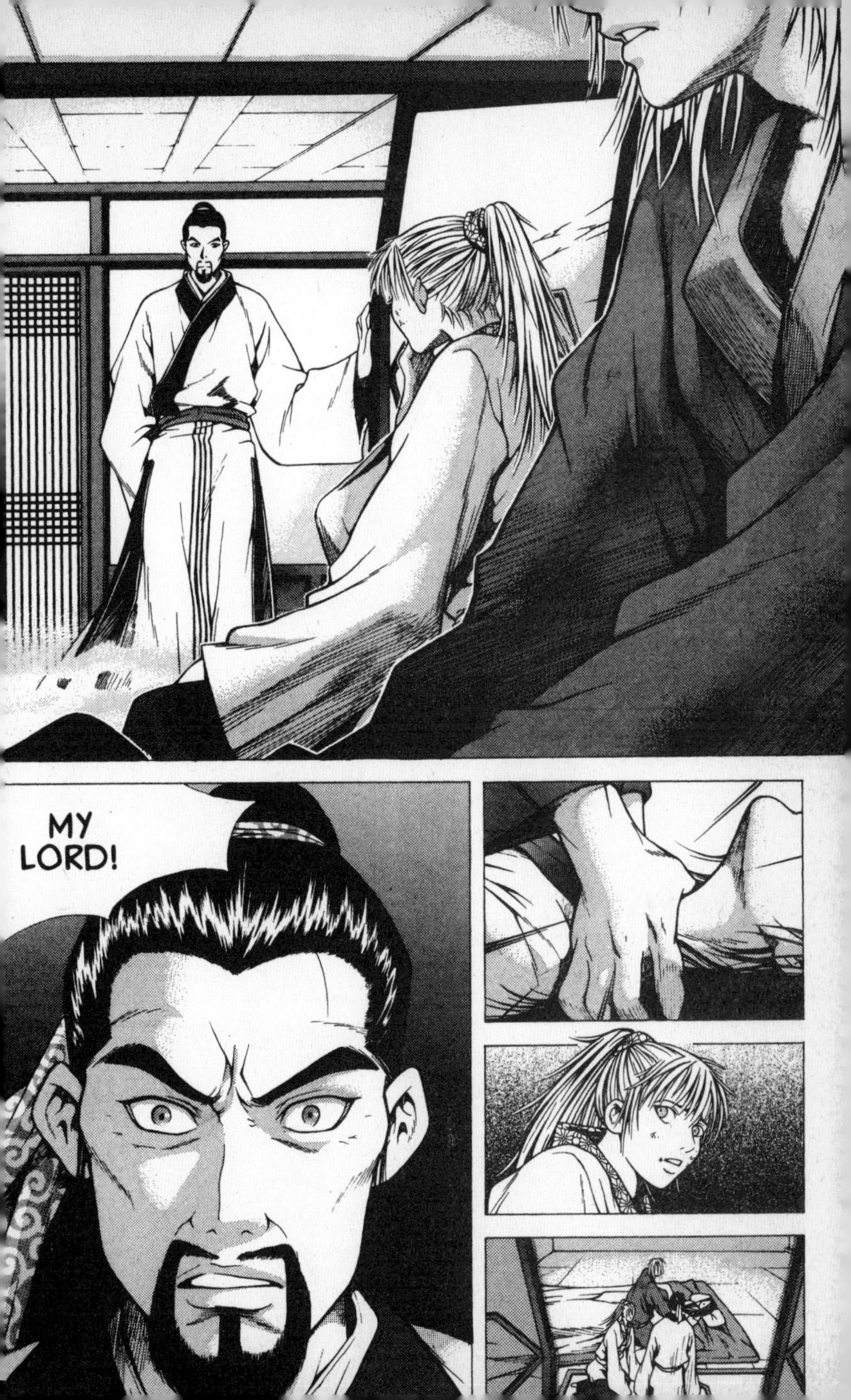
MY LORD!

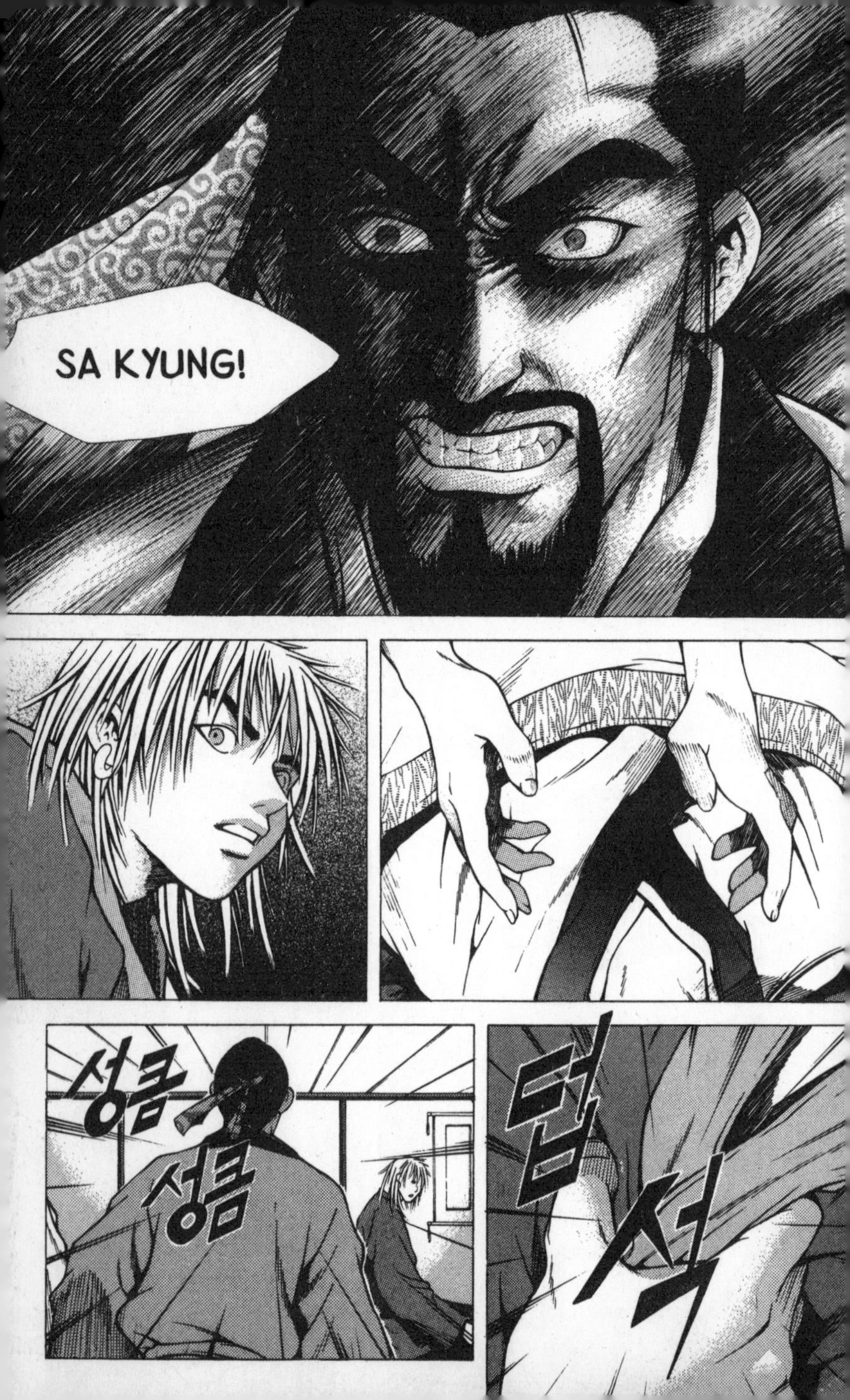
SA KYUNG!
성큼
성큼
덥석

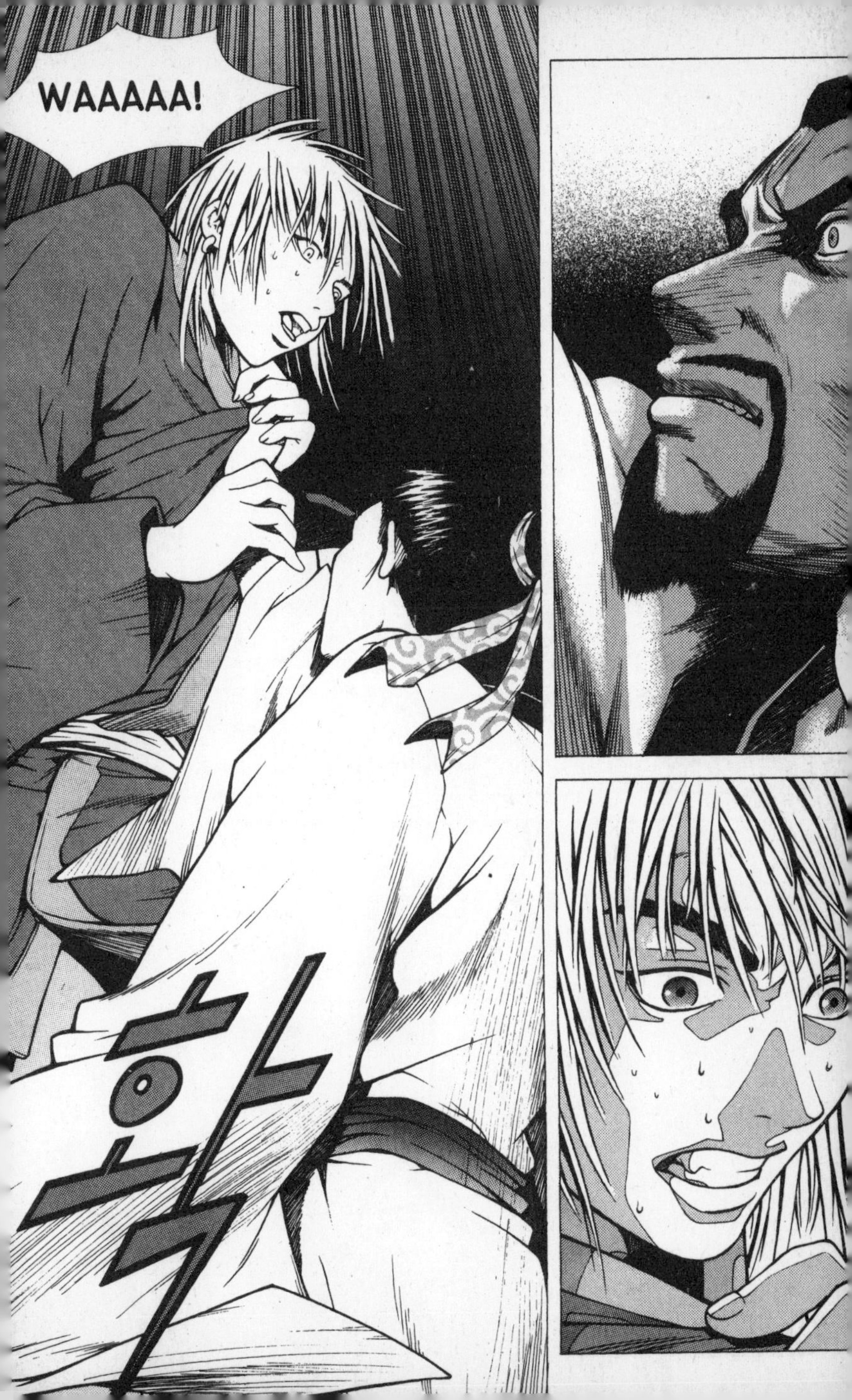
WAAAAA!

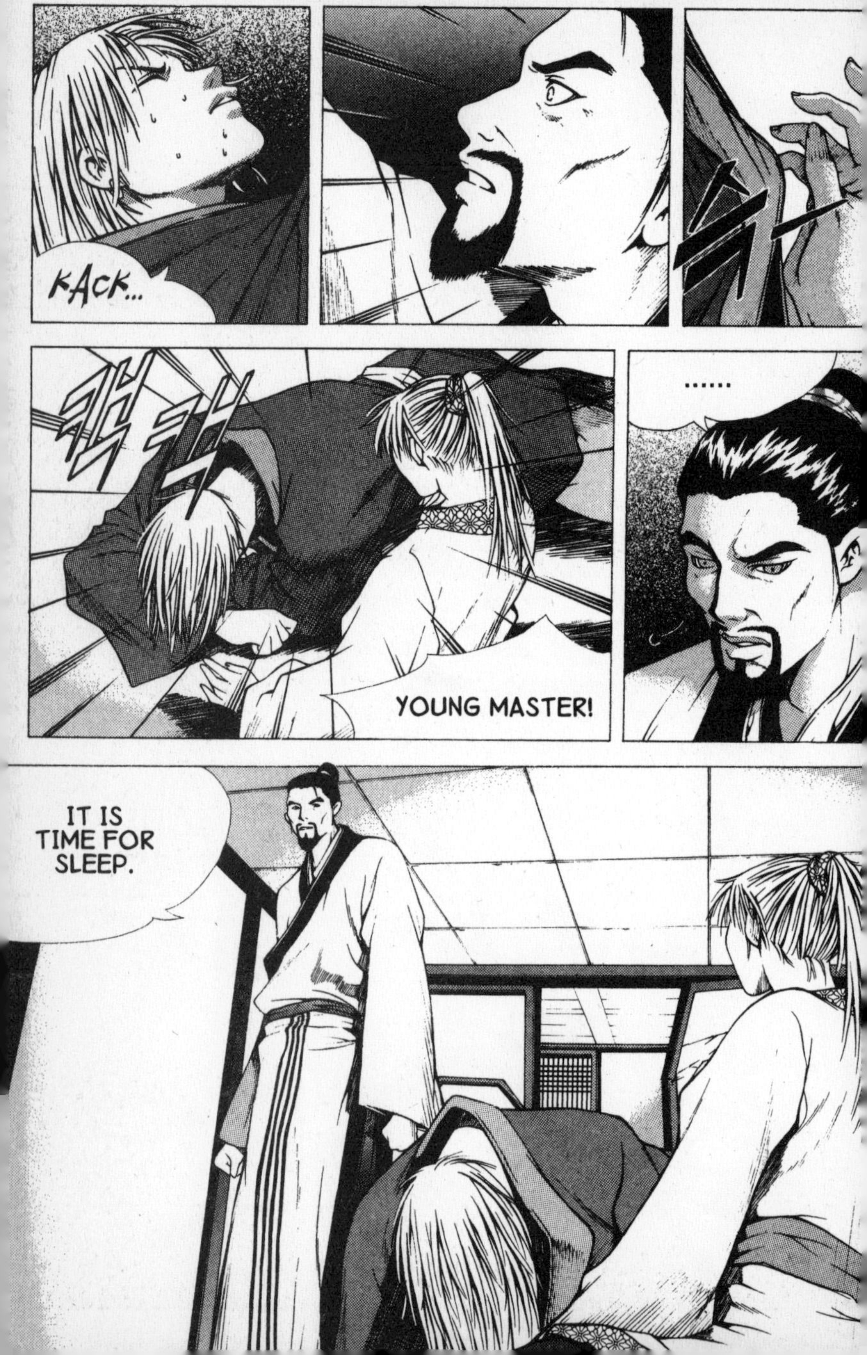
KACK...
YOUNG MASTER!
......
IT IS TIME FOR SLEEP.

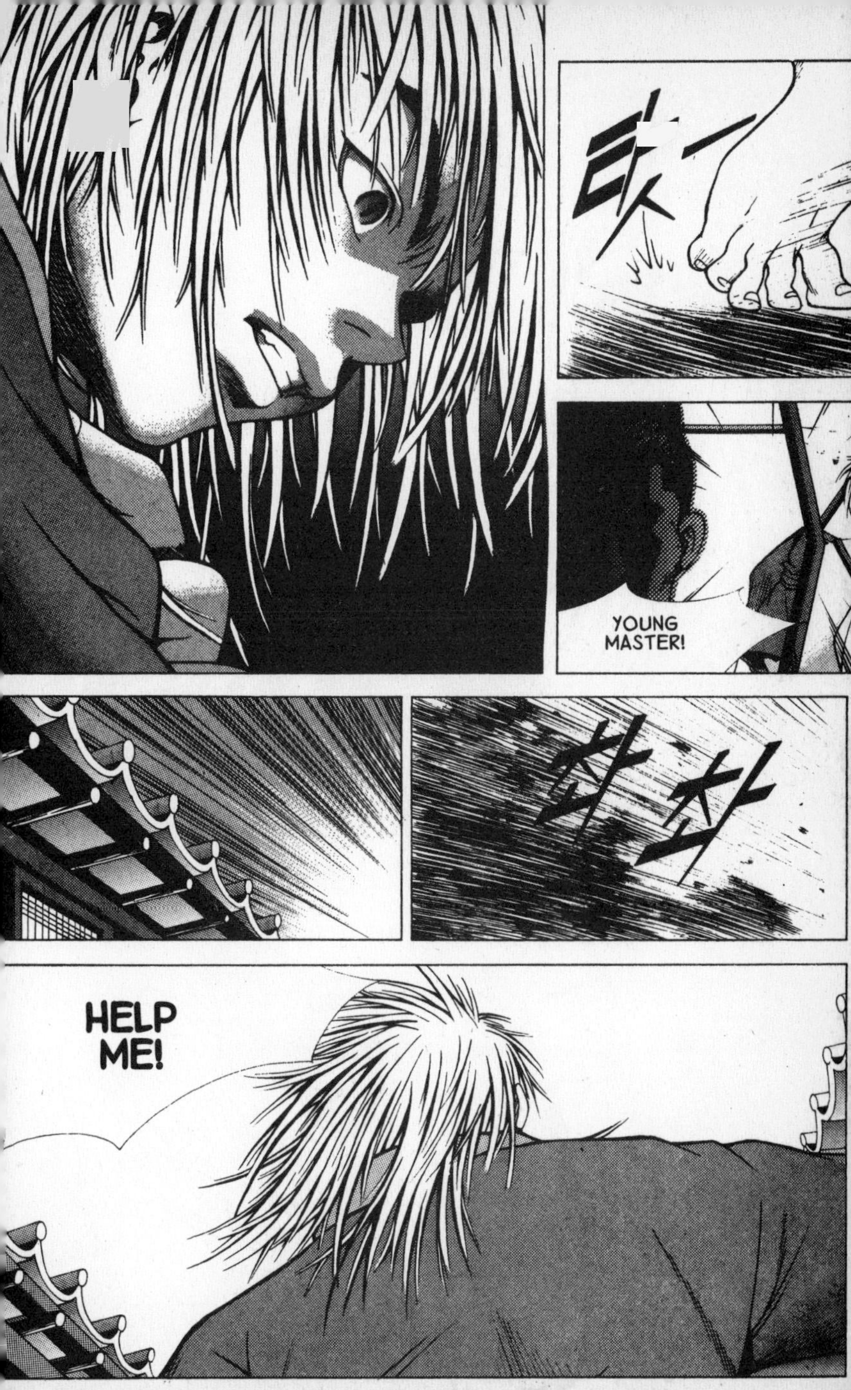
YOUNG MASTER!
HELP ME!

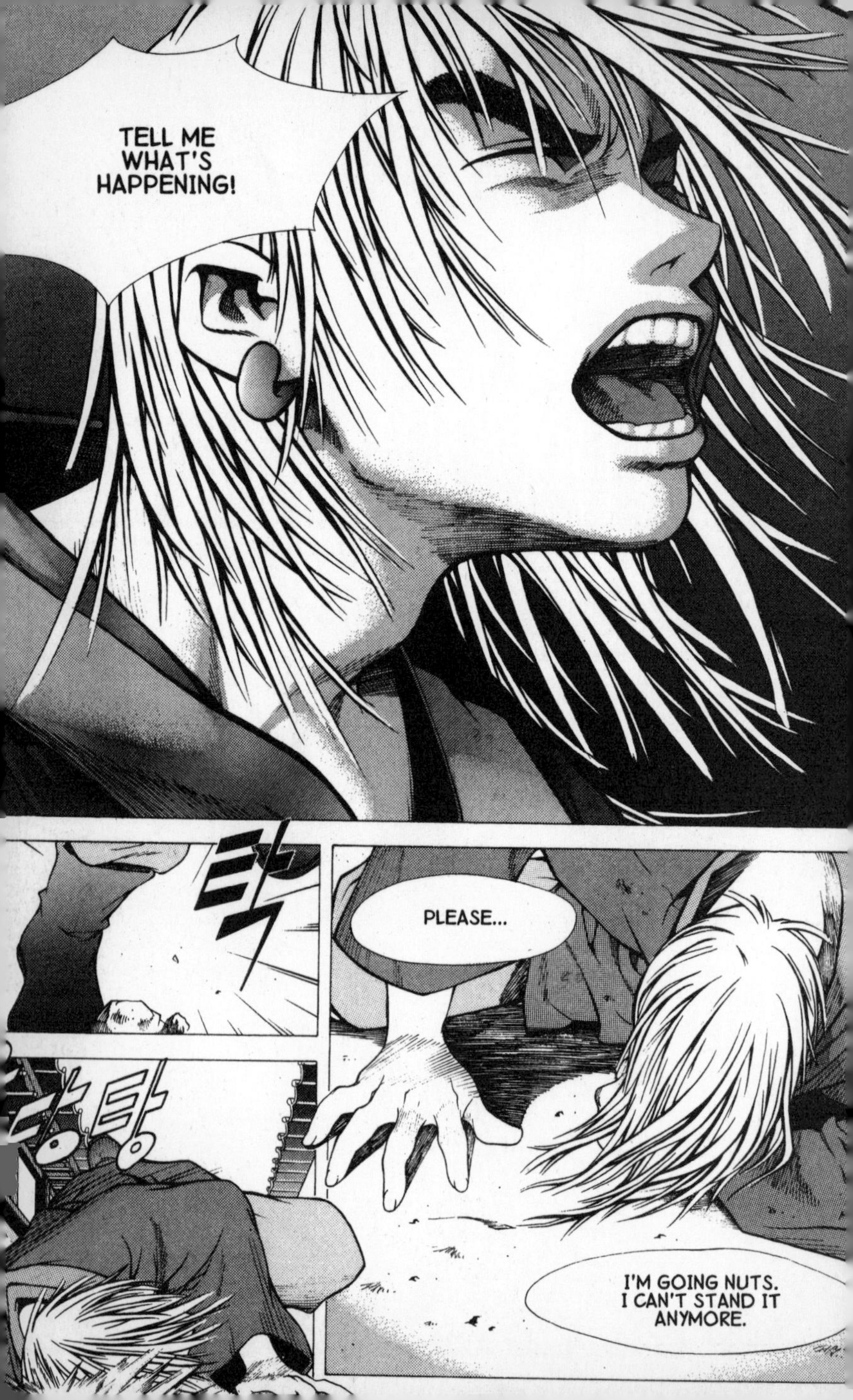
TELL ME WHAT'S HAPPENING!
PLEASE...
I'M GOING NUTS. I CAN'T STAND IT ANYMORE.

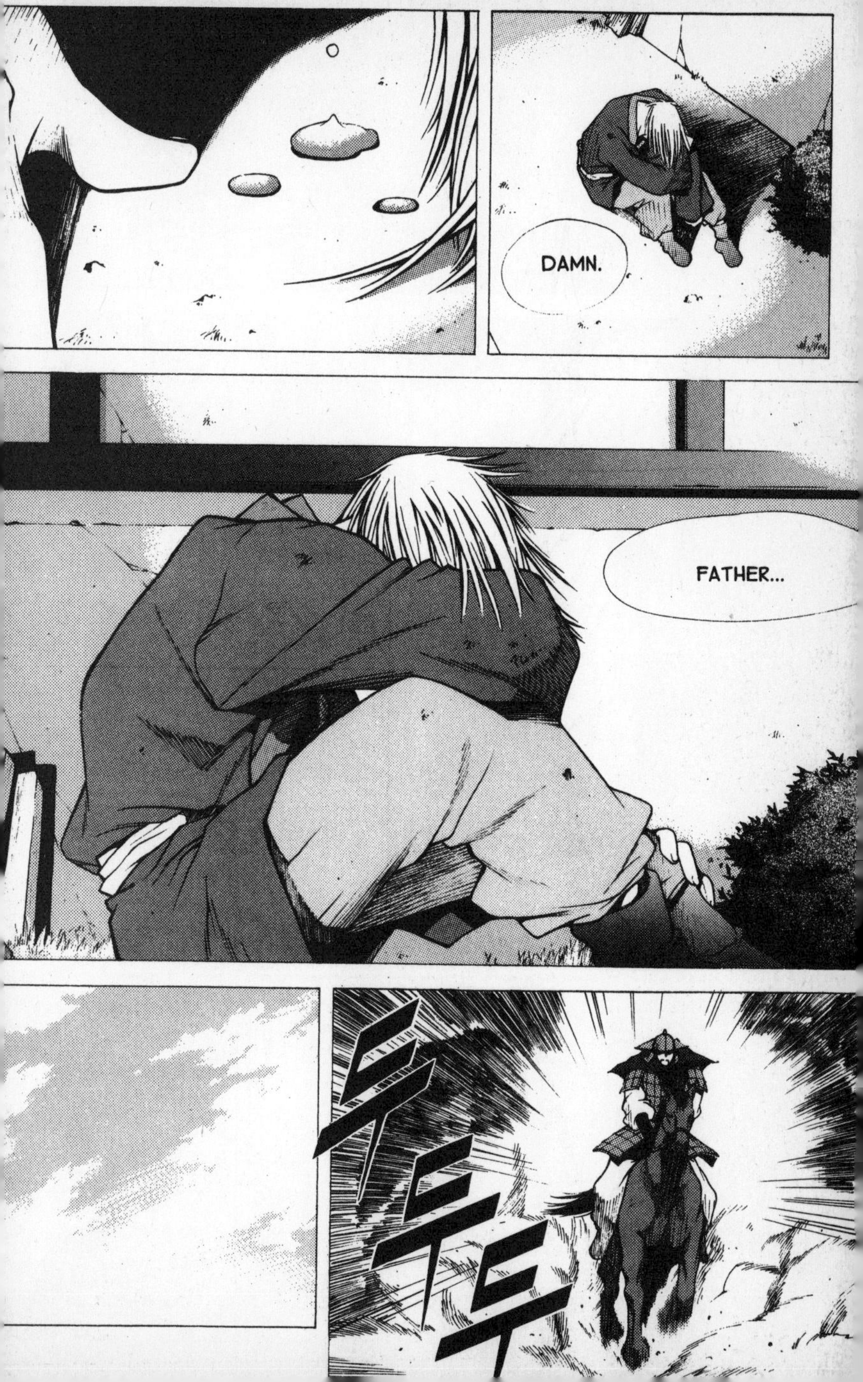
DAMN.
FATHER...

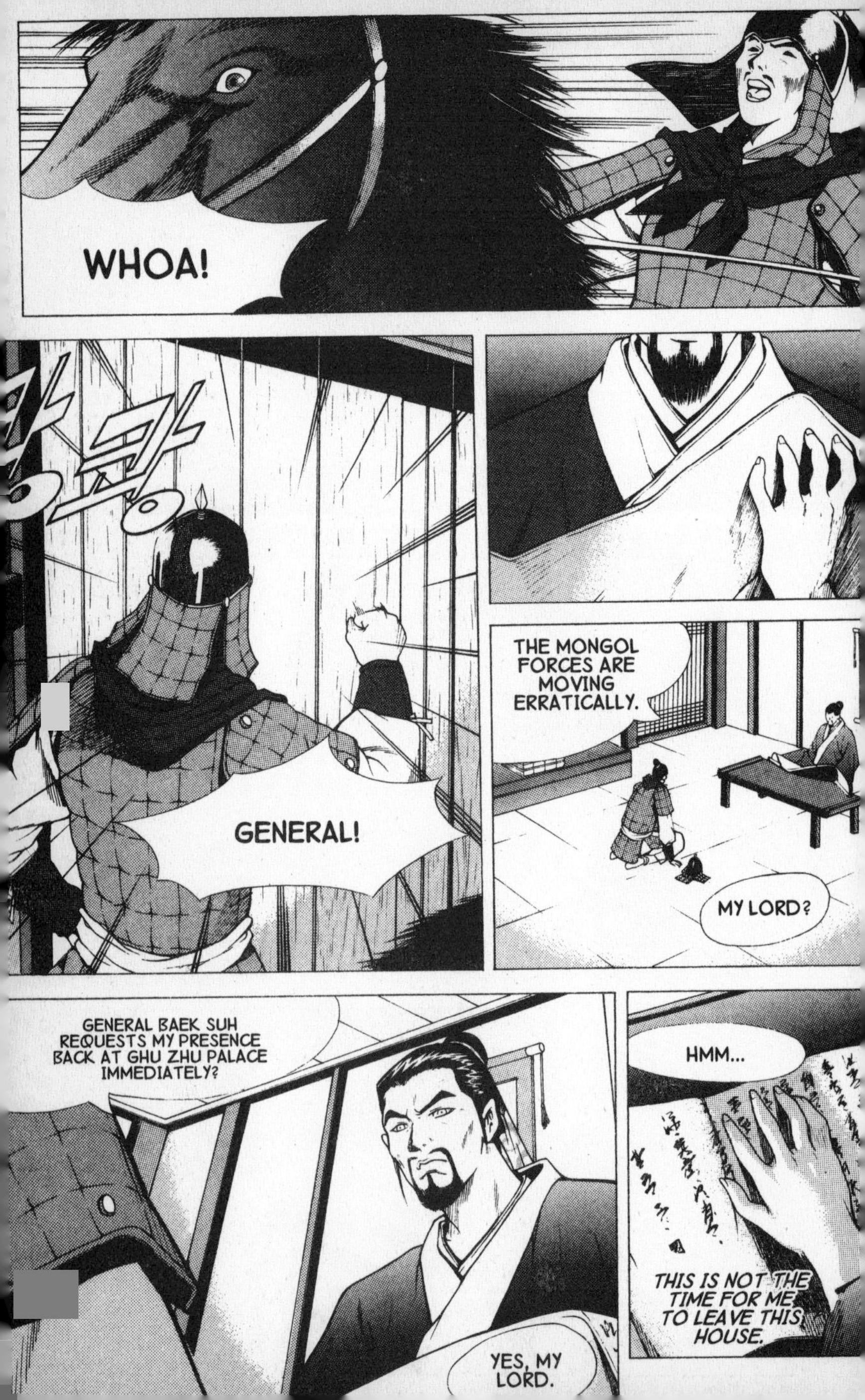
WHOA!
GENERAL!
THE MONGOL FORCES ARE MOVING ERRATICALLY.
MY LORD?
GENERAL BAEK SUH REQUESTS MY PRESENCE BACK AT GHU ZHU PALACE IMMEDIATELY?
YES, MY LORD.
HMM...
THIS IS NOT THE TIME FOR ME TO LEAVE THIS HOUSE.

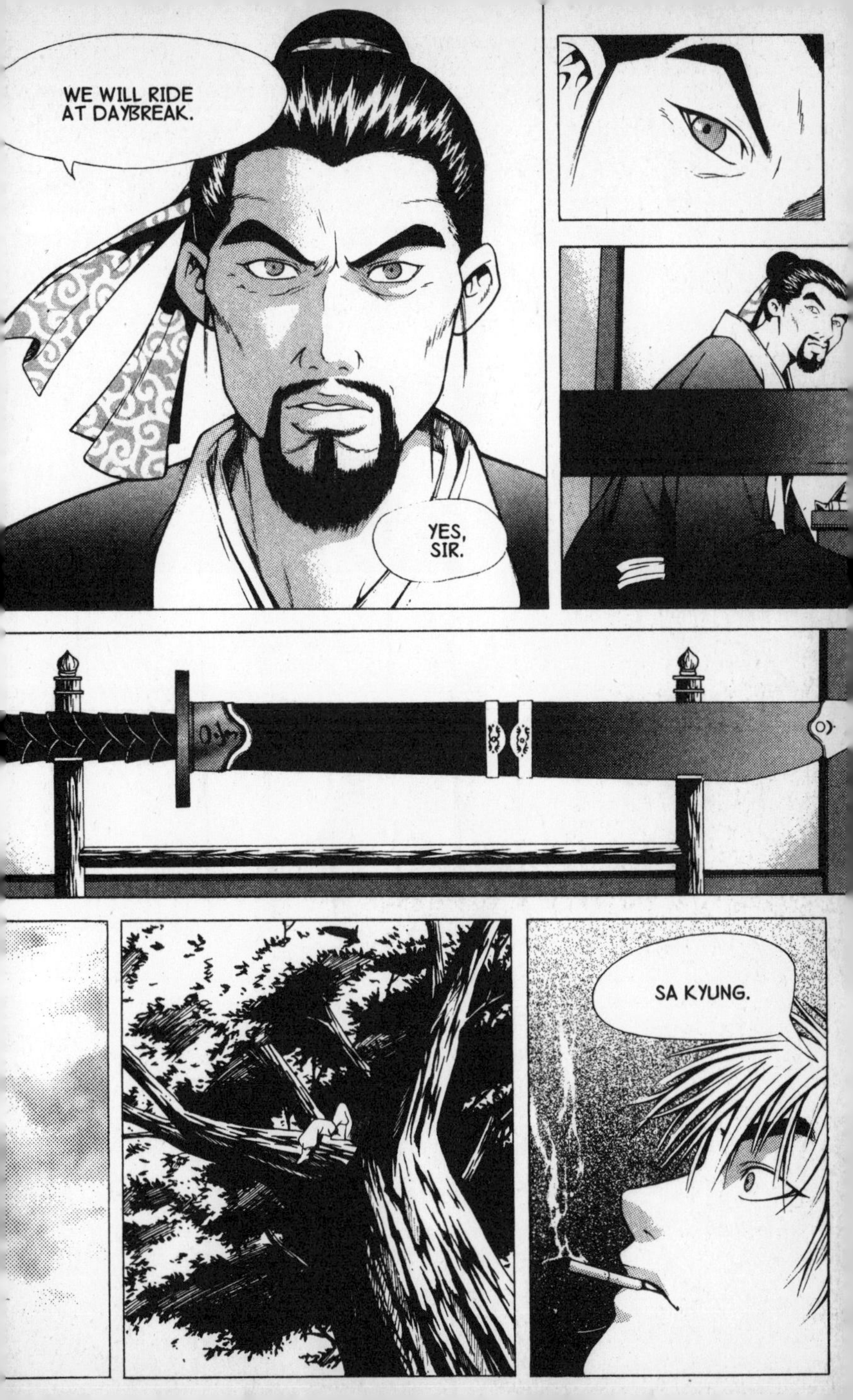
WE WILL RIDE AT DAYBREAK.
YES, SIR.
SA KYUNG.

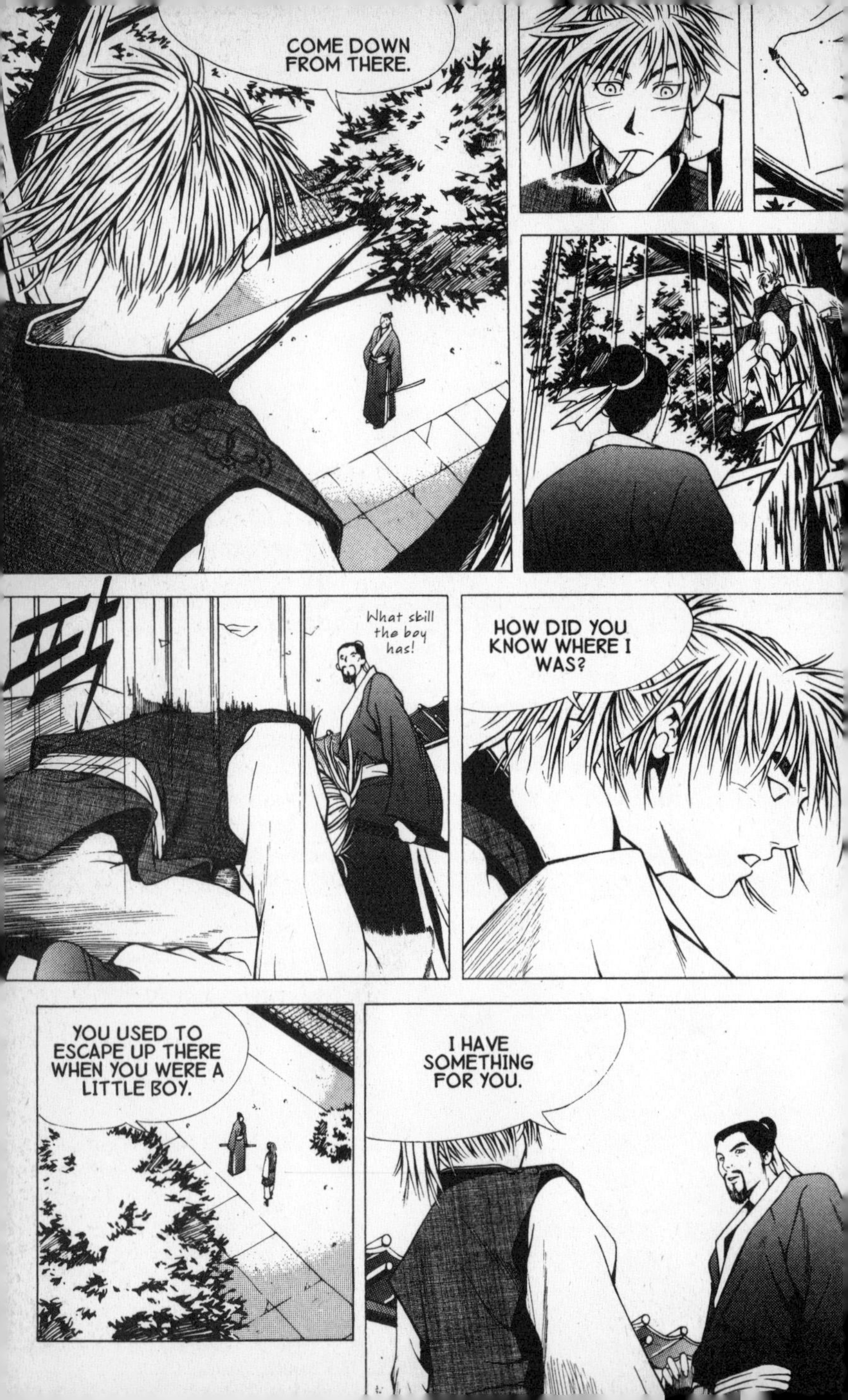
COME DOWN FROM THERE.
What skill the boy has!
HOW DID YOU KNOW WHERE I WAS?
YOU USED TO ESCAPE UP THERE WHEN YOU WERE A LITTLE BOY.
I HAVE SOMETHING FOR YOU.

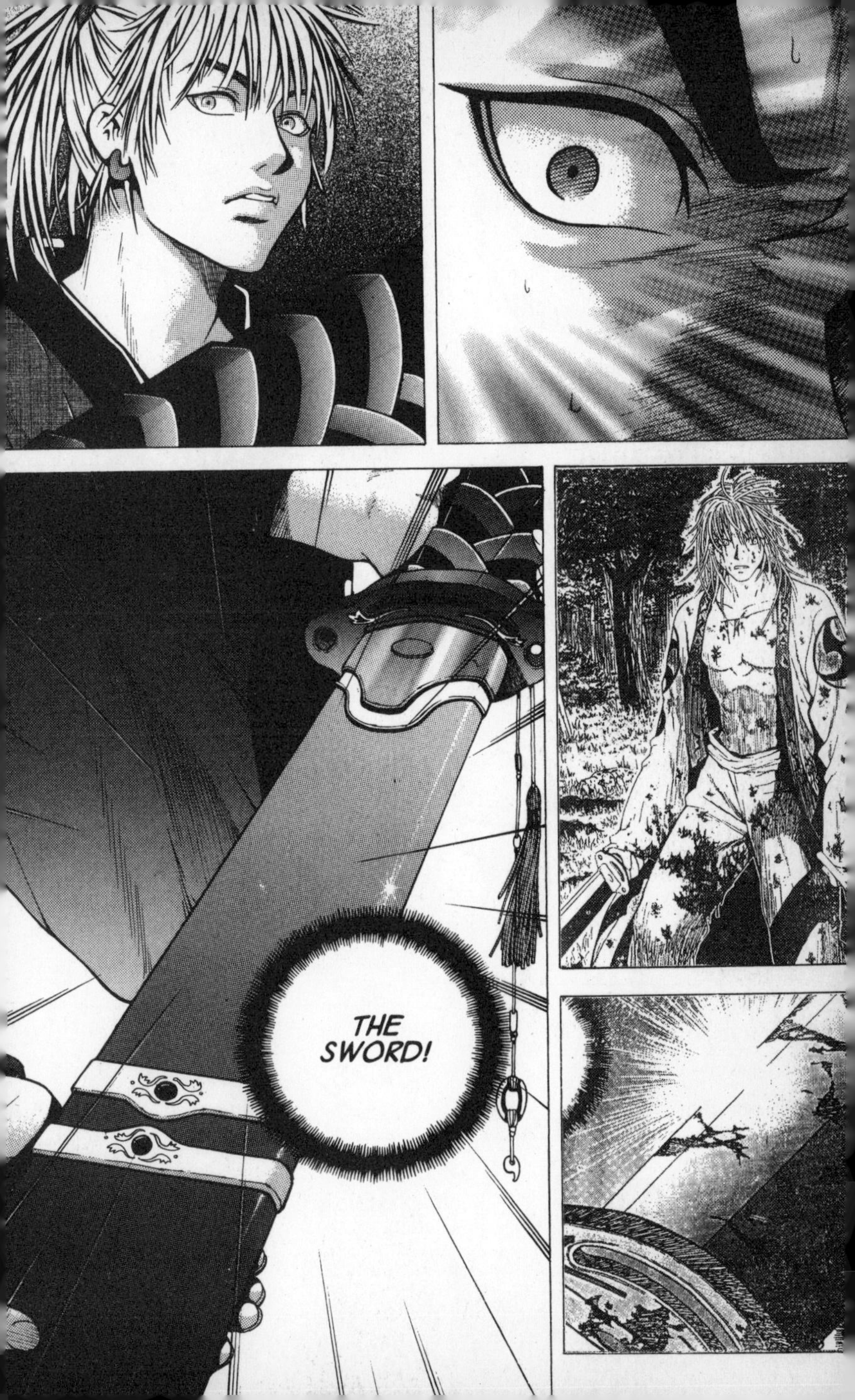
THE SWORD!

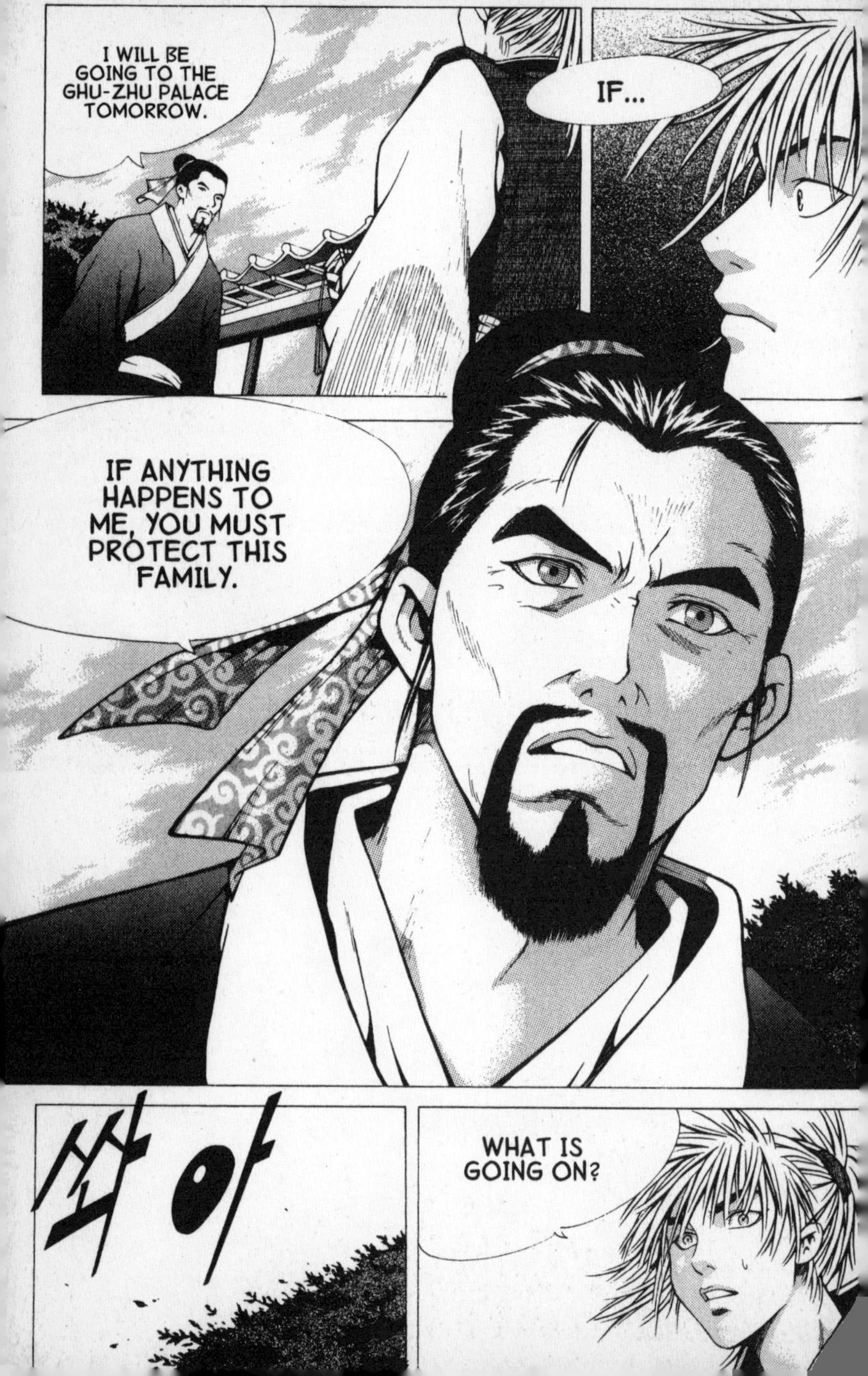
I WILL BE GOING TO THE GHU-ZHU PALACE TOMORROW.
IF...
IF ANYTHING HAPPENS TO ME, YOU MUST PROTECT THIS FAMILY.
쏴아
WHAT IS GOING ON?

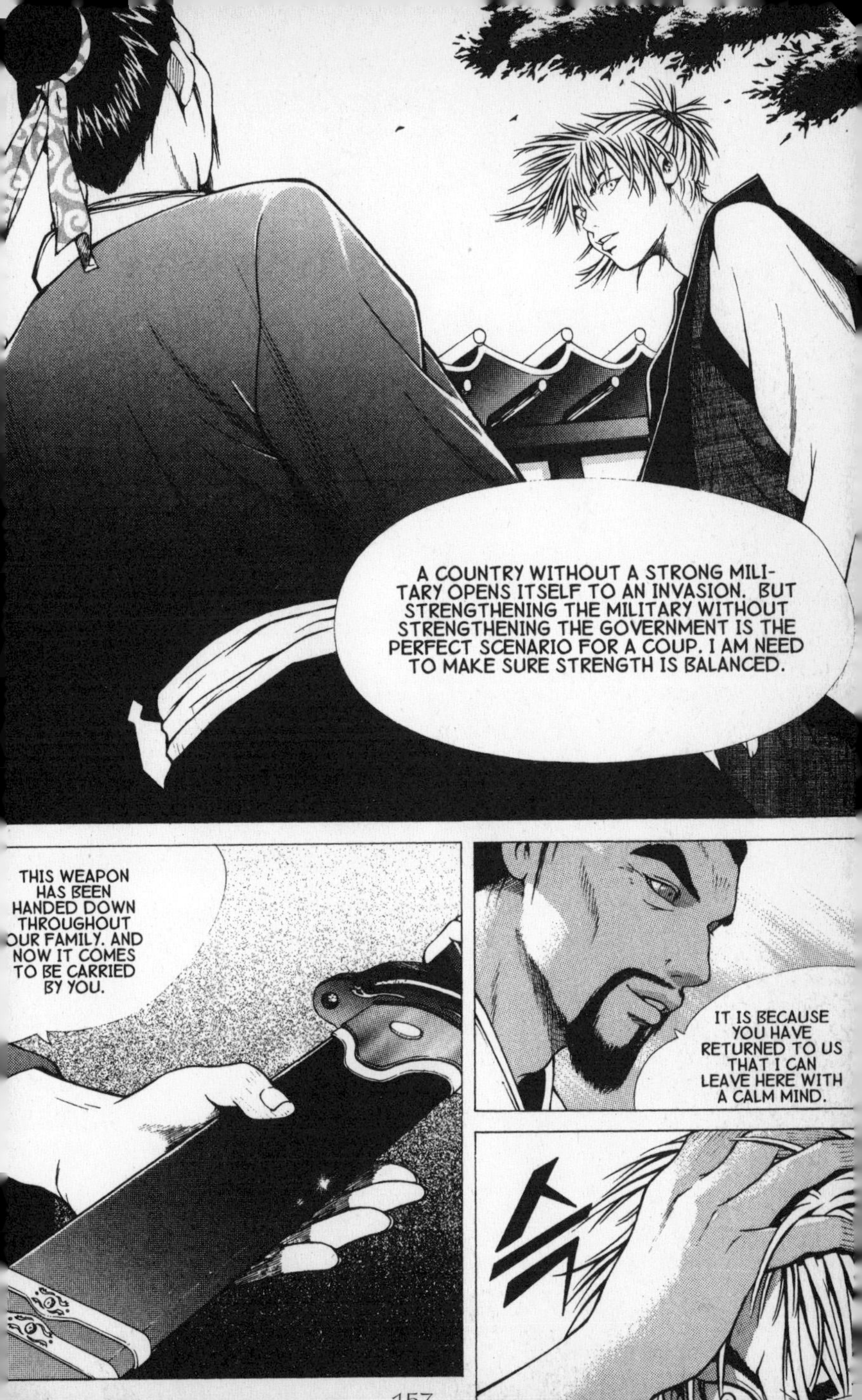
A COUNTRY WITHOUT A STRONG MILITARY OPENS ITSELF TO AN INVASION. BUT STRENGTHENING THE MILITARY WITHOUT STRENGTHENING THE GOVERNMENT IS THE PERFECT SCENARIO FOR A COUP. I AM NEED TO MAKE SURE STRENGTH IS BALANCED.
THIS WEAPON HAS BEEN HANDED DOWN THROUGHOUT OUR FAMILY. AND NOW IT COMES TO BE CARRIED BY YOU.
IT IS BECAUSE YOU HAVE RETURNED TO US THAT I CAN LEAVE HERE WITH A CALM MIND.

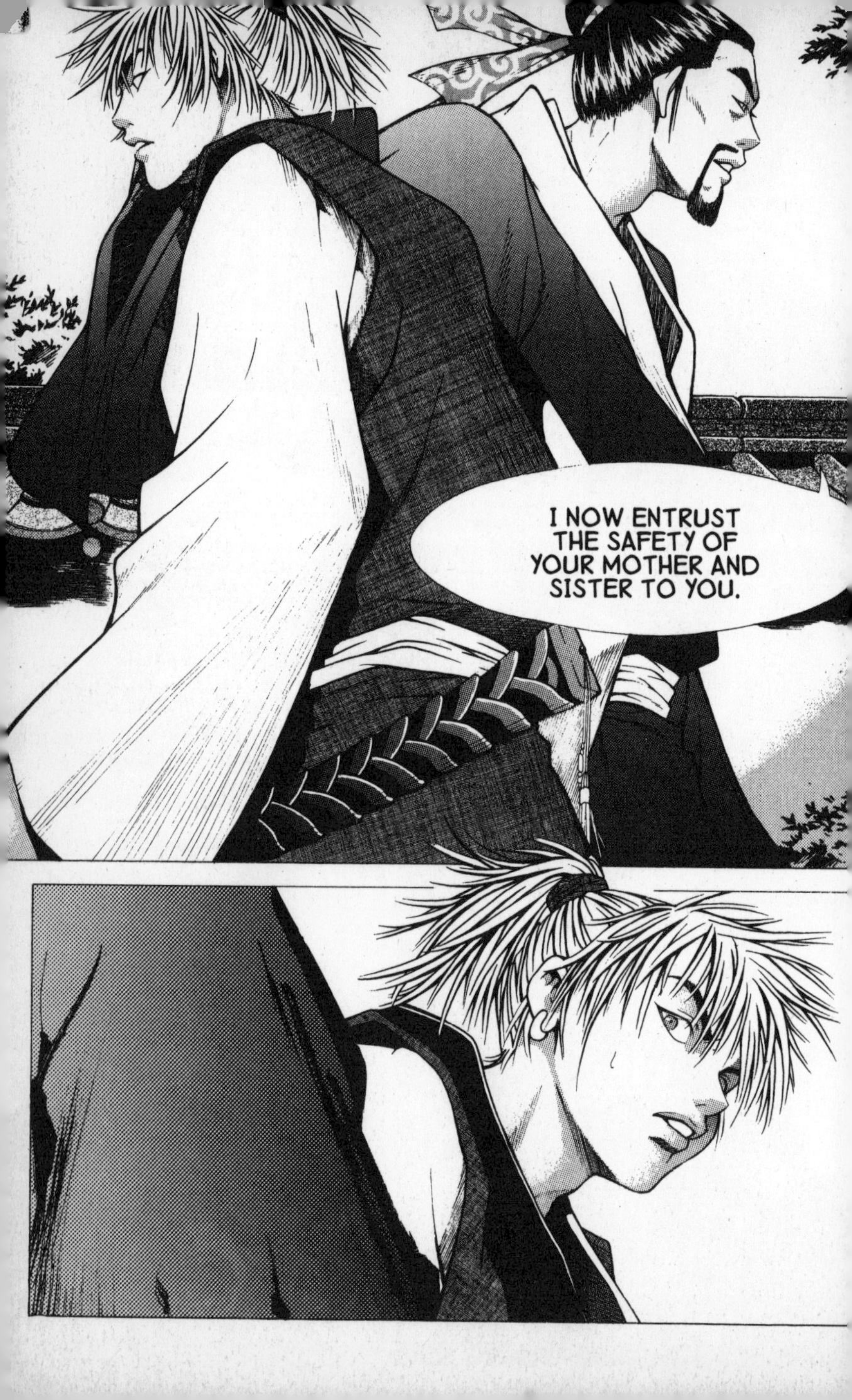
I NOW ENTRUST THE SAFETY OF YOUR MOTHER AND SISTER TO YOU.

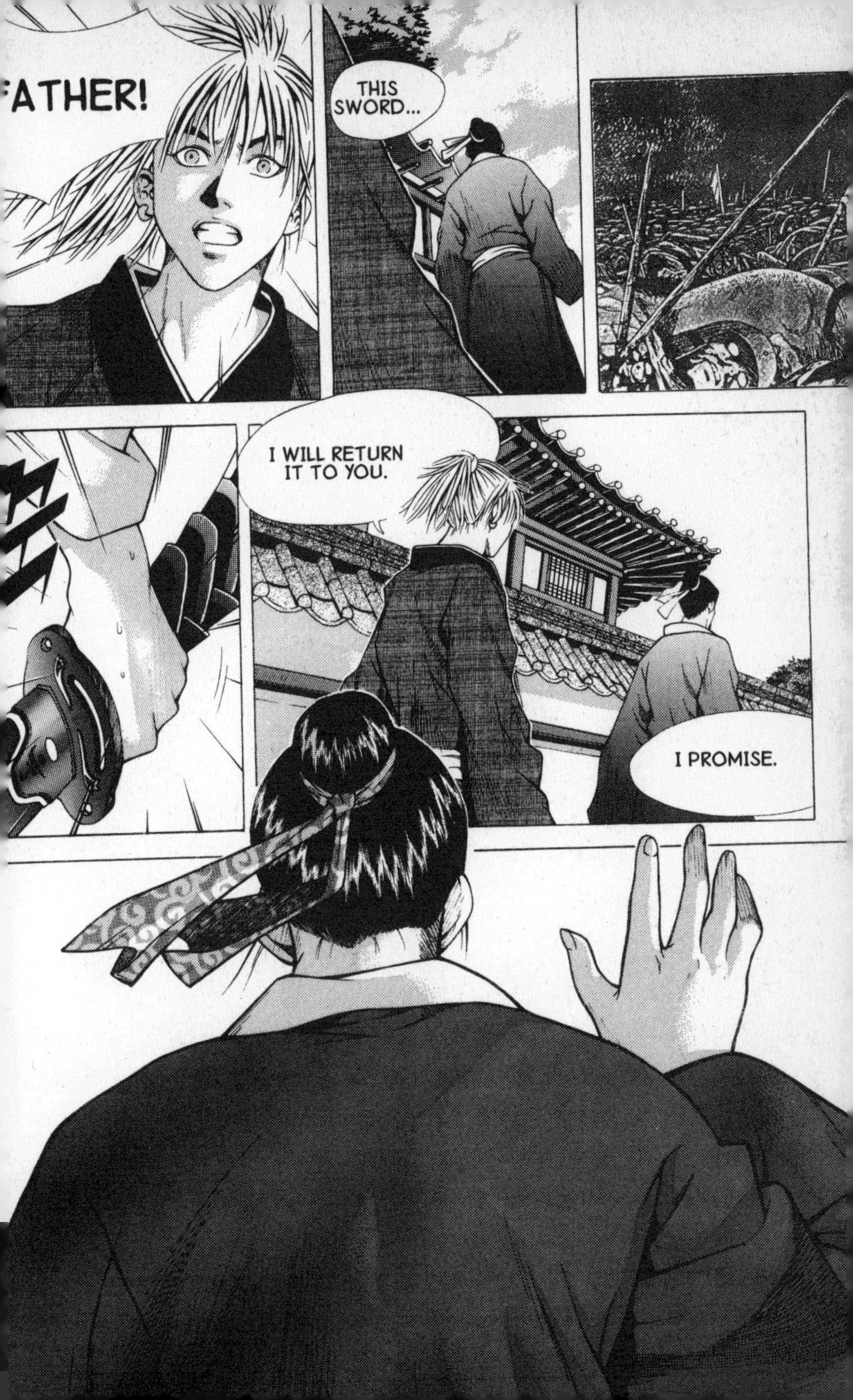
FATHER!
THIS SWORD...
I WILL RETURN IT TO YOU.
I PROMISE.

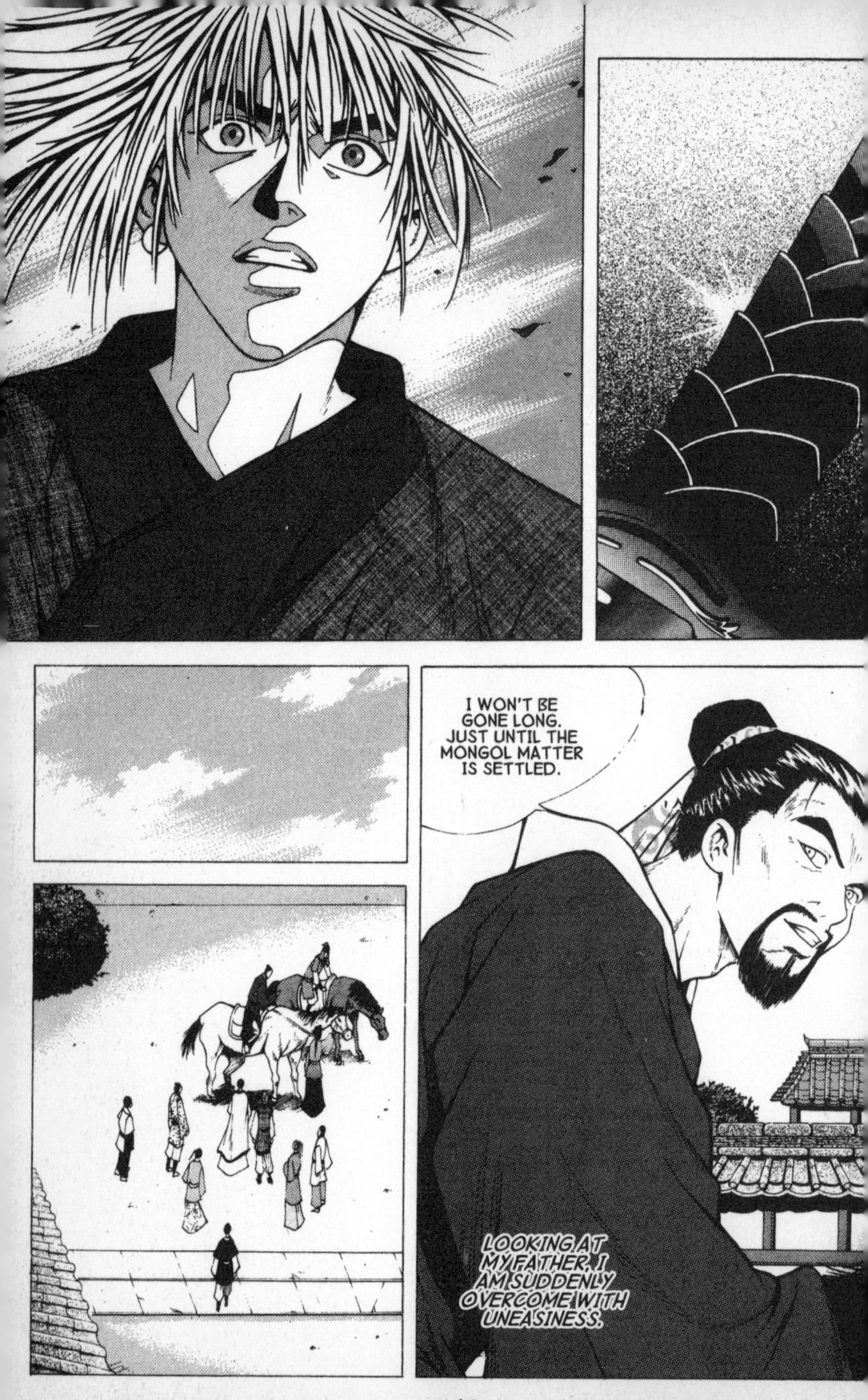
I WON'T BE GONE LONG. JUST UNTIL THE MONGOL MATTER IS SETTLED.
LOOKING AT MY FATHER, I AM SUDDENLY OVERCOME WITH UNEASINESS.

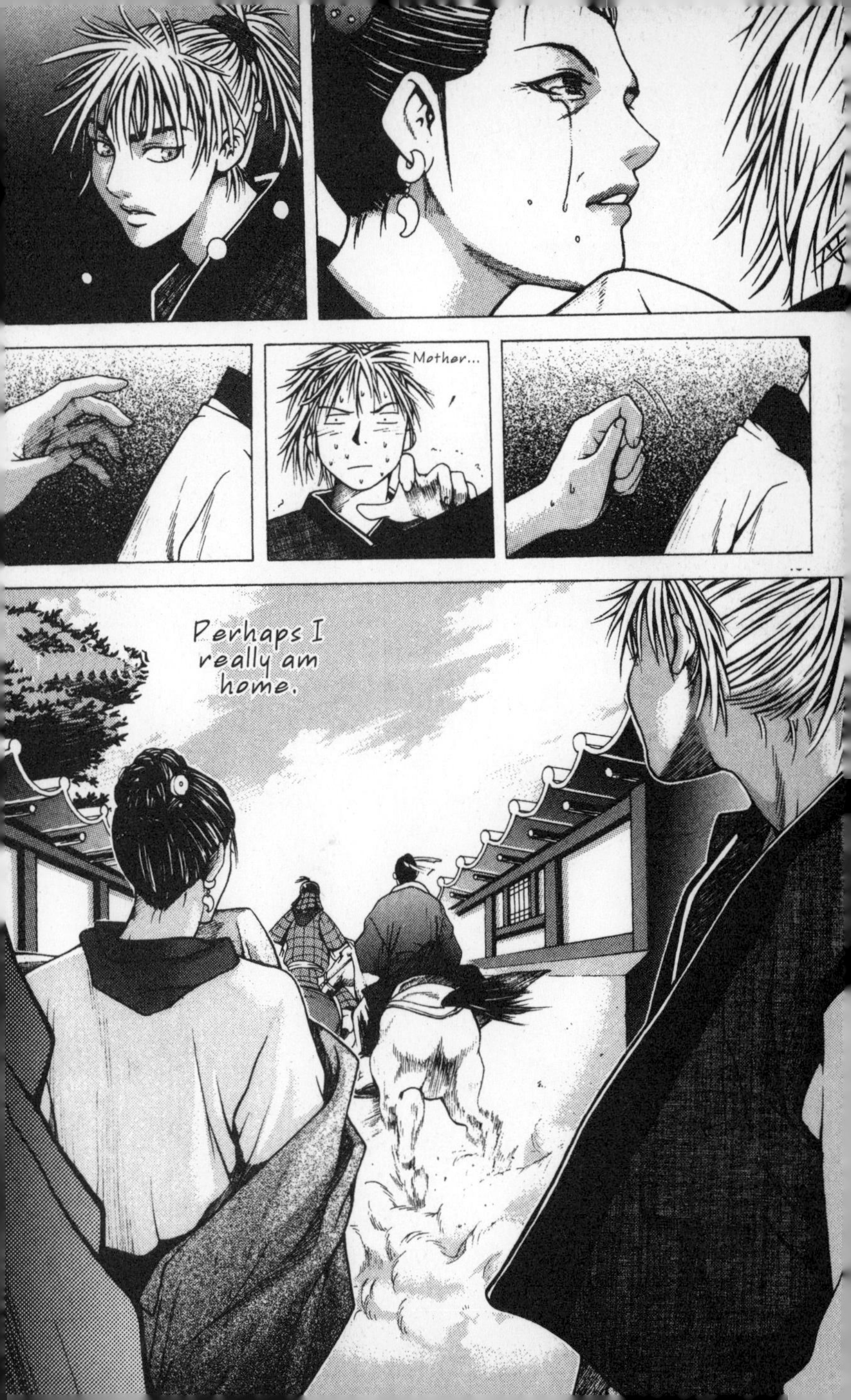
Mother...
Perhaps I really am home.

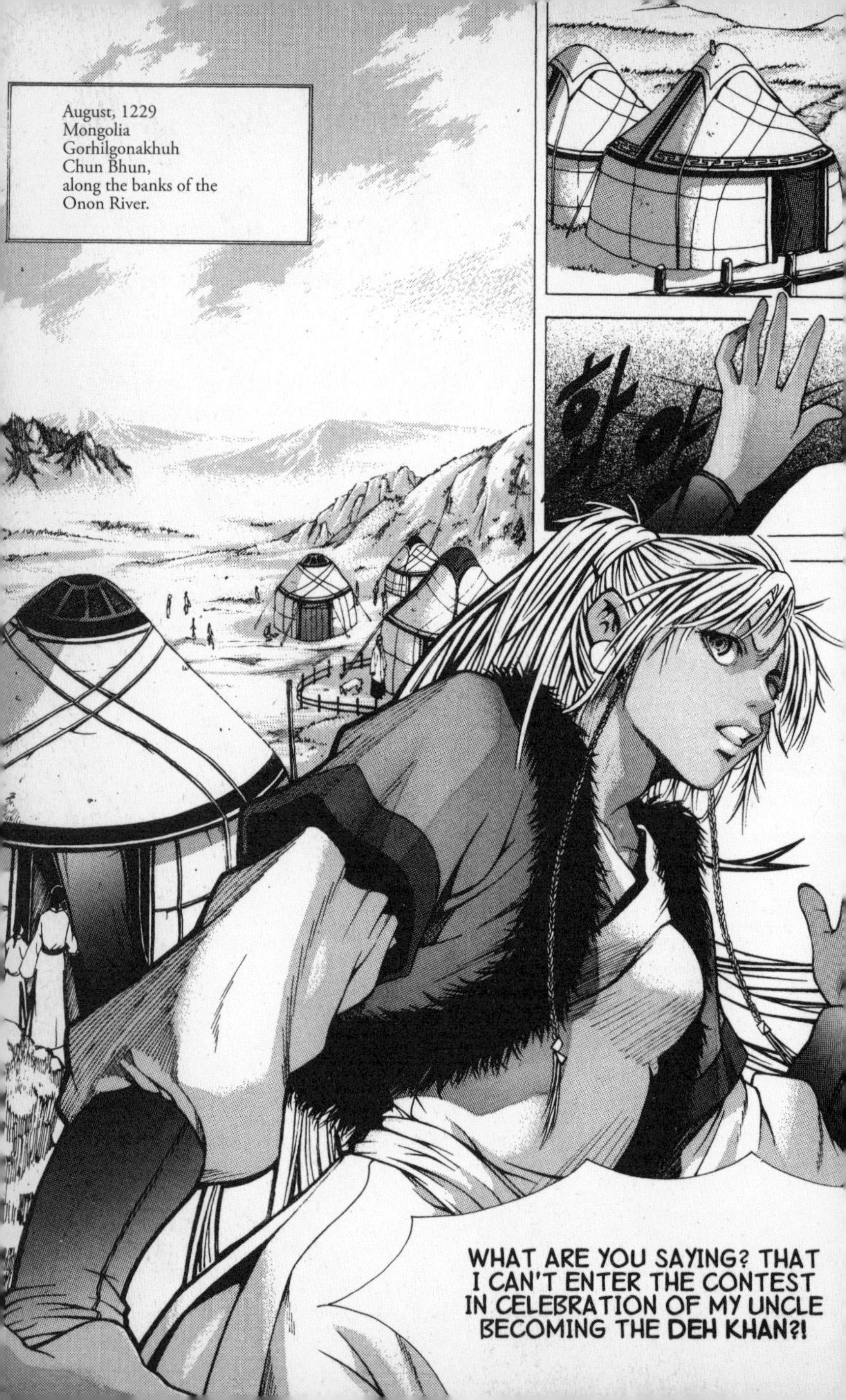
August, 1229
Mongolia
Gorhilgonakhuh
Chun Bhun,
along the banks of the
Onon River.
WHAT ARE YOU SAYING? THAT I CAN'T ENTER THE CONTEST IN CELEBRATION OF MY UNCLE BECOMING THE DEH KHAN?!

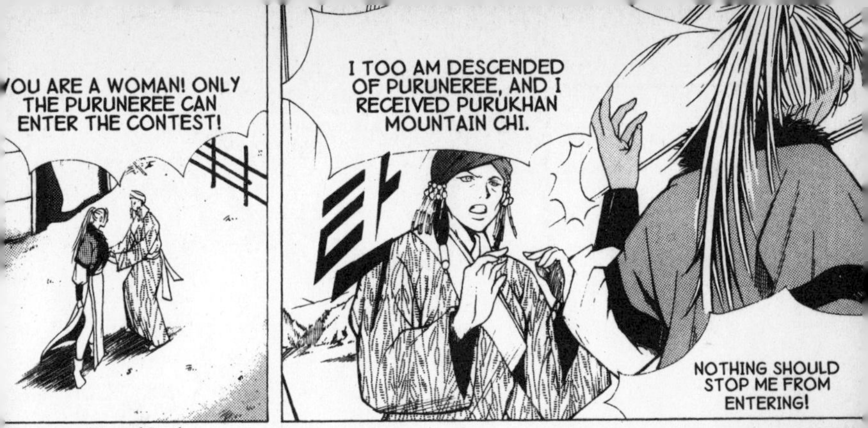

YOU ARE A WOMAN! ONLY THE PURUNEREE CAN ENTER THE CONTEST!
I TOO AM DESCENDED OF PURUNEREE, AND I RECEIVED PURUKHAN MOUNTAIN CHI.
NOTHING SHOULD STOP ME FROM ENTERING!

Puruneree: Mongol Lords

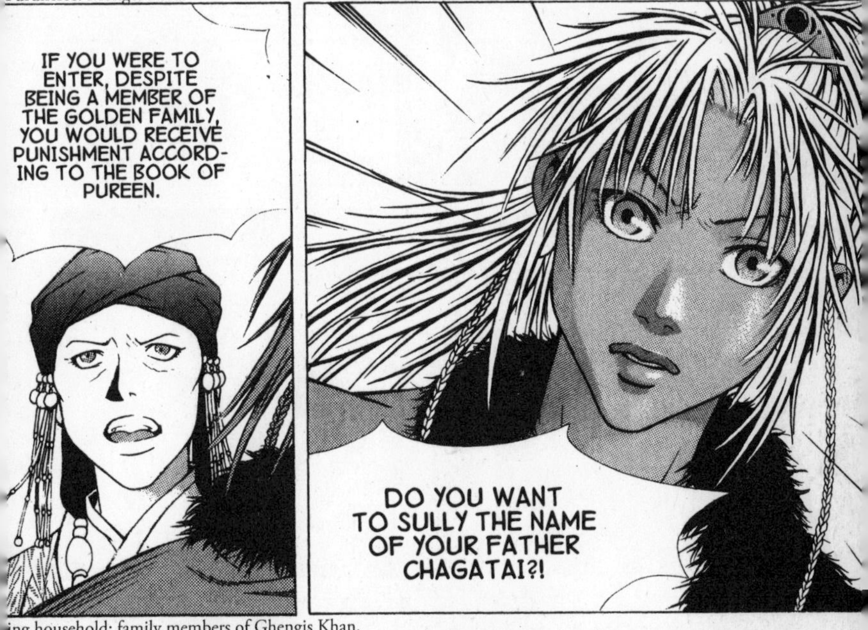

IF YOU WERE TO ENTER, DESPITE BEING A MEMBER OF THE GOLDEN FAMILY, YOU WOULD RECEIVE PUNISHMENT ACCORDING TO THE BOOK OF PUREEN.
DO YOU WANT TO SULLY THE NAME OF YOUR FATHER CHAGATAI?!

ing household: family members of Ghengis Khan.
ook of Pureen: Book of recorded sayings from Ghengis Khan. The book doesn't really exist.

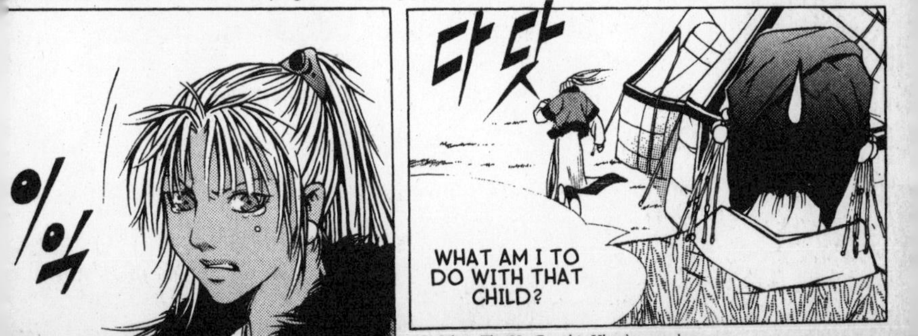

WHAT AM I TO DO WITH THAT CHILD?

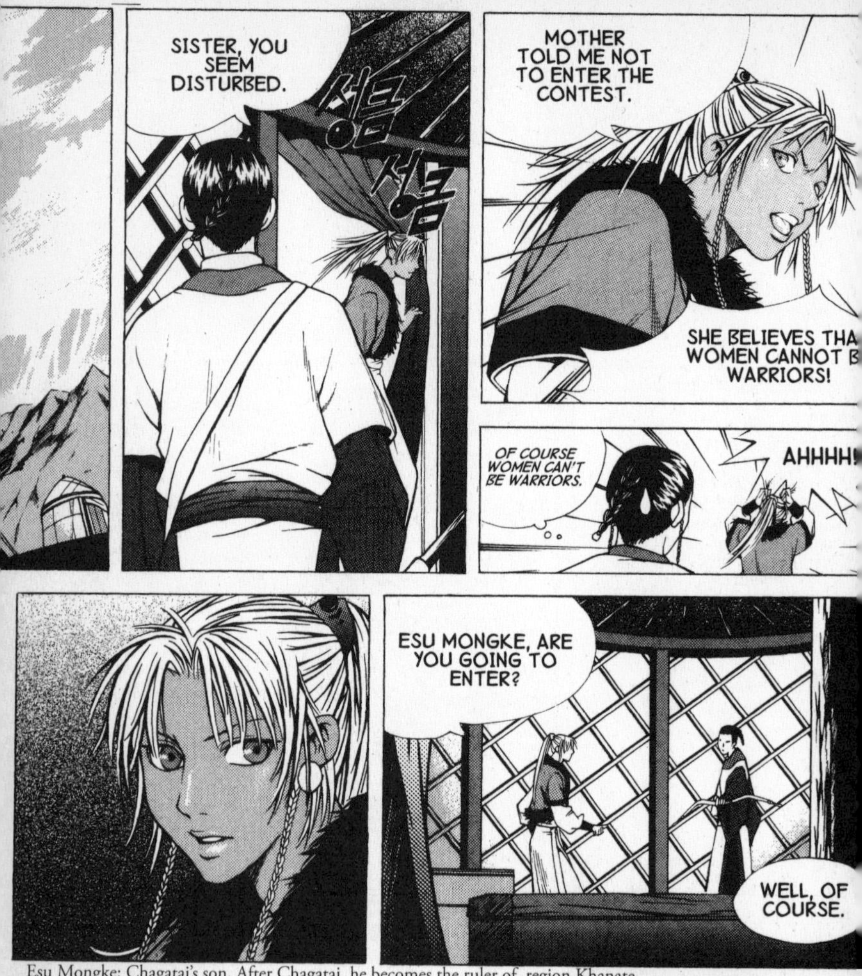
SISTER, YOU SEEM DISTURBED.
MOTHER TOLD ME NOT TO ENTER THE CONTEST.
SHE BELIEVES THA WOMEN CANNOT B WARRIORS!
OF COURSE WOMEN CAN'T BE WARRIORS.
AHHHH
ESU MONGKE, ARE YOU GOING TO ENTER?
WELL, OF COURSE.

Esu Mongke: Chagatai's son. After Chagatai, he becomes the ruler of region Khanate.

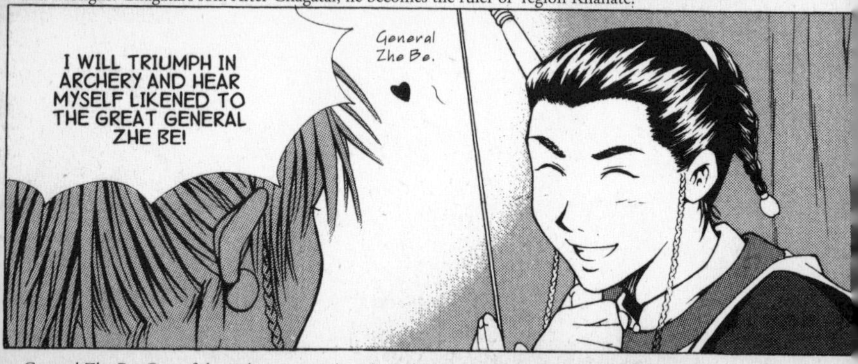
I WILL TRIUMPH IN ARCHERY AND HEAR MYSELF LIKENED TO THE GREAT GENERAL ZHE BE!
General Zhe Be.

General Zhe Be: One of the eight warriors directly under Genghiskhan; famous for his archery.

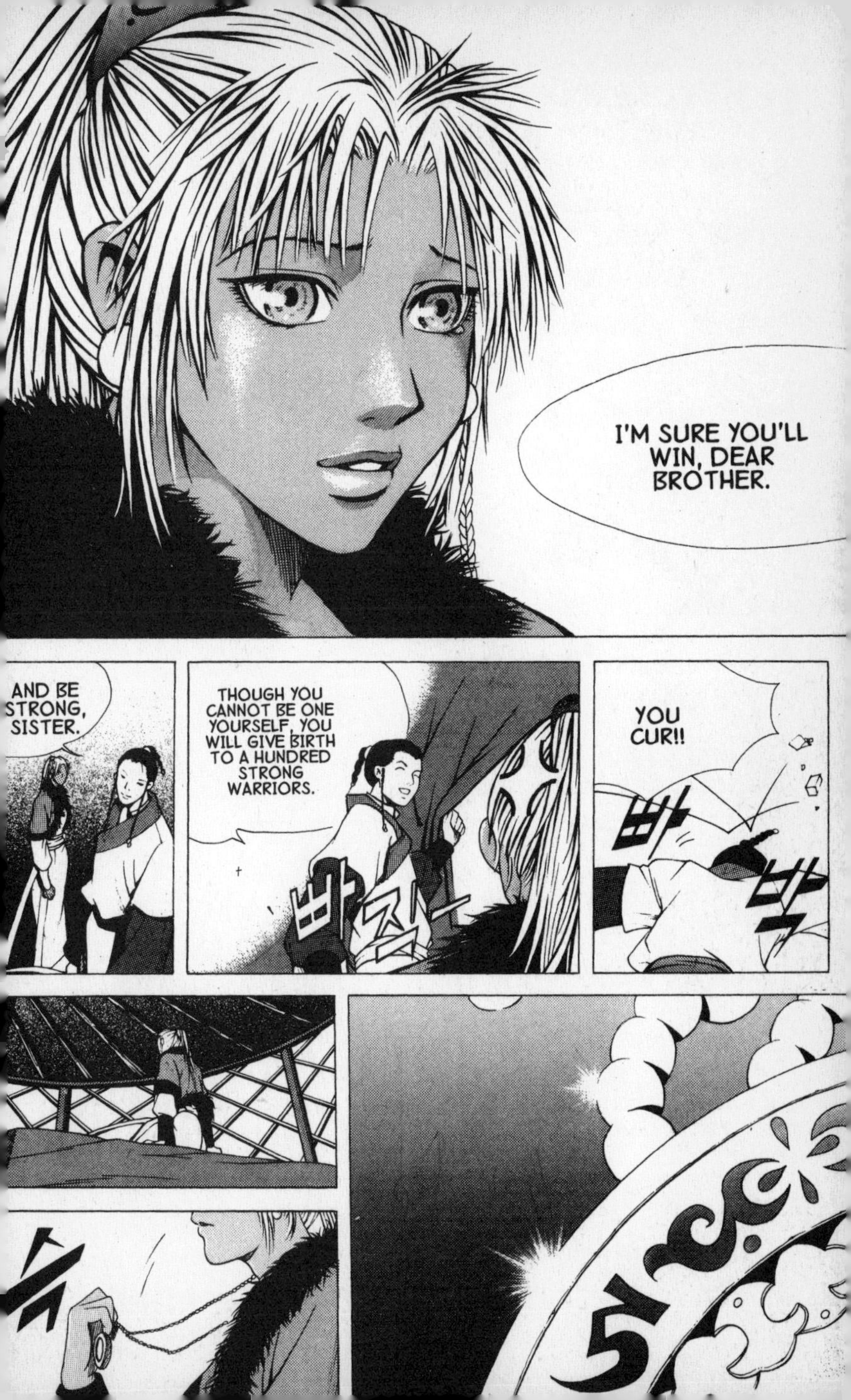
I'M SURE YOU'LL WIN, DEAR BROTHER.
AND BE STRONG, SISTER.
THOUGH YOU CANNOT BE ONE YOURSELF, YOU WILL GIVE BIRTH TO A HUNDRED STRONG WARRIORS.
YOU CUR!!

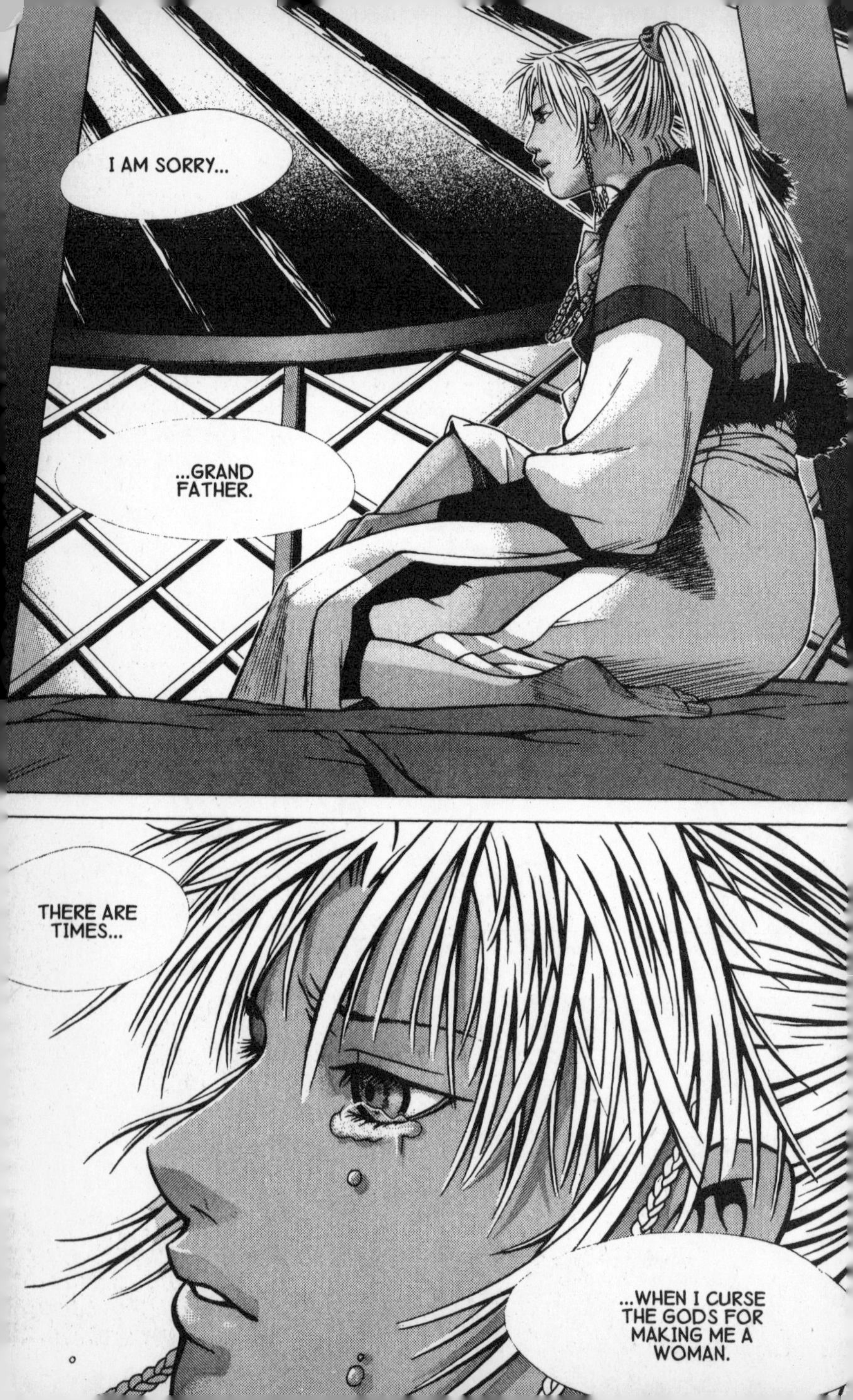
I AM SORRY...
...GRAND FATHER.
THERE ARE TIMES...
...WHEN I CURSE THE GODS FOR MAKING ME A WOMAN.

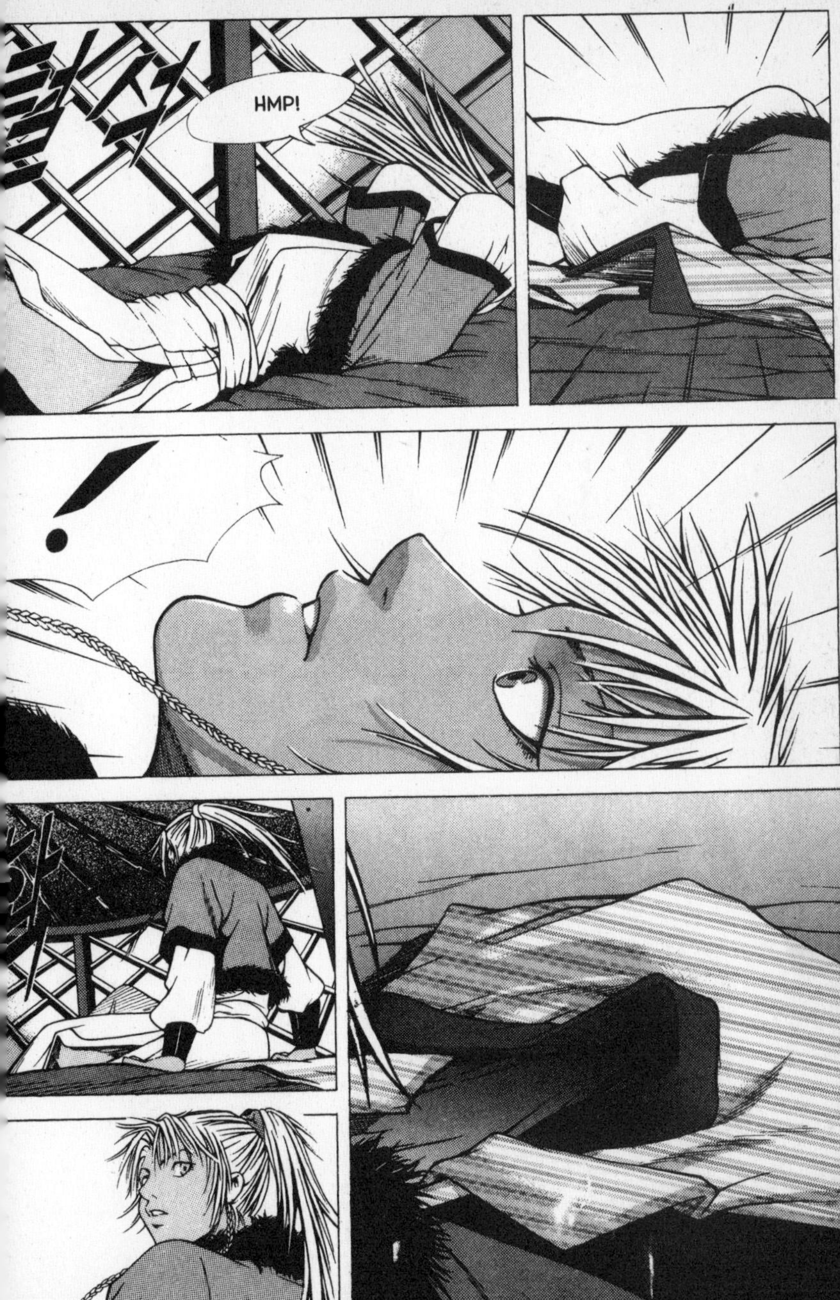
HMP!
!

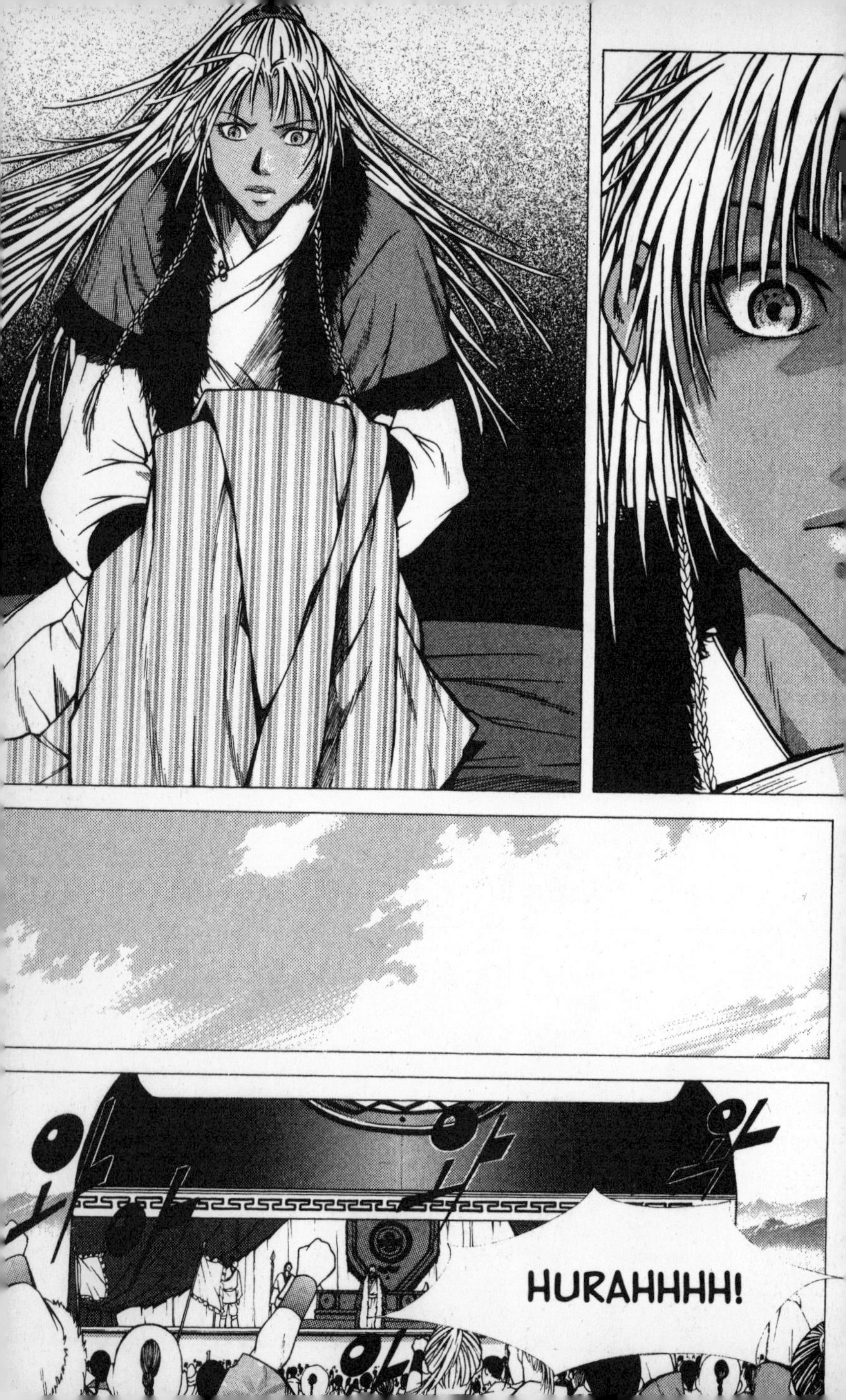
HURAHHHH!

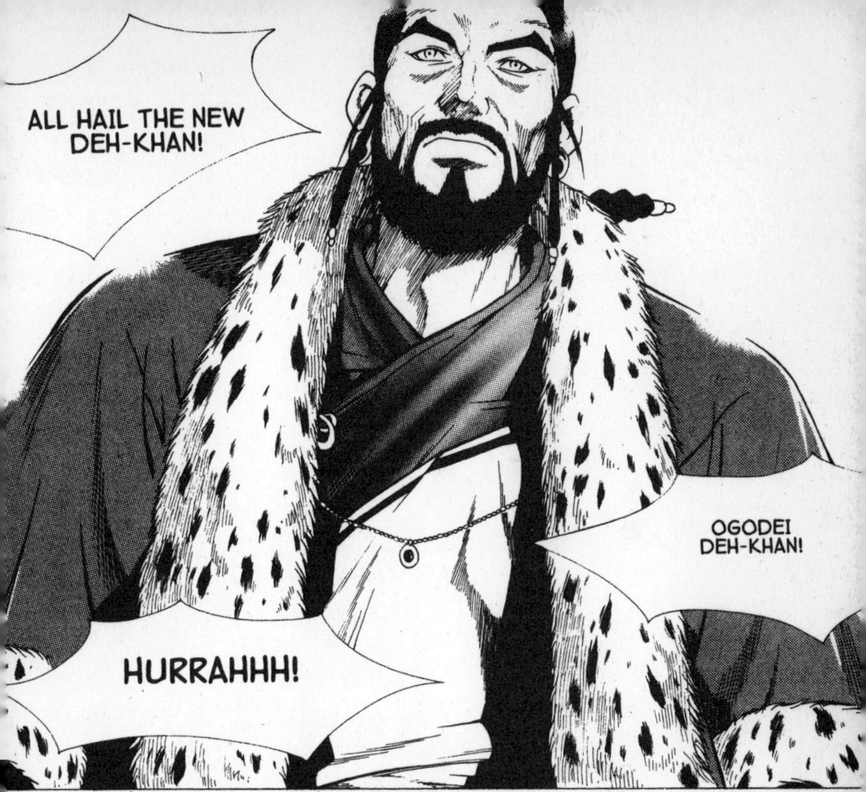
ALL HAIL THE NEW DEH-KHAN!
OGODEI DEH-KHAN!
HURRAHHH!

Deh-Khan: great king or emperor

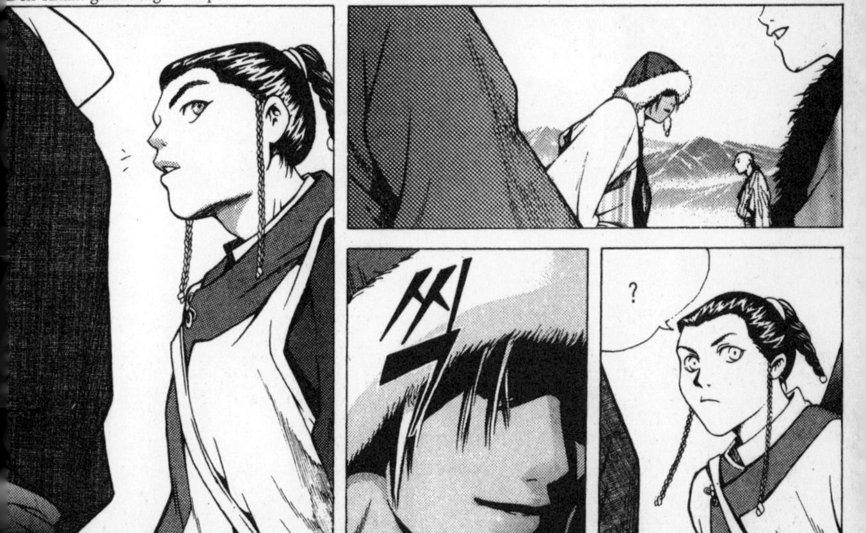
?

godei: Genghis Khan's third son. According to Genghis Khan's will, he becomes
e Deh-Khan of the region.

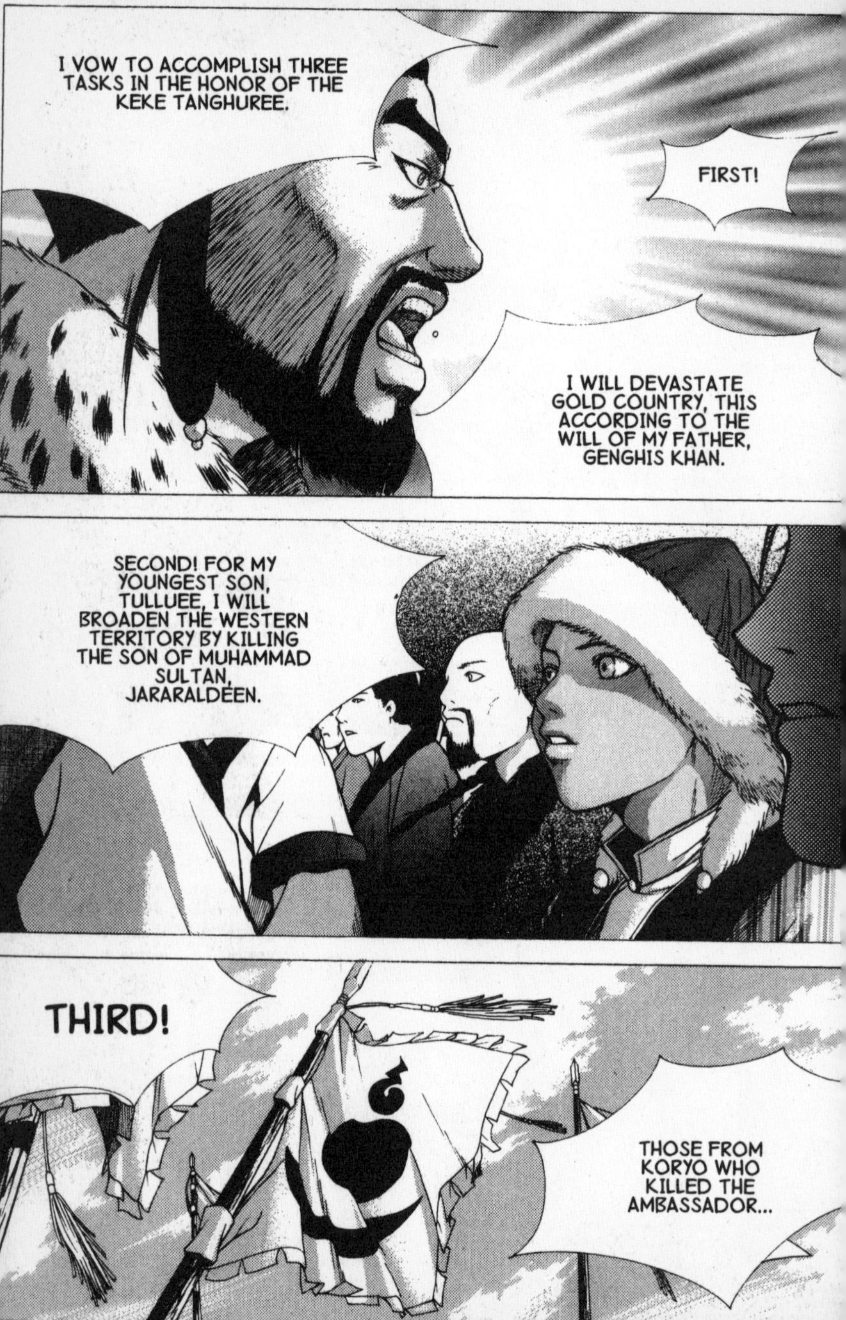
I VOW TO ACCOMPLISH THREE TASKS IN THE HONOR OF THE KEKE TANGHUREE.
FIRST!
I WILL DEVASTATE GOLD COUNTRY, THIS ACCORDING TO THE WILL OF MY FATHER, GENGHIS KHAN.
SECOND! FOR MY YOUNGEST SON, TULLUEE, I WILL BROADEN THE WESTERN TERRITORY BY KILLING THE SON OF MUHAMMAD SULTAN, JARARALDEEN.
THIRD!
THOSE FROM KORYO WHO KILLED THE AMBASSADOR...

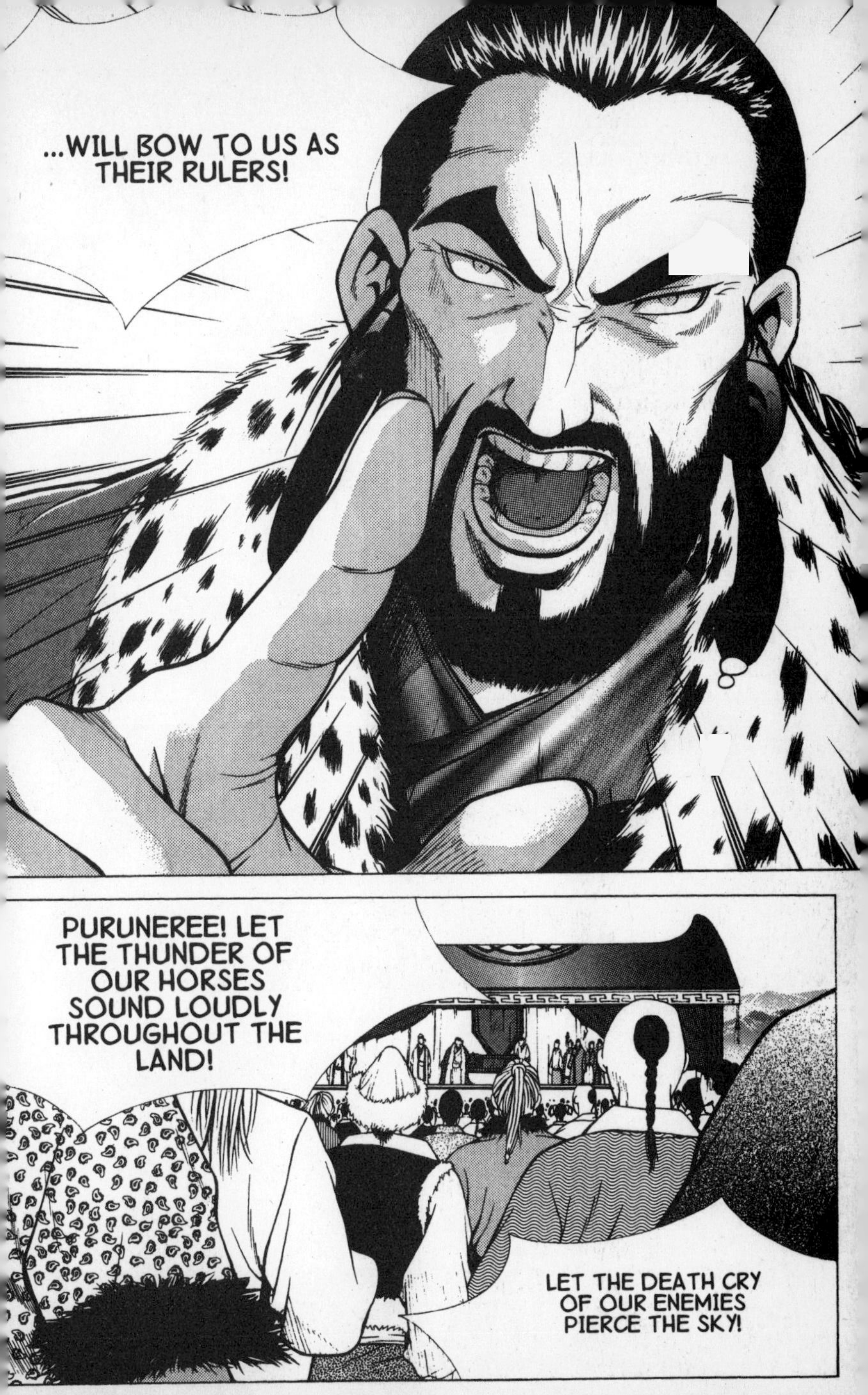
...WILL BOW TO US AS THEIR RULERS!
PURUNEREE! LET THE THUNDER OF OUR HORSES SOUND LOUDLY THROUGHOUT THE LAND!
LET THE DEATH CRY OF OUR ENEMIES PIERCE THE SKY!

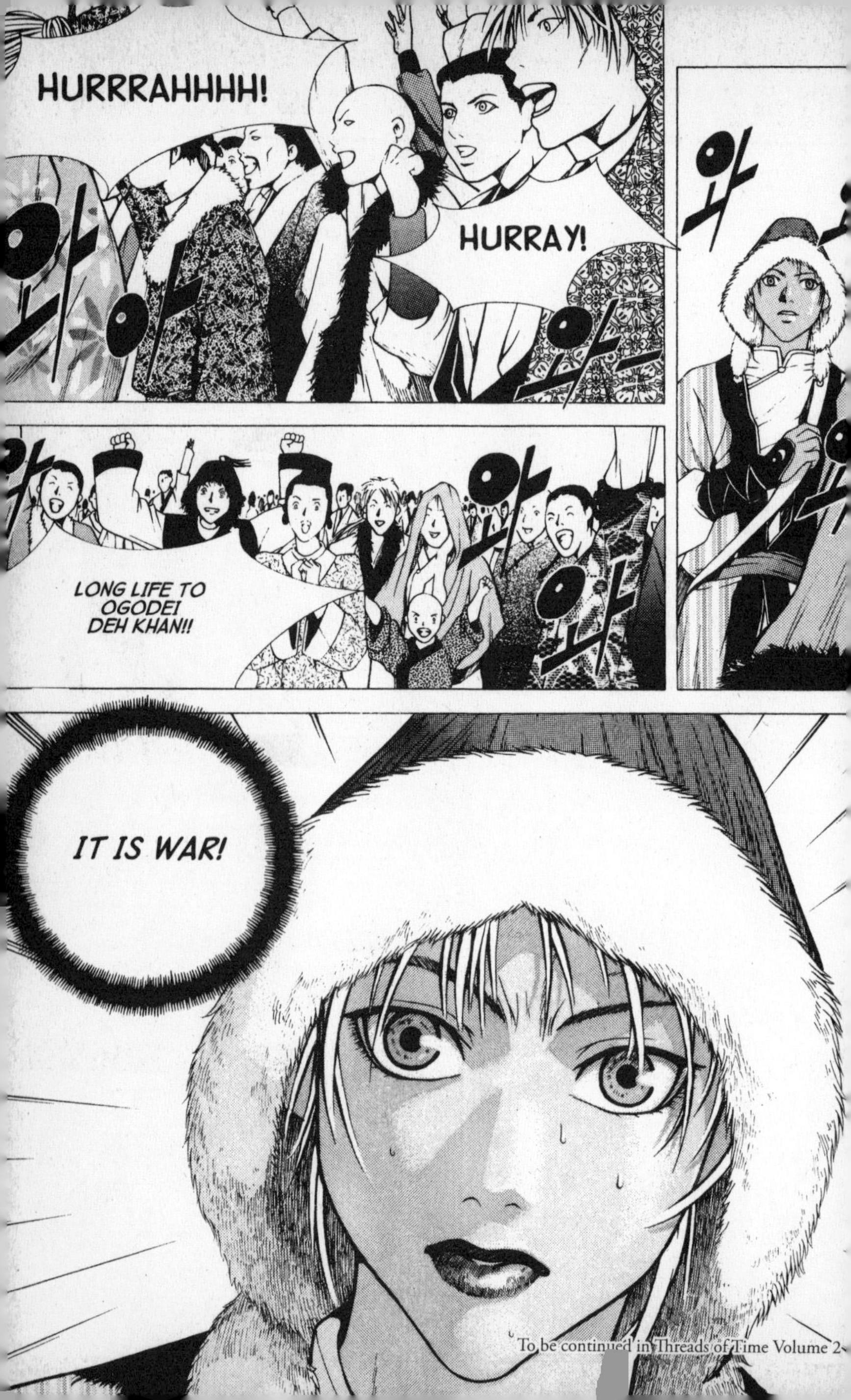
HURRRAHHHH!
와
와
HURRAY!
와—
와
와
LONG LIFE TO OGODEI DEH KHAN!!
와
와
IT IS WAR!
To be continued in Threads of Time Volume 2

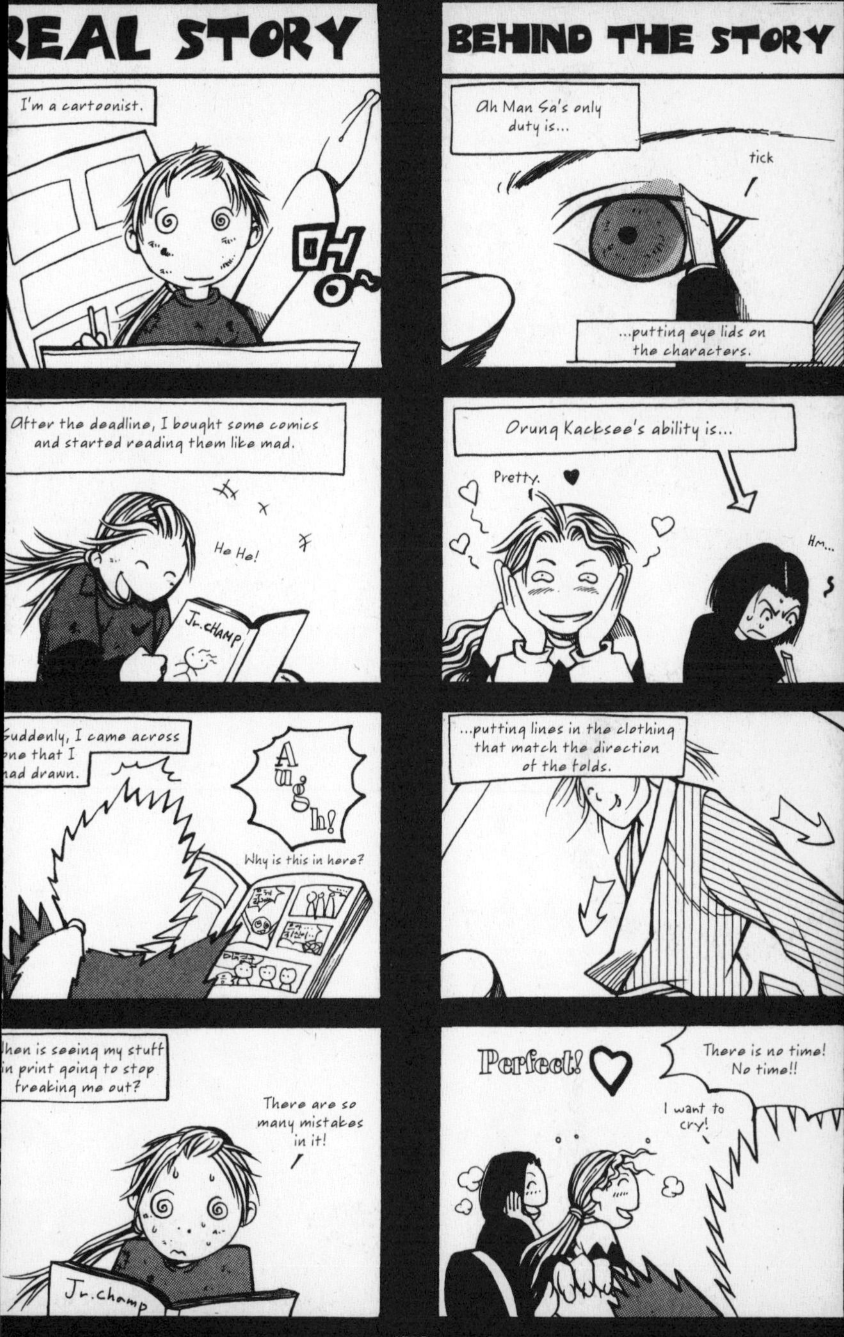
REAL STORY
I'm a cartoonist.
After the deadline, I bought some comics and started reading them like mad.
He He!
Jr. CHAMP
Suddenly, I came across one that I had drawn.
Augh!
Why is this in here?
When is seeing my stuff in print going to stop freaking me out?
There are so many mistakes in it!
Jr. champ
BEHIND THE STORY
Ah Man Sa's only duty is...
tick
...putting eye lids on the characters.
Orung Kacksee's ability is...
Pretty.
Hm...
...putting lines in the clothing that match the direction of the folds.
Perfect!
There is no time! No time!!
I want to cry!

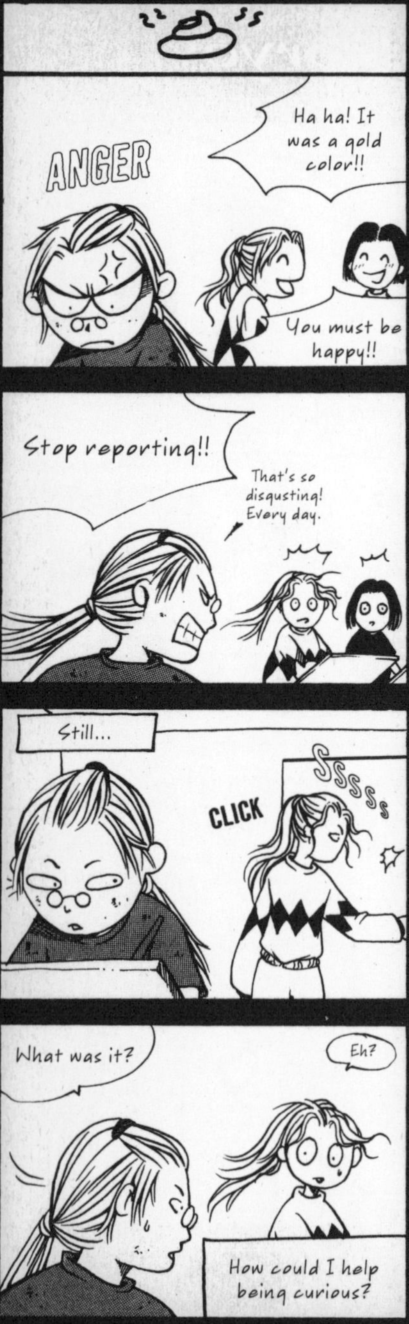
ANGER
Ha ha! It was a gold color!!
You must be happy!!
Stop reporting!!
That's so disgusting! Every day.
Still...
SSSSSs
CLICK
What was it?
Eh?
How could I help being curious?

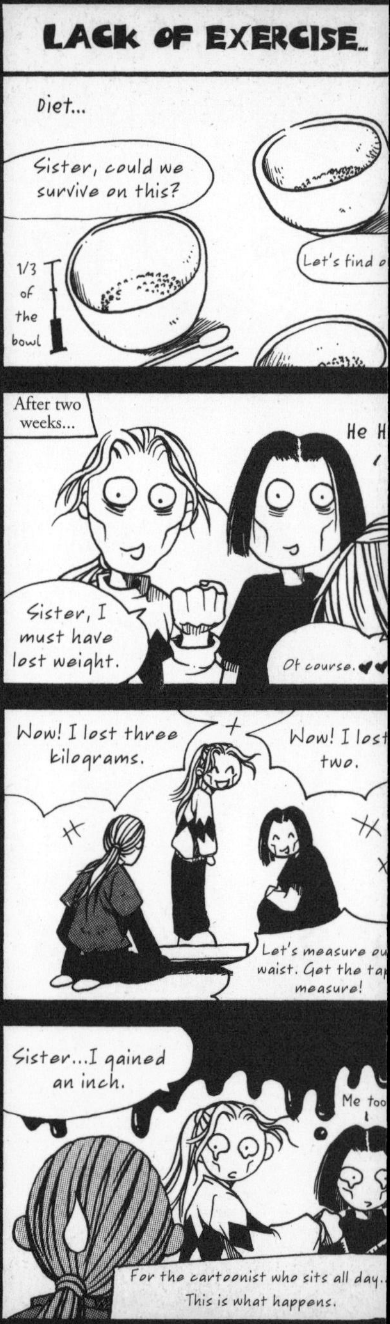
LACK OF EXERCISE..
Diet...
Sister, could we survive on this?
1/3 of the bowl
Let's find o
After two weeks...
He H
Sister, I must have lost weight.
Of course.♥♥
Wow! I lost three kilograms.
Wow! I lost two.
Let's measure ou waist. Get the ta measure!
Sister...I gained an inch.
Me too
For the cartoonist who sits all day...
This is what happens.

What was Koryo?

Threads of Time is set in ancient Korea,
at a time when most of North Korea and South Korea was unified as Koryo.

Timeline

918 — Koryo unified by general Wang Kon

1231 — Mongol army advances on the capital, Kaesong. Koryo negotiates peace.
Mongols leave military governors behind

1232 — Koryo general Ch'oe rejects peace proposal and moves Koryo court to
Kanghwa Island

1239 — Successful Mongol invasion. Koryo court attempts to maintain autonomy,
despite swearing fealty to the Khan

1260 — Mongolian Empire begins to fracture

1300–1392 — Koryo factions vie for power in the shadow of the rapidly declining
Mongol empire

1392 — Koryo breaks into smaller principalities and ceases to be a unified entity

Who was Genghis Khan?

Temujin, meaning "of iron". Genghis Khan means "universal ruler" in Turkic,
now an extinct language.

Probably born in 1162, Genghis Khan, along with his mother, was ostracized from
his tribe in 1175 following the poisoning death of his father by Tartars. By 1206, he had unified all Mongolian nomadic tribes under his direct control. At its height, the Mongolian Empire
spread from the Caspian Sea to the tip of Korea (see accompanying map). Genghis Khan,
however, did not live to see his greatest goal, capturing the Jurchen Empire of Manchuria, as
he died of injuries incurred by falling off his horse (or so the official report goes) in 1227.

Who were his sons?

In the timeline of Threads of Time, Genghis Khan died before Moon Bin Kim
ever reaches Koryo. But the emperor's sons, Jochi, Chagatai, Ogodei and Tolui
still threaten Asia through the strength of their Khanates.

Jochi — The West
Though Jochi died before Genghis Khan, his son Batu led the "Golden Horde" through
Russia and Eastern Europe from 1235-41.

Chagatai — Central Asia
After experiencing fierce resistance from natives, the Khanate was eventually broken into
Chagatai and Jl-Khanate. Chagatai is Atan and Esu's father.

Ogodei — The East
At the end of Threads of Time Volume 1, Ogodei, the third son of Genghis Khan, ascends
to the position of Den-Khan. Named as successor to the empire by Genghis himself, the
Mongol invasion of Koryo began to lose momentum after his death in 1241.
His son Guyuk reigned until 1248.

Tolui — North China and Mongolia
Despite naming Ogodei his heir, Genghis Khan entrusted Tolui with his plans to invade the
Jurchen Empire in modern-day North China. His son, Mongke, ruled Ogodei's empire from
1251 until his death in 1259, at which time his brother Kublai Khan succeeded him
and conquered southern China.

The Asia of Genghis Kha

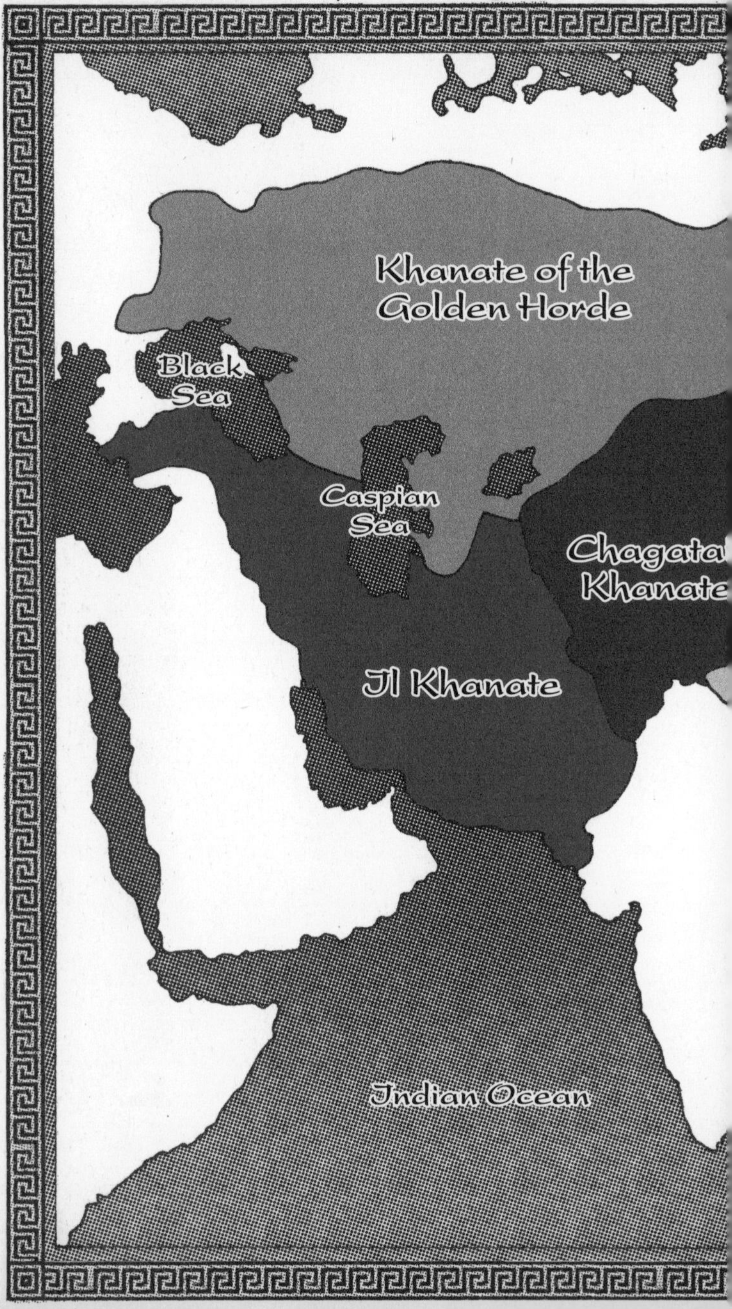
Khanate of the
Golden Horde
Black
Sea
Caspian
Sea
Chagata
Khanate
Il Khanate
Indian Ocean

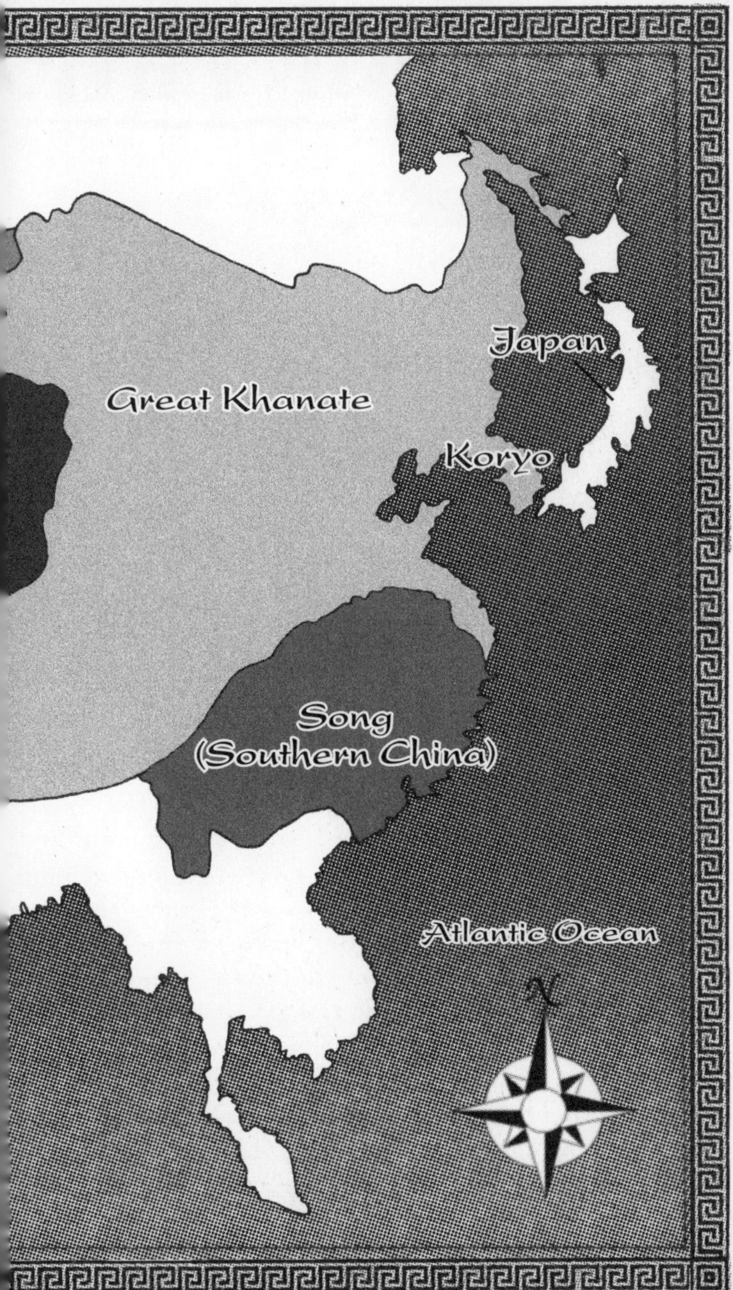
Japan
Great Khanate
Koryo
Song
(Southern China)
Atlantic Ocean

Threads of Time

撤神塔

The princess Atan Hadas will hardly let bull-headed, male ignorance keep her from becoming a warrior. She enters the archery competition despite the protestations of her mother, brother and elders, though she enters it disguised as a boy...and wins. But thumbing her nose at the foundations of her culture may prove less dangerous than meeting and befriending a royal son of the enemy. Rescued by Sa Kyung Kim from assassins, Atan Hadas must reconcile her gratitude to the young man from Koryo with her filial responsibility to destroy the Mongol army's enemies. Meanwhile, Sa Kyung Kim continues to suffer from delusions of the future, seeing in the people around him as counterparts from his 20th century life.

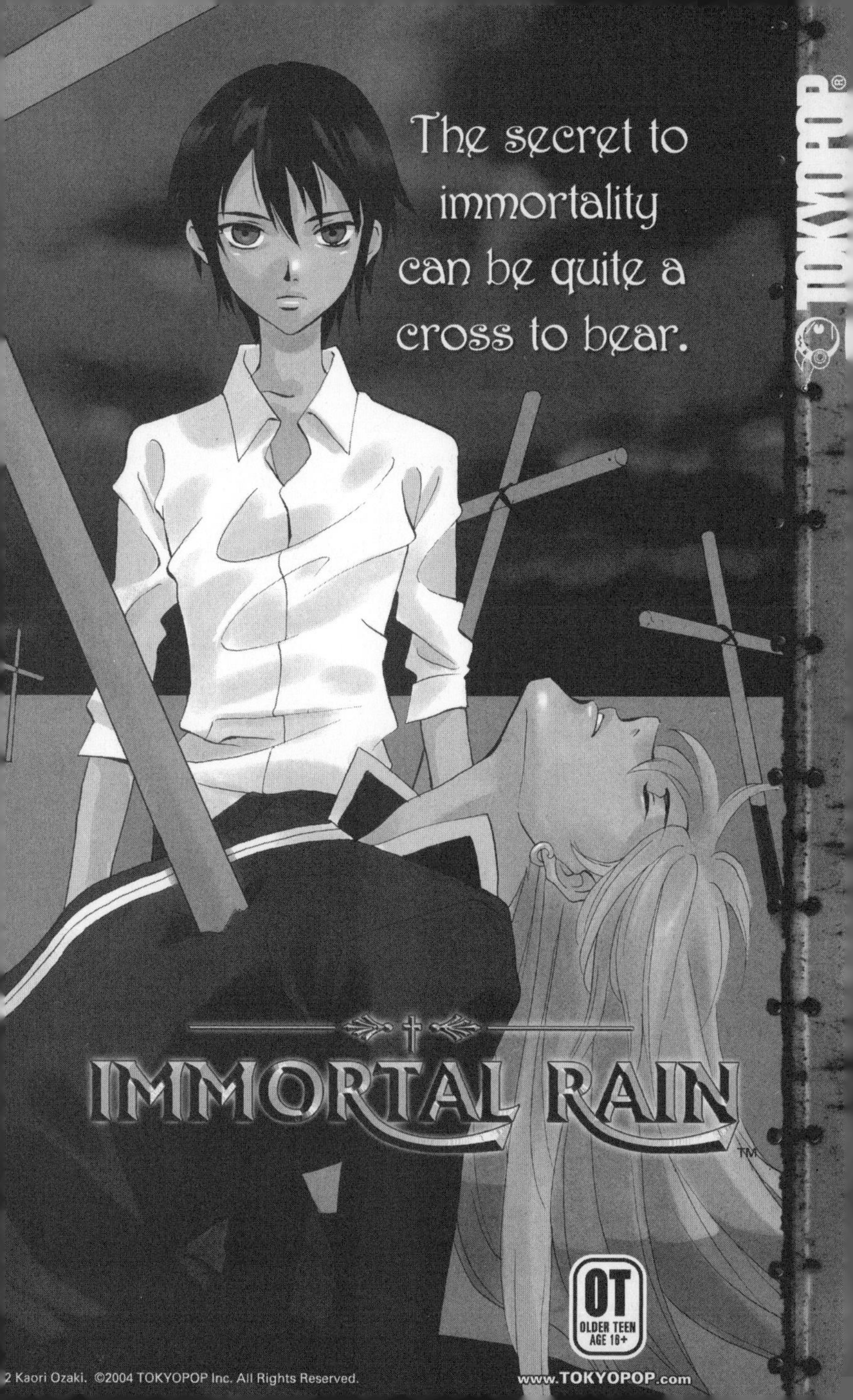

The secret to immortality can be quite a cross to bear.
IMMORTAL RAIN
TM
TOKYOPOP
OT
OLDER TEEN AGE 16+
2 Kaori Ozaki. ©2004 TOKYOPOP Inc. All Rights Reserved.
www.TOKYOPOP.com

ALSO AVAILABLE FROM TOKYOPOP®

MANGA

.HACK//LEGEND OF THE TWILIGHT
@LARGE
ABENOBASHI: MAGICAL SHOPPING ARCADE
A.I. LOVE YOU
AI YORI AOSHI
ANGELIC LAYER
ARM OF KANNON
BABY BIRTH
BATTLE ROYALE
BATTLE VIXENS
BOYS BE...
BRAIN POWERED
BRIGADOON
B'TX
CANDIDATE FOR GODDESS, THE
CARDCAPTOR SAKURA
CARDCAPTOR SAKURA - MASTER OF THE CLOW
CHOBITS
CHRONICLES OF THE CURSED SWORD
CLAMP SCHOOL DETECTIVES
CLOVER
COMIC PARTY
CONFIDENTIAL CONFESSIONS
CORRECTOR YUI
COWBOY BEBOP
COWBOY BEBOP: SHOOTING STAR
CRAZY LOVE STORY
CRESCENT MOON
CROSS
CULDCEPT
CYBORG 009
D•N•ANGEL
DEMON DIARY
DEMON OROARON, THE
DEUS VITAE
DIABOLO
DIGIMON
DIGIMON TAMERS
DIGIMON ZERO TWO
DOLL
DRAGON HUNTER
DRAGON KNIGHTS
DRAGON VOICE
DREAM SAGA
DUKLYON: CLAMP SCHOOL DEFENDERS
EERIE QUEERIE!
ERICA SAKURAZAWA: COLLECTED WORKS
ET CETERA
ETERNITY
EVIL'S RETURN
FAERIES' LANDING
FAKE
FLCL
FLOWER OF THE DEEP SLEEP
FORBIDDEN DANCE
FRUITS BASKET

G GUNDAM
GATEKEEPERS
GETBACKERS
GIRL GOT GAME
GIRLS EDUCATIONAL CHARTER
GRAVITATION
GTO
GUNDAM BLUE DESTINY
GUNDAM SEED ASTRAY
GUNDAM WING
GUNDAM WING: BATTLEFIELD OF PACIFISTS
GUNDAM WING: ENDLESS WALTZ
GUNDAM WING: THE LAST OUTPOST (G-UNIT)
HANDS OFF!
HAPPY MANIA
HARLEM BEAT
HYPER RUNE
I.N.V.U.
IMMORTAL RAIN
INITIAL D
INSTANT TEEN: JUST ADD NUTS
ISLAND
JING: KING OF BANDITS
JING: KING OF BANDITS - TWILIGHT TALES
JULINE
KARE KANO
KILL ME, KISS ME
KINDAICHI CASE FILES, THE
KING OF HELL
KODOCHA: SANA'S STAGE
LAMENT OF THE LAMB
LEGAL DRUG
LEGEND OF CHUN HYANG, THE
LES BIJOUX
LOVE HINA
LUPIN III
LUPIN III: WORLD'S MOST WANTED
MAGIC KNIGHT RAYEARTH I
MAGIC KNIGHT RAYEARTH II
MAHOROMATIC: AUTOMATIC MAIDEN
MAN OF MANY FACES
MARMALADE BOY
MARS
MARS: HORSE WITH NO NAME
MINK
MIRACLE GIRLS
MIYUKI-CHAN IN WONDERLAND
MODEL
MOURYOU KIDEN
MY LOVE
NECK AND NECK
ONE
ONE I LOVE, THE
PARADISE KISS
PARASYTE
PASSION FRUIT
PEACH GIRL
PEACH GIRL: CHANGE OF HEART

06.21.04T

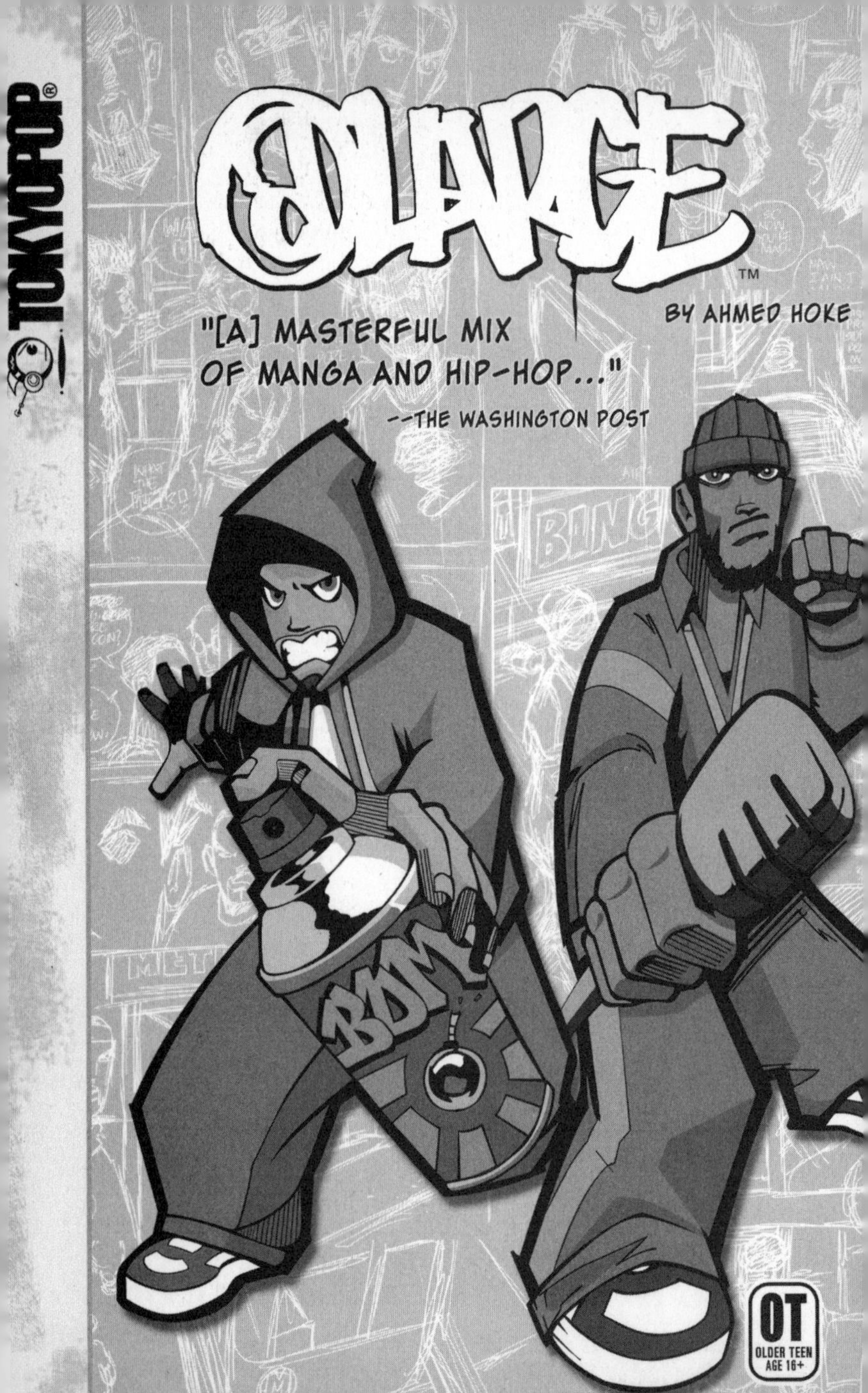
TOKYOPOP®
@LARGE™
BY AHMED HOKE
"[A] MASTERFUL MIX
OF MANGA AND HIP-HOP..."
--THE WASHINGTON POST
OT
OLDER TEEN
AGE 16+

ETERNITY™

Not all legends are timeless.

www.TOKYOPOP.com

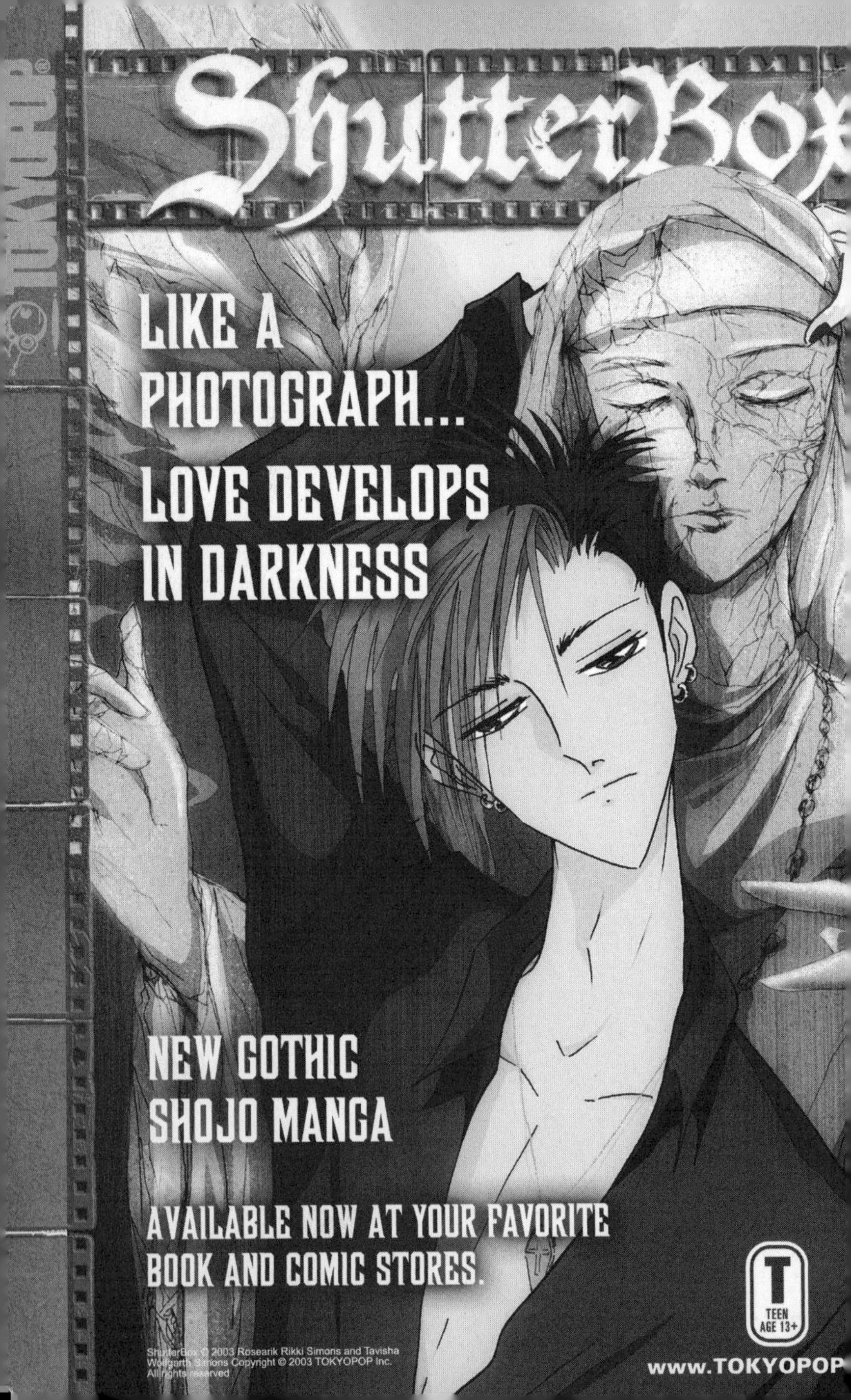

ShutterBox

LIKE A PHOTOGRAPH... LOVE DEVELOPS IN DARKNESS

NEW GOTHIC SHOJO MANGA

AVAILABLE NOW AT YOUR FAVORITE BOOK AND COMIC STORES.

www.TOKYOPOP.com